DIVINE MADNESS

DIVINE MADNESS

On Interpreting Literature, Music, and the Visual Arts Ironically

Lars Elleström

Lewisburg
Bucknell University Press
London: Associated University Presses

Associated University Presses
440 Forsgate Drive
Cranbury, NJ 08512

Associated University Presses
16 Barter Street
London WC1A 2AH, England

Associated University Presses
P.O. Box 338, Port Credit
Mississauga, Ontario
Canada L5G 4L8

The paper used in this publication meets the requirements of the American National Standard for Permanence of Paper for Printed Library Materials Z39.48-1984.

Library of Congress Cataloging-in-Publication Data

Elleström, Lars, 1960–
    Divine madness : on interpreting literature, music, and the visual arts ironically / Lars Elleström
      p.   cm.
    Includes bibliographical references and index.
    ISBN 0-8387-5491-0 (alk. paper)
    1. Irony in art criticism.   2. Arts, Modern.   I. Title.
NX640 .E45   2002
700′.1—dc21   2001043238

To my beloved children, Julia and Joakim,
who invented the ''other way 'round'' language
and thus made my life more complicated.

Irony is divine madness.
—Søren Kierkegaard

Contents

Acknowledgments

MY GRATITUDE GOES TO THE ERIK PHILIP-SÖRENSEN FOUNDATION, WHICH gave me a grant for the initial research, and to the Swedish Council for Research in the Humanities and Social Sciences, which financed the bulk of the research. Among colleagues and friends who have read the manuscript and encouraged me, especially Bengt Edlund, Magnus Nilsson, Patricia Wetterberg, and Caroline Wintersgill should be mentioned. Thanks!

DIVINE MADNESS

Prolegomena

In the beginning the Word already was.
—The Gospel according to John

WHEN GOD CREATED THE WORLD HE TRANSFORMED CHAOS TO COSMOS. In chaos no distinctions exist. Everything is everything and nothing. However, when heaven is separated from earth, when light is separated from darkness, day from night, good from evil, and woman from man, order arises: cosmos. In the Christian cosmogony this figure of thought is thoroughly developed, but also in many other religions and cultures the basic pattern chaos–separation–cosmos is of the utmost importance. The separation of heaven from earth is the cosmogonic germ not only within Christianity, but also in Babylonian, Egyptian, Indian, Greek, and Icelandic myths.

The cosmic order is therefore built upon separation. Yet, how is this done? The answer is, with the aid of language. In the Old Testament one reads about a God who *speaks*. It is the articulation of divine words that transforms chaos into intelligible units and hence creates order. First God, and later on Adam, gives names to phenomena, things and creatures. In the opening sentences of the Gospel according to John we even read that God "is" the word: "In the beginning the Word already was. The Word was in God's presence, and what God was, the Word was. He was with God at the beginning, and through him all things came to be; without him no created thing came into being."[1] According to this view, a view that has stimulated many Christian and Jewish mystics, language and divinity are practically one and the same, and furthermore inseparably connected to the "act" of separation. Language and the world as one knows it, as one sees it, and as one describes it, are fundamentally connected—if not literally "the same," they are at least not possible to imagine without each other. Without language, no world. Without the world, no language.

Consequently, the cosmogonic myths are in a way also meta-

13

phors for the rise of consciousness, perception, judgment, intelligence, language—and literature. The myths of creation are not only literally the historic origin of literature; they also form the original narrative pattern of the epic. They can even be said to be first and foremost stories *about* language and literature. To tell about the creation of the world (of which rather little is actually known) is in a way to tell about *how the story may be told at all*; it is to tell a story about the telling of stories, about language.

Actually, the myths of creation may remind us about how language works according to post-saussurean linguistics: through separation, difference, *différance*. Language is an immensely refined system of distinctions and phonetic differences. If God "is" language "is" the world, it all makes sense. Everything is ordered for the best.

However, the cosmic order is threatened. The cosmogonic myths have their destructive equivalents in apocalyptic myths. Apocalypse represents destruction of order. Through the forces of evil and darkness cosmos may be transformed back into chaos in a reversed creation. The Greek word from which the name *Devil* originates, *diaballein,* means "to throw around," and this is exactly what the Devil represents to us. God is order, the Devil is the one that destroys order. The Devil is thus the enemy of not only the cosmic separations in the material world, but also of the linguistic separations in language.

This is where irony comes in. In a way, irony represents the apocalyptic regression back to chaos. If irony is accepted, anything can mean everything or nothing. When irony reigns, the divine names are reversed and the distinctions are withdrawn: light may mean darkness, good may mean evil. It seems as if irony is closely allied to the chaos of the Devil. For Victor Hugo, irony is "the Devil's face."[2] Yet, we all know that it is possible to live, write, and speak even in a world contaminated by irony. There is, or there may be, some sort of order also in ironic language. Is irony then a human perversion of the divine order, or is it divine madness; a chaotic dream created by *the silence* of God when he rested on the seventh day?

Let us once again start from the beginning.

1
History

Only concepts without history can be defined.
—Friedrich Nietzsche

THE CONCEPT OF IRONY: AN HISTORICAL SURVEY

To TRACE THE HISTORY OF IRONY IS TO TRACE TWO COMPLEX HISTORIES that are intimately related to each other but not identical: the history of *the word* irony and its many derivations, and the history of the changing *concepts* of irony. In a way, this whole book will continuously be dealing with the problematic relationship between words and concepts, but I believe that it is a good idea to construct some kind of skeleton before trying to build a body. No doubt the body of irony that will finally be completed when the reader reaches the last chapter will, for some, bear a resemblance to the famous monster of Dr. Frankenstein—but I will do my best to instill some life into it.

There is no general agreement concerning the etymology of the word *irony*. One approach is that the Greek word *eironeia* could stem from *iron* [opposite] and *onoma* [term], which would fit the most common definition of irony very well: to say one thing and mean the opposite.[1] As far as is known, irony was from the beginning understood as a kind of dissimulation (*dissimulatio, simulatio*). It is reasonable to assume that ironic phenomena of various kinds were recognized in classical antiquity, but when defined in *Rhetorica ad Alexandrum* (formerly credited to Aristotle, now to Anaximenes of Lampsacus, an historian of the fourth century B.C.) irony was pinned down as one of the tropes.[2] The word *irony* thus became part of the rhetorical vocabulary, authorized by among others Cicero and Quintilian, and the concept was defined as stating the opposite of the intended meaning.[3] The trope irony could even be reduced to one single word, and was then often labeled *antiphrasis.*

15

However, irony was initially also understood as an attitude or a mode of behavior. The irony of Socrates is the best known example of this. Socrates' attitude of pretended ignorance, as it appears in the dialogues by Plato, can by no means be reduced to *antiphrasis*, the irony of single words, although many classical and Renaissance authors held that the irony of Socrates is theoretically indistinguishable from rhetorical irony. On the contrary, the irony of Socrates permeates the discourse in its entirety—and from this conception it is only a short step to accepting irony as a general philosophy of life that sees truth as the result of a fundamentally dialectic attitude.

Irony as a philosophy of life or an all-embracing mode of discourse brings one back to the history of the word *eironeia*. After Cicero, who distinguished between irony as a figure and as a pervasive habit of discourse, Socratic irony has by many been highly regarded from a philosophical point of view. Yet, when Socrates was initially called an *eiron*, the word was not necessarily associated with his philosophical virtues.[4] The *eiron* is a deceiver and a mocker, one of the standard characters in Greek comedy. In the plays of Aristophanes, the *eiron* is a cunning and sly figure who talks a lot but never says much. He gives the impression of being an ignorant fool, but regularly he triumphs in the end, thanks to his cleverness. In Aristophanes' *Clouds* the word *eironeia* is, although indirectly, connected to Socrates in a derogatory way.[5]

The opposite stock character of early Greek comedy, the figure who boasts, exaggerates, and tries to give an impression of superior knowledge, is called the *alazon*. Of course, the *alazon* is in fact the true fool. Still, both these figures are in a sense "false," and well-balanced men by the time of Socrates, and later philosophers such as Aristotle, were not in favor of the deceptive behavior of either of them.[6] In a way, they are both ironic figures, being something quite different than they appear to be, and not always distinguishable.[7]

Eironeia, in Latin transcription *ironia*, was thus originally something vulgar as opposed to established ethical values—although the concept was not at all clear-cut even in classical Greece.[8] The *eiron*, as the Greeks most often understood him, was intent on deceiving. However, when finally defined by the rhetoricians, the negative connotations of *irony* were excluded. Cicero and Quintilian did not see the pretense of irony as deceptive. Instead, irony was treated as a trope or a figure of speech; an ornament associated with elegance and refinement. Simultaneously, Socratic irony—an ironic attitude prevailing throughout a whole life—was recognized and praised by Quintilian.[9]

In many respects, the discussion concerning irony during the Middle Ages and the Renaissance was a simple continuation of the ideas presented in classical antiquity. The meaning of the word *ironia*, however, became more thoroughly circumscribed. Some of its original significance was discarded in favor of rhetorical irony: irony as a figure of speech. In the Middle Ages, the most derogatory meanings of *ironia* were largely forgotten (although St. Thomas Aquinas believed irony, "which consists in belittling oneself," to be a sinful vice).[10] The *ironia socratica* appears to have been almost completely unknown—as a term, not as a phenomenon. Most of the medieval authors dealt with *ironia* as a trope or a figure, an instrument for embellishing discourse, but often included phenomena that both earlier and later have been called Socratic irony.[11]

It was with Petrarch and the Renaissance that Socrates once again became a central figure in the discourse on irony. During the Renaissance, Socratic irony was often understood as witty irony filled with enigmatic humor, but everybody did not hold it in high esteem. Some claimed it to be boastful and mocking, not at all modest.[12] Anyhow, the theoreticians of the Renaissance distinguished between irony as a trope, stating the opposite of the intended meaning, and irony as self-depreciation.

When *irony* appeared as an available English word by the first half of the seventeenth century, it was the classical definition of irony as a trope or a figure that stuck to it. Irony was conceived to be a rather technical and elegant mode of speech, whereas the more popular word *raillery* covered the controversial mockery of the time. With the writings of Defoe and Swift in the beginning of the eighteenth century, however, the word *irony* gained ground and soon came to include mockery also. Eventually, efforts were made to distinguish irony from raillery, banter and other notions, but no major changes in the conception of irony occurred. The age-old definition of irony as saying the contrary of the intended meaning dominated these centuries, and in practice the method of "blame-by-praise" was believed to be the most important incarnation of irony. Irony as an all-embracing, dialectic method was not discussed at all. When the irony of Socrates was mentioned, it was conceived to be a skillful blend of "blame-by-praise" and "praise-by-blame."[13]

Yet, radical change was to come. With the writings of Friedrich Schlegel at the turn of the nineteenth century a new notion of irony emerged: Romantic irony. Irony is the most famous and perhaps also the most important part of Romantic literary theory, and the two are so closely associated that irony and Romanticism are now and then regarded as indistinguishable.[14] But when Schlegel himself used the word *romantic,* he did not refer to his own time. It is hence not at all obvious that Schlegel's notion of "romantic irony," mentioned by himself only a few times, must mean the same as it normally does today. However, the term *Romantic irony* has for long been so firmly associated with the notion of irony developed by Schlegel that abandoning it would be confusing.

The heart of Romantic irony lies in a conjunction of opposites: *both/and* is the formula for Romantic irony rather than *either/or.* Classical, rhetorical irony implies a stable truth and a clear-cut intention, whereas Romantic irony implies a fundamental ambiguity of the world. The word *romantic* was already associated with paradox and incongruity before Schlegel wrote about the irony of Socrates, Shakespeare, Cervantes, Sterne, and others,[15] but undoubtedly it was Schlegel who for the first time since antiquity formulated new ideas of irony. However, it is perhaps not reasonable to call his ideas a *theory* of irony. The word *irony* is mentioned only a few times in his early writings and then almost completely abandoned. The notion of Romantic irony is to a large extent a product of later writers who have built upon some of the more striking implications of his critical ideas.[16]

The innovations of Schlegel were based upon a discussion with the past. He is always thoroughly historical, and when writing about irony he often mentions Socrates. One might say that Romantic irony is the Socratic mode of thinking carried to extremes and transformed into literary praxis, and one might even find the seeds of Romantic irony in Quintilian's description of Socrates. For Schlegel, an ironic text is paradoxical and dialectic in its entirety. Irony as a trope is not rejected, but it is the holistic view of irony that is innovative and that characterizes his whole project. Fragment 42 of the "Kritische Fragmente" thus emphasizes that irony is something to be found as a whole and in every detail of the literary work.[17]

It is important to note that Romantic irony is not only an artistic approach, but also a philosophical conception of the world. According to Schlegel, the world is in its essence paradoxical, and the only way to grasp its contradictory totality is to hold an ambivalent attitude. "Irony is clear awareness of the eternal agility; the endless, complete chaos," Schlegel writes in fragment 69 of

"Ideen."[18] In a world where no firm points or absolute truths exist, it is of course consistent to write about irony in fragments, as Schlegel did, and to be sometimes slightly contradictory. If irony is connected to chaos, it cannot be completely ordered without being destroyed.

As stated before, *both/and* is the formula for Romantic irony. Almost all of Schlegel's writings about irony deal with juxtaposed opposites of various kinds. One of his most famous statements is found in fragment 108 of the "Kritische Fragmente," where Socratic irony is discussed: "Everything should be in jest and everything should be in earnest, everything true-heartedly open, and everything deeply dissimulated." In the same fragment Schlegel mentions "the impossibility and necessity of a complete communication."[19] The very act of communication is thus fraught with paradox: it is impossible to really communicate, yet it is necessary to do so—and the only possible means of achieving understanding is to be fundamentally paradoxical: to combine chaos and order in systematized confusion; to mix sincerity and jesting in a symmetry of contradictions.

To attain this mode of communication, *Mitteilung,* to be true to the chaos of the world, Schlegel insists that there be a reference to literature within literature itself. The text must exhibit constant reflection, annihilation, and transcendence. A literary text enclosed in firm fictionality does not mirror the ambiguities of the universe. The bald rupture of illusion, however, often identified as the essence of Romantic irony, is only implied by Schlegel but systematically practiced in the plays of his contemporary Ludwig Tieck.

Schlegel is thus engaged in the shape and content of the literary texts themselves. Authors such as Boccaccio, Shakespeare, Ariosto, Cervantes, and Goethe offer him possibilities to discuss literary devices. Yet, the concept of irony is often also applied to the creative process. Schlegel here draws upon the philosophy of Johann Gottlieb Fichte that focuses on the alternation of affirmation and negation, expansion and contraction, and emerging from and returning to the self.[20] According to Schlegel, the romanticist is characterized by an interaction of creative enthusiasm and restraining self-criticism and is constantly engaged in simultaneous creation and de-creation.

Schlegel's fragmentary ideas of irony are in many ways progressive. He anticipates the philosophy of Nietzsche and the epistemology of the poststructuralists when insisting that existence permits mutually exclusive interpretations and implying that language is trapped in an infinite game of signification that can give nothing but secondary reflections of the various aspects of truth and reality.

However, his influence started much earlier. In Germany, Friedrich Schlegel's evasive notion of irony was adapted and simplified by Adam Müller, who developed a philosophy in which the idea of "mediation" of contradictions was central.[21] For Schlegel, the contradictions of life and literature could never be mediated; they were bound to exist in constant tension. Karl Wilhelm Ferdinand Solger, too, built upon the ideas of Schlegel. In Solger's notoriously obscure dialogue *Erwin* of 1815, it is maintained that all art is dialectic, a juxtaposing and merging of opposites; and that irony is the very mode of comprehending this dialectics. Hence, there can be no art without irony. The artistic irony is the spirit of all art.[22] Perhaps this is as far as the concept of irony can possibly be stretched.

Quite soon, however, critical voices were also heard. Hegel criticized the notion of Romantic irony for being a principle of the hollow and the bad. Romantic irony represents, Hegel held, "the infinite absolute negativity."[23] Yet, Hegel also coined the expression "universal irony of the world," later developed by Kierkegaard, Heine, and Nietzsche with increasing emphasis on the lack of order and meaning in an ateleological world abandoned by God. According to Hegel, however, history proceeds strictly through contradictions: destruction and creation; thesis, antithesis, and synthesis.[24] There is a resemblance between this dialectics of Hegel and the ideas of Friedrich Schlegel, but the difference is important.[25] Hegel's dialectics is transcendental and progressive, Schlegel's "dialectics" allows no genuine synthesis, no mediation—it is rather a duality.

In 1841, Søren Kierkegaard's thesis *Om Begrebet Ironi: Med stadigt Hensyn til Socrates* [*The Concept of Irony: With Constant Reference to Socrates*] was published. Kierkegaard, too, criticized Romantic irony, but in an ambiguous way. For Kierkegaard, as for the Romanticists, irony is not merely a figure of speech or a certain behavior, but a capacity to view existence from contrasting points of view. Irony is the unity of opposites, and irony in a literary text is a product of the whole work.[26] Irony is "a dialectics that in permanent movement sees to that the question does not get entangled in a temporary comprehension; that never gets tired and always is ready to pull the problem afloat when it is grounded, in short: that always knows to keep the problem hovering, and precisely hereby will solve it."[27]

According to Kierkegaard, irony thus keeps everything hovering. As a kind of dialectics, in Hegel's sense of the word, irony has both a positive and a negative aspect, although Kierkegaard tends to put emphasis on the negative.[28] It is often noted that Kierkegaard cites Hegel's opinion that irony is "the infinite absolute negativity," but Kierkegaard does not accept Hegel's criticism wholeheartedly.[29] Kierkegaard is himself skeptical about the irony of Tieck and Friedrich Schlegel—because of its subjectivity "of the second power" (the ego observing the ego)—but enthusiastic about earlier irony, principally the irony of Socrates. However, it is the irony of Schlegel's novel *Lucinde* that is being criticized. The fragments are not mentioned. When Kierkegaard praises Socrates and Shakespeare, he actually indirectly adopts the ideas on irony put forth in the fragments of Schlegel.[30]

Kierkegaard consequently distinguishes between the concept of irony before and after Fichte, but it is not always easy to discover where the difference lies—apart from the fact that the former is accepted and the later not. The distinctions made by Kierkegaard rather seem to be academic camouflage for a fundamental ambiguity in his relation to irony. Socrates, like irony itself, is often described as divine, but nevertheless defective. Kierkegaard writes about *"the irony* in all its divine *infinity,* which lets nothing at all remain." Irony is the "infinite freedom;" though "negative," it is imaginative. For Kierkegaard there is truth, *Sandhed,* in irony, but the enthusiasm of the ironist accomplishes nothing.[31]

Perhaps the essence of Kierkegaard's influential ideas on irony is to be found in thesis number XV: "Ut a dubitatione philosophia sic ab ironia vita digna, quæ humana vocetur, incipit." [Just as philosophy begins with doubt, a life of human dignity begins with irony.][32] This thesis is explained by the end of the book, where irony again is praised. Yet, one does not dive into the sea of irony to stay there, Kierkegaard writes, rather to free one's mind, and then "sound and happy and light" get dressed again.[33] It is thus necessary to *begin* with irony, but it is also necessary to abandon it. Irony is *"the infinite negativity,"* but it is also "positive"—that is, *"infinitely ambiguous."*[34] According to Kierkegaard, irony is ambiguous both in its essence and in its ethics.

In 1833, Connop Thirlwall published an essay called "On the Irony of Sophocles." In this influential text, Thirlwall distinguished between *verbal irony,* equivalent to rhetorical irony; *dialectic irony,* also verbal in its nature and equivalent to Socratic irony; and *practical irony,* irony that is "independent of all forms of speech."[35] Practical irony is nowadays normally called *situational irony*. The main reason for mentioning Thirlwall in this brief history of the concept of irony is that he acknowledges that irony and the tragic are compatible. Schlegel, Müller, and Solger had already discussed irony in tragic plays,[36] but the essay by Thirlwall came to establish the notion of *tragic irony*. This is a little peculiar, as Thirlwall uses the expressions "irony of fate" and "tragic irony" only incidentally, without connecting them to any elaborated concepts.[37]

Instead, Thirlwall's business is to examine the various kinds of irony in the dramas of Sophocles. "Tragic irony" seems to mean simply any kind of irony in tragedy. Oddly enough, it is often claimed that Thirlwall's discussion on Sophoclean irony ends up in a definition of what later has come to be called *dramatic* or *tragic irony*, while as a matter of fact he circumscribes irony on many "totally different" levels in the plays of Sophocles.[38] Thirlwall does not use the term *dramatic irony* at all. It was not until the twentieth century that dramatic irony came to be defined as a discrepancy between the knowledge of the spectator and the knowledge of the protagonist of a drama. Dramatic irony, or tragic irony, as we understand it today, occurs when a character acts in a way that leads to the opposite result of what was intended, or, more specifically, when a speaker uses words that for the audience bear an ominous sense that is not understood by the character himself or herself—a phenomenon noted but in no way highlighted by Thirlwall.[39]

No radical changes can be noted in the development of the concept of irony during the remaining part of the nineteenth century. Situational irony and irony of fate were established as nonverbal variants of irony. Generally, irony gained ground as a tool for positive evaluation, which eventually made it possible for New Criticism to propose an extended usage of irony as a critical concept. As a forerunner of this critical school, I. A. Richards laid the foundation for some of its ideas on ambiguity and irony. In *Principles of Literary Criticism* from 1925, Richards refers to Coleridge's high evaluation of the reconciliation of opposite qualities. Because Coleridge's ideas are related to Schlegel's, Richards indirectly opens up a connection to the German Romanticists. According to Richards, the "æsthetic experiences" of the best poems have their roots in "a balance of opposites" and "mediating relations"; they bear "an ironical contemplation."[40] Also, for Cleanth Brooks, "balance," "stability," "unity," and "complexity" are key notions, and in *The Well Wrought Urn*, first published in 1947, Brooks too connects to Coleridge's idea of the reconciliation of opposites. For Brooks, the three terms "ambiguity," "paradox," and "irony" are very intimately related.

Brooks's main project, in *The Well Wrought Urn* and in two articles dedicated to irony, is to circumscribe a certain quality of poetry that is highly regarded by him.[41] He argues that a poem is not reducible to a simple "statement." Rather, the meaning of a successful poem is to be found in the hovering of paradoxes and ambiguities. Brooks maintains that every single part of a poem is constantly modified by the other parts, and "irony is the most general term that we have for the kind of qualification which the various elements in a context receive from the context." Moreover, he continues, "irony is our most general term for indicating that recognition of incongruities—which, again, pervades all poetry to a degree far beyond what our conventional criticism has been heretofore willing to allow."[42]

Here Brooks is only a hair's breadth from Karl Solger's very general conception of irony as the dialectics of all art. Although not discussed at all, the thoughts of Friedrich Schlegel lie in the background. As we have seen, Schlegel treats irony mainly as a phenomenon of contrasts on various levels that permeate the whole work of art. An important difference, however, is that Schlegel is not interested in the mediation or reconciliation of opposites. For New Criticism, as is known, this is of the utmost importance.

It is significant to note that it is not really the *term* irony that is of interest to Brooks, but rather the phenomenon of parts being qualified by the context in a poem.[43] His point is that this qualification is indistinguishable from what is habitually called irony. According to Brooks, there is no difference in principle, only in degree, between the obvious, sharp contrasts involved in what has normally been called irony, and the more subtle reversals of meaning generated by contextual relations within a text, or the coexistence of competing meanings. Hence, it is quite consistent with his theory to use the word *irony* also in a fairly traditional way, as he himself often does; to denote a certain tone, mood, or contrast in particular words or short passages.[44] Brooks obviously finds it appropriate to apply the term *irony* to the whole scale between the two extreme levels already established in antiquity: from the simplest rhetorical irony to the most elusive variation of Socratic (or Romantic) irony. Actually, I believe that it is this old dichotomy that is revised and adapted to the domain of lyric poetry by Brooks in a controversial but prolific way.

Finally, a few words must be said about poststructuralism and postmodernism. The deconstructive method of Jacques Derrida, which aimed at revealing widely diverging possible interpretations and postponing any certain meaning of texts, is often associated with irony—not so much by Derrida himself as by other theorists that are more or less in favor of poststructuralism. A wide range of notions associated with Derrida, Paul de Man, and other poststructuralists—such as "différance" and "indeterminacy"—are from a historical point of view closely related to irony.[45] Deconstruction, one may maintain, is a method designed to indicate the ironic potential of all texts: *nothing* is what it appears to be.

For de Man, irony is explicitly the condition for undecidability in literature and critical discourse; it represents the lack of determinate meaning. At least this is what the closing sentences in *Allegories of Reading* imply: "Irony is . . . the systematic undoing . . . of understanding. As such, far from closing off the tropological system, irony enforces the repetition of its aberration."[46] In his early essay "Allegory and Irony in Baudelaire," de Man seems to understand irony as Socratic irony when he associates it with a "dominant overlooking position" and "a different and higher point of view."[47] In his much debated essay "The Rhetoric of Temporality," however, his notion of irony is more difficult to grasp. The word *irony* is given different meanings in different parts of the essay, which makes his arguments somehow deceptive. The essay ends up being strangely normative in favor of allegory. Actually, de Man here treats irony chiefly as a classical trope. This becomes apparent when he analyses the same poem by Wordsworth as Cleanth Brooks once did, but compared to Brooks he uses the word *irony* in a much more restricted way.[48] Allegory, on the other hand, ascends to the status of an all-embracing, critical tool. It seems as if "allegory" in "The Rhetoric of Temporality" means much the same as "irony" in *Allegories of Reading*.

The reading method of poststructuralism is generally called *deconstruction*, and the literature of the latter half of the twentieth century that has been favored by it is generally called *postmodern*. The alleged radical undecidability of these texts is now and then given the name "postmodern irony." Postmodern irony may be said to take Romantic irony one step further. As one knows, the creative subject was central to the Romanticists, and it was supposed to transcend the characters and events of the text. In postmodern irony, the subject is withdrawn from the text to such an extent that it becomes practically annihilated. The postmodern text must instead be circumscribed in negative terms: it lacks closure, it is dedicated to uncertainty and randomness—and its self-referentiality is brought to the surface.[49] Clearly, there is a strong link between writing fragments,[50] Romantic irony, the impersonal narrator of Flaubert's *Madame Bovary*, and, later, modernist novels and postmodern irony with its emphasis on texts without coherent subjects—a link that can be traced all the way back to the *eiron* figure of antiquity who refused to reveal his "real" opinions in a straightforward way.

The difference between the notions of irony tied to Romanticism and poststructuralism is important, however. Deconstruction favors skeptical analysis in a radical and rather one-sided way. It differs from the Romantic attitude in that it does not accept—theoretically—the creative "enthusiasm" that is so crucial to Friedrich Schlegel. For de Man, the distinction between allegory and symbol is important, and he argues that allegory, the trope of difference, is more authentic than symbol, the figure of unity. Schlegel, on the other hand, if confronted with this distinction, would have accepted the two figural modes as necessarily complementary.[51]

The Beginning of a New Story

To define irony is not, I would say, all that wise. As we have seen, the concept of irony has undergone considerable changes. Its history arguably comprises more extensions and modifications than that of most literary concepts, and, as Nietzsche points out, one can only define concepts that lack history.[52] This multitude of approaches is reflected in theoretical discourse, interpretive practice, and everyday language. Most people use the word *irony* in many different and indeed vague senses, including the sly, subversive, and self-depreciating ones, but when asked to define irony, they almost always fall back on the rhetorical formula of saying one thing and meaning the opposite.

There is nothing strange or objectionable about this use of words. Although the concept of irony has changed through history, the basis for even the most recent extensions was established already more than two thousand years ago. At the core of the concept one can find the notion of incompatible meanings. This is a necessary but perhaps not sufficient condition for irony. The variants of irony have differed in aspects that may primarily be reduced to questions concerning how narrowly or how widely irony can be defined: Do we find irony in one single word, in a sentence, in a text in its entirety, in a whole life, or in the whole world? Does irony require an absolute contradiction of meaning, or does it suffice that there are opposites of a slightly less pronounced character, or even quite vague ambiguities? Is the effect of irony necessarily some kind of consensus where one of the opposed meanings wins, or may irony include a floating meaning that perhaps never comes to an end?

All these questions are fundamental and will continuously be considered in this book. In addition, at least two more approaches have been prominent in the history of irony: the normative and the hermeneutical questions. I will return to the normative question toward the end of the book, whereas the hermeneutical question will be of prime importance from the beginning. Surprisingly enough, the question of "where" irony emerges has very often been neglected. To put it simply, is irony in the author, the text, or the reader? This negligence in even quite recent texts on irony is probably due to a presupposed consensus on the authority of the author—as the word suggests. Sometimes the hermeneutical question is treated as if it were of only secondary interest.

No matter how one defines it or values it, however, the concept of irony has its historical and theoretical roots in the realm of words and literature. The more penetrating discussions concerning irony have been almost exclusively limited to literary theory. A quick investigation of a major database indicates that there are thousands of books and articles dealing with irony in literature. In the case of music and art, this is not so. The word *irony* is hardly found in dictionaries covering these disciplines.

Yet, it is also true that the concept of irony *is* being used to interpret paintings, sculptures, buildings, films, advertisements, videos, symphonies, songs, dances, industrial photos,[53] political utopias,[54] and shoes,[55] and this usage has increased rather dramatically in the last few decades. Today, one may find the word *irony* in not a few texts concerning visual art and music, but it is still relatively rare for visual works of art, or specific pieces of music, to be described as ironic in a more concise manner. It is not hard to see why: as the concept of irony is basically connected to the use of words and literary meaning, it is easy to hesitate before trying to say where the irony is to be found if nothing is really "said" in the work of art. If nothing is "stated," there can be no implied opposite "meaning"—or can there?

Certainly, many visual and musical works of art have been interpreted as ironic because of their literary aspects. When titles or other words are involved, it is relatively easy to discuss ironic aspects in traditional terms. The title of a painting or a piece of music explicitly makes some kind of proposition, and when words are inscribed in paintings or sung to music, literary aspects are stressed. A more challenging question that will be posed in this book is whether it is reasonable to speak of irony in images and pieces of music that lack verbal elements altogether—and if so, what does this imply?

The aim of the book is thus to provide a theory that enables the concept of irony to be transferred from the literary to the visual and audible domains. In practice, this transfer is already on its way, and it is high time that theory followed practice. In 1970, William August Becker finished a dissertation with the title "Concepts of Irony with Special Reference to Applications in the Visual Arts," in which he stated that "The field of art criticism . . . has been handicapped by a lack of tradition of the discussion of irony."[56] Becker wanted to initiate a new discussion, and I agree that it is an urgent task to remedy this lack in the criticism of both art and music. Never before in history, I believe, has the concept of irony been so widely acknowledged and so often made use of as during the last decade of the twentieth century: in the streets of big cities, in the pubs of small towns and villages, in the fields in the countryside, and in the lecture rooms at the universities. Even the appearance of an "ironic generation" has been proclaimed. Never before in history have the concepts of culture and literature been so wide. The cultural field covers a very wide area of multimedia and mixed-media art: concepts of art and works of art that, with increasing frequency, are being interpreted in terms of irony. Still, the efforts to examine, understand, and describe what happens when the range of the already wide concept of irony increases in such a fundamental way have been very limited.

It goes without saying that the subject of this book requires an interdisciplinary approach. Perhaps this necessity can lead not only to an understanding of what irony in visual art and music might be, but also to an increased awareness of how ironic interpretations of literary texts work; and perhaps even to the highlighting of a few fundamental similarities between the various art forms. If this is achieved before reaching the Bibliography, I will certainly be lucky. Irony is a notoriously elusive concept, but I believe that this theoretical elusiveness might be mitigated rather than aggravated through the widening of frames. Visual and musical irony is not a "problem"—on the contrary.

In any case, some interesting dilemmas of human expression, thinking, and communication will be highlighted in the forthcoming chapters. First, some important theoretical and terminological issues will be scrutinized within the well-established framework of literary criticism, and then the concept of irony will be gradually transposed to discussions on images and music.

As have few other phenomena, irony has challenged, and continues to challenge, the ability to interpret and understand what happens in art and in ordinary life. My ambition in this book, however, is to establish a discourse that is as earnest as possible. "Irony is definitely no laughing matter,"[57] Friedrich Schlegel writes, and I interpret the statement to be as serious as might be expected of an essay on a phenomenon that Kierkegaard believes to be "a divine madness."[58] Yet, perhaps an effort to write a book on irony completely without irony would be human madness.

2

Irony and the Problem of Intentionalism

> The painter's products stand before us as though they were
> alive, but if you question them, they maintain a most majestic
> silence.
>
> —Plato

IRONY AND ORALITY

IN ITS WIDEST SENSE *HERMENEUTICS* IS BOTH THE SCIENCE AND THE PRAG-
matics of interpretation. What does one do when one interprets
texts, for instance? How does one do it, and why does one do it
the way one does? The hermeneutics of irony is, of course, subor-
dinated to the premises of hermeneutics in general. There is
nothing in irony that gives one the right to treat it as something
exclusive. I believe it is true that irony has the ability to both confuse and illuminate in quite special ways—once one has incorpo-
rated irony into one's mode of thinking, it might very well invade
the universe of one's mind—but it is nevertheless possible to discuss it rationally and with the aid of established conceptual tools.

The hermeneutics of irony thus includes the standard hermeneutical questions "how?" and "why?". One of the reasons for
studying irony is that the hermeneutical problems become radically acute as soon as the question of irony is raised. Irony sharp-
ens all discussions of interpretation. Its existence proves that
hermeneutics is not an esoteric issue for dry scholars, but something that is a part of everyone's life—at least in its pragmatic aspect. In my view the excitement, dedication, bewilderment, and
perhaps frustration of interpreting are never more pronounced
than when irony is involved. Why is this so? Because irony allows
one the possibility of not only modifying or changing meaning,
but also of reversing it. Irony includes both vague nuances and
fundamental contradictions. Therefore it is perhaps the most inclusive discursive phenomenon, impossible to ignore.

The classical hermeneutical question of irony is easy to pose but not as easy to answer: how does one know when irony is at work? This problem is centered on the question of intentionality. The standard definition of *irony* found in most dictionaries involves an opposition between something that is *said* and what is *meant* by it, and as this rhetorical definition is rarely questioned, irony is almost always treated as a verbal phenomenon that is a result of an intentional act. Oddly enough, this standard definition that includes the intention of a writer or a speaker is often understood to be a definition of a *textual* phenomenon—even by philosophically minded literary critics. Not so seldom irony is even highlighted as the rhetorical device that "proves" the necessity of including authorial intention in the interpretation of literature. This is an illusion resulting from a vicious circle. If one accepts a definition of irony that includes intentionality, intentionality is self-evidently impossible to ignore. If one does not, however, the importance of intentionality is open to dispute. Questioning intentionality thus includes questioning the standard definition of *irony*.

Why, then, is intentionality so firmly rooted in the hermeneutics of irony? Naturally, the answer lies in the history of irony and the history of hermeneutics. When the ancient thinkers initially defined the concept of irony, it was modeled on the hermeneutical pattern of orality. In Plato, the written text is understood as a special case of oral discourse, sharing much of its characteristics but lacking its communicative strength. Plato prefers the spoken language, as it is always possible to ask interlocutors what they mean by using certain words. According to the dialogue *Phaedrus*, a written text remains silent if one puts a question to it; hence it is inferior as a philosophical instrument. Socrates says:

> You know, Phaedrus, that's the strange thing about writing, which makes it truly analogous to painting. The painter's products stand before us as though they were alive, but if you question them, they maintain a most majestic silence. It is the same with written words; they seem to talk to you as though they were intelligent, but if you ask them anything about what they say, from a desire to be instructed, they go on telling you just the same thing forever. . . . And when it [the written] is ill-treated and unfairly abused it always needs its parent to come to its help, being unable to defend or help itself.

To this Phaedrus replies, of course: "Once again you are perfectly right," and then, with the aid of Socrates, he reaches the conclusion that "the living speech, [is] the original of which the written discourse may fairly be called a kind of image."[1]

It is certainly a paradox, and one not without its irony, that the discussion between Socrates and Phaedrus is a written text formed by the author Plato. Certainly, the dialectic designs of Plato's texts suggest an oral communication of a rather stiff kind, but if, "from a desire to be instructed," one asks the words of Plato what they mean, "they go on telling you just the same thing forever."

This inherent paradox of Plato's argument for the superiority of oral communication does not, however, invalidate it. It is true that spoken words are often superior in communicating feelings, pieces of information, and ideas. One knows that from everyday experience. People all go on talking to each other without very often feeling an urge to write articles or poems in order to make things clearer. Yet, it is also true that written words are sometimes superior. For instance, when it comes to getting a grip on a large amount of information or a complex web of arguments or feelings, it is convenient to write the words down. Furthermore, one often has to rely on written words in order to be able to reach people that one cannot meet eye to eye, either because they are too far away or because they are not yet born.

This is self-evident, but it is perhaps not self-evident that written words are not only sometimes superior, but also somehow different. If the written discourse is "a kind of image" of the living speech, it is certainly not only a distorted image, but an image with its own, original life. The ontology of a written word is different from the ontology of a spoken word. As this difference is both factual and normative, the exact nature of it cannot be established—but it exists. Walter J. Ong summarizes: "After the invention of writing, and much more after the invention of print, the question of who is saying what to whom becomes confusingly and sometimes devastatingly complicated. The writer's audience is always a fiction."[2] This is correct, I think, and it entails certain consequences for irony.

The referentiality of spoken words is *in general* more clear-cut than the referentiality of written words. Oral communication always includes at least one physical context that to some extent determines both the "who," the "what," and the "whom" of the utterances. The speaker and the listener share their experience of time and space, and unless the speaker quotes or acts, the word "I" refers to the person who talks. Whereas spoken words generally may be said to communicate in one way or another (to communicate means "to share"), written words tend to liberate themselves from communication in a narrow sense. The "I" of a written text does not necessarily refer to the writer, partly due to the fact that the temporal and spatial contexts of writer and reader differ. It is a historical fact that written texts characterized as "literature" have developed a status of certain autonomy. All texts are sooner or later physically removed from their creators, and it is possible (although not in any way necessary) to regard them as independent keepers of meaning.

The great majority of differences between the spoken and the written word are not of a logical nature, but rather the result of conventions that make life easier and a little bit more pleasant or interesting to live. If my neighbor says to me, "I saw one of your cats on my roof some minutes ago," I accept that as a statement that involves some facts about the physical world around me. Because I am not the only owner of black and white cats, my neighbor may be mistaken, and so may I when I trust her words—but from a pragmatic point of view it is a good, general rule to presume that oral communication includes a factual link between the uttered words and the real world. Life would simply be too complicated if one did not.

However, if I read the same words in a novel, it is equally convenient to presume that there is not necessarily a factual link between the words and the real world around me. No doubt it would be an absurd action, and a severe waste of time and energy, if I went out looking for my cat after having read the sentence. Of course, there *may* be factual connections between what we call fiction and the real world; but if I feel that a novel loses power and existential depth when its plot is being connected to the factual world, I have good reason for treating the novel as a text that does not work in the same way as oral communication.

This is self-evident also, I think, but nevertheless the difference must be emphasized because its implications are often neglected in the discussions on irony. The border between the ontology of oral and written discourse is, however, vague. My neighbor's words "I saw one of your cats on my roof some minutes ago" may be part of an amusing story about what happened yesterday many miles from our houses, they may report what happened in her dream when taking a nap after dinner, or they may be the result of an impulse to deceive me. To put it briefly, her words may be "fictitious." On the other hand, the very same words in a novel *might* say something very factual—about the author, about what has happened in the real world, or even (although it is perhaps not very likely) about the reader's cat. It is not compulsory to read novels and poems as pure fiction.

The distinction between oral and written words is thus not definite. Typical characteristics of both oral and textual "communication" are found in, for instance, hand-written letters, E-mails, and telephone conversations. Lyrics in popular songs are by some people comprehended as literary texts and by others as communicative statements made by the artist himself or herself. On the basis of a wide range of personal motivations and circumstances, the listener/reader estimates the relevance of various contexts, ranging from the situation of the "sender" to the interests of the "receiver"—and his or her choice of context might very well be decisive for the interpretation of the words.

As far as I can see, there is no method for establishing general rules for the interpretation of orally and textually mediated words, respectively. However, hermeneutical research has offered not only descriptive investigations. On the contrary, statements about interpretation are often heavily biased toward the normative. When trying to explain "how" a text means, many writers in fact make statements on how it *ought* to mean. This is the case also in the history of the concept of irony, and the most decisive feature of this history is the tendency to reduce irony to a phenomenon that is defined by the characteristics of oral communication. Although it is not always made quite explicit, many hold the opinion that irony ought to be understood as something that cannot be properly dealt with distinct from the conventions of oral discourse.

Because this connection between irony and oral communication is normative rather than descriptive, it is certainly impossible to prove that it is invalid. Instead, I want to argue for another normative standpoint: that it is a great disadvantage to connect irony and oral communication too strongly. It is true that irony historically has relied very much on extralinguistic features, but I suggest that there is good reason for treating irony apart from the paradigm of orality. Orality favors intentionalism, and intentionalism is problematic. The words of Plato arguing that a written text "always needs its parent to come to its help, being unable to defend or help itself," imply a concept of meaning that is far too authoritative for my personal taste. I interpret Plato's words as stating the law of the Father: there is right, and there is wrong, and only the divine *I* knows how and why. In oral communication "truth" is always productive, but in other discourses it is sometimes reductive.

The hermeneutical primacy of intentionalism in the theories of irony has caused endless debates on whether this or that text is "really" ironic, and on whether this or that author has been mis-construed or not. The law of the Father has led many a good critic to "ask daddy" instead of making his or her own interpretation of the meaning of the text. Classical, medieval, and Renaissance authors treat irony mainly as a direct result of an intention of a speaker, and the hermeneutical question is often reduced to a question of how to interpret this speaker's intonation and ges-tures.[3] The listener hears the speaker say one thing; but if the speaker pulls faces at the same time, the listener may suspect that he or she means something else—and if one feels uncertain, one just asks the speaker what he or she actually means. Then one is on safe ground as far as irony is concerned, the argument goes—unless, of course, the speaker tells a lie.

According to traditional hermeneutics, it is taken for granted that irony necessarily originates from the speaker/author. The problem is how to "reveal" the irony, and the solution is to look for "signals" that indicate the true intentions. Another problem, unfortunately not considered at all by most rhetoricians, is that what is understood as "signals" of irony, mainly intonation and gestures, are actually part of the communicative situation and hence strictly speaking no more in direct alliance with the inten-tion than the words. Gestures, also, have to be "decoded."

However, there are other ways of dealing with irony.

IRONY AND WRITING

Although the classical, medieval, and Renaissance philoso-phers and authors did not omit discussing ironic traits in the texts themselves, the dominance of intentionalism was not bro-ken until Friedrich Schlegel put forth his ideas of irony. From German Romanticism and onward, irony is treated variously as something intended by the author, something inherent in the text, or something generated by the interpretation of the reader. By this time, D. C. Muecke notes, it became possible to think of irony as "unintentional, something observable and hence repre-sentable in art, something that happened or that one became or could be made aware of."[4] With Romanticism, Ong concludes, the textual mode associated with writing and print reaches its first climax. Ong is not explicitly concerned with the question of intention, but his description of the development "From Mimesis to Irony," as the title of an essay of his reads, gives an adequate picture of how one eventually reaches "the multiple layers of irony in creative writing and the resulting critical fascination with irony in literature and critical discussion."[5] The subtitle of the essay is "The Distancing of Voice." If the question of intentionalism that is suggested by this subtitle were to be answered, the result might be an essay with the clumsy but adequate title "From Rhetorical, Univocal, Intentional Irony to Romantic, Multilayered, Hovering Irony."

It is not easy to disentangle Schlegel's thoughts about intentionality in his scattered fragments—the subject is naturally not treated very systematically—but a few words might be said. As Schlegel accepts the existence of rhetorical as well as Socratic and Romantic irony, and as he does not seem to be interested in redefining rhetorical irony, intentionality is undoubtedly part of his ideas of irony at large. Furthermore, Romantic irony is, according to Schlegel, to a large extent a concept of poetic creation, which makes it deeply associated with intentionality. However, it is understood that Romantic irony is manifested in the work itself. The sovereignty of the poet consists in an ability to exercise complete control over the written text, which is almost synonymous with a withdrawal from it. Schlegel's and other Romanticists' emphasis on the creative subject thus implies a kind of objectivity of the created text. One might say that irony in a Romantic text is the result of conflicts in the text that are not resolved by any authorial subject; it is not a figure that is dependent on an intention outside the text. Clearly, the intentionality related to Schlegel's ideas of irony is something quite different from the intentionality of rhetorical irony.

There are certain passages in the writings of Schlegel that explicitly support such an interpretation of his ideas. In "Fragmente" number 51, he discusses irony and naïveté in Homer and states that, even if the author had no intentions, *Absichten*, the true authoress, Nature, and the Poetry itself, had intentions.[6] The Romantic conception of irony as something that may be found not only in texts, but also in the world around us, is here mirrored in an interesting way. Schlegel suggests that nature itself may have an intention. Irony in a text may emerge independently, he asserts; it need not be intended by the author.

When Schlegel writes about the irony of irony in "Über die Unverständlichkeit" [On Incomprehensibility], it becomes even more apparent that he believes that irony may be something that arises, *entsteht*, quite out of the author's control. One may talk

ironically about irony without noticing, "ohne zu merken," that
one is part of a much more remarkable irony. The irony of irony
arises "if irony becomes wild and escapes all control"—irony
may well refuse to let itself be tamed.[7] Kierkegaard, too, sometimes treats irony as a phenomenon created by an interpreter
rather than an author. After citing a passage by G. H. Schubert
describing ironic constellations in nature, Kierkegaard remarks
that "all such things are not in nature, but *the ironic subject* sees
them in it."[8]

A more systematic discussion of intentionality did not arise
until the 1940s and the heyday of New Criticism. In their famous
essay, "The Intentional Fallacy," W. K. Wimsatt and Monroe C.
Beardsley assert that the intention of the author is irrelevant if
not manifested in the text, and superfluous if manifested. The intention is on the one hand not "desirable," on the other hand
not "available."[9] Wimsatt and Beardsley do not discuss irony, but
their thoughts are related to Cleanth Brooks's notion of irony.
Clearly, Brooks is not interested in the intentions of the author.
He does not explicitly discuss intentionality in relation to irony,
but he defines irony as a textual phenomenon, as "the kind of
qualification which the various elements in a context receive
from the context."[10]

Brooks's focus is definitely on the intrinsic characteristics of
texts, but he is well aware of the fact that irony is a descriptive
category that may be relevant for one reader, but not for another,
when confronted with the same text.[11] It is not a main question
for him to argue that the interpreter is the creator of irony, but
he clearly recognizes the role of the reader. Consequently, he
may write about a "recognition of incongruities" rather than
about incongruities inherent in the text.[12] In the writings of
Brooks, Joseph A. Dane remarks, irony has already become "a
critical problem."[13]

It is quite difficult to find defenders of irony as a purely textual
phenomenon in recent critical discourse, but there are excep-
tions. In an article from 1982, Daniel O. Nathan rejects intentionalism as the key to interpreting irony and asks for "*textual*
evidence." He is convinced that irony always emerges from traits
in the written text itself, which is "the sole source of evidence in
interpretation."[14] Irony as a result of an interpretive act of the
reader does not seem to be a possibility for Nathan.

It has thus become unusual to describe irony as an intrinsic
quality of texts, but intentionalism lives on. In some of the most
influential books on irony from the last decades, intention is still

the heart of the matter. In *The Compass of Irony* from 1969, D. C. Muecke initially asserts that irony "is in the eye of the beholder," but he also maintains that one has to ask the question *"Was it meant ironically?"* if one wants to know whether something is ironic or not.[15] He repeatedly states that intention is a necessary condition for irony.[16]

There is, however, one exception to this rule. Muecke explains: "I have said several times that a work can be ironical only by intention; being ironical means deliberately being ironical. It is only events and situations which may be unintentionally ironic."[17] In *Irony and the Ironic* from 1982, Muecke submits that "while we may legitimately question whether or not something has been said or done with ironical intent, we cannot question anyone's right to see something as ironic. We may question his sense of taste though."[18]

Still, Muecke prefers to linger on the comprehension of texts as communicative in a narrow sense. He does not abandon the idea of a "correct interpretation" of irony and maintains that the term *irony* ought to be reserved for intentionally based interpretations of texts.[19] In order to be able to deal with phenomena that, ever since the beginning of the nineteenth century, have been called ironic, although they are clearly not related to any intention of an ironist—cosmic irony, irony of events, and so forth—Muecke is forced to uphold a distinction between verbal and situational irony. Although he admits that it is impossible to draw a sharp line between verbal and situational irony, he finds himself obliged to accept that there are two "types" of irony that are distinguished from each other in the issue of intentionality: verbal irony that is the result of an intention and situational irony that is the result of an interpretation.

Wayne C. Booth's *A Rhetoric of Irony* from 1974, like Muecke's *The Compass of Irony* one of the modern standard works on irony, is also firmly grounded on intentionalism. Booth's notion of "stable irony" implicitly depends on the view that at least some intentions are accessible, unambiguous, and of significant hermeneutical value.[20] In a few passages in the book Booth suggests that it is really the texts in themselves that comprise the intentions, but the evocation of his notion of "implied author"— his proposal that one should "for some critical purposes . . . talk only of the *work's* intentions, not the author's"—and his idea of "reconstructing" stable ironies, seem to be inconsistent with his obvious reliance on traditionally conceived authorial intention.[21] As Susan Suleiman puts it, when writing about the work's intentions, Booth "simply effects a metonymic displacement and treats the text as a hypostatized subject."[22] Although Booth is very well aware of the difficulties involved in the act of interpretation, he thinks that there is always right and wrong in irony. If there is not—if the irony is "unstable" rather than "stable"—it is because the author did *not* intend it to be stable.

In an article published in 1983, "The Empire of Irony," Booth seems to reduce his claims concerning the relevance of intention. He here states that, "of those ironies that are embodied in language, some are the results of human intentions and some are not," and with discreet reluctance he admits that nobody can prevent a reader from interpreting a text against the author's intentions.[23]

It is certainly true that authors sometimes intend to be ironic and that readers sometimes find irony in texts that are not intended to be ironic. Booth's acceptance of this truth, however, does not change the hermeneutical basis for his notion of irony. Rather, it indicates some inherent difficulties in his theory. If one assumes that there are verbal ironies that are intended, and verbal ironies that are not intended—how does one know *when* one is dealing with a stable, intended irony? If the intended ironies actually have to be "reconstructed" on textual evidence, as Booth suggests in *The Rhetoric of Irony*, is it not extremely difficult to tell the difference between a "reconstructed," stable irony and a "constructed" irony created by the reader? Is not the stability of the reconstruction an illusion built upon a base of interpretive prejudices? Even if one maintains that there are verbal ironies that are intended and stable, and verbal ironies that are not intended, and that it is somehow possible to tell the difference between them—what *reason* does the reader have for assuming that it is relevant to consider the intention of being ironic in one instance, while at the same time the reader may choose to neglect the intention of *not* being ironic in another instance?

Muecke and Booth both recognize many of the problematic implications of an intentionalistic kind of hermeneutics, but they seem to accept authorial intention as something so deeply rooted in the concept of irony that it is meaningless to really question its relevance. In an article that aims at being unbiased, Göran Hermerén, however, attempts to clarify some of the assumptions made by intentionalists and nonintentionalists respectively. Hermerén's discussion concerning irony and intention is in many ways very informative, but his conclusion that intention is at least partly relevant to the interpretation of irony, no matter which theory of meaning one supports, is based on his opinion that an explanation of irony "should not depart too much from ordinary usage."[24] With this assumption, fair enough in itself, it seems to follow that one is obliged to adopt the standard descriptions of rhetorical irony in dictionaries, and hence one is left with no other choice than to accept that intention is the *sine qua non* of irony. It is certainly reasonable to demand that an explanation be in fair accordance with ordinary usage—that is one of the basic assumptions of this book—but the problem is that ordinary usage of the word *irony* shifts. Various kinds of ordinary usage are incompatible, and hence a circumscription of irony, if possible, must be performed on the basis of other arguments. One cannot cite ordinary usage as *evidence* for the "true meaning" of a concept, but if it loses contact with ordinary usage altogether the concept becomes worthless, of course.

Now and then, however, efforts are still made to prove that irony *necessarily* implies the hermeneutical sovereignty of authorial intention. As a rule, the model of oral communication forms the basis of the arguments. In his extensive book, *Interpretation,* P. D. Juhl makes no effort to distinguish between speaking and writing. In his quest for a general theory of interpretation, he takes it for granted that not only oral communication but also the writing and reading of literary texts are always characterized by an aim to uphold a univocal delivery of meaning. Among his arguments for intentionalism—he wants to show "that the anti-intentionalist thesis is incorrect"—are found discussions on allusion and irony, among other phenomena.[25] Unfortunately, his arguments are circular. As both allusion and the very narrow notion of rhetorical irony that Juhl discusses include intention by definition (in the case of rhetorical irony, to say something and *mean* the opposite), it is self-evident and empty to conclude that the intention of the author is relevant to the interpretation of allusion and irony. Juhl is putting the cart before the horse. If Juhl were to choose the notions "intertextuality" and "situational irony" instead, his system would break down. "When intentionality becomes suspect, the standard definitions of irony come to seem inadequate," Lilian R. Furst remarks[26]—and to insist on the standard definitions the way Juhl does is to treat the symptoms of an illness instead of the illness itself. If one should define irony in a way that excludes intention, or reject the oral model of communication, then the arguments of Juhl collapse.[27]

Speech act theories of irony also are, as might be expected, firmly rooted in the rhetorical definition of irony and of little help to the interpretation of more complex, written literature. In an article called "The Theory of Ironic Speech Acts," David J. Amante analyzes ironic communication without questioning the relevance of principles of oral communication for the understanding of written texts. He takes it to be "self-evident" that "the speaker must intend his irony and must be capable of giving signals to his ironic meaning."[28] If he were to deal with, for instance, Romantic irony, the result would be very strange. Amante leaves us with a good description of rhetorical irony on the basis of traditional hermeneutics, but without a clue as to how to handle more complex types of ironies in literature or elsewhere. Although effective within the rather narrow range of oral communication,[29] speech act theory seems to be incapable of aiding one's understanding of the majority of ironic phenomena.

IRONY AND INTERPRETATION

As a consequence of the strong impact of reception theory and reader-oriented criticism over the last twenty-five years, however, voices have been raised in favor of the view that irony is a phenomenon created by the interpreter rather than by the writer or the text itself. It has become possible to think that perhaps the answer to the question "how do we know when irony is at work?" is that we cannot definitely "know": irony is not an objective quality; it is not "there" until one "sees" it.

In an essay on irony and intention published in 1979, William E. Tolhurst maintains that "the work is a public object and the reader is as qualified to interpret it as is the author." This is a good starting point, but his strange notion of an "intended audience" makes his line of argument collapse into quite ordinary intentionalism.[30] Like so many before him, Tolhurst takes it for granted that the interpretation of written literature must necessarily follow the basic rules of oral discourse. One year later, Paul A. Bové claims that no text " 'is' or 'is not' 'ironic.' " Bové's conception of irony is consistent and symptomatic of the dominating hermeneutics of the time: "Since no text has meaning apart from the interpretations of it, no statement can be made about what a poem 'is,' but only about what certain interpretations let it 'mean.' "[31]

Bové's assertions are feasible but not really supported by arguments. Instead, it was Stanley Fish who in 1983, building upon ideas of meaning and interpretation developed during the preceding decade, formulated the first consistent, reader-oriented theory of irony. In "Short People Got No Reason to Live: Reading Irony," Fish convincingly demonstrates that, as a matter of empirical fact, it is virtually impossible to agree upon what the intention of the author—in spite of his or her explicit statements—"really" is. Fish chooses to discuss the reception of Randy Newman's song "Short People," stating that they "got no reason to live." When the meaning of this caustic text was excitedly debated, Newman himself declared that it was ironically intended. However, "rather than providing a point of clarity and stability," Fish asserts, this authorial statement "merely extended the area of interpretive dispute."[32] Was Newman in fact lying, telling the truth, rationalizing, revealing unconscious opinions, or what?

Fish argues that every conception of an author's intention is in itself an interpretation, and hence no more—or less—valid than more overtly presented interpretations. For Fish, irony is an "interpretive strategy." In polemics with Wayne C. Booth, he effectively demonstrates that irony is never "in" the texts and that there are no "stable" ironies. Fish observes that a poem by Swift that was read straightforwardly by "everybody" for two hundred years—a seemingly perfect proof of the existence of stability—suddenly came to be interpreted ironically by "everybody."[33]

Fish's stance is well motivated, but his valuable insights into the nature of irony and interpretation do not in themselves rule out intentionalism. It can be argued that even if the intention of an author is empirically inaccessible, perhaps even nonexistent, one has a moral obligation to interpret the meaning of a text as much as possible in accordance with the most reasonable account of what the author "meant"—the difficulty of the task should not prevent the reader from trying to fulfil it.[34] Again, it all depends on which hermeneutical stance one takes: should one try to read books more or less as one talks to people, or should one read them as texts written by authors that are necessarily "dead," as Barthes would put it?

Two major works on irony from the last decade, written by Joseph A. Dane and Linda Hutcheon, must also be mentioned in this context. Although Dane's business in his most valuable book *The Critical Mythology of Irony* from 1991 is metacritical, a nonintentional type of hermeneutics of irony is implied by his approach. Dane maintains that irony is created by readers, and among them critics. What I recognize as my own irony, Dane asserts, "is not something that really exists at all except in my own

claim that it does." That does not mean, however, that statements about irony are without implications: "They set an activity
within a particular institutional context."[35] Dane seems to imply
that even if irony is not really embedded in the intentions or the
texts themselves, but is rather a product of a critical activity, it is
not free to move unrestrictedly. Hutcheon too follows the path
set out by Stanley Fish in arguing that irony is produced by interpretation, not by intention. In her stimulating book, *Irony's Edge*
from 1994, Hutcheon adopts a terminology that subordinates authorial intention to interpretive activity. In Hutcheon's words,
the interpreter does not "get" irony, he or she makes it; irony
"happens."[36]

A crude summary of the history of irony and hermeneutics
would read thus: from authorial intention, via textual traits, to
the interpretation of the reader. Of course, this is a very simple
way of describing it. A polarization of meaning as on the one
hand a product of authorial intention, and on the other hand a
product of (critical) interpretation, leaves out some important
nuances. Furthermore, the history of the hermeneutics of irony
in this brief form is only a reflection of the history of hermeneutics in general.

Yet, there is a validity in simplifying it this way, if one bears in
mind that the various hermeneutical approaches today flourish
side by side and are intermingled. It is true that irony has developed into a popular, and perhaps often vaguely outlined, critical
category, but it is also true that ironic interpretations are most
often anchored in one trait or another in the text, and that intentionalism has a rather firm grip on hermeneutical practice. It
is not difficult to see why: everyday experience tells one that
irony is an oral and intentional phenomenon—as it certainly is,
too—which might lead one to conclude that the same is true for
written texts. It is a well-known fact that many interpretive disagreements arise from conflicts between different hermeneutical
views of the readers, but the case of irony makes it extremely
clear that conflicting notions and modes of interpretation mirror
the different, partly incompatible layers of the history of hermeneutics. To put it simply, there are various ways of interpreting
what one reads, sees, and hears, and if one does not realize that
the interpretive modes are *different*, one might conclude that the
world consists of stupid, ignorant, and/or evil people. Conflicts
arising at the pub, at the seminar, or at the dinner party may develop into small disasters if they are a result of different hermeneutical approaches and become invaded by irony. Such

conflicts can never be solved unless one takes a step backward and considers the hermeneutical stances.

Obviously, there is no mode of interpretation that is "right" or "wrong." When one ascribes irony to something, one builds one's interpretation on a conception of what the hermeneutical basis of irony is or ought to be. If one believes that the hermeneutics of intentionality ought to be the guideline, one may of course be mistaken as to what the intention of an author really is; if one chooses to look for ironic traits manifested in what one takes to be the text itself, one may overlook certain important passages; and if one sees irony as an interpretive strategy of the reader, one may simply perform an interpretation that is so private that nobody cares about it. In this way, it is certainly possible to be wrong or to make poor ironic interpretations. I think that the value of an ironic interpretation depends on its relevance (which may always be disputed, of course, and of which very little is known beforehand) and its consistency. As long as the "rules" of the chosen, hermeneutical basis are followed, the serious game of irony may be played.

Every ironic interpretation thus implies a hermeneutical stance: a concept of meaning. This concept of meaning is often vague, or even confused, but it is there—ready to end up in conflict with other concepts of meaning. One might say that the common comprehension of what is ironic or not ironic is formed by battles on an interpretive field. The various concepts of meaning are the actors on this field, and every single person may prefer to favor one or another of these actors. The actors are not soldiers who kill each other, however, but rather artists who try to catch one's attention by way of performing intricate dances. The dances may be beautiful and forceful, ugly or weak, but they are never meaningless because they are reflections of people's very lives.

Which hermeneutical stance is to be preferred, then? I believe that it has already become clear that I prefer to see irony as an interpretive strategy, and that I am not fond of intentionalism. Why am I not fond of intentionalism? As Hermerén points out, the question of the relevance of intention is very much a question of how to define literary meaning. The decision that must be made is normative rather than descriptive. Depending on what one means by "meaning," authorial intention may or may not be relevant evidence for an interpretation.[37] However, as Hermerén states, the area in semantics that involves theories of meaning "is one of the most difficult and also most confused areas in contemporary philosophy."[38]

In this book, I will continue to be descriptive, but also normative. Among other ideas, I will try to demonstrate that the hermeneutics of intentionalism is problematic, and sometimes even fallacious. When it comes to interpreting irony in artistic texts, it is, I believe, almost always reductive. This is certainly a value judgment. In the following pages, and then successively through the book, I want to give some reasons for holding this belief rather than argue for its correctness.

THE IRONY OF INTENTIONS

The first question we have to ask when scrutinizing irony and intentionality is, what really *is intention?* It is easy to supply more or less adequate synonyms—*purpose, object, design, motive, aim*—and it is easy to grasp roughly what it means. Yet, it is difficult to discriminate between different kinds of intentions—intentions that are related to each other but nevertheless may be difficult to unite—even if one limits oneself to the range of the intended *meaning* of an utterance or a text. The risk of getting lost once the reader has penetrated the cerebral cortex of the author, if the reader manages to get that far, is imminent.

One way of approaching the troublesome aspects of intentionalism, is to focus on the disputed notion of "unconscious irony." Frank Stringfellow rightly questions the rhetorical model of irony that emphasizes the importance of a hidden but conscious intention. In his book, *The Meaning of Irony: A Psychoanalytical Investigation*, Stringfellow argues that there may exist unconscious intentions, and that one person may have many, even contradictory intentions. Therefore, it is not always obvious whether a text is ironic or not, even if one asks the author himself or herself. Due to the psychological complexity of intentions, even the "simplest" forms of irony are always multilayered.[39]

I believe that Stringfellow is basically right, but even though he argues against the traditional concept of intention, he is still trapped in the mode of thinking defined by intentionalists. Emphasizing unconscious intentions is only a variation on emphasizing conscious intentions, a variation within the same hermeneutical field. If one wants to know a person better, it is of course extremely interesting to look for unconscious ironies (I am convinced that they exist), but if one wants to know a text better, it is better to look for something else.

Perhaps the most severe difficulty for intentionalism is the problem of accessibility. The notion of unconscious irony gives a hint of the interpreter's predicament when trying to find the correct intention, but it removes the problem rather than solving it. Trying to identify conscious intentions is like fumbling in the dark, but perhaps the darkness grows even thicker when one is trying to identify unconscious intentions.

The problem of accessibility is a major argument against intentionalism already in Wimsatt and Beardsley's "The Intentional Fallacy." The intention of an author, they argue, is not "available" for the reader, and often not even for the author himself or herself.[40] One problem is that it is very difficult to say in a more precise way what an intention really is when emerging in the conscious or unconscious spheres of the author's brain. Another problem is that intentions are manifested only very haphazardly and sometimes in biased ways.

By far the most common type of "evidence" for intentions is written texts and orally communicated material. These texts must evidently be submitted to interpretation—and if one believes in intentionalism it is implied that one has to look for intentional evidence for the meaning of the alleged intention also, and so on *ad infinitum*. In most cases, probably there is no such thing as *one* definite *intention*, only a collection of perhaps incoherent and vague *intentions*. Every person with the faintest idea of what it means to create, knows that the mental activity involved is very complex and partly situated on nonverbal (perhaps unconscious) levels. Statements about intentions made by the author himself or herself or by some other person are hence necessarily both simplifying and selective. The "intentions" that reach the reader are always already interpreted, by the author or by someone else. Marike Finlay puts it in Lacanian terms: it is not the subject that is the origin of ironic discourse, it is the subject that has its origin in discourse.[41]

Many defenders of intentionalism are well aware of these problems, and there is a point in emphasizing that communication, no matter how many theoretical problems can be raised, actually works rather well most of the time. Following E. D. Hirsch, Wendell V. Harris admits that a "reconstruction" of intentional meaning can only be "probabilistic," a fact that does not bother him very much.[42] Like so many other defenders of intentionalism, Harris sees no fundamental difference between oral com-

munication and literature. When people speak to each other, it is
no doubt almost always possible to "narrow down" each other's
probable intentions, but when it comes to reading literature
things get more complicated. The fact that a reconstruction of
intention is necessarily "probabilistic" is the very problem when
interpreting literature. Sometimes two or more interpreters
might think that they "narrow down" the probable intention,
when they in fact construct meanings that are incompatible or
even contradictory. That happens all the time. Again, irony may
be said to be the phenomenon that undermines rather than supports intentionalism. The problem of accessibility is grave in all
types of interpretation, but it becomes acute when the issue of
irony is involved. A slight vagueness in an alleged intention is
perhaps permissible in the interpretation of texts as long as irony
is kept at a distance—but if just one little unsteadiness of intention might make a little stone of irony roll . . . and if just one single word is mistakenly inverted, or not inverted, one soon loses
control. In the end, the intentionalist interpreter becomes
crushed by the rocks.

More questions can and have been asked. What if the author
had varying intentions in different stretches of the writing? What
if there are serious inconsistencies in the material used as evidence for the existence of intention? These are well-known problems for intentionalists, but one might continue to ask: What if
the author is ironic every single time he or she says or writes
something about the intentions of his or her own work? What if
he or she is sometimes ironic and at other times not? What if the
interpreter becomes trapped in an endless series of clues—true
or false, who knows the difference? What if the author's whole
life is so utterly ironic, in Kierkegaard's most negative sense, that
it is impossible to disentangle one single instance of stability? For
an intentionalist, looking for stabilizing intentions but finding
only new potential ironies in an endless series as in a hall of mirrors, this truly is an ironic situation.

The intentionalist's situation does not become more comfortable when artistic texts created by more than one person are
drawn into the discussion. Many works of art, such as films, are
results of teamwork, and I think that it would be a strange use of
words to say that there are "intentions" that determine the
meaning of these artistic objects. The *auteur*-theory is an attempt
to focus the creative force on the director as far as film is concerned, but it is certainly superfluous to argue for the existence
of various different intentions in the minds of the actors, the pro-

ducer, and the director—to mention only some of the partici-
pants in the creation of a film. When interpreting a piece of
artistic teamwork, the recipient may of course utilize strategies
similar to those being used when dealing with multilayered intentions in the unconsciousness of one single creator, but the
basic problem remains: lacking the authority of one, univocal intention, one is forced back into the field of "free" interpretation.

Another problem that will be discussed in more detail later is
the existence of so-called situational irony: ironic situations
found in real life and not created by an "ironist" (if one does not
regard God, Faith, or some other personification as the "person"
who intends to be ironic). Many theoreticians of irony that hold
to intentionalism accept situational irony as "true" irony, and
are consequently obliged to make a distinction between two
types of irony: one that is in need of intentional support, one that
is not.

Should one then, in order to be able to rescue intentionalism,
make a distinction between "verbal" and "situational" irony? I
can see no reason why. My point is simply that the problems associated with intentionalism are so severe that it is an easier and
more pragmatic solution to abandon intentionalism when dealing with "texts" of various kinds. If one does so, the concept of
irony becomes more coherent, less confusing, and in no need of
the fundamental distinction between verbal and situational
irony. The advantages of this solution become even more apparent when ironic interpretation of the visual arts and music is included in the discussion, as will be demonstrated later.

Still, it is a fact that many interpretations emerge out of a
knowledge of what is understood to be the author's intentions.
These interpretations may be relevant, interesting, and stimulating, although they do not hold an authoritative position—
according to my view. What is one to do, then, with these
fragments of alleged intention that are traced, rescued, and made
fruitful?

My suggestion is that one avoid talking about intentions altogether and treat the alleged intentions of an author simply as the
author's interpretations of his or her own text. The swamp of fascinating but insoluble questions about "intended meaning" and
"true meaning" is avoided if one concentrates instead on the
possible interpretations of a text. A person who writes something
may or may not, consciously or unconsciously, intend to be
ironic—but that does not mean any more than that he or she interprets his or her own words as either completely ironic, partly

ironic, or not ironic at all, just as the reader of his or her text, depending on norms and supplied contexts, interprets it as ironic or not. In my view, the ambiguity of so-called unconscious irony is only one specific case of the overall ambiguity of ironic interpretation. The author's interpretation of his or her own text may be vague and even contradictory, just as interpretations performed by various readers may differ substantially. Of course, the interpretation of a reader might coincide with the interpretation of the writer, but there is no method of really knowing when this happens. Sometimes one thinks one knows—but that is not the same as knowing.

My arguments are thus, in short: When one asserts that some specific meaning is the intention of an author, one has always already performed an interpretation. Because an intention is such an obscure phenomenon, it is more convenient and I think also more correct to say that the author interprets his or her own text and that this interpretation has the same hermeneutical value as an interpretation by an "ordinary" reader. If the notion is to be used at all, its meaning must be reduced to a suggestion and a wish to have one's own text read in a certain manner. The writer, like the reader, may of course argue about how to interpret the text. One of them, or both, might shift meanings if new aspects of the text or some context should be brought to light. Consequently, irony may come and go. Indeed it does: from age to age, from reader to reader, from culture to culture.

To treat irony as an interpretive strategy, rather than something that exists objectively in the mind of the author or in the text itself, does not of course imply that the interpreted text is irrelevant. Later in this book, textual traits that tend to be perceived as ironic within certain contexts will be discussed. Irony "happens," as Hutcheon puts it, when a certain reader responds to a certain text, and of course this "happening" is dependent upon the features of both the text and the reader. The existence of irony is unthinkable—I would even say logically impossible— without the existence of a "text," in the broadest sense of the word, *and* an interpreter. The interpreter *may* be, but not necessarily, the author himself or herself. The moment one accepts the existence of "situational" irony, however, the relationship between author and "text" is definitely dissolved. Both literary texts and "the text of the world" necessarily need an interpreter to produce meaning, but they do not necessarily need an author. The possible ironic meaning of the world is written by the interpreter.

I thus choose to reject the theological, intentionalist hermeneutics of irony and place our Father among the rest of us. However, I do not wish to assert that irony is solely a product of the
interpreter. The *material* of irony is found in the text, but it is
formed by the reader. Some materials seem to be easier to give
ironic shape, once one has seen their potentialities, but on the
other hand the textual material is *never* in itself ironic—and it can
always be formed otherwise. To try to separate the reader or the
ironic interpretation from the text would nevertheless certainly
be vain, because, as Yeats puts it in a famous line: "How can we
know the dancer from the dance?"[43]

3
Classifications of Irony

It is equally fatal for the spirit to have a system and to have
none. One must thus decide to join the two.
—Friedrich Schlegel

DISTINCTIONS

BEFORE CONTINUING TO DISCUSS HOW IRONIC MEANING IS CREATED IN
the act of interpretation, one must inquire into some of the most
common classifications of irony. Because irony has been subject
to distinctions and classifications executed on widely differing
hermeneutical premises, it is impossible to collect all the "subcategories" of irony in a united system. The various distinctions
overlap and interfere with each other. This has caused quite severe confusion and might be one of the reasons for the inclination to describe the concept of irony as notoriously elusive.

As some of the classifications are both habitual and useful, it
would be foolish to abandon them completely. However, they
must be used with caution and an awareness of their hermeneutical foundations. In this chapter I will give a description of the
most common subcategories of irony. Some efforts will be made
to make them reasonably compatible, which has to involve some
slight simplifications.

Verbal irony is almost always understood as a synonym for *rhetorical irony*. It is commonly defined as a sharp opposition between what is said or written and what is meant. The term was
coined by Thirlwall, who describes it as "a figure which enables
the speaker to convey his meaning with greater force by means
of a contrast between his thought and his expression, or, to speak
more accurately, between the thought which he evidently designs to express, and that which his words properly signify."[1] *Verbal irony* is thus defined in terms of intention and expression. A
common example of verbal irony is the remark "What lovely

weather!," uttered by someone who looks sadly at the rain outside the window. In this situation, the utterance is evidently in conflict with a context of great relevance.

The most common distinction nowadays is the one between *verbal irony* and *situational irony*. In spite of the problems related to it, which I discussed earlier, it is almost universally accepted and very often found in dictionaries. *Situational irony*, sometimes called *irony of events*, is most broadly defined as a situation where the outcome is incongruous with what was expected, but it is also more generally understood as a situation that includes contradictions or sharp contrasts. Thirlwall calls this type of irony *practical irony*. Practical irony, he states, "is independent of all forms of speech, and needs not the aid of words."[2] *Situational irony* is thus clearly not defined in terms of intention. It is commonly accepted that it emerges in the eye of the beholder. An example would be a man who takes a step aside in order to avoid getting sprinkled by a wet dog, and falls into a swimming pool.

The distinction between *verbal irony* and *structural irony* is almost as common as the one between *verbal irony* and *situational irony*. *Structural irony* is most often understood as situational irony given shape or acted out in a text. More specifically, *structural irony* may be defined as irony that involves a naive hero or an unreliable narrator whose view of the world differs from the circumstances recognized by the readers and the implied author (in Booth's *The Rhetoric of Fiction*, the notion of "unreliable narrator" is frequently coupled with irony).[3] Jonathan Swift's "A Modest Proposal" is a famous text that may be said to convey structural irony. The narrator's detailed proposal to breed, slaughter, and eat children contrasts sharply with the norms of most readers.

Some specific subcategories of situational irony are the almost identical notions *cosmic irony, irony of God,* and *irony of Fate.* They were first circumscribed by the Romanticists and imply the view that people are the dupes of a mocking God or Fate. These variations of situational irony may be found in real life, but of course also in texts, in which case they are variations of structural irony. As an example of cosmic irony, the situational irony of a man falling into a swimming pool may serve the reader well. One only needs to add the idea that it was God's finger who pushed the dog in front of the man in order to make him take the fatal step into the pool.

Some very important subcategories of situational irony that are almost always treated as structural ironies are *Socratic irony, Romantic irony,* and *dramatic irony* or *tragic irony. Socratic irony,* circumscribed already in antiquity, is mostly understood as pretended ignorance or naïveté on the part of an interlocutor in a text, a pretense that results in a sharp contrast between the ignorance of the person who at first seems to be wise and the gradually revealed wisdom of the person who pretends to be ignorant. Thirlwall calls this form of irony *dialectic irony,* and the classical example is, needless to say, Plato's dialogues.[4] As I have already noted, Romantic irony is a complex category associated with literary texts that express the paradoxical nature of reality and fiction. Laurence Sterne's *Tristram Shandy* and Thomas Mann's novels are among the most frequently cited examples of Romantic irony.

The terms *dramatic irony* or *tragic irony* denote a situation where the reader or audience knows more about a character's situation than the character himself or herself. Consequently, the audience can foresee an outcome of the events that is contrary to the character's expectations. A character involved in dramatic irony is, as G. G. Sedgewick expresses it, "acting in ignorance of his condition."[5] As a consequence of this state of affairs, the audience ascribes meaning to the character's utterances that sharply differs from the character's own comprehension of what he or she says. Here one comes close to verbal irony: the uttered words mean one thing to the character, quite another to the audience. Of course, dramatic irony may be found also in texts belonging to other genres than the drama (or in real life), and, as Booth suggests, it might be defined less strictly. It is a category that arguably can be said to include also discrepancies between "what two or more characters say of each other," or between "what a character says now" and "what he says or does later."[6]

The terms *dramatic irony* and *tragic irony* have their origins in the first decades of the nineteenth century and are by most writers on irony considered synonymous, but now and then efforts are made to distinguish them. For instance, it is sometimes suggested that tragic irony is dramatic irony in tragedies. Be that as it may, dramatic irony and tragic irony are clearly variations of situational irony, and perhaps it ought to be added that other variations of situational irony, such as cosmic irony, are often closely associated with dramatic irony. The classic example of dramatic irony is Sophocles' tragedy *Oedipus Rex,* in which Oedipus tries to avoid his predicted fate but nevertheless, without realizing it, systematically acts to fulfill it. He seeks the murderer of

Laius, the former king of Thebes, only to find that he himself is the guilty one. *Oedipus Rex* also offers many examples of utterances that are of no great significance for Oedipus himself, but to the reader or spectator convey insights into the ignorance of Oedipus and the cruelty of his destiny.

Clearly, many of these categories overlap and merge into each other. The most distinct difference seems to be found between situational irony and verbal irony. Situational irony may be found practically everywhere and is in no need of language to come into existence. Structural irony is also a very broad category: it is restricted to texts but might involve an almost unlimited variety of extensive contrasts. Verbal irony, on the other hand, is limited to a few words or sentences and involves only an opposition between explicit and implicit meaning. The definition of *situational irony* is thus the most inclusive one, and the definition of *verbal irony* the most exclusive.

INDISTINCTIONS

Now, *how* are these categories of irony related to each other? Are they variations on one and the same *concept,* or are they united only through the *word* irony? This has been an important question right from the beginning. Originally, the relation between rhetorical and Socratic irony was disputed, and Quintilian recognized the difficulties involved in classifying irony as a trope or as a figure. Over the centuries all the new categories have been questioned. Is Romantic irony *really* irony? If it is, is it a variation on verbal irony, or is it significantly distinct? Is irony in Cleanth Brooks's sense *really* related to the "original" notion of irony, or is their relationship only terminological? To put it differently, *are* the various categories of irony essentially related, or *should* they—for pragmatic reasons—be seen as related? Are they successively "found," or are they rather "invented"?

As long as one does not expect to find definite answers, I do not think that it is meaningless to ask questions like these. However, with the view that all irony is fundamentally in the eye of the beholder, the need to put forth essential claims disappears. Consequently, I find it difficult, for instance, to argue for or against Uwe Japp's claim that all ironies can be reduced to variations on rhetorical irony. According to Japp, the complex ironies are nothing more than applications, *Anwendungen.*[7] Booth's almost contrary claim that the various notions of irony are related to each other "at best" by family resemblance is equally open to dispute.[8] Dane's view that the danger in any discussion of irony is "the assumption that the word must have a coherent and universal referent in the objects to which it is applied" is certainly reasonable,[9] but it is also reasonable to assume that there are some common denominators in the phenomena that with some agreement have been called ironic.

In this discussion, it is very difficult not to hover between the level of "texts" and the level of "interpretations." On the one hand, one must acknowledge that Dane is right when he claims that "ironies are not embedded in texts awaiting discovery and classification by me or by any other critic,"[10] and on the other hand one must assume that ironies do not arise in the brain of the interpreter independently of the texts and the world. It should be beyond dispute that the many categories of irony (among which only the most commonly accepted were discussed above) are based on various contradictory or contrasting elements, principles, and phenomena. The difficulties start when one asks exactly *where* these contrasts are located. One reason for continuing to hover between the levels of text and interpretation is that some texts have a remarkably strong inclination to generate irony under certain circumstances, whereas other texts are interpreted in terms of irony much more incidentally. Both the textual traits that somehow involve contrasts and the contrasts that emerge out of the meeting between a text and the assumptions and associations of an interpreter are obviously relevant to the production of ironic meaning. This will be discussed in more detail later.

The tendency to classify irony on the level of texts has, however, dominated. Yet, if one chooses to treat irony as a critical strategy rather than as something created in intentional acts or embedded in texts, differences are seen. Some of the various subcategories of irony simply lose their shape when treated as critical tools. The explanation of this lies in the history of the notions of irony.

At first, many considered it to be an awkward use of words to talk about Romantic or tragic irony.[11] In 1833, Thirlwall opened his essay "On the Irony of Sophocles" with an understatement: "Some readers may be a little surprised to see *irony* attributed to a tragic poet."[12] At that time, it was not common terminology, but now one has become accustomed to it. Although they did not always formulate it explicitly, the Romanticists started to circumscribe irony mainly as a mode of *seeing, reading,* and *compre-*

hending contrasts and paradoxes. The "content"—comedy or tragedy—became in a way less important. The classical notion of irony as a rhetorical device was not rejected, but perhaps due to its connection to the hermeneutics of intentionality it lost its attraction. In a way, the theory of irony went through a change of paradigms in the era of Romanticism.

From the point of view of classical intentionalistic hermeneutics, the "new" notions of irony are abnormal as they imply that irony exists, if anywhere, in the eye of the beholder. Of course, one can maintain that it is "as if" the intention of God lies behind cosmic irony, but such a view only reflects the condition that irony through the centuries has been interpreted mainly as a phenomenon created by an ironist. The indisputable fact remains that there is no intention (in any reasonable meaning of the word) behind what is seen as situational irony in the world of events. When such a situation is presented in a text (and perhaps interpreted as structural irony), the intention of the author is of course part of the genesis of the irony in the respect that the text was written by the author; but as far as I can see, it would be absurd to distinguish between ironic events in reality and ironic events given form or described by texts. That is what one is obliged to do if, like Leon Satterfield, one argues that situational irony too is a function of an author's intention.[13] The result would be that a situation that is understood to be ironic when described in a text or by a speaker could not properly be called ironic at all when perceived in reality—as there is no intention behind the events in the world.

Situational irony was thus initially regarded as an anomaly, but the now almost unanimous acceptance of this notion indicates that the standards have changed. Yet, it is also true that irony is still mainly understood to be verbal in the old sense. Clearly, two hermeneutical stances operate side by side, united by the term *irony* and, perhaps, the concept of irony, but distinct in interpretive practice. The initial suspiciousness toward "situational" ironies is certainly one explanation of the urge for keeping verbal and situational ironies distinct. Another explanation is the incapacity of intentionalism to deal with situational ironies.

If irony is seen as a critical strategy rather than an intentional act, the distinction between verbal irony and situational irony becomes problematic. I think that verbal irony is best understood as something that does not differ much from situational irony. In theory, verbal irony is a clear-cut phenomenon; in practice, however, it is highly problematic to establish what the author "evidently" (as Thirlwall puts it) wants to express. Often it is not at all evident what is meant—especially not when one interprets texts rather than oral statements. The act of establishing an "intention" is in itself, as I have already noted, an interpretive act.

To me, it is strange that so many theoreticians have distinguished so emphatically between irony in verbal language and irony in the world "outside" the text. The historical reasons for it are obvious, but does the distinction fulfill a purpose, or is it rather upholding a pointless conflict between incompatible hermeneutical views? Henceforth I will argue that the act of interpreting an utterance or a text ironically, even if it be only one single word, does not differ in any fundamental way from the act of interpreting events in the world ironically. A line in a poem, an image, a scene in the street, a punk rock song, a TV program, a strange sound from the neighbor's bedroom, an opera, an article in a newspaper—they are all phenomena that are given meaning in acts of interpretation: phenomena that may be seen as ironic if conflicts of meaning emerge somewhere in the field between the observer and the observed.

Booth argues that "If tornadoes can be ironic or appear ironically, they do so in a different sense from that in which Jonathan Swift is ironic."[14] Because it is a truism that only human beings can be ironists, he is certainly right in claiming this fundamental difference. This fact, however, gives us no clue as to why so many agree upon the feasibility of continuing to speak of irony in both cases, in spite of the alleged fundamental difference between verbal irony and situational irony. In my view, it is because both Swift and his readers may arguably be said to be interpreters of his texts, and because all readers, as interpreters, "observe" texts in the same way as they "observe" the world—including tornadoes. For people who live, read, and interpret, there ought to be no qualitative difference between interpreting some words in a text and an event in life as ironic. Even in a situation of oral communication, dominated by the hermeneutics of intentionality, irony emerges out of interpretation. If a question concerning the intended or nonintended irony in an utterance is posed, it is the verbal and contextual situation created by the initial utterance *and* the answer that are the basis for a new interpretation.

There is thus reason for using the distinction between verbal irony and situational irony, or between *instrumental irony* and *observable irony,* as it is also termed by Muecke,[15] with discrimination. All irony is in a way "situational" and "observable." "Verbal" irony also is "observed" as a textual "situation." All irony is created by the observer, it might be maintained, and the so-called intention of the ironist is nothing more than the ironist's observation of the verbal situation created by his or her own utterance, connected with his or her own ironic interpretation of it. I do not know whether this is the definite "essence" of all irony, but it is at least a pragmatic solution to some major theoretical problems.

Muecke, for whom the difference between verbal irony and situational irony is very important to uphold, admits that they are not always possible to distinguish.[16] Yet, why are they not always distinguishable when, according to Muecke himself, one of them includes the intention of an ironist, whereas the other does not? Obviously, Muecke's own interpretive practice reveals to him that the author's "intention"—which theoretically ought to be indisputably demarcated, as it allegedly belongs to a distinct field of hermeneutics—in practice merges with "situations" of irony. The qualitative difference that is implied by the theoretical distinction between verbal irony and situational irony vanishes in the actual act of interpretation. Does one need a distinction that is not possible to uphold when one tries to use it? I believe that the hermeneutics of intentionality leads to more confusion than clarity.

4

The Creation of Irony

The reader said: "Let there be irony!", and there was irony.
—Unknown

THE IRONIC STRATEGY

ARE LESS CONFUSION AND MORE CLARITY NEEDED? YES, I THINK THEY ARE. Understanding irony better does not mean getting rid of the confusion it might cause, but getting rid of the confusion that poor explanations of it might cause. In my view, the critical advantages of dealing with irony as an interpretive act (or the "result" of an interpretive act) are considerable. Irony is one option for understanding the world and everything that is in it. When confronted with a phenomenon that is considered to have certain incompatible qualities, one may apply the ironic strategy in order to "make sense" of it all. According to this hermeneutical view, ironic meaning is never really "found" in a text or in the world: it is always "created" in an act of interpretation. To be strict, then, it is a misleading expression to say that readers "find" irony in a text. Actually, readers "find" irony in a poem because they themselves "place" it there.

However, as readers are not always aware of the fact that they do "place" irony, it is indeed a subjective truth that they "find" it. One does not see the world "as it is" but rather as one conceives it, and that is why it is after all reasonable to say about something that one "finds it" ironic. The troubles start when two or more individuals disagree on what is "really" to be found. Such disagreements can often be resolved if one assumes that ironies are creations of the interpreters and not proper qualities. That does not lead to the end of all discussions, but it gives one the possibility to fight more meaningful interpretive fights— creative fights in which readers are included as readers of the world.

58

From this it follows that irony may be "placed" and "found" almost anywhere. That might be considered a somewhat disturbing fact, but it is a fact that must be lived with. Irony being placed and found here, there, and everywhere is already the state of affairs, and one can either try to change the situation or try to understand it and accept it. The first solution has proved not to work. It is vain to define irony as an objective quality in order to try to resolve disagreements. That has been done for some thousand years, and people still go on quarreling about who has "found" the proper ironies.

Nevertheless, it is also known that strategies of ironic interpretation are often being used in considerable agreement, sometimes with seemingly universal consensus. The kingdom of irony is clearly not ruled by complete anarchy. There are rules; not rules that one is obliged to follow, but pragmatic ones that are sometimes followed because one is used to them and because, under certain circumstances, they enable one to communicate the way one wishes. Sometimes, however, the rules are being "misused," and it is the nature of irony that one can never really tell the difference between used and abused rules. That is why the rules of irony are not really rules.

However, the existence of this seemingly universal consensus on how and why certain phenomena are ironic has led to the emergence of some rather deceptive notions. Perhaps the most important of these is *irony marker* or *irony signal*. Once again, one must go back to antiquity in order to be able to explain why this notion is so predominant—and why it is so deceptive.

For the classical, medieval, and Renaissance authors, irony was first and foremost a phenomenon generated by the intention of a speaker and inherent in the words and the context of this speaker's utterance. They focused mainly on *pronuntiatio*—that is, intonation and gesture—as the means by which irony might be disclosed in oral communication.[1] The tone of the voice and the appearance of face and body are parts of the context in oral communication, and there have been conventions of interpreting certain physical behavior as signs meaning "not." If one thus considers an ironic meaning "hidden" in the words, it might nevertheless be "apparent" in the totality of communicative signs.

Although the stress was on oral communication, some writers had ideas of how irony may be "revealed" by signals in written texts, too. As literary texts are not always read aloud by the author himself or herself, parallels to gestures and mimicry must sometimes be traced in the texts themselves if one wants to find irony

signals. Texts, too, if one thinks of them as people, can cross their
fingers and wrinkle their noses. Among other techniques, word
order, contrasts between a proposition and the context of the
text, and oppositions between the description of the text and
known facts of reality were discussed.[2] Quintilian boils it all down
to three types of incongruities: irony is disclosed if the words are
out of keeping with either "the delivery, the character of the
speaker or the nature of the subject."[3]

When contrasts and oppositions in written texts were defined
as irony signals, the limits of the cultural context were probably
taken for granted. Deviations and incongruities were generally
understood to be characteristics of the text itself or to be
definitely placed in the relationship between text and context.
However, an agreement on what is incongruous or deviating presupposes a consensus on what "normal" language, "normal" behavior, "correct" norms, and a "true" description of the world
are. For those living today, having knowledge of the multiplicity
of cultures and norms in the world and perhaps lacking the inclination to put everything into hierarchies (which is indeed in itself
a situation conditioned by culture and norms), it is easy to see
that no such consensus exists.

In fact, all the "signals" of irony that have been recognized
from antiquity and onwards are culturally and conventionally
coded. Most writers on irony have probably realized this, but
without letting it interfere with their hermeneutics. Already in *Reflections upon Laughter* from 1750, Francis Hutcheson emphasized that both individual, social, and temporal conditions are of
relevance for what is considered mean or dignified, and hence for
what will cause laughter.[4] On the analogue of this, the creation of
irony is heavily dependent upon the ever-changing views on
what is, for instance, mean or dignified.

Irony signals consequently exist (if at all) only in relationship
to cultural codes. Linda Hutcheon states that "nothing is an
irony signal in and of itself."[5] She maintains that it is only within
certain discursive communities that certain textual traits may be
understood to be irony signals. Rainer Warning, however, accurately notes that irony signals do not definitely obey even codes;
they are located not on the *langue* level, but on the *parole* level:
"irony signals function as such only in a particular speech act."[6]
Warning correctly notes that hyperbole, for example, may "signal" irony but also a lot of other phenomena. A very troublesome
aspect of the notion of irony signal is that it gives the impression
of something that unambiguously "shows the way" to irony,

whereas all so-called irony signals are subject to interpretation and might be ironically reversed. How can one tell the difference between a "straight" irony signal and an ironic irony signal?

Writers on irony have emphasized various types of incongruity, sometimes limited to the level of the text, sometimes including contexts of all sorts. I do not wish to argue for the unimportance of making distinctions between types of incongruity, but I believe that it is more urgent to point out that a common hermeneutical stance does in fact unite all the attempts to circumscribe irony signals: the view that irony is embedded in the words and their contexts, and that there are a set of signals, markers, signs, or clues (several other semi-synonyms are also being used) that lead the interpreter to identify this irony. Of course, it is the model of oral communication that defines this view on how irony is "revealed." According to this model the speaker intends to convey something but for some reason chooses to hide his or her message by way of reversing it; however, signals are given in the message (or in the context of the message) that enable the listener to "find" the correct, intended message. The interpreter is thus seen as a detective in search of the truth about what "really happened."

If irony is seen instead as a creation of the interpreter, it makes no sense to talk about signals of or clues to irony. No detective who reveals the truth by means of clues placed at the scene of the crime by himself or herself is worthy of the name. In the game of irony, as in the game of all interpretation, no one is definitely guilty or innocent. In my view, irony signals are simply products of interpretation, as is irony in itself. The interpretive act that involves the creation of irony in a text is certainly dependent on perceived verbal traits—but the "incongruities" or "deviations" that are formed in the reading of the text do not lead to the "revelation" of irony; they are connected to the "creation" of irony. The "irony signal" does not reveal an irony embedded in a text, but mirrors the interpreter's recognition of his or her own interpretive strategy. To say that something is a signal of irony implies that one has already employed the strategy of ironic interpretation. The use of the notion of irony signal is in itself a signal of irony—not in the text, but in the mind of the reader.

Nevertheless, the notion of irony signal is still widely applied in ways that imply a stable relation between irony and text. Muecke's distinction between overt, covert, and private irony (differing in grade, not in kind) is only one example of an influential, relatively recent approach to irony that suggests a scale

between ironies that are accessible to everyone and ironies that
are accessible only to the ironist himself or herself.[7] In my view,
this kind of distinction is of little value. It neglects the fact that
the same text might very well be described as covert by one person and as overt by another, depending on the various norms
and contexts brought to the text by different interpreters. The
problem is that Muecke's distinction aims at classifying texts
rather than interpretations.

Muecke does not apply the notion of irony signal in his books,
but his view implies that irony is more or less "visible" or "hidden," meaning that it is "placed" in the text by the author and
revealed by more or less apparent clues. In his article "Irony
Markers," however, Muecke says that "in any particular case of
irony the irony-marker can be *confirmed* as such only retrospec-
tively, that is when one has understood the irony."[8] There are no
linguistic or formal devices that automatically lead to irony,
Muecke argues (correctly, I believe), only conventions with limited range of validity. He equates literature and oral communication and presupposes that intention, as well as irony markers of
some sort, is a necessary condition for irony.

Yet, if an irony marker can be "confirmed" only when the
ironic interpretation has already been performed, why should
one bother with such an awkward notion at all? To assume,
as Muecke does in his article, that only *some* intended ironies
are "really" ironies—namely, those that are successfully
"marked"—is to open the way to a kind of arbitrariness that is
inconsistent with intentionalistic hermeneutics. Who decides
when a marker is confirmative enough? Obviously the author
does not. Muecke's line of argument indicates that both intentionalism and the notion of irony marker are troublesome.

Similarly, it is problematic to delineate a semiotics of irony.
One of the semi-synonyms for *irony marker* is *irony sign*. This notion, put into a semiotic framework, implies that certain textual
or extratextual traits are symbolic or indexical signs of irony; it
implies that irony exists "in itself" as an "object" of some kind
under the surface of the text and that it may be revealed by irony
signs. In his article "Toward a Poetics of the Ironic Sign," Leon
Satterfield writes about "ironic signs" as if the relationship between irony and text were the same as between a treasure and a
treasure map: if one simply follows the indexical signs designed
by the pirate, one will find the hidden gold. However, I maintain
that there are no ironic signs of this kind, only ironic interpretations. All irony is certainly a product of semiosis, but that does

not mean that there are signs of irony that it is possible to circumscribe and isolate. Irony comes into existence in the eyes of the beholder, and the "ironic sign" is created simultaneously with irony itself.

Yet, the semiosis of irony is not entirely a product of individual interpreters, although the "psychorhetorical" contexts are doubtless of immense importance both in oral communication and in the interpretation of texts.[9] Within interpretive communities, conventions of ironic communication are established. These conventions might be said to form "codes" of irony that under some circumstances are valid for the people who are part of the community.[10] However, the "ironic signs" that are at work within these codes are not univocal. Incongruities and contradictions do not automatically lead to ironic interpretations: they may be understood to be ironic,[11] but also nonironic, and there are multiple ways of performing ironic interpretations that are not in accordance with the established codes. The "ironic signs," if the terminology of semiotics is insisted on, must definitely not be understood to be fixed building blocks that form the codes—they are rather products of fluctuating codes or deviations from codes.

It is thus necessary to distinguish between on the one hand the misconception of "signs of irony," and on the other hand the fact that ironic interpretation is part of the general semiosis of reading. Peirce's wide definition of a sign, or *representamen*, as "something which stands to somebody for something in some respect or capacity," makes it clear that irony cannot be a "something" (a sign or its *object*).[12] Rather, irony is an aspect of the relation between *representamen*, *interpretant*, and *object*. To be more precise, irony may be seen as a specific variation of the semiosis connected to what Peirce calls the icon, and even more specifically to the metaphor (the vaguest variation of the icon, generated through some kind of parallelism).[13] Peirce actually discusses the possibility of "a drunken man" representing iconically—by contrast—"temperance."[14] He does not mention the concept of irony, but, as I shall demonstrate later, metaphor and irony are intimately connected although they are in a way opposites: the one operates through resemblance, the other through opposition.

Unfortunately, Peirce dismisses as "trivial" the question of the relationship between iconicity through resemblance and iconicity through opposition.[15] To me, the difference between these two variations seems to be decisive for the role the concept of irony may be allowed to play within semiotics. If one emphasizes the difference between the principles of resemblance and opposition, one may even argue that irony is an a-representational mode of communication or interpretation that disrupts all representational theories of language such as rhetoric and semiotics. In her book, *The Romantic Irony of Semiotics*, Marike Finlay successfully maintains that "rather than using representational semiotic models to describe ironic communication, it is more fruitful to use romantic irony's theories of communication to criticize and surpass semiotics."[16]

The relationship between irony and semiotics is certainly interesting, but it has not been focused on at all in the bulk of theoretical studies of irony. Instead, the relationship between irony and rhetoric has gained considerable attention. Wayne C. Booth's list of irony signals in *A Rhetoric of Irony* has been influential. It is a list that in many ways connects to the ancient writers and builds upon the hermeneutical presuppositions that were valid already for Plato and Quintilian. Booth is interested in the process by which one comes to one's "convictions about the intentions of the authors." When describing this process, he uses a very typical vocabulary that gives associations to the investigations of a detective: "Every clue thus depends for its validity on norms (generally unspoken) which the reader embraces and which he infers, rightly or wrongly, that his author intends."[17] As irony is determined by the intention of the author, according to Booth's hermeneutical view, the interpreting detective has to look for clues that might lead him or her to a reconstruction of the author's act of verbal creation. The detective then has to decide whether a crime has been committed: has the author intended to be ironic or not?

The advantage of Booth's description of this interpretive process is that he clearly recognizes the importance of norms. The clues to irony, Booth stresses, have no objective existence. They are dependent on the way the reader values and interprets phenomena in the world. This important insight does not, however, lead Booth to abandon the notion of irony signals. On the contrary, the task of the interpreting detective seems to become even more intricate if one supposes that the norms of the author can be reconstructed and somehow matched with the norms of the reader. Booth suggests that, although sometimes difficult to know definitely, the clues to irony are either valid or not valid, and the interpreter of irony is either right or wrong.

Booth's clues to irony are ordered into five categories: "1. Straightforward warnings in the author's own voice"; "2. Known

Error Proclaimed"; "3. Conflicts of Facts within the Work"; "4. Clashes of Style"; "5. Conflicts of Belief."[18] As one can see, this rather condensed list includes various kinds of incongruities and deviations both on the level of the text and between text and contexts. Booth is well aware of the fact that these clues are dependent upon a number of shifting factors, but he nevertheless feels confident that the irony intended by the author exists somewhere under the textual surface. It is not always easy to find the intention, or to be sure that one has found it—but it is there. One may feel more or less convinced of the ironic dimension of this intention, but in principle it either exists or it does not. In Booth's view, the only problem connected to the interpretation of irony is that it is sometimes difficult to determine how "reliable" the clues are.

I have already criticized intentionalism in detail, and there is no point in repeating my line of argument here. Suffice it to say that Booth's standpoint makes all the cases where ambiguous intentions are involved into anomalies that are not possible to deal with properly. The most problematic aspect of Booth's hermeneutics, however, apart from the difficulties connected with intentionalism in itself, is its hovering between the intention of the author and the text itself. As I have already noted, Booth suggests that the intended ironies as a matter of fact have to be "reconstructed" on textual evidence. Yet, what happens to the intention? What does one have that is more than a text and an interpreter if the intention must be "reconstructed"? In my view, it is impossible to tell the difference between a "reconstructed" intentional irony and a "constructed" irony created by the reader.

It is remarkable that Booth puts such emphasis on the importance of the norms of the reader, and, furthermore, that through his way of suggesting that intention must be reconstructed on a basis of textual evidence, he implies that the accessibility to the authorial intention is limited—and yet he does not recognize the implications. His acceptance of the great relevance of the interpreter's norms, and the difficulty of reaching definite knowledge of the author's intention, points to a position that Booth himself is definitely not ready to embrace: the hermeneutical view that irony is always created by the interpreter, even when he or she believes that he or she re-creates an ironic intention.

If one examines the "clues" to irony suggested by Booth, one realizes that they are not really irony signals but rather descriptions of the interpretive result of a reader's ironic strategy. His first and fifth categories, "Straightforward warnings in the author's own voice" and "Conflicts of Belief" ("between the beliefs expressed and the beliefs we hold *and suspect the author of holding*") are based on the fact that the reader must initially interpret the text in order to find the "true" voice of the "author"—which the reader cannot do without involving his or her own norms and prejudices. His fourth category, "Clashes of Style," involves a conception of what a homogeneous style is and what significance should be attached to perceived incongruities. His second and third categories, "Known Error Proclaimed" and "Conflicts of Facts within the Work," likewise involve a conception of what the facts of the world really are and what significance should be attached to perceived conflicts between these facts. Even if one recognizes that there are, for instance, certain "indisputable" historical facts (which I think there are), a violation of these facts in a text does not automatically lead to the existence of irony. There is no irony until the reader has created an ironic interpretation of the conflict, and the ironic interpretation is only one out of many options. Finding conflicts in a text might lead to calling it ironic, but one might also call it mistaken, bad, ill-considered, stupid, or mendacious.

Booth's claimed "stability" of irony is thus an illusion, I argue: an illusion that cannot become real even in a utopian state of maximum accessibility of intentions. Yet, ironic interpretation often proves to be a successful strategy both in oral communication and in the reading of texts. Stanley Fish's notion of "interpretive communities" offers an explanation of the area of *relative* stability that makes it possible for different readers to sometimes agree upon ironic interpretations. According to Fish, interpretive communities consist of those who share interpretive strategies. All meaning that one ascribes to texts is a product of rules and codes that are accepted as valid within an interpretive community. These rules form our interpretations from the very moment we begin to read: there are no innocent readings that avoid the rules of one community or another. Even when one says that something is self-evident, normal, or beyond dispute, it is so only within the limits of an interpretive community. Often, however, the communities that one belongs to are so dominant that one tends to consider "the normal" a general state of the world rather than a product of conventions.[19] Hutcheon, who adopts the views of Fish, prefers to use the term "discursive communities."[20]

Interpretive communities are not fixed entities, however. That is why disputes arise all the same even between very old friends or between members of the same faculty. Fish summarizes: "Interpretive communities grow larger and decline, and individuals move from one to another; thus, while the alignments are not permanent, they are always there, providing just enough stability for the interpretive battles to go on, and just enough shift and slippage to assure that they will never be settled."[21]

The notions of interpretive communities and interpretive strategies are certainly fruitful, but they are not without their problems. As every notion of what an interpretive community really consists of is dependent upon an interpretation of it— necessarily performed on the basis of the interpreter's own strategies—there is no way of definitely grasping an interpretive community and knowing when one reader shares interpretive strategies with another reader. An interpretive community exists only *ad hoc*: as an interpretive construction. It is consequently an abstraction that vanishes as soon as one tries to describe it in detail. Through the spiral of interpretations, one can reach only very approximate agreement on where a particular community begins and ends. Yet, that does not lessen the value of the notion. It explains both why interpretation is possible and why it is impossible. It also explains why irony sometimes looks like a sitting duck that moves as soon as one aims at it and puts one's finger to the trigger.

UNSTABLE STABILITIES IN DICKENS'S *OLIVER TWIST*

It is now time to read some literature, starting with Charles Dickens, whose irony is seldom questioned or taken to be very problematic. I would like to discuss some passages in the first chapter of *Oliver Twist* in order to show that even ironies that tend to be interpreted as "stable," "overt," "universal," and certainly "intended" by the author, ironies that are described as verbal, local, and firmly established in the text itself, are in fact results of a construction of the reader. This does not mean that I find most conventional interpretations of *Oliver Twist* wrong or bad. On the contrary, I think that the general view of Dickens as the author of ironic texts is very well motivated, considering the interpretive communities and codes of reading into which his novels are normally inscribed. I do not wish to launch a new interpretation of *Oliver Twist*, only to argue that the ironies found in the novel are not as stable as one might think, and that they are primarily a result of interpretive maneuvers—not of textual traits or authorial intentions.

In the opening of the novel, little Oliver's pale and weak mother wants to see her newborn child, "and die." The surgeon replies: "Oh, you must not talk about dying yet," and the conversation continues:

> "Lor bless her dear heart, no!" interposed the nurse, hastily depositing in her pocket a green glass bottle, the contents of which she had been tasting in a corner with evident satisfaction. "Lor bless her dear heart, when she has lived as long as I have, sir, and had thirteen children of her own, and all on 'em dead except two, and them in the wurkus with me, she'll know better than to take on in that way, bless her dear heart! Think what it is to be a mother, there's a dear young lamb, do."
>
> Apparently this consolatory perspective of a mother's prospects, failed in producing its due effect. The patient shook her head, and stretched out her hands towards the child.
>
> The surgeon deposited it in her arms. She imprinted her cold white lips passionately on its forehead; passed her hands over her face; gazed wildly round; shuddered; fell back—and died.[22]

The most important common denominator of an interpretive community is knowledge of a language and the phenomena and items described by it. To be able to perform an ironic reading of the above cited passage, one must know English and one must have some idea of what it is to "die" and what may be contained in "a bottle." However, as every individual has more or less private associations and valuations attached to, say, nurses, liquor, and little babies, the boundaries of every interpretive community are necessarily very blurred. The "members" of an interpretive community share strategies of reading and basic norms concerning political, religious, and other important matters. Yet, the complexity of life makes sure that every human being embraces knowledge, beliefs, and norms that are uniquely combined.

The reason for the strong inclination to interpret Dickens's description of the mother's death as ironic is, I believe, the author's tendency to use words and descriptive categories that for most readers are heavily loaded with emotions of a pronounced character. I assume that most interpretive communities consider it a sad event when a newborn child's mother dies. I also assume that most people consider it a sad life when one is forced to work very hard and yet dwell in poverty while one's children die.

How, then, is irony created in the reading of Dickens's text?

What the reader learns from the cited passage is this, in short: Oliver's mother believes that she will soon die. The nurse, though, holds the opinion that the mother has no reason to pity herself. She summarily describes her own miserable life, but seems to enjoy the content of the bottle and feel rather fine while doing it. Oliver's mother is, however, very weak and dies only a few moments later.

If one accepts this paraphrase of the described events in the cited passage, the situation may be said to include sharp contrasts and perhaps even incongruities. As I read the situation of the text, Oliver's mother is worthy of pity and comfort, and yet she receives nothing of this. On the contrary, the nurse (who does not seem to have very many troubles, at least not for the moment) pities herself. Furthermore, the narrator calls the nurse's description of her own life, filled with poverty, hard work, and her children's death, a "consolatory perspective." I know that I myself would not be consoled by such a prospect, and neither, I infer, is Oliver's mother—or rather she would not be if she were in a state of being able to comprehend the full meaning of the nurse's words. On the contrary, I find it very likely that the effect of the nurse's words would be the opposite of what the narrator implies by using the word "consolatory"—and I am not the least surprised when the narrator states that "this consolatory perspective of a mother's prospects, failed in producing its due effect."

On the basis of certain values connected to life and death, I hence apply the strategy of irony and interpret the word "consolatory" in opposition to its lexical meaning. Those values are embraced by me personally, which explains my inclination to interpret the text ironically, but they are also shared by many other people who together form an interpretive community— which explains the rather extensive but nevertheless limited consensus on the ironic dimension in Dickens's text. Most interpreters take it for granted that the prospect of living a life similar to the nurse's is discouraging, not consolatory. That is why we are tempted to say that the ironic interpretation is self-evident.

It is, however, important to note that one may recognize that the conventional implications of the word "consolatory" are in conflict with the norms of most people even if one does not share those norms. One can never escape the norms and interpretive strategies that one holds at a certain time, but one may identify and understand the standards of interpretive communities that one does not belong to. One may even create ironic readings that one does not fully sympathize with. If this were not possible, every interpretive community would be an interpretive trap. Often such communities are just this, but it is after all possible to rethink, change one's mind, and gain access to new interpretive communities. If it were not, I would never have tried to write this book, and I would definitely not have bothered to get it published and read.

However, I did bother to write it, and I will continue interpreting Dickens for a few more pages. As one knows, Oliver's mother dies, but Oliver himself lives on: "Oliver cried lustily. If he could have known that he was an orphan, left to the tender mercies of churchwardens and overseers, perhaps he would have cried the louder."[23]

I suppose that for most readers the narrator's words "tender mercies" are in strong conflict with what is understood to be the selfish, cruel behavior of the "churchwardens and overseers" that is described in detail later in the novel. This behavior is implied already in the cited passage by the narrator's suggestion that Oliver "would have cried the louder" if he had known what was to come. An ironic interpretation thus presupposes that it is not seen as merciful to let orphans starve and die, and that it is seen as a natural behavior to cry if one is mistreated.

As in the case of the description of the mother's death, doubtless very few readers would not apply an ironic strategy when reading this passage, especially not if it is seen in relation to the entire novel. My conviction and, I hope, that of most people is that "mercy" belongs to a descriptive category that is incompatible with the act of voluntarily letting children who could have been saved starve to death. Indeed, the ironic interpretation seems to be so evident that the irony appears to be "in" the text. It might seem to be hard to even hypothetically imagine a reader who would not find the words "tender mercies" to be ironic in the context of Dickens's novel. Yet, the basis of the ironic interpretation is made up of the norms of an interpretive community even if those norms are so firmly rooted in one's mind that one more or less takes them to be facts of the world. It is, after all, not at all impossible to imagine a reader belonging to an extreme community of, for instance, a religious nature that believes that it is merciful to let children die even if they want to live, because they will then be definitely saved from the hardships of life. It is possible to imagine a reader who believes this so strongly that the possibility of an ironic interpretation does not even occur to him or her. If the irony is not placed in the text by this reader, it is not there. If it is not there, all the reader can do is to place it there and say: there it is, can you not see it? Then the answer might be: yes, I can see it because you have placed it there, but it is not in the text itself.

It might seem far-fetched, perhaps even absurd, to imagine such a reader, but they do definitely exist, and I believe that the interpreter who does not see any irony in Dickens's words is right. He or she might have a hard time construing a "coherent," nonironic meaning of the novel, and he or she will run the risk of being laughed to scorn by those who think that they know better, but there is no way of showing that the text "is" or "is not" ironic. All one can do, and that is perhaps not so little, is to quarrel about the norms and the standards of interpretation that one brings to the reading of the text. In order to convince one's opponents about the feasibility of an ironic interpretation, one has to convince them of the moral or cognitive value of one's opinions, or demonstrate that there exists an interpretive community that holds those opinions, and furthermore argue for the advantages of an ironic "solution" of perceived "conflicts." It is meaningless to point at the incongruities of a text and say that, for instance, the words "tender mercies" are "irony signals" because of their conflict with the context of the novel and with facts of the world, because these conflicts are part of the ironic interpretation and do not exist independent of the norms embraced by the reader who creates the irony. In Fish's words, "incongruities do not announce themselves, as Booth assumes they do; rather, they emerge in the context of interpretive assumptions, and therefore the registering of an incongruity cannot be the basis of an interpretation, since it is the product of one."[24] Similarly, contradictions do not exist independent of interpretations—not even in *Oliver Twist*.[25]

Fish is right, I think, but it must be added that Booth recognizes the problem of establishing a "relevant" context for the interpretation of irony: the impossibility of keeping the contexts within the text itself. Booth thus asserts that ironic communication presupposes a kind of "agreement" between author and reader. The two must have a common experience of vocabulary and grammar, of cultural experience (including its meaning and value), and of literary genres.[26] He seems to believe that ironic communication necessarily can take place only *within* an interpretive community, and that it is after all at least theoretically possible to know exactly which is *the* correct community.

If one instead adopts a kind of hermeneutics that gives no predominant position to the intention of the author, one must accept that the interpreter creates rather than perceives irony; that he or she writes it rather than reads it. The writing of irony may certainly be a very pleasurable occupation, to talk in Barthesian terms. It may include a questioning of values and norms, but also a sharpening of one's own norms. I presume that this is what happens when readers create irony in *Oliver Twist*:

> For the next eight or ten months, Oliver was the victim of a systematic course of treachery and deception. He was brought up by hand. The hungry and destitute situation of the infant orphan was duly reported by the workhouse authorities to the parish authorities. The parish authorities inquired with dignity of the workhouse authorities, whether there was no female then domiciled in 'the house' who was in a situation to impart to Oliver Twist, the consolation and nourishment of which he stood in need. The workhouse authorities replied with humility, that there was not. Upon this, the parish authorities magnanimously and humanely resolved, that Oliver should be 'farmed', or, in other words, that he should be despatched to a branch-workhouse some three miles off, where twenty or thirty other juvenile offenders against the poor-laws, rolled about the floor all day, without the inconvenience of too much food or too much clothing, under the parental superintendence of an elderly female, who received the culprits at and for the consideration of sevenpence-halfpenny per small head per week. Sevenpence-halfpenny's worth per week is a good round diet for a child; a great deal may be got for sevenpence-halfpenny: quite enough to overload its stomach, and make it uncomfortable. The elderly female was a woman of wisdom and experience; she knew what was good for children; and she had a very accurate perception of what was good for herself. So, she appropriated the greater part of the weekly stipend to her own use, and consigned the rising parochial generation to even a shorter allowance than was originally provided for them. Thereby finding in the lowest depth a deeper still; and proving herself a very great experimental philosopher.[27]

Dickens's novel certainly gives readers many opportunities to confront their own benevolent minds and high moral standards with the terrible descriptions of poor relief. The innocent orphans are called "culprits" and "juvenile offenders against the poor-laws," they are accused of rolling about the floor all day "without the inconvenience of too much food or too much clothing," and their stomachs are said to get overloaded by a minimum of food. One finds, however, two descriptions of their diet that are difficult to harmonize from the point of view of general benevolence. First it is called "a good round diet for a child" (I believe that most readers imply that it is the opinion of the woman that is echoed in these words), and then one reads about "even a shorter allowance than was originally provided for them."

Readers are consequently in a position to be able to construct an incongruity between what they take to be two narrative levels of the text. Two voices are heard, it might be argued: one belonging to a character in the novel, another belonging to the narrator (whom one may also identify as the implied author). The insoluble conflict between these two narrative levels is a product of a reading rooted in a normative conception, and it is certainly a vital part of the creation of irony in *Oliver Twist*. Some other conflicts that may be perceived in the text are also products of the norms of the interpreter. The text does not explicitly suggest that there is a conflict between what is "good for children" and what is "good for herself" (the elderly female). Nor does the text in itself deny the validity of its description of the woman as "a very great experimental philosopher." *Philosopher* means lover of wisdom, but if one finds it wise to steal from orphans in order to lead a more comfortable life for oneself, one does not see a conflict in this passage.

Again, the ironies in *Oliver Twist* are there because readers place them there, and they place them in the text because of their deep conviction of the correctness of certain moral values— values that are part of a widespread but nevertheless not universal interpretive community. Still, the irony of Dickens is generally seen as a stable quality of the texts.[28]

Because interpretive communities are partly products of historical circumstances, all texts are transformed when moved from one historical context to another. Certainly, the interpretation of irony may be dependent on the historical contexts, and perhaps readers of today are even more inclined to see irony in Dickens's descriptions than the readers of the nineteenth century. Poverty in Western societies is not as widespread nowadays as it was a few hundred years ago, and as a consequence more people can "afford" to be altruistic today.

To interpret ironically is often stimulating, but it also includes a risk. The ironic reading of Dickens may include a confirmation of one's own moral judgments—a confirmation that allows one to feel morally superior to those that belong to the category of people that is rejected in the creation of irony. If limited to the acknowledgment of two mutually exclusive moral standards of

which one is preferable, the ironic strategy may bring about a
false sense of being in a position "above" the opposite. It is easy
to feel anger and contempt directed toward the characters who
embrace moral standards that one would never accept as one's
own—that one at least *assumes* that one would never accept as
one's own, perhaps without noticing the consequences of this
conclusion. However, if one places Dickens's novel into a larger,
contemporary context, it might very well be read as a metaphor
for capitalism in Western society. Is not everyone who belongs to
the interpretive community that rejects the behavior of the mean
characters in *Oliver Twist* part of a political structure that lets
children starve to death while one goes to bed with a clean con-
science (perhaps after having read *Oliver Twist* and nursed one's
alleged benevolence), the only difference of importance being
that one is able to zap to another TV channel if the dying children
should happen to come into sight?

My reading of some passages in *Oliver Twist* has hopefully
made it clear that, even if irony is considered an interpretive
strategy rather than an intentional act or a collection of textual
traits, that does not mean that total subjectivity rules. To those
who read with the same strategy, the object produced by this interpretive act is "perspicuous," as Fish puts it.[29] In this sense,
there certainly "is" irony "in" *Oliver Twist*. It is, however, necessary to accept an important consequence of this line of reasoning: that the statements about irony made here are possible to
accept as "true" or "valid" only if one already belongs to, or becomes persuaded to convert to, the interpretive community that
determines the limits within which the ironic incongruities are
created.

My reason for putting such a strong emphasis on the notion of
interpretive community is that it gives a fairly clear account of
how the creation of irony emerges and finds its place in critical
discourse, but it must be remembered that the notion is only a
theoretical simulation of the very complicated interpretive activity that is constantly going on around us. Every reader is part of
at least one interpretive community, I think, but even if readers
agree upon which are the relevant interpretive strategies, the very
individual norms concerning the values of life may cause different reactions to the same text. Every person who has ever argued
about irony knows from experience that there are always at least
important details in the readings that differ from the readings of
even the most kindred spirits.

The ironic interpretation of *Oliver Twist* just performed was mainly limited to shorter passages. Examples of what would be called verbal irony within the traditional taxonomies were discussed, such as the use of the words "tender mercies" to describe a behavior that is arguably the opposite of merciful. Yet, it became apparent that the creation of these limited ironies is intimately related to very extensive contexts in and outside the novel. The interpretation also showed, I believe, that the so-called verbal ironies are often intermingled with the situation described to such an extent that it is very difficult to make a tenable distinction between verbal irony and situational irony. The words "consolatory perspective," certainly not unlikely to be seen as an example of verbal irony, are found in a context that might be categorized as an example of situational irony. Oliver's mother is not expected to die—or so it is said—and yet that is exactly what she does, only a few moments after the lamentations of the nurse who is obviously in a much better condition than the mother.

These perceived oppositions and contrasts between life, health, illness and death, may be interpreted as forming an ironic situation, but the situation is not only *described* in Dickens's text, it is *formed* by every word in it. I submit that the ironic reader does not on the one hand interpret "consolatory perspective" as a verbal irony, and on the other hand the whole scene as a situational irony. The "verbal" irony is one small but vital part of the "situational" irony as the existence of the latter is dependent on every word of the text—and vice versa. There is a dialectics in the relation between the single words and the context, and I do not think that it would be entirely correct to say that the words "consolatory perspective" are interpreted ironically because of the context, if one did not at the same time recognize that the interpretation of these words is affecting the context. This is, I believe, a parallel to the impossibility (in theory and in practice) of distinguishing between irony as a trope and irony as a figure, recognized by scholars during the Renaissance who opposed Quintilian.[30]

It is especially important to note that the reader confers different narrative functions on different segments of the text, and that the relation between these segments is a "verbal situation" that may form the basis of ironic interpretation. I suggest that the overarching irony in the situation when Oliver's mother dies is generated (but not determined) by verbal factors. The heart of the matter is *how* the situation is described, but only if one interprets certain descriptions of the narrator as ironic, or finds incompatible contrasts between the "voices" of the implied author, the narrator, and the characters does so-called situational irony emerge. Much irony in literature is thus basically interpretations of *verbal* situations.[31]

Oliver Twist is a novel that is generally seen as ironic "in part," but there are also books that most of the time are interpreted ironically "in entirety." A text that nicely lends itself to the illustration of this fact is *Praise of Folly* by Erasmus of Rotterdam, written in Latin almost five hundred years ago and below cited from the translation of Betty Radice.[32] The general view of *Praise of Folly* is very different from the general view of *Oliver Twist.* Dickens's novel is most often understood to be a text consisting of local, "verbal" ironies and with a stable norm, whereas Erasmus's text as a rule is considered problematic because of the ambiguity of its "structural" irony.[33] I think that there might be important differences between these texts in themselves, but the point of comparing them is to show that the creation of irony is similar in the reading of both of them. In practice, the alleged "verbal" ironies in *Oliver Twist* are not separable from the interpretation of the narrative structure of the text, and conversely the alleged structural irony of *Praise of Folly* is not separable from the interpretation of certain separate words. In a way, this is perfectly self-evident—and yet it is much too often neglected by routine.

When reading Erasmus's *Praise of Folly*, one must ask oneself, what are the true values of life? I think it is quite difficult to interpret this text in a way that successfully harmonizes its various statements on folly and wisdom. This is not to say, though, that *Praise of Folly* essentially requires an ironic reading. The ironic strategy is certainly a very helpful interpretive device that has proved to be successful within various interpretive communities, but the potential ironies of *Praise of Folly* are manifold, and none of them is evidently correct. Erasmus's text may be and has been read as a slightly self-contradictory satire that fails to maintain a narrative coherence.[34] However, once one starts to apply the ironic strategy, one is faced with an inescapable predicament: the questions one poses to the text are returned to oneself. To interpret *Praise of Folly* ironically is to interpret one's own life values. It is a business to which Booth's statement that wrestling with irony drives one "into debate about how a man should live" is more appropriate than ever: "In reading any irony worth bothering about, we read life itself, and we work on our relations to others as they deal with it. We read character and value, we refer to our deepest convictions."[35]

Henceforth I will hint at some of the fruitful or perhaps disturbing questions that might emerge from an ironic reading of *Praise of Folly*. In a short preface "Erasmus" suggests that "unless my 'self-love' entirely deceives me, my *praise of folly* has not been altogether foolish,"[36] but the narrative situation in the bulk of the text is that a woman, the personification of folly, makes a speech. Folly's intention, she declares in the opening, is to praise herself as nobody else will: "Yet there has been no lack of persons ready to spend lamp-oil and lose their sleep working out elaborate speeches in honour of tyrants like Busiris and Phalaris, quartan fever, flies, baldness and plagues of that sort."[37] Already here, the reader who does not approve of tyrants has reason to believe that Folly is quite wise in praising herself rather than tyrants. A first question arises: Is Folly really foolish, or is she wise?

Praise of Folly consists of a succession of normative descriptions of various categories of people, or rather various categories of behavior. Folly argues that wisdom makes people unhappy and that only folly renders them satisfied with life. Yet, the sum of Folly's descriptions does definitely not end up in a holy, foolish alliance of the true, the good, and the beautiful. According to Folly, rhetoricians who "dig four or five obsolete words out of mouldy manuscripts with which to cloud the meaning for the reader" are happy.[38] However, the same is true for deceived men:

> A husband is laughed at, cuckolded, called a worm and who knows what else when he kisses away the tears of his unfaithful wife, but how much happier it is for him to be thus deceived than to wear himself out with unremitting jealousy, strike a tragic attitude and ruin everything![39]

Wisdom, on the other hand, is a misery: "Ask a wise man to dinner and he'll upset everyone by his gloomy silence or tiresome questions. Invite him to a dance and you'll have a camel prancing about."[40] This line of argument is summarized in a comparison with the animals. Folly considers the "happiness" of animals equivalent to the "happiness" of men: "a horse who knows nothing of grammar isn't unhappy, and a foolish man is not unfortunate, because this is in keeping with his nature."[41] This comparison is of course unthinkable for all who embrace the pre-

Darwinistic view on life that is paradigmatic within Christian interpretive communities.

What is likely to happen for a secularized reader who is not immune to hedonism is that he or she interprets Folly's arguments as "serious" and perhaps, at least to a certain extent, valid. If Folly is wise in opposing the praise of tyrants, she may very well be wise also in praising a hedonism stating that a man is much happier when he is unaware of the misfortunes of his life. However, if one also considers wisdom and folly mutually exclusive categories, it follows that Folly's speech (taken that she is a fool) is ambivalent. She is a fool being wise. If one maintains that she *is* wise, she is surely wise enough to see through herself and her alleged folly. This ambivalence that may be interpreted as being an aspect of the relation between Folly's statements can also be seen as inherent in some individual statements:

> What would this life be, or would it seem worth calling life at all, if its pleasure was taken away? I hear you applause, and in fact I've always felt sure that none of you was so wise or rather so foolish—no, I mean so wise—as to think it could.[42]

Either Folly is a whimsical fool who does not know what she is talking about, blurring such profound contradictions as folly and wisdom, or she is a wise fool who skillfully (and with the aid of the narrator, of course) reveals that her discourse is double-layered. If one is looking for coherence, certain passages may be cited that might support the latter possibility: "no one can approach that perfect wisdom which the wise call the citadel of bliss unless Folly shows the way"; "Perhaps what I'm saying seems foolish and absurd at first sight, but really it's a profound truth."[43]

Still, nothing very much is settled as long as one asks only the text and oneself whether Folly is foolish or wise. What may be stated so far is that *Praise of Folly*, especially in its beginning, reverses the norms of what might loosely be called the interpretive community of educated, Christian men with knowledge of classical philosophy. The quality that is commonly called folly within this community is said to guarantee happiness, and the quality that is commonly called wisdom, or more generally knowledge, is said to guarantee unhappiness. Consequently, a conflict between two views of life arises, each of which may be said to be supported by the ambivalent speech of Folly: Christian-Stoic philosophy and hedonism—two views of life that are rooted in the realms of mind and body respectively; two views of life that see the true happiness of humans as dependent upon their status either as a replica of God, or as a creature comparable to animals such as horses. A second question arises: What *is* wisdom, and what *is* folly?

This question is perhaps no easier to answer than Pontius Pilatus's famous question "What is Truth?". Because every reading is a product of the norms of the reader, answers can be found only in individual readings of texts—and if one does not know what one's norms are, perhaps *Praise of Folly* is a text that can help one find the decisive questions. Clearly, there are some structural traits in *Praise of Folly* that make it *possible*—not compulsory—to utilize an ironic strategy when reading the text, but the shapes of all ironies that emerge from the readings of *Praise of Folly* are determined by the attitude of each reader. Because these attitudes are likely to be related to serious convictions concerning life values, it is not surprising that Erasmus's text has been the subject of some harsh disagreements. I will continue to penetrate Folly's arguments and the way she delivers them in order to see how conflicts and conflicting ironies may be created.

The two paradigms of wisdom and happiness that are echoed in Folly's speech are sometimes made clearly visible. In other words, if one knows the two differing views of life and identifies them as Christian-Stoic philosophy and hedonism, one may project these views to the differing arguments of Folly. In this way, the conflict between the two norm systems is "obvious" when life is described as a battle between reason and passion. Jupiter "confined reason to a cramped corner of the head and left all the rest of the body to the passions," Folly says.[44] The real complication for any reader who wants to reach a smooth interpretation arises when he or she comes to the many passages in the text where "folly" hovers between something that seems to be either sincerely praised or seriously disliked. Consider, for instance, the following sentences:

> But I don't think the female sex is so foolish as to be angry with me for attributing folly to them, seeing that I *am* Folly, and a woman myself. If they look at the matter in the right way they must see that it's entirely due to folly that they are better off than men in many respects.[45]

Folly repeatedly declares that it is folly that makes people happy, and yet it would be "foolish" to get angry. Is anger then compatible with happiness? The same sort of question may be asked

when a schoolmaster is described as being "pitiable afraid that
someone will win the prize," because then "all his labours of so
many years will be wasted," and yet he is so happy "that he
wouldn't want to change places with the kings of Persia."[46] Is
fright then compatible with happiness?

It would seem not, not even from the perspective of hedonism.
Yet, Folly's argument for the superiority of folly is valid only if
anger and fright are accepted as parts of happiness—at least this
is one way of reading her arguments that I find relevant. It is also
noteworthy that Folly distinguishes between two types of insanity—insanity being folly in its extremity. In Folly's view, one kind
of insanity is associated with war, forbidden love, and sacrilege,
the other is "quite different, desirable above everything, and is
known to come from me."[47] There is folly, and there is folly, even
the way Folly sees it—wise or foolish enough as she is to see the
distinctions that have to be made when dealing with such a
broad concept as folly.

It may be argued that *Praise of Folly* changes character in its
final sections. This shift is prepared by the extensive descriptions
of the happy and self-satisfied theologians, some of whom hold
the opinion "that it is a lesser crime to butcher a thousand men
than for a poor man to cobble his shoe on a single occasion on
the Lord's day."[48] The happy monks, also, are of interest for Folly:
"Then when they bray like donkeys in church, repeating by rote
the psalms they haven't understood, they imagine they are
charming the ears of their heavenly audience with infinite
delight."[49] To me, it is not very surprising that most readers understand descriptions like these as satiric. At one instant, a reser-
vation is made that seems to exclude the hedonists, also, from
the perspective of appraisal: "for the moment," Folly says, and at
least for that very moment she seems to be giving up her project
to praise her own, nominal character of folly; "for the moment
they're happy in their expectations."[50]

The theologians and the monks do not live in accordance with
the teachings of Christ, Folly implies, and are therefore happy
only "for the moment." By the end of her praise of herself, Folly
starts to undermine her own arguments as I have interpreted
them so far. In order to show how folly renders people happy,
she describes the vices of these people with increasing intensity—that is, what are seen as vices from the Christian point of
view. The theologians and the monks are people who gain happiness from these vices but are supposed to be Christians. A conflict between the Christian-Stoic philosophy and hedonism is

thus enacted. Folly seems to be aware of the interpretations that may be generated by her speech and declares that "I don't want to look as though I'm writing satire when I should be delivering a eulogy."[51] For the reader who has already seen Folly's descriptions as satire, this aspect is hereby confirmed, and for the reader who has clung to the pattern of a eulogy, it now becomes possible to see Folly's words as an ironically masked suggestion to interpret the eulogy as satire.

If one holds on to the strategy of seeing *Praise of Folly* as a text that puts Christian-Stoic philosophy and hedonism into conflict, the stage is now set for the presentation of a slightly different kind of folly. This folly is not in keeping with the hedonistic folly, and it is definitely not compatible with the veiled vices of theologians and monks, the folly that enables one to feel happy while deceiving oneself—and yet it is in alliance with Christianity: the folly that, according to St. Paul, is necessary in order to be accepted by Christ:

> Finally, the biggest fools of all appear to be those who have once been wholly possessed by zeal for Christian piety. They squander their possessions, ignore insults, submit to being cheated, make no distinction between friends and enemies, shun pleasure, sustain themselves on fasting, vigils, tears, toil and humiliations, scorn life and desire only death—in short, they seem to be dead to any normal feelings, as if their spirit dwelt elsewhere than in their body. What else can that be but madness?[52]

This folly undoubtedly resembles the folly of the stupid hedonist, but there is a decisive difference: it is a folly that does not favor the happiness and pleasure of the body; it is a folly that is somehow chosen. The happy, deceived man is cheated without knowing it, the Christian fool submits to being cheated.

By the very end of her eulogy, Folly says:

> But I've long been forgetting who I am, and I've "overshot the mark". If anything I've said seems rather imprudent or garrulous, you must remember it's Folly and a woman who's been speaking. At the same time, don't forget the Greek proverb "Often a foolish man speaks a word in season", though of course you may think this doesn't apply to women.[53]

Once again, and for the last time, Folly indirectly invites one to ask oneself: Is Folly really foolish, or is she wise? What *is* wisdom, and what *is* folly? Furthermore, as a consequence of these questions, what is happiness?

I have argued that it is very difficult, perhaps impossible, to find a position from which *Praise of Folly* can be seen as a coherent text that univocally supports an established set of norms. I have read it from the positions of what I take to be some dominant interpretive communities and thus tried to demonstrate that the text is open to interpretations that highlight important normative conflicts in and outside the text. The last question that the reader following my path will be confronted with is, may ignorance go hand in hand with true happiness?

I will finally isolate some of the extreme positions that may be held in relation to this question. If the reader's answer is yes, then Folly must be considered right when claiming that ignorance guarantees happiness, which does not exclude that even the Christian, "informed" fool, as described by the end of the text, may be happy. This reading implies that Folly speaks with the voice of Wisdom, which is a state of affairs that may be seen as ironic. If the reader's answer is no, then Folly is wrong when claiming that ignorance and happiness are compatible. However, presupposing a coherence in her views, Folly is also wrong when implying that the theologians and monks are living sinful lives. This reading furthermore leads one to suppose that Folly, who is wrong in praising the unchristian lives of people that are comparable to the lives of horses, is at the same time wrong in blaming the vices of theologians and monks. This also is a state of affairs that lends itself to an ironic interpretation.

What if the reader's answer is neither yes nor no? What if one supposes that Folly is neither completely right nor completely wrong? Then one is left with the decision about *where* and *why* distinctions must be made. Performing that task is a very lonely and very instructive business.

It thus seems to be difficult for the reader of Erasmus to avoid discrepancies and to collect Folly's arguments in a coherent system. Depending on what norms one relies on, one may try to arrange the opinions and statements on wisdom, folly, misfortune, and happiness in various positions. The results will vary widely. In each of the positions that I have proposed and outlined, discrepancies emerge that I would call ironic. These ironies are created by strategies that aim at giving the text some sort of meaningful structure. However, although the ironies are of a similar nature, they are (and now I am reading the already read ironies from a normative position) not possible to keep together.

Hence, my reading of my proposed ironic readings of Erasmus's text produces another, overarching irony.

The final result of the ironic strategies set into play in these readings is a penetration of a philosophical issue that has forced me over and over again to reconsider the nature of true happiness. If I am still not wiser than the experimental philosopher in *Oliver Twist*, the nurse who found "in the lowest depth a deeper still," irony is not to blame, but rather folly. Yet, if I am not entirely foolish, I am right in suggesting that the ironies I see in *Praise of Folly* are of a magnitude that could justify the designation *structural ironies*. Still, they are definitely the results of ironies that I place in single words too and that could be called *verbal ironies*: change the interpretation of a short passage, and the whole structure changes; change the interpretation of the structure, and the single words change. As in *Oliver Twist*, no ironies that are definitely stable or overt can be found. The ironies in *Praise of Folly* are all results of interpretations of verbal situations in which the readers are themselves involved.

5

Irony, Obliqueness, and Incongruities

A concept, statically defined, represents what a number of
separate entities have in common. Quite often, however, a
concept is instead a kind of highspot within a sweep of con-
tinuous transformations.

—Rudolf Arnheim

IRONY AND RELATED NOTIONS

WHAT IS THE DIFFERENCE BETWEEN THE VARIABLE CONCEPT OF IRONY AND
the many notions that it has been attached to through history?
Where is the difference? Are the various notions mutually exclusive? In his eminently informative book, *Ironia: Medieval and Renaissance Ideas on Irony*, Dilwyn Knox opens every chapter with
a summary. The first two propositions in the summary of chapter
3 read: "Any type of sentence may be ironic—*Ironia* can combine
with any figure or trope."[1] Renaissance authors in particular held
the rather modern view that irony can be combined with other
tropes or figures. That is reasonable, I think: if irony is seen as
an interpretive strategy dependent on interpretive communities,
individual norms, and certain qualities of the text, it should be
obvious that other interpretive strategies may not only compete
with but also be combined with the ironic strategy. As no textual
quality exists definitely, until it has been created in the reading,
it should also be obvious that no clear-cut system of textual traits
may be upheld. In theory it is easy to make sharp, "objective"
distinctions, but in practice these distinctions often prove
vague—but of course that does not mean that it is impossible to
delimit irony altogether.

The difficulty of getting a firm grip on irony is one that applies
to other literary concepts also, but the problems seem to be more
acute for irony. Antiquity produced some quite clear-cut rhetorical definitions of irony, but since then irony has over and over

84

again escaped the simple duality between intended and expressed meaning. According to Knox, the word *ironicum* is
glossed simply as *obliquum* [covert] in a thirteenth-century vocabulary.[2] The opinion that irony is basically identifiable with
obliqueness is today widespread, and it is certainly not impossible to argue for it. In any case, it explains why irony has a tendency to interfere with such a wide range of textual notions and
devices: the meaning of all figurative language is "oblique," and
if irony is the same as obliqueness, all figurative language is
ironic, it might be maintained. From this it follows that all literature, if one defines it as figurative language, is ironic. This conclusion has been drawn by some theoreticians, from Solger to
Brooks and (perhaps) de Man. Irony has been treated as both a
very limited trope and the sine qua non of literature.

Seen in this perspective, irony is a scandal of literary criticism.
Due to its unwillingness to be tamed conceptually, it has caused
disorder and confusion, and furthermore it has a strong historical
connection to abuse. Nevertheless it is fully possible to understand how, and partly also why, irony has navigated its way between so many different notions: sarcasm, humor, allegory,
satire, parody, ambiguity, and so forth. In the following I wish to
discuss some of the implications of adhering to nonintentionalis-
tic hermeneutics. What happens to the relationship between
irony and all the notions that it is so strongly linked to, historically and theoretically, if one sees irony as an interpretive strategy? Is the scandal restored to peace and order?

Lying

Literature, irony, and lying are in many ways closely associated. Some people, though perhaps not as many now as in
former days, believe that all literature is "deceptive," "mendacious," or "untruthful"; literary stories are "made up" and not in
accordance with what has "really happened." The notion of a
poem or a novel that lies is in a way certainly naive, based as it
is on an extremely consistent intentionalism, assuming that all
uttered or written words are intended to convey, and ought to be
interpreted as conveying, only factual references. Nevertheless,
the "naive" opinion that all literature is mendacious corresponds
to the more "sophisticated," opposite opinion that all literature
is ironic.

Irony and lying are intimately connected not the least from an
historical point of view. As is already known, there has been sus-

picion about irony from the beginning: a suspicion that on a
more general level has included all kinds of rhetorical devices. To
speak and write figuratively is to violate the "natural" order of
language, it has been argued, and because irony is a reversal of
meaning it must be the worst of all abuses against language and
honesty. The link between rhetoric, irony, and lying is particularly obvious in the critique of the Sophists, who were accused of
using figurative language in order to violate truth and deceive
their public. Even Socrates, the ironist who was eventually sen-
tenced to death, was sometimes included in the group of the
Sophists.[3] According to Theophrastus's description in *Characters*,
the ironist is simply a liar.[4] It goes without saying that this conception of irony is contrary to the alleged nobility of Socratic
irony.

The close relationship between irony and deception was manifested in the translation of the Greek word *eironeia*. When it was
adopted into Latin, it was most often translated as either *ironia*
or *dissimulatio*, and from the notion of dissimulation it is only a
short step to deception.[5] Soon, the negative values attached to
irony were partly replaced by appraisal, especially among rhetoricians (texts by whom dominated the theoretical writing on
irony until the eighteenth century). Yet, in spite of this revaluation
and in spite of the often highlighted contrast of "appearance"
and "reality" in irony, the sense of deceitfulness has remained
linked to irony until this very day.

As irony has been and can be defined in a number of ways, it
is impossible to claim that there is one and only one theoretical
relation between irony and lying. In antiquity, and also later,
there are many varying conceptions of irony: irony as pretense;
irony as *deceitful* pretense, irony as simple mockery, and so
forth.[6] Often it is maintained that being ironic may be distinguished from lying on the ground that the deceitfulness of the
ironist is intended to be seen through (at least by some), whereas
the deceitfulness of the liar is intended not to be revealed.[7] This
is, I would say, a valid description of the standard conceptions of
"being ironic" and "lying" in oral communication.

However, as every little child knows, it is impossible to distinguish definitely between lying and irony in practice. If someone
intends to be ironic, but is understood to be lying, he or she *is*
lying—from the point of view of the listener. The difference between being ironic and lying, I argue, lies in the eyes of the beholder. To say that someone is not lying when he or she states
something that is understood not to be in accordance with truth

is to assert that the speaker interprets his or her own utterance as ironic rather than untruthful. Yet, the "intention" of an alleged ironist or liar is always an interpretation, as I have earlier advocated. The speaker who claims to be interpreting his or her own utterance as ironic might be lying when it comes to the alleged ironic intention. The speaker who claims to be interpreting his or her own utterance as a lie might be ironic when it comes to the alleged deceitful intention, and so on ad infinitum.

These are not, I would claim, far-fetched, hypothetical examples, but communicative realities. There are no manifest differences between lies and ironies of the sort that are made up of a contrast between an "apparent" and a "hidden" meaning. The difference lies on an ethical level. To call someone an ironist is a hermeneutical judgment that does not have to include a moral dimension. To call someone a liar is a hermeneutical but also a moral judgment. To put it bluntly, a liar is punished, an ironist is at most disliked.

To call someone a liar is thus an interpretive strategy that is not distinguishable from the ironic strategy if no moral dimension is considered. Both include an utterance that is perceived as stating something that is in opposition to a belief about some state of affairs that the interpreter holds, but to interpret the utterance as deceptive or untruthful is to add a moral verdict. Naturally, this distinction is often of immense importance in many areas of society, but it must be recognized that untruthfulness can be decided only on circumstantial evidence, as the legal term reads.

Again, it is necessary to remember the importance of discursive practice and norms. Perhaps it is easier to see the very close connection between irony and lies if one applies the notion of interpretive community to lies also. Truth is at least partly a product of the beliefs one holds, and hence truth may change from one interpretive community to another. What the Muslim with all his or her heart and intellect involved calls a lie might very well be called truth by a Christian who tries to be as just as possible. Irony, I have maintained, may emerge and disappear when texts are moved between interpretive communities, and similarly lies may emerge and disappear. What is understood to be ironic or figurative in one interpretive community may be understood to be a lie in another. As the intention is always a product of an interpretation, and as the moral dimension connected to an alleged lie is a product of the values of an interpretive community, there is no way of definitely deciding who is "right."

To argue about the difference between ironies and lies is

thus—to repeat something very important—to argue about our deepest convictions and values of life. A very extreme example of an interpretive battle closely related to this discussion is the *fatwa* on Salman Rushdie caused by his novel *The Satanic Verses*—a novel that was hailed as sublime literature by some and judged as a mendacious and revolting text by others because of its questionable connections to Islam. On moral grounds, one can argue that it is wrong and perhaps even absurd to sentence someone to death because of heresy (a sort of lie), but one cannot argue that Rushdie is not *in some sense* "lying" in his novel if one admits that his language is somehow figurative. The dimension of "deceitfulness" is not, I believe, possible to extract from a text.

This discussion has now moved from oral communication to literature, and some demarcations must be made. Because the concept of meaning that I advocate involves a nonoral, noncommunicative conception of literature, the concept of lying is for me irrelevant when it comes to literary criticism. This is well in line with established views on literature in Western societies: a literary text cannot lie because it does not assert anything in the communicative, referential sense of the word. Lies can come into existence only within an intentional kind of hermeneutics based on a situation of oral communication and including a moral dimension. Within nonintentional hermeneutics, it is not appropriate to use the concept of lying. The same words, uttered in court and written in a poem, ought to be interpreted using differing hermeneutical postulates. Even if interpreted within the same interpretive community, and in light of similar contexts, exactly the same word might be said to be untruthful in court and ironic in a poem—the only difference being the relevance of moral judgment.

This might seem to be self-evident, and yet it is not. The existence of these two sometimes competing hermeneutical approaches explains why hostile discussions may emerge about truth-value in texts that are situated on the borderline between fiction and nonfiction. Nonfictional texts are generally interpreted as communicative in the same sense as oral messages, and they may hence be seen as both ironic and mendacious. In most modern Western interpretive communities, however, literary texts are generally interpreted by means of a theory of meaning that excludes the simplest forms of intentionality and hence also the notion of lying. Clearly, the stage is set for disagreement about whether a text is figuratively ironic or mendacious if one does not agree on the fictional status of the text.

From the line of reasoning that I have developed so far, it follows that I consider all efforts to distinguish between irony and lying on other than moral grounds as vain. Those who insist on the distinction are obliged to lean on intentionality, with all that it includes. In the article "L'ironie comme trope," Catherine Kerbrat-Orecchioni asserts that it is impossible to distinguish between irony and lying on linguistic grounds and concludes that it is the intention to deceive that marks the difference between lying and being ironic. Her problems begin when *intention*, much as in Booth's book, is defined as something that is reconstructed on textual grounds.[8] If the "intention" is reconstructed it is in fact an interpretation and not necessarily a very strong ground for accusations of lying, for instance.

In a similar way, Linda Hutcheon comes into severe difficulties when she maintains that the notion of intentionality is necessary in order to keep irony and lies distinct. She wants to avoid the implications of intentionality and claims, as I have earlier noted, that all irony "happens" in the act of interpretation. However, she also wants to be able to separate irony from lying and thus feels obliged not to get rid of intentionality altogether. She therefore asserts that interpretation is an intentional act: "all irony happens intentionally, whether the attribution be made by the encoder or the decoder."[9] Yet, is intentionality on the part of the "encoder" really equivalent to the strange notion of intended interpretations of the "decoder" when it comes to rescuing the distinction between irony and lying? Certainly not. I think that the proposition "I intend the words of X to be a lie" is rather meaningless compared to the propositions "I interpret the words of X to be a lie," "I intend my words to be a lie," or "I interpret my words to be a lie." Lies "happen" in the same way that ironies "happen," the only (but very important) difference being that it makes sense to pass moral judgments on some "happenings." What I argue is consequently not that the hermeneutics of intentionalism ought to be abandoned when it comes to practical life, only that it is fraught with such complications that it causes more confusion than order when practiced in literary interpretation.

Sarcasm

Another notion that is often associated with irony is sarcasm. Being sarcastic, like lying, is generally seen as something bad;

some believe that the word means "biting of flesh."[10] In modern dictionaries *sarcasm* is often defined as a crude and blatant use of apparent praise for dispraise, which indicates that sarcasm is seen as a variation of ironic blame-by-praise. Within classical rhetoric, *sarcasmos* is as a rule defined as harsh derision, and it is very often connected to irony. Sometimes it is even classified as a specific species of *ironia*: "bitter irony."[11]

Sarcasm and irony may obviously be very intimately related, but they are by no means necessarily connected (unless, of course, one narrowly defines sarcasm as "bitter irony" and nothing more). A text may be interpreted as both conveying bitterness or derision and involving a double-layered meaning—in which case it is both sarcastic and ironic—but a text may also be seen as straightforwardly bitter or derisive, which means that it is interpreted as sarcastic but not ironic. Like irony, it should be noted, sarcasm is often seen as an aspect of oral communication directed by gestures and, most importantly, the tone of the voice.

Humor

As I understand it, the relation between irony and sarcasm is quite unproblematic. Perhaps more intricate, but basically of the same nature, is the relation between irony and humor. As it is associated with laughter rather than bitterness, humor might be said to be the opposite of sarcasm, but this is certainly a simplistic view of humor. Sick jokes and black humor may be both derisive and bitter.

The connection between irony and humor has been a rather popular topic for a long time.[12] The outcome of a comparison between the two notions obviously depends on how one defines humor, and to define humor satisfactorily is perhaps as problematic as to define irony. Be that as it may, humor and jokes, like sarcasm, are closely related to irony already in the works of the classical authors. Some of these believe that all jokes include an opposition that is basically ironic, whereas others are content to recognize that humor may include irony. According to some authors, irony depends on explicit propositions that are somehow reversed, whereas jokes are said to depend on implied propositions.[13]

Some writers from more recent times also have described or defined humor in ways that strongly relate it to irony. Kant's famous definition of the comic is strongly reminiscent of how situational irony is commonly described: "Laughter is an emotion derived from the sudden transformation of a tensed expectation into nothing."[14] Among the Romanticists, Jean Paul Richter in particular circumscribes *Humor* in a manner that makes it very similar to Schlegel's conception of irony. For Jean Paul, humor is a transcendent unification of opposites such as the finite and the infinite, or realism and idealism.[15] In addition, most post-Romantic writers who have dealt with humor and the comic—notably Schopenhauer, Baudelaire, Bergson, Freud, and Koestler—rely on a perception of opposites and contrasting situations. In her book, *Nonrepresentational Forms of the Comic: Humor, Irony, and Jokes*, Marcella Tarozzi Goldsmith labels this dominant trend "the incongruity theory."[16]

Humor and irony are thus generally seen as closely related, and it might be argued that the two terms are to a large extent interchangeable.[17] To put it pragmatically, the oppositions and contrasts that according to all leading definitions are fundamental for both *humor* and *irony* may be understood to be both "humorous" and "ironic" in various cases, depending on the interpreter's attitudes, view of life, and sense of humor. A whole range of questions must be answered before one can definitely distinguish between irony and humor: Is "the tragic" compatible with "humor"? Is "the tragic" compatible with "irony"? Is "humor" compatible with "irony"? Is all "humor" really dependent on opposites and contrasts? Can something be "humorous" if one does not laugh or smile? Furthermore, it might be asked whether or not the humorous and the comic ought to be seen as two different notions.

I believe that the answers given to these and many other questions vary fundamentally among both scholars and laypersons. Of course, they depend partly on the norms and discursive practices of interpretive communities, and partly on individual preferences. To be able to make a tenable distinction between irony and humor, one must postulate so many factors that the distinction becomes heavily normative. Therefore, I do not find Goldsmith's attempt to distinguish between humor, irony, and jokes as three differing variations of the comic very successful. On the other hand, it is difficult to argue against postulations that do not rest on argumentation at all, as when Vladimir Jankélévitch writes that irony is "too cruel to be really comic," whereas the irony that is "ultimately serious" is called *l'Humour*.[18]

Of course, one may make ad hoc distinctions that do not claim to be generally valid. This is how I understand the proceeding in Candace D. Lang's book *Irony/Humor: Critical Paradigms*. Lang treats irony and humor as closely associated phenomena, but she postulates rather than argues that irony "implies an intender" whereas humor "is a textual phenomenon." Irony is said to be associated with "a position of superiority" for the critic who, with the aid of intention, is able to "step outside and beyond the language of the literary texts he interprets."[19] In its attempt to keep irony within the domains of rhetoric, this distinction resembles Jean Paul's view of irony. For him, humor is warm and free, irony cold and constrained. Irony has been strongly connected to rhetoric, and it is often regarded as a trope or a figure, whereas humor has been discussed in these terms only incidentally. Seen in this perspective, irony is more hard-boiled than humor.

It is of course legitimate to define the two concepts the way Lang does, but the distinction collapses if irony is seen as an interpretive strategy that is independent of the author's intention. The development of the concept of irony during the last two centuries has inevitably drawn it closer to humor. The moment one accepts that it makes sense to call situations and states of affairs ironic without there being an ironist, irony falls into the same category as humor. If one does not accept this conception of irony, one may feel forced (as Jean Paul did) to keep irony and humor distinct. In my view, however, both irony and humor "happen" as reactions to (textual) events. Most people, I believe, would find it absurd to deny the existence of humor if someone laughs at something, and analogously I find it absurd to deny the existence of irony if it is clearly "seen" by someone.

According to my hermeneutical view, humor, like lying, is thus indistinguishable from irony on linguistic grounds or in terms of intention. From this it follows that humor and lying are also fundamentally indistinguishable, which I believe is the case. Irony, humor, and lying are products of perceived opposites and incompatibilities that are interpreted in various ways. They are all "interpretive strategies" or "reactions" that supply us with different but not necessarily mutually exclusive "answers" to the questions that emerge from the perceived incompatibilities: why is it that this (textual) situation is incongruous, and what am I to do with it? One calls the situation ironic if one finds that the incongruity conveys some sort of meaning or truth that is not possible to pin down in unambiguous terms; one calls it humorous if one laughs at it; and one calls it a lie if one believes that one has moral reasons to condemn it. This is why both ironies and lies may be funny; this is why the same text may generate laughter, admiration, and condemnation in various readers; and this is why the three notions may be separated by individuals in interpretive practice and to a certain extent also within interpretive communities, but never definitely distinguished from each other.

Dialectics

The concept of dialectics, also, has rather strong historical and theoretical connections to irony. Most writers who have dealt with the relationship between irony and dialectics refer to Plato's dialogues and Socratic irony in one way or another, but it was not highlighted until the time of Romanticism and Hegel.[20] Thirlwall calls what was then known as Socratic irony *dialectic irony*. In the historical survey that opened this book, I briefly discussed the very intimate connections between these two notions in the theories of Schlegel, Müller, Solger, and Kierkegaard. Here I only wish to restate the important difference between Hegel's transcendental and progressive dialectics of history and Schlegel's dialectics of irony that allows no genuine synthesis, and point to the fact that irony and dialectics are still regarded as closely related phenomena that have "common roots," as René Schaerer puts it.[21]

The way I see it, dialectics is an interpretive strategy that is compatible with and sometimes almost identical to post-Romantic notions of irony. Like irony, the dialectic interpretation is certainly dependent on the norms and discursive context of the interpreter. To perform a dialectic interpretation (in Hegel's sense) of a (textual) situation, one must perceive a tension between opposites and argue that the "result" of this opposition is a third state that is in some sense "higher" than the two initial ones. To perform an ironic interpretation (in Schlegel's sense) of a (textual) situation, however, one must perceive a tension between opposites and maintain that the "result" of this opposition is a third state that does not transcend the two opposites but instead lets them operate in a creative conflict. It should be obvious that the borderline between these two modes of interpretation is not always very sharp in practice.

In any case, dialectics is one of the most important of the critical concepts that was related to irony by the Romanticists and the post-Romanticists. The notions of arabesque and grotesque were also important for a rather short period but have then disappeared out of focus in the discourse concerning irony. The arabesque and the grotesque, notions borrowed from art criticism,

were for Schlegel important aspects of irony—so important that
the terms *irony, arabesque,* and *grotesque* were used almost as
synonyms, although the latter ones were most often associated
with aspects that concern form and technique.[22]

Metaphor

As I have noted, irony has traditionally been grouped among
the tropes. Often it is considered one of the most important,
together with metaphor, metonymy, and synecdoche.[23] Even
within the field of rhetoric these tropes have been defined in different ways, but it is common to mark a resemblance between
metonymy and synecdoche. Irony and metaphor, on the other
hand, are commonly defined in distinct opposition: metaphor as
a trope of similarity, irony as a trope of contrariety. Still, a resemblance between metaphor and irony is sometimes remarked.[24]

This might seem strange, but it is quite easily explained. *Figural language* is by definition language that is assigned two or
more levels of meaning, and the distinction between various
tropes is but an attempt to create some order in the boundless
semiosis of language. I have argued that the creation of irony involves a construction of contrariety based on norms and contexts
that are partly individual and partly shared by interpretive communities. Similarly, the creation of metaphor often involves a
construction of similarity performed by the reader—a construction that is more or less in accordance with comparisons suggested by words and linguistic constructions in the text (what
one calls a simile is a metaphor that is linguistically indicated in
a definite way).[25] Because the interpretation of a text is dependent on norms and contexts, the same words may certainly be
interpreted in opposite ways. One opposite to ironic meaning is
"literal" meaning; another opposite is "figural" meaning based
on difference; and yet another opposite is "metaphorical" meaning—and as contrariety actually requires some sort of similarity,
it might be argued that the ironic contrariety is more closely associated with metaphoric similarity than with other sorts of figural "difference."

These opposite readings may be created by different readers,
but also by one and the same reader. Consider these famous
words from Shakespeare's *As You Like It,* cited by Booth in his
discussion on metaphor: "All the world's a stage."[26] This is, as I
understand it, either a metaphor, an irony, or both (or, for that
matter, something else). If one believes that there are some as-

pects of life as lived in this world that are similar to aspects of life acted on the stage—pretense, tediousness, comedy, and so on—it makes sense to perform a metaphorical reading. If, on the other hand, one believes that real life is (or should be) contrary to life given shape in theater—that it is *not* acted, *not* limited to a few hours, *not* possible to ignore, and so on—an ironic reading is plausible. If one recognizes both the similarities and the contrarieties, Shakespeare's statement may very well be interpreted as metaphoric *and* ironic. Indeed, this double, "contradictory" interpretation may in turn be seen as ironic, in which case the metaphor and the "limited" irony become parts of an "all-embracing" irony. Then one comes close to the notions of irony introduced by Schlegel and the other German Romanticists: irony as *both* earnestness/similarity *and* irony/contrariety.

Although possible to distinguish in theory, irony and metaphor (and many other tropes and figures) are thus not always possible to disentangle from each other in interpretive practice. Irony and metaphor are related, it might be argued, not *in spite* of their opposite positions in the rhetorical system, but *because* of them.

Allegory

Much more often than metaphor, however, allegory is put in relation to irony. Allegory is a figure the etymology of which simply indicates that it means "to say something else." It is, however, sometimes seen as an "extended" metaphor—the figural equivalent of the trope. According to this neat definition, an allegory is simply a long metaphor. This presupposes that allegory is treated as a figure based on similarity, which is common today but has not always been the case. If defined as a figure of similarity, *allegory* is anyhow quite clearly distinguished from *irony*, which is based on contrariety.[27]

As a matter of fact, however, *allegory* has also been defined in terms of contrariety. Already a comparison of Cicero and Quintilian makes evident that the demarcation lines between allegory, irony, and the figure *inversio* are extremely fragile. Sometimes allegory is defined in words that are in other instances reserved for the definition of irony; sometimes the definitions merge. From late antiquity to the seventeenth century the notion of allegory *ex contrario* is habitually identified as irony in rhetorical manuals; irony is consequently seen as a species of allegory. In fact, most other species of allegory in rhetorical taxonomies of this period, such as antiphrasis and *sarcasmos*, are strongly related to irony.[28]

Although allegory and irony are not very often lumped together nowadays, it still happens that they are.[29]

The classification of *ironia* as a species of *allegoria* rests on the shared element of *obscuritas* [opacity].[30] This opacity is, I would say, a vital element also in de Man's discussion of the concepts of irony and allegory in his essay "The Rhetoric of Temporality." De Man's metaphorical use of the notion of "temporality" as a distinctive feature of symbol, allegory, and irony is not, in my opinion, very informative. Irony is described as "a synchronic structure" and a "staccato," whereas allegory is described as "a successive mode" and as connected to "duration"—and yet they are "the two faces of the same fundamental experience of time."[31] De Man thus adopts and tries to fuse two views: allegory and irony are opposed, he sometimes asserts, and yet they are basically the same.[32] Still he treats irony almost as a trope in the classical sense in this essay: it is limited to one single moment. Allegory, on the other hand, ascends to the status of a critical, all-embracing tool and is closely related not only to Romantic irony, but also to the medieval notion of allegory as a figure *ex contrario*—which is in its turn often identified as irony. De Man's distinction between irony and allegory seems to be very close to the distinction between irony as a trope and irony as a figure made already by Quintilian.

When defined in terms of contrariety, allegory is consequently more or less identical to irony seen as a figure. When defined in terms of similarity, on the other hand, allegory becomes the figural equivalent of the trope metaphor. To put it briefly, no matter what it is, an allegory is always long.

Litotes and Hyperbole

There are some other critical concepts that have as strong historical and theoretical connections to irony as allegory, but that are easier to keep distinct because their definitions have been more uniform: *litotes* (*meiosis*) and *hyperbole*—that is, approximately, understatement and exaggeration. If one expands the trope litotes to a philosophy of life, one gets an important aspect of Socratic irony. For Aristotle, in the *Nicomachean Ethics*, irony is a constant pretense of self-depreciation, and he defines irony as "a pretence tending toward the under-side."[33] The opposite of the vice of *eironeia* is, according to Aristotle, *alazoneia* [boastfulness].[34] Neither the *eiron* nor the *alazon* is truthful (irony is thus not distinguished from lying), but for Aristotle it is only the "pretence tending toward the under-side" that is considered ironic by way of terminology. Posterity, however, has preferred to put the term *alazoneia* aside and instead associate both pretended self-depreciation and boastfulness with irony.

Irony in this broad sense has often been distinguished from irony as a trope, and yet they are of course closely related. The trope has also been connected to understatement and exaggeration. In the sixteenth century, understatement was for the first time called *irony* instead of *litotes* or *meiosis* in an English rhetoric manual, and eventually it came to be accepted as a standard ironic device.[35] Also exaggeration, hyperbole, is commonly seen as one of the most frequent ironic devices.

Undoubtedly both litotes and hyperbole are intimately related to irony, but it must be noted that an understatement or an exaggeration does not exist until it has been interpreted as one. Only the norms of individual readers and interpretive communities can provide the standards of comparison. Litotes and hyperbole can thus not be seen as irony markers, which is very commonly done, as an ironic reading *includes* an interpretation of what might be seen as understated or exaggerated. Furthermore, an apprehended understatement or exaggeration does not necessarily involve an ironic reading. It is mainly when the understatement or exaggeration is seen as so significant that a conflict tending toward an opposition emerges that irony *might* be used as an interpretive category.

To illustrate the complications that are involved in this area, it may suffice to ask one question: Are the texts of Marquis de Sade ironic? The answer to this question depends on several factors, some of the most important of which are moral and sexual norms; comprehension of how "detailed," "perverse," or "lengthy" a description of sexual actions should be to be considered "very" hyperbolic; the inclination to create irony out of hyperbole; and of course the ability to find an ironic "meaning" that somehow transcends the face value of pornography. It is necessary to scrutinize in detail how these factors are related to different interpretive communities if one wants to reach an explanation of why de Sade may be read both as a dirty, philosophical pig and an ironic satirist. The only thing that is clear, as far as I can see, is that both interpretations emerge from the same texts but are products of widely differing norms and interpretive strategies, none of which is unreasonable.

Satire

As noted, irony was originally seen as almost identical to mockery, which means that it was close to satire in the modern sense: a critique directed chiefly toward the authorities. In antiquity, however, the term *satire* meant something rather different than today, but although the terms have shifted meaning, satire may be said to be a vital part of the early notions of irony.

A historical development to be observed here is that the age of satire, beginning in the second half of the seventeenth century, coincides with a growing interest in the concept of irony. The English term *irony* came into general use at that time, and since then most writers who are habitually characterized as satirists are also called ironists. Indeed, irony and satire are frequently found in the same texts, although they are by no means necessarily connected. From a historical point of view, their relationship is immensely important: irony and satire have been discussed together and confused or mingled with each other in innumerable books and articles—but theoretically the relationship is rather casual. There are many ways of making someone or something look stupid. Irony may certainly be effective, but satire may also be totally straightforward. Irony is a strategy that often victimizes someone or something—but not always.

Parody

Another notion that must be discussed in this context is parody. The relationship between irony and parody is in a way reversed compared to the rather unambiguous relationship between irony and satire. Historically, irony and parody have been connected rather casually, whereas their theoretical connections, on the other hand, have been quite intricate. Yet, irony, satire, parody, and also hyperbole form a complicated web that may appear to be confusing. Muecke states quite correctly that "The word 'parody' more commonly in English means not the adoption or inversion of a style but the exaggerated imitation of a style in order to satirise or ridicule either stylistic mannerisms or mannered ways of thought or both."[36]

In the context of literature, parody is thus seen as a phenomenon dependent on exaggeration of "style" or "thought" that involves satire. Parody would consequently be a result of the same interpretive procedures as hyperbole, with the addition that the reader is somehow amused at the cost of some text or author.

Linda Hutcheon has argued that parody does not necessarily ridicule its "object" (it may also pay "reverential homage"), but her
notion of parody is a deliberate extension that serves the purpose
of discussing intertextual phenomena in twentieth-century art
forms.[37] In the context of music, the notion of parody is partly
different from literary parody. This will be discussed in detail
later.

Parody is, as I see it, a species of irony. It is an ironic interpretation of the relationship between two texts, or between a text and
a genre, a text and a style, a text and an authorship, a text and a
standard plot, a text and standard characters or standard values
in literature—and so forth. Parody may be called "intertextual
irony" with an addition of satire. As such, it is of course formed
in interpretive and discursive communities. More than other
variants of irony, parody is dependent on the reader's supplement of the special type of context that intertexts constitute. If
the reader does not supply any contrasting intertext, no ironic
interpretation of a parodic kind may be performed.

As I understand it, there is no fundamental difference between
the creation of ironic meaning based on contexts and intertexts,
respectively. All irony is a result of interpretation, the only difference being that the conflicts and incongruities that are seen as
ironic are found in different areas and on different levels. Nevertheless, a terminological distinction between irony and parody is
usually upheld. A more neutral and historically less burdened
distinction could possibly be maintained with the three terms
"intratextual irony," "intertextual irony," and "extratextual
irony." Intratextual irony would thus be understood as irony created out of incongruities that a reader understands to be part of
one and the same text; intertextual irony would be irony that
emerges from an apprehended relationship between two or more
texts; and extratextual irony, finally, would be irony resulting
from a perceived conflict between a text and some context in the
"extratextual" world.

Naturally, these distinctions are not in any way definite, and I
refrain from discussing the question of whether ideas can really
be situated "inside" or "outside" texts. Because all irony is a result of individual norms and interpretive communities, all irony
is in a way extratextual. Yet, it is an inescapable fact that one may
tie some phenomena closer than others to the texts themselves.
The distinction between intratextual and extratextual irony is
thus more a distinction within the phenomenology of reading
than within the factual world. The ironies that Cleanth Brooks,

for example, is interested in are definitely intratextual. This is, I submit, the greatest weakness of Brooks's notion of irony: his insistent discussion of contexts is limited to the contexts of the texts themselves and does not really recognize the importance of the contexts "in the world" supplied by the reader's knowledge and norms. Wide-ranging as it is, Brooks's notion of irony is still paradoxically narrow.

To conclude this discussion of parody, I suggest that at least two interpretive maneuvers must be performed in the creation of this type of intertextual irony: the "choice" of a contrasting intertext and the "construction" of ironic meaning in their relationship; an ironic meaning that somehow involves laughter at a "victim." Of course, parody is no more a fixed entity than other ironies. It is a well-known empirical fact that opinions often differ on which text is a parody and why. Comparisons of intertexts may be more or less convincing, but there is nothing in the texts themselves that guarantees an ironic relationship between them. How can one, by way of example, discriminate between a "real" nazi-propaganda pamphlet and a "parody" of one? If written proposals are understood to be "wrong," "exaggerated," "stylistically pompous," "contradictory," and in grave conflict with "normal" political discourse, then they *are* parodic, from the point of view of the reader. If, for instance, the author of the pamphlet himself or herself says that it is not parodic, this is an interpretation that may be considered—but the author, I think, and especially the author of fiction, is simply a reader of his or her own text with no more and no less right to interpret his or her own text.

Ambiguity

Ambiguity, too, is a notion that is often fused or combined with irony in critical discourse from the last few centuries. Both *ironia* and *ambiguitas* are tropes within the rhetoric of antiquity, but originally they were not very intimately connected. In classical, medieval, and Renaissance texts, the notions of ambiguity and irony are only distantly related.[38] They are considered to be loosely connected but clearly distinct: irony, according to rhetoric, is a trope that indicates *one* meaning, although in a roundabout way; ambiguity includes *many* meanings. As Dane puts it, "Irony is the authoritative solution to the ambiguous text."[39] For many critics, this distinction is still valid. Even today, it is common to firmly separate irony and ambiguity on the basis of singularity and plurality. Irony, it is said, implies that among two or more competing meanings there is one that is "correct." Ambiguity, on the other hand, implies that it is not possible to choose between the competing meanings in any definite way.[40]

Yet, there is also another story to tell about irony and ambiguity. When the concept of irony is expanded in the writings of German Romanticism, it comes near to ambiguity. Romantic irony is not authoritative. Rather, it consists of a juxtaposing of discourses that are in conflict with each other but are nevertheless nonhierarchic. Perhaps one can say that ambiguity and Romantic irony are related to each other in a way analogous to the often noted relationship between metaphor and allegory: ambiguity is primarily multiplicity of meaning in a limited part of a text, whereas Romantic irony is multiplicity of meaning in a text in its entirety. The notion of dramatic irony is a concrete example of this close connection between ambiguity and irony in the writings of the Romanticists. Certain ambiguities of speech in the Greek drama were on one level seen as ordinary verbal ambiguities, but on another level as segments of an overarching ambiguity connected to the fate of humanity that received the name *dramatic irony*. In this way, the boundaries between ambiguity and irony have come to be partly dissolved.

In the twentieth century, the two notions are often understood to be more or less synonymous. In William Empson's famous book *Seven Types of Ambiguity*, many interpretations of poems would pass as ironic interpretations according to the terminology of New Criticism. His first type of ambiguity explicitly includes dramatic irony.[41] On the whole, the New Critics' interest in both ambiguity and irony is a symptom of the close relationship between the two notions in modern critical discourse. For Brooks, irony and ambiguity are very intimately related. He even stresses (which those who criticize Brooks for his terminological abusiveness often neglect) that the "terms as such" are not important. His major point is that poems make no "statements": their meaning is complex and multilayered, always a result of the intricate context of the whole poem and never reducible to a univocal "message."[42] Perhaps he would agree that a poem is ambiguous in its parts and ironic in its entity.

For critics such as Muecke, however, who see literary texts as messages that are not distinguishable from messages of oral communication, and who insist on the author's intention as a corrective instance, irony is definitely not related to or even compatible with "uncertainty" of any kind.[43] For them, irony and ambiguity are as clearly distinct as they were in antiquity. For critics who on the other hand want to avoid the authoritative aspect of irony, difficulties in holding the two notions apart may arise—difficulties that are often neglected or considered irrelevant. One critic who does not neglect the problem is Linda Hutcheon. Her opinion is that what distinguishes irony from ambiguity is the "edge" of irony: "the ambiguous lacks the ironic's critical differential impact."[44] What this "edge" consists of more precisely is, of course, an open question. Suffice it to say that Hutcheon's conception of irony as a notion with a "critical differential impact" rests heavily on the age-old idea that irony always strikes a "victim."

New Criticism has been attacked by poststructuralist critics innumerable times, but there are—and that has been pointed out before—important connections between the two critical schools. The interest in irony and ambiguity is a characteristic that relates them, and although the New Critics sometimes heavily emphasize "closure" and "autonomy" of texts in a biased way, they are often apt to see a relationship between irony and uncertainty. Their rejection of authorial intention as an instrument of pinning down the meaning of texts opens the way for a critical discourse that aims at indicating the hovering status of interpretation. Certainly, the interpretive uncertainties that are circumscribed by Brooks and others are more "limited" than the radical, "unlimited" uncertainties that interest Derrida and de Man, but often they meet somewhere in the middle. Their readings of texts may lead to similar or at least related results, but when it comes to terminology the New Critics choose to say that the ironies and ambiguities are "united" or "resolved" by the artistic frame of the text, whereas poststructuralists choose to say that the boundaries of a single text are always blurred by epistemological uncertainties of an endless range. It is, I believe, impossible to say who is "right" in this matter. New Critics and poststructuralists employ critical strategies that are both defensible, but they emphasize different levels of the textual interpretation.

Poststructuralism has given birth to a wide range of terms that are closely related to *ambiguity* and *irony.* The term *ambiguity* itself is almost always avoided by the poststructuralists because it is heavily associated with the "limited" polyvalence of New Criticism, whereas the term *irony,* as I have already shown, is adopted in what I would call an ambiguous way by Paul de Man and others. De Man's favorite term is *allegory,* but during the last decades the impossibility of ascertaining meaning has been also labeled "indeterminacy," "undecidability," and "unreadability," to mention only the most common terms that suggest an "unlimited" polyvalence.

What is certain, if I dare say so, is that the praxis of reading texts that has been elaborated by Derrida, de Man, and others is centered on the insight that everything always means, also, "something else" than it appears to do. Deconstruction, it might be said, is an interpretive practice of poststructuralism that radically stresses the ironic potential of all texts. In this way, irony (as it has been conceived for the last two centuries) is the master figure of poststructuralism, although the term *irony* itself, consistently enough, has been deconstructed.

Heteroglossia

In this context, it is appropriate also to discuss Mikhail Bakhtin's fascinating and influential notion of *heteroglossia*. Especially in the extensive essay "Discourse in the Novel," this notion has been employed in a way that actualizes the concept of irony.[45] Like the poststructuralists, Bakhtin dismisses ambiguity as simply a multiplicity of limited meanings; "*single-voiced* double or multiple meaning." Heteroglossia, Bakhtin states, adds to ambiguity "an ironic accent" and transforms it to *double-voicedness*.[46] In Bakhtin's view, a novel, a *real* novel, is not written in one authoritative language: it is "a diversity of social speech types (sometimes even diversity of languages) and a diversity of individual voices, artistically organized."[47] None of these languages are normative. They do not exclude each other but exist together in dynamic tension.

This implies that there is no center in a heteroglossic text: it juxtaposes different sorts of languages without trying to subsume them in a master language that is analyzable by linguistic tools. Heteroglossia, Bakhtin emphasizes, escapes the methods of rhetoric and linguistics. Hence, rhetorical irony is a notion of little interest to him. In a more general sense, though, irony and parody are often associated with heteroglossia (or "dialogical texts," or "polyphony")—by Bakhtin himself or by his interpreters.[48]

Heteroglossia is thus an overarching, textual ambiguity with "an ironic accent." Without mentioning Friedrich Schlegel or Romantic irony, Bakhtin often comes close to the philosophical and literary ideas of the German Romanticists, as when he states that "we must deal with the life and behavior of discourse in a contradictory and multi-languaged world."[49] Furthermore, Bakhtin

praises Cervantes and Sterne for much the same reasons as
Schlegel: Bakhtin in terms of heteroglossia, Schlegel in terms of
irony. It is also interesting to note that both put great emphasis
on meta-language and favor novels where the fictionality of the
text is accepted and laid bare.[50]

Clearly, heteroglossia is Bakhtin's formula for literature's ability to embody and give form to the contradictions and instabili-
ties of society and its languages. Therefore, the wide interest in
Bakhtin's writings, as well as the considerable impact of poststructuralism, might be said to be a late offspring of the Romanticists' fascination with irony. However, perhaps as a result of
some sort of anxiety of influence, both Bakhtin and the poststructuralists hesitate to make use of the concept of irony as
established by the Romanticists and prefer to invent new terms—
terms that undoubtedly give important, new shades to the interpreted texts, but nevertheless can be seen as variations of irony
in its broadest sense. It should be added, however, that Bakhtin,
in spite of his hostility toward authoritative language and his admiration of novels that engage the reader in a multilayered interpretive activity, does not hesitate to speak of the "author" and
his or her "intention" as if he or she were in perfect control of
the text. In this respect, the ironic "accent" of heteroglossia is
limited, and the role of the reader is unduly diminished.

Opposition

Finally, some additional notions that are of prime importance
for ironic interpretation must be considered: antithesis, contradiction, paradox, oxymoron, incongruity, incompatibility, and
some others. They differ in various ways, but they all imply
modes of opposition. Both theoretically and historically, irony
and opposition seem to be indistinguishable. Classical, medieval,
and Renaissance definitions of irony all include opposition or
some very similar notion,[51] which is the case also for Romantic
and modern definitions. In different times and in different theories various basic kinds of opposition have been stressed, most
notably oppositions related to appearance and reality, words and
their meanings, affirmation and denial, saying and doing, and actions and their results.

Although terminology has been refined, contemporary definitions also—especially those that are placed within linguistic, rhetorical, and semiotic frameworks—try to capture the essential
oppositions of irony. Thus Rice and Schofer maintain that *"Irony*

is characterised by a semantic and referential relationship of op-
position made possible by the possession of one or more contrary
semantic features," and that "An ironic relationship occurs when
the signifier is opposed to the signified."[52] No matter how eminently definitions like these are worked out, it is extremely difficult to cover the wide field of oppositions that can be and have
been involved in ironic interpretations. The meaning of a text is
always a product of an interpretation, and all interpretation also
includes a relation between the interpreter and the world. As the
reading of the world always invades the reading of a text, it is
often difficult to see the difference between opposites that are
"located," or rather "placed," in a text, and opposites that are
"located" or "placed" in the world or between the interpreter
and the world. Perceived oppositions are very often dependent
on contexts that are in no way given or self-evident, although certain areas of "reasonable" contexts are accepted within interpretive communities.[53]

A definition of *irony* as an interpretive mode that includes oppositional elements is thus theoretically reasonable, and I think
the best one available, but often of little or no help when it comes
to settling interpretive disputes. Elements that are clear-cut oppositions for one reader are by another often either not apprehended as such, or regarded as irrelevant. Consequently, the
definition above displaces the problem from being a question of
locating irony to being a question of locating oppositions. Unfortunately, there is no end to this hermeneutical chain of displacements. There is, as poststructuralism has taught, no meta-
language that offers a safe island from which it is possible to control the waves of meaning. This, however, does not imply that it
is meaningless to swim. I will therefore discuss some of the most
important of the oppositional modes within rhetoric and literary
criticism.

Antithesis

Antithesis, one of the classical rhetorical figures, is perhaps the
simplest of the oppositional modes. An antithetical relation includes two "theses" that are perceived as oppositional but not
necessarily as in conflict with each other. In one of the passages
of *Oliver Twist* that was discussed earlier, it is rather easy to identify an antithesis in the relationship between life and death. After
having drunk from the green bottle, the nurse says: "when she
has lived as long as I have, sir, and had thirteen children of her

own, and all on 'em dead except two, and them in the wurkus with me, she'll know better." A few sentences later, the following is narrated about the pregnant woman: "She . . . passed her hands over her face; gazed wildly round; shuddered; fell back— and died." All that is needed to perceive this antithesis, is knowl- edge of the English language and an ambition to read the sentences of Dickens literally. An antithesis, it might thus be maintained, *may* be a characteristic of a text that exists without interpretation of a kind more complicated than the most basic decoding of well-established conventions of language. However, any antithesis may also be part of an ironic interpretation. As I have shown, life and death might be regarded as involved in an ironic dimension of *Oliver Twist.* Vital elements in an interpreta- tion of this kind are the word "consolatory," the whole situation of Dickens's novel, and the existential norms of the reader. Yet, the hermeneutical maneuvers connected to an ironic interpreta- tion are more complicated and definitely more far-reaching than the ones that are required for antithesis.

Contrariety

Two notions that are closely related both to each other and to irony are contrariety and contradiction. Aristotle distinguishes between four kinds of opposites: *contraries,* like "tall" and "short"; *contradictories,* like "he is good" and "he is not good"; *relatives,* like "double" and "half"; and *privation/possession,* like "sight" and "blindness"—that is, "not-sight."[54] Life and death in the Dickens example above are consequently an opposition of privation/possession. These distinctions have been modified in many logical models, but from an historical point of view it is the system of Aristotle that has been most important. In definitions of *ironia* from classical antiquity to the Renaissance, *contrarium* could mean "opposite" in a sense that either included all four Aristotelian modes or more narrowly only "contradictory" and "contrary."[55]

It is clear that *contrarium* is the heart of the matter in virtually all older definitions of irony, but opinions have differed on how narrowly it ought to be defined. Some theoreticians held a rather strict view: that only contradictions and contraries concern irony.[56] Yet, many writers on irony found the narrowest delimit- ations untenable, and much looser differences were also involved in the discussions.[57] The differences of opinion have caused a great deal of terminological confusion, but the result has been a rather wide acceptance of the view that many kinds of opposition, and also only *implied* propositions, may be ironic. When interpreted, texts certainly often display oppositions that are not definitely encoded in the language. On the whole, contrariety (like similarity) is by no means a philosophically irreproachable concept.

In this context, it should also be pointed out that some tropes and figures that are based on oppositions, although not propositional or dependent on a concealed meaning, were sometimes seen as species of irony: for instance, *antiphrasis*, which, besides being a synonym for *ironia*, is "an etymological principle by which a word supposedly derived from its opposite," and *preterition*, "a figure in which a speaker mentions something while claiming not to do so."[58] Definitions of *antithesis* have never, to my knowledge, merged with definitions of *irony*.

Clearly, the Romantic and post-Romantic widening of the concept of irony was on its way much earlier. When Schlegel circumscribed irony in a radically open way, a wide range of opposites had already been discussed and, from time to time, accepted by rhetoricians. The terminological confusion waited for its solution by a concept of irony that accepted all the many possible levels of opposition. Of course, there are still discussions now and then concerning what qualities of opposition should be requisite for irony, but the notion of opposition in itself is never called into question. Uwe Japp's closing sentence in his book *Theorie der Ironie* is an eloquent example of this fact: "Irony is an attempt to create a linguistic equivalence to the world in the form of a simultaneous contradiction."[59]

Paradox

Paradox is a notion that is closely related to contrariety and contradiction, and sometimes even used synonymously. The standard definition of a *paradox* is that it is a contradiction that somehow makes sense. The most explicit contradictions are purely linguistic phenomena, like "he is good and he is not good." "Technical" contradictions like this and also more vaguely oppositional statements are neither meaningful nor meaningless in themselves, and in order to "make sense" they must be part of a context and related to the norms of the reader. In other words, a contradiction must be interpreted if it is to be understood as a paradox. In a literal sense, an explicit contradiction is always by definition false. If the contradiction is only

seemingly a genuine contradiction, however, or if truth and false-
ness are seen as nonlogical, more or less metaphorical qualities,
it may very well be true—and hence described as a paradox. A
paradox may thus be defined as a contradiction that is interpreted as somehow revealing a "truth." In practice, it is often a matter of interpreting the two contrary propositions as referring to
two closely related but yet distinct phenomena. "He is good and
he is not good" might, for instance, mean that a man is generous,
benevolent, and mild, but not suited to be the leader of a multi-
national company.

Of the four Aristotelian opposites, only contradictions can be
described in terms of logical truthfulness and falsehood. As a
concept within literary criticism, however, paradox crosses the
borderlines between all sorts of oppositions. The definition
above must thus be slightly widened, but there is no need to
worry about that. Literary texts are always complicated enough
not to be disentangled by the Aristotelian modes of opposition.
The moment one begins to read and interpret a text (two acts
that are indistinguishable), innumerable opposites and similarities are created: textual relations that are not surface qualities of
the language but constructions of one's individual experiences
and the interpretive communities to which one belongs. Among
these oppositional and even contradictory relations that are
taken to be implied by the text, some are seen to reveal aspects
of life and reality that are regarded as somehow true. These are
called paradoxes.

The notion of paradox is obviously highly usable, and it is also
closely related to irony. Both paradox and irony are inseparably
connected to a state of opposition, and both offer some kind of
"solution" to this state. Until the eighteenth century, a dominant
trend in the efforts to define *irony* was to emphasize that the
ironic relationship between opposites is situated between words
in presentia and a meaning *in absentia*. Paradox, on the other
hand, was seen mainly as a relationship between opposites that
are both *in presentia*. When the concept of irony was widened by
Schlegel and the other German Romanticists, the polarity between *in presentia* and *in absentia* disappeared to the background of theoretical speculations. Romantic irony is structural
irony, and structural irony implies that the ironic opposites are
perceived as qualities that are displayed in the "visible" structure
of the text. From Romanticism and onward the distinction between irony and paradox is hence no longer very sharp.

The classical opposition between words *in presentia* and

meaning *in absentia* is valid chiefly for what has been called verbal or rhetorical irony. Socratic irony, on the other hand (although it is said to also embody a measure of verbal irony; the "pretense" of Socrates), is a variation of structural irony as it is circumscribed as a contrast between the ignorance of the person who initially seemed to be wise, and the gradually revealed wisdom of the person who appeared to be ignorant. The opposites of Socratic irony are thus both *in presentia*, although it might be argued that the dichotomy *in presentia / in absentia* becomes less usable the more complicated the text is.

Nevertheless it makes perfect sense that Schlegel, who built on definitions of Socratic irony when developing what came to be called Romantic irony, also adopted the notion of paradox. In an often-cited note, he writes that paradox is the *conditio sine qua non* of irony.[60] Number 48 in "Kritische Fragmente" reads in its entirety, "Irony is the form of paradoxes. Paradox is everything that is good and great at one and the same time."[61] Schlegel is apparently not eager to follow the traditional definitions of *irony* and *paradox* very closely, but his conjunction of the two notions nevertheless makes sense. One way to interpret Schlegel—if one supposes that it is fruitful to read the two fragments together—is to see paradox and irony as two aspects of the same phenomenon: paradox represents the "literary," "textual" aspect of the oppositional modes, irony represents the "philosophical" aspect of it; irony is the all-embracing *Form*—in life and in literature. This is, I repeat, only one way to interpret Schlegel's fragments, and it does not fully consider the puzzling statement that paradox is everything that is "zugleich gut und groß." Perhaps one may see *gut* as a synonym for "true" and *groß* as a term for the junction of opposites. If so, one comes close to *paradox* as it is commonly defined.

After Schlegel, irony and paradox have come to be commonly joined and often treated more or less as synonyms. In New Criticism, irony, ambiguity, and paradox are a critical trinity that are at once three and one. Brooks may, for instance, write that the paradoxes in a specific poem "insist on the irony."[62] Alan Wilde, to pick a more recent example, identifies what he calls "absolute irony" with "the shape of an indestructible, unresolvable paradox."[63] The paradigmatic examples of ironic interpretation that merges with paradoxical interpretation are found, however, among the exegetes of Plato. The source of the alleged Socratic statement "I know that I know nothing" is *Apology*, where Plato puts these words into Socrates' mouth:

I am only too conscious that I have no claim to wisdom, great or small. . . . Then when I began to try to show him that he only thought he was wise and was not really so, my efforts were resented both by him and by many of the other people present. However, I reflected as I walked away, Well, I am certainly wiser than this man. It is only too likely that neither of us has any knowledge to boast of, but he thinks that he knows something which he does not know, whereas I am quite conscious of my ignorance. At any rate it seems that I am wiser than he is to this small extent, that I do not think that I know what I do not know.[64]

In a condensed form, this certainly may be expressed as "I know that I know nothing," although the words of Plato are much more elaborated.

Kierkegaard holds that the words of Socrates are ironic, because his ignorance is, as Kierkegaard puts it, at once serious and not serious: serious in the sense that he really knows that he does not know, and not serious in the sense that the recognition of his ignorance is the beginning of knowledge.[65] This interpretation is by Kierkegaard himself held to be an ironic interpretation, but it is written with words that suggest paradox. According to Kierkegaard as I interpret him, the words of Socrates are contradictory on a linguistic level—but the contradiction is annihilated on an interpretive, existential level. The contradiction conveys a "truth," and consequently one has a paradox.

Similarly, the contemporary philosopher Gregory Vlastos interprets Socrates' words in terms of irony, but he explicitly also uses the notion of paradox. He gives Plato's "great philosophical paradoxes" the name "complex irony." Vlastos, like Kierkegaard, distinguishes between two levels of knowledge: one "moral," on which Socrates is held to admit ignorance, and one of "justified true belief," on which he is supposed to claim knowledge. Vlastos writes: "When he professes to have no knowledge he both does and does not mean what he says."[66] The implicit contradiction in Socrates' words is thus interpreted as only ostensibly contradictory—as conveying a truth. His irony is paradoxical.

Incongruity

The notion of oxymoron is at times associated with irony. As it is quite unanimously defined as a paradox expressed in one or a few words, it would, however, be of little use to discuss the oxymoron. Instead, some much vaguer and more important notions must be brought to attention: incongruity, incompatibility, contrast, and conflict. Because there will be an ongoing discussion of these notions throughout the book, it is not my object to scrutinize them here. Yet, it should already have been noted that there exists a wide range of terms that are very often used to characterize ironic texts and situations—terms that do not denote contradictions or even opposites, but vaguer (sometimes very much vaguer) relationships.

This widening of terminology seems to be inevitable. The moment one leaves one-word ironies and attempts to describe more complex, textual relationships in terms of irony, the Aristotelian logic—and any other logic for that matter—disappoints the interpreter. Literature is very much about feelings and moods, and it might be misleading to talk about contradictory or even opposite feelings if one wants to use the terms in a stricter sense. Ironic readings of texts must therefore make use of more relative terms such as incongruity and contrast. As David S. Kaufer notes, the metric for the incompatibilities involved in irony "is aesthetic, not logical"; ironic oppositions may also be "psychological."[67]

This is not a modern insight. Cicero noted that the ironic meaning was either something "contrary," "the exact reverse," or something "other," "different."[68] Quintilian distinguished between irony as a trope and a schema (figure): when irony leaves the linguistic level of tropes and permeates "an entire life" it is no longer possible to articulate.[69] Although this insight that irony is not always easily pinned down in terms of strict contrariety or opposition has been ignored by most rhetoricians (perhaps because it would make their systems less symmetric), it has been drawn to attention now and then even before the nineteenth century. Today it is often part of the standard definitions of *irony*. Simple reversals of meaning are not always seen as very interesting by critics of the late twentieth century, whereas "otherness" fascinates all the more. Lilian Furst may thus write about the "elusiveness" of irony: "the capacity to imply other and more than is actually said." In this respect, Furst continues—and I do not disagree with her—"irony represents a tremendous enrichment of literary expression."[70] Similarly, Hutcheon states that the ironic meaning is "always different—*other than* and more than the said."[71] Philippe Hamon suggests that the notions of "tension" or "distance" should be preferred.[72] In his dissertation from 1985, "Reading Irony," Mark Jeffry Dicks emphasizes that irony "manages a radical foregrounding of the essential arbitrariness of the sign," and instead of relying on the spatial/structural categories of duality and negation, Dicks introduces four "principles" of irony: disjunction, disclosure, imminence, and play.[73]

Critics who aim at systematization of a more traditional kind also often stress the necessity of accepting some amount of vagueness in ironic meaning. Muecke writes about oppositions that may take the form of contradiction, incongruity, or incompatibility, and he suggests that "other things being equal, the greater the contrast the more striking the irony."[74] Booth demonstrates the complexity of the relationship between levels of meaning in "A Modest Proposal," and he firmly states that it is not possible to settle for "simple inversion to contraries" when interpreting a literary text.[75]

The vaguer the terms used to describe ironic opposites, the more reasonable it is to assume that irony is created in an act of interpretation. "Incongruities," "contrasts," and "conflicts" are far from always definite qualities of texts: they are most often created by the reader—sometimes simultaneously with irony. Jonathan Culler states that "no sentence is ironic *per se*,"[76] and it should be added that few sentences or texts or anything is incongruous per se. I suggest that irony and paradox are always creations of interpretation, whereas more limited, oppositional modes (such as contradiction) are sometimes encoded in the very linguistic construction. Of course, it is not always possible to say exactly where the decoding of linguistic conventions ends and where "free" interpretation begins. However, when the reader starts using vaguer terms such as "contrast" and "conflict," terms that are generally focused on the "content" of a text rather than its linguistic "form," one may feel sure that extralinguistic interpretation has started.

I hope that by now I have made clear that the many variations of opposites involved in ironic interpretation in no way self-evidently announce themselves to every reader of a text, and that there is not one strategy of ironic interpretation, but rather many strategies. When reading a text and finding its "surface" meaning unsatisfying in the sense that there is something in it that "does not work," a reader may construct an ironic meaning that is situated somewhere "beyond" the text—a meaning being something "other." However, this does not mean that the "surface" meaning simply disappears. I think that the conflict between opposite meanings often also remains as a vital part of the ironic meaning in relatively simple, limited textual ironies. This is one reason why the difference between "verbal" irony and "structural" irony is questionable: in both types of irony the interpreted meaning may engraft conflicting levels. Perhaps this is also why rather simple ironies may be understood to be offensive: even if one inverts the said or the written, there is always a risk that a double meaning remains in the interpretation. Perhaps, finally, this is what distinguishes irony from other phenomena (even those that are seen as closely related according to the terminology of today's literary criticism, ambiguity and paradox): irony never comes to rest. The (at least) two levels of opposed meaning that form the basis of ironic interpretation may be seen to exclude each other (and perhaps it is not sure which one is to go), annihilate each other, or complement each other.

There are, consequently, three basic variations of the ironic strategy of interpretation: either/or, neither/nor, and both/and.[77] "Either/or" is mainly associated with the so-called verbal irony; "neither/nor" with critics of irony such as Theophrastus, Hegel, and to a certain extent Kierkegaard; and "both/and" with the notions of irony of Romanticism, New Criticism, and poststructuralism. It must be emphasized that these three modes of ironic strategies are applicable to the very same texts. One's choice of ironic strategy often mirrors one's own aesthetic ideals and ideologies rather than textual traits. Perhaps this radical openness that yet demands some sort of position on the part of the reader—a state of affairs that may force one to consider existentially important possibilities of interpretation—perhaps this is what lies behind Hutcheon's claim that "edge is the primary distinguishing feature of irony."[78] I am not sure where this edge is to be found, though. I agree with her (I think) on the point that "unlike paradox, irony is decidedly edgy,"[79] but I would not want to be a professional edge-hunter—I am not sure that I would recognize one if I saw one.

In any case, the incongruities and contrasts that over the years have been seen as ironic in one way or another have been found within a huge range of levels in literary texts and in reality. Some of the most widely known levels are well-established categories of irony, and yet these ironies can hardly be described in terms as precise as contrariety or contradiction. Dramatic irony involves a conflict between a character's actions and what the reader, but not the character, knows about the narrative. Irony in novels, a popular topic in literary scholarship, is often described in terms of conflicts between implied author and narrator, or between implied reader and narratee. In the reading of Dickens above, I argued that narrative levels might even be construed on the basis of what is understood to be ironic conflicts in the text. To argue

for irony in terms of incongruity between one or a few of an author's texts and his or her complete oeuvre is also a very common
device.

Among the many applications of the theories of Romantic
irony, by far the most popular is to look for ruptures in the fiction—that is, conflicts between textual fictionality and textual illusion of reality. The mixture of tragedy and humor is also an
aspect of Romantic irony that is very often highlighted because
of the conflict between or incongruity of feelings. Of course, it is
an open question whether these conflicts of feelings (if they are
at all interpreted as such) are understood to be instances of
"true" complexity (then one may talk in terms of both/and
irony), of "artistically failed" plurality (neither/nor irony, or perhaps no irony at all) or of a complexity of feelings where one of
them "loses" (either/or irony). Shakespeare, who was praised by
Schlegel, wrote tragedies that include scenes of comedy, and
Henrik Ibsen's *The Wild Duck* is often praised for its ironic blend-
ing of tragedy and humor,[80] but from the many varying interpretations of these authors one learns that irony may always also be
something else.

SIMILES AND INCONGRUITIES IN KAFKA

To conclude this chapter, I will shortly discuss two texts by
Franz Kafka, an author who is frequently called ironic. Both these
texts may illustrate the open character of the opposites that are
involved in ironic interpretations.

As I read "Ein Bericht für eine Akademie" [An Account for an
Academy], the difference between humans and animals is central
for this short story. A chimpanzee tells the tale of his life as it
turned out after he was captured and brought to civilization.
Soon, he tells the reader (or rather, he tells the members of a scientific academy), he found out that the only way for him to escape his cage was to become human. He learned to speak,
smoke, and drink alcohol.

The ironic inversion, as I see it, consists of a contrast between
what might be expected to be qualities of humans and apes, respectively. In one respect, the chimpanzee certainly learned to
become a man, with "the average education of an European,"
but in another respect he learned to become less human: his
greatest victory was when he managed for the first time to empty

a bottle as a "professional drunkard"—which was immediately followed by the utterance of his first word.[81]

In this story, irony may be created out of many opposites.[82] Depending on how one interprets the story, these opposites may be labeled by many different terms, such as the "difference" between man and ape, the "inverted contrasts" between human nature and the behavior of animals, and the "discrepancy" between the ape's alleged victory, his *Sieg,* and his true humiliation that might be inferred by the reader. Yet, the chimpanzee also acquired qualities that are perhaps not so readily seen as human in an ironic sense. His story is, I would say, well balanced, and he is wise enough to realize that humans are not very much less apelike than he himself.

I thus maintain that it is not possible to find, or construct, contradictions, firm oppositions, or univocal contraries in "Ein Bericht für eine Akademie." The only way to reach a description of something that would come close to the definite ironic status of Kafka's story would be to once and for all prove and impeccably describe what human nature really is like.

"Von den Gleichnissen" [On Similes, or On Parables] is a short piece of prose, the reading of which also may give a nice illustration of the hovering oppositional positions in irony. It reads as follows:

> Viele beklagen sich, daß die Worte der Weisen immer wieder nur Gleichnisse seien, aber unverwendbar im täglichen Leben, und nur dieses allein haben wir. Wenn der Weise sagt: "Gehe hinüber," so meint er nicht, daß man auf die andere Seite hinübergehen solle, was man immerhin noch leisten könnte, wenn das Ergebnis des Weges wert wäre, sondern er meint irgendein sagenhaftes Drüben, etwas, das wir nicht kennen, das auch von ihm nicht näher zu bezeichnen ist und das uns also hier gar nichts helfen kann. Alle diese Gleichnisse wollen eigentlich nur sagen, daß das Unfaßbare unfaßbar ist, und das haben wir gewußt. Aber das, womit wir uns jeden Tag abmühen, sind andere Dinge.
>
> Darauf sagte einer: "Warum wehrt ihr euch? Würdet ihr den Gleichnissen folgen, dann wäret ihr selbst Gleichnisse geworden und damit schon der täglichen Mühe frei."
>
> Ein anderer sagte: "Ich wette, daß auch das ein Gleichnis ist."
>
> Der erste sagte: "Du hast gewonnen."
>
> Der zweite sagte: "Aber leider nur im Gleichnis."
>
> Der erste sagte: "Nein, in Wirklichkeit; im Gleichnis hast du verloren."[83]

Willa and Edwin Muir have translated the text:

Many complain that the words of the wise are always merely parables and of no use in daily life, which is the only life we have. When the sage says: "Go over," he does not mean that we should cross to some actual place, which we could do anyhow if the labor were worth it; he means some fabulous yonder, something unknown to us, something too that he cannot designate more precisely, and therefore cannot help us here in the very least. All these parables really set out to say merely that the incomprehensible is incomprehensible, and we know that already. But the cares we have to struggle with every day: that is a different matter.

Concerning this a man once said: Why such reluctance? If you only followed the parables you yourselves would become parables and with that rid of all your daily cares.

Another said: I bet that is also a parable.

The first said: You have won.

The second said: But unfortunately only in parable.

The first said: No, in reality: in parable you have lost.[84]

This little text may be described as a sophisticated and very teasing verbal game that invites the reader to set opposites into play: wisdom versus skepticism, winning versus losing, reality versus simile. There are many ways that lead into this text, but I doubt whether there is any way out. To put it another way, one never gets in but always gets out of this text, as it constantly exhorts one to see everything as similes.

Now, as the reader might have noticed, I too talk in similes, or rather metaphors—the slight difference is here unimportant. However, because this statement of mine is only a reflection of my own interpretation of what I have written myself (so I say), one might as well claim that my statements are ironic. It all depends on how I am interpreted, and, of course, on how "Von den Gleichnissen" is interpreted.

Starting from the beginning, are the incongruities in Kafka's text ironic? Are there any incongruities? Is "Der erste" right in stating that "Der zweite" is right in claiming that "Der erste" talks in similes? If so, what does it mean that "Der zweite" has lost his bet "im Gleichnis"? Is there a similarity between reality and similes, or between winning and losing? Is it then not reasonable to call this similarity, that is based on opposites, ironic? Or does everyone lose when trying to understand the "reality" that is hidden (one might believe) behind the similes (or ironies) of language? Then again, is it not ironic that one loses when one believes that one is able to say that something is ironic in some other way than in similes—which would mean that one is right after all in believing in irony, which would mean that one wins, which would mean that there are only similes?

Perhaps it would be best to conclude with this sentence: "Alle diese Gleichnisse wollen eigentlich nur sagen, daß das Unfaß-bare unfaßbar ist, und das haben wir gewußt." [All these parables really set out to say merely that the incomprehensible is incomprehensible, and we know that already.] So why waste energy on writing and reading this book? Because, in reality one wins.

Is that not ironic?

6

Irony and Mysticism

Praised be your name, no one.
—Paul Celan

IRONY, MYSTICISM, AND DECONSTRUCTION

PERHAPS THE CONCLUSION OF THE LAST CHAPTER TURNED OUT TO BE somewhat mysterious. For that, I apologize, but there is nothing I can do about it—except to write some pages about irony and mysticism. For me, mysticism is the great, verbal code for describing what might seem impossible to describe with the aid of contraries and contradictions, and I find it surprising that the close relationship between irony and mysticism is virtually never discussed.

It is of course impossible to scrutinize mysticism very deeply in a few pages, so I will have to settle for some rather brief, but nevertheless important aspects of it. It is chiefly the language of mysticism that must be considered, a language that is almost always characterized as paradoxical. To put it the other way around, texts that are understood to be religious and paradoxical are as a rule called mystical. However, the language of religion in general is certainly not always straightforward. The Holy Trinity is said to be at once One and Three, to take a familiar example from the dogmas of Christianity. This assertion might very well be called a paradox because it involves a contradictive conflict between being both One and not One, which makes sense for those who believe in the Christian God. Yet, this is not an example of what is normally called mysticism. However, my object is not to try to distinguish between mystical and other paradoxical, religious language. Suffice it to say that mysticism is related to a mode of religious thinking that is characterized by a tendency toward heresy or atheism.

Religious language that may be described in terms of contrari-

118

ety, contradiction, and paradox is found in both Occidental and Oriental texts; within Buddhism, Hinduism, Judaism, Islam, Christianity, and many more religions (and quasi-religious philosophical systems) of all kinds. According to Taoism, to take one initial example, the experience of the world can be described only in terms of a play between incompatible, and yet in a paradoxical way unified contraries. Heracleitus and Blaise Pascal,[1] as well as Simone Weil, to mention a writer from the twentieth century, are all "mystics" in some respect and might successfully be related to Taoism, for instance. Other authors such as Dionysius the Pseudo-Areopagite, Meister Eckhart, and St. Teresa of Avila are universally called mystics.

Texts by all these authors, and from all these religious traditions, are thus united by their inclination to be interpreted in terms of opposition, contrariety, contradiction, and paradox. In his book, *Mysticism and Philosophy*, W. T. Stace notes (and he is far from unique) that "we may be surprised to find how remarkably similar is the language of the Upanishads to the language of some of the Christian mystics so long as these latter confine themselves as much as possible to uninterpreted description" (that is, so long as the specific terminologies of the belief systems of the various religions do not dominate the descriptions).[2] Among the characteristics of what is called *mystical language* one finds the habit of describing God as a "Void" and/or a "One"; a "Nothingness" and/or an "All"; an infinite "Absence" and/or an infinite "Presence."

The relation between these aspects of mystical language and the religious experience of mysticism is a controversial question. Steven T. Katz maintains that there is an "inherent linguistic element in spirituality: language is integral to mystical practice," but the dominant trend has been to emphasize a qualitative distance between language and mystical experience. A premise of this "dominant theory regarding the insufficient fit between language and transcendental experience is," Katz states, "that language is a human convention."[3] It is indeed common to find reservations associated with descriptions of mystical experience and mystical characterizations of God. Language is a human device and as such it is incapable of reaching the divine truth. This is why mystics, the explanation goes, are forced to use a language of contradiction and paradox. Katz opposes this view and asserts that "mystics reveal, however unintentionally, more of the 'truth' they have come to know in language than their overt negations of meaning and content would suggest." It is, he maintains, "their *success* at just this sort of substantive communication that allows us to speak of, to learn of, and to participate in mystical traditions at all."[4]

Stace, on the other hand, does not believe that there is a linguistic element in mystical spirituality, but he also argues against the belief that there is an insurmountable gap between mystical experience and language. Stace advocates that mystical categories (that may be put into the logical and rhetorical categories "contradiction" and "paradox") need not necessarily be understood to be in conflict with logic. Everyday experiences are based on multiplicity, whereas mystical experiences of infinite unity annul multiplicity. If the claims of mystical experiences are taken seriously, it follows that they do not adhere to the same mental laws as ordinary experiences: "The laws of logic are in fact simply the *definition* of the word 'multiplicity.' The essence of any multiplicity is that it consists of self-identical distinguishable items. But in the One there are no separate items to be kept distinct, and therefore logic has no meaning for it."[5] To put it simply, language gives an accurate description of the mystical experience, an experience that according to the laws of logic is impossible. The mystical experience is not ineffable, Stace asserts: it is paradoxical in its nature, beyond the logical categories of differentiation, and hence possible to describe satisfactorily in paradoxical language.[6]

My own opinion is that Katz is probably right in submitting that mystical language and mystical experience are intimately integrated. Also the traditional view that some phenomena are out of reach of language is plausible, I think, although there is reason to believe that the capacity of language is great indeed. Why, again, should one otherwise bother to write a book like this? This is, however, not the place for arguing extensively for this belief, and it is definitely not the place for penetrating the fascinating problem of the relation between *unio mystica* and how it may be interpreted in the verbal expressions of different religions and different individuals. Instead, I will comment on some interesting resemblances between the two categories *mysticism* and *irony*. If one wishes to see them, similarities between *mysticism* and *irony* can be found on many levels: the level of language and linguistics, the level of interpretation, the level of evaluation, the level of "truth-claims," and so forth.

As a rule, however, irony is not associated with mysticism, not even when literary aspects of mysticism are stressed. Shira Wolosky does not even hint at possible ironic interpretations of

Eliot, Beckett, or Celan in her intriguing book *Language Mysti-cism*, in which she investigates texts of these authors in the light of the negative language of mysticism.[7] This is noteworthy, be-cause all these authors, perhaps especially Beckett, have been seen as ironic in other contexts. There is, I would say, a general resistance to letting irony and mysticism live in the same house.

This becomes apparent if one considers the role paradox plays in this context. As I have shown, irony and paradox are a well-established couple, as are mysticism and paradox—but not irony and mysticism. In fact, it is as unusual to find the notions of mys-ticism and irony together as it is common to find mysticism and paradox joined. Stace, as an example, notes that mysticism draws paradox to its extreme. All mystical categories "are incompre-hensible to the logical understanding." In spite of his general be-lief in the power of language, he submits that "even to call them 'paradoxical' is to apply to them a logical category which misrep-resents them," and to say " 'they are' or 'they are not' is only to utter vain words about the Unutterable."[8] Stephen H. Phillips, to take another example, claims that the "seemingly paradoxical language" of Zen Buddhism is an extreme case of "figurative speech as reflecting the peculiarity of mystical experience and a corresponding peculiarity of the spiritual object(s)."[9]

It seems as if the notion of paradox is, for many writers on mys-ticism, as close as one can get to the "peculiarity" of mystical experience—and yet it is not quite sufficient. Perhaps one some-times forgets that a paradox is not the same as a contradiction or an opposition of whatever kind. A paradox, as pointed out, is generally distinguished by its "truth." The paradoxical truth is certainly created by the interpreter, and because of this openness in the notion of paradox it is, I believe, a highly usable tool for comprehending the "ineffable."

If I understand the nature of alleged mystical experience cor-rectly, it consists of mental categories that are incompatible when verbalized within logic and yet are fundamentally compati-ble within the experience itself. When described in language, the experience thus seems to be "impossible," because its verbaliza-tion is contradictory. Yet, this verbalization is "correct" if one considers that the "laws" of mystical experience are not of the same "nature" as the laws of everyday experiences. Language *may* be used to describe a mystical experience—if one accepts that a contradictory proposition that would be invalid as a de-scription of "normal" events might be valid as a description of a mystical experience, as it reveals the "truth" of a category of experience that does not follow the laws of logic.

According to the standard definition of *paradox,* very many descriptions of mystical experiences may certainly fit into the pattern of paradoxical interpretation. Still, this notion seems to be insufficient for many mystics and scholars. Knowledge of the intimate conceptual relationships between contrariety, paradox, and irony hence allows one to ask whether *irony* is not a proper term for describing both the mystical experience and the mystical language.

My not necessarily modest proposal, in favor of which I will argue below, is thus that mysticism and irony are very closely related—in certain respects almost identical. Both, I submit, are best comprehended as interpretive strategies that aim at coming to terms with what are understood to be inconsistencies in language, thought, and experiences of various kinds. The resistance to this junction of mysticism and irony is sometimes tangible, especially when mysticism is discussed in a terminology that is very close to discourse on irony—as when Bimal Krishna Matilal refers to the perhaps "bizarre" mode of "saying something and then adding, 'I did not say it.' "[10]

This resistance might have historical reasons. The aspect of dissimulation that traditionally has been connected to irony is perhaps not desirable when divine matters are in focus. As irony and lying are often seen as closely related, and for good reasons too, it is not difficult to trace the reluctance to the concept of irony in a wish to keep religious terminology as pure as possible in its associations with truth.

It is indeed true that irony and deceitfulness, satire, and the comic have been and still are associated with each other. Yet, it is also true that the normative implications of irony have been and still are also of a wholly different nature. Socratic irony, a notion that was almost forgotten for a long time, is generally highly esteemed. With Romanticism, irony became compatible with the grand feelings of the tragic and was again associated with philosophy and the great questions of life and destiny. From then on, the stage was set for a more friendly relation between irony and religion.

To be sure, this is a simplification of the historical development, but it is true enough to be considered seriously. Two extreme positions may be confronted: Theophrastus's revolting description of an ironic person and modern books on irony in religious texts. If Christ were to be characterized as an ironist in

Theophrastus's sense, it would certainly clash with all that Christianity stands for, but nowadays it is fully possible to write books on irony in the Bible without running the risk of being accused of heresy.[11]

Yet, irony and mysticism are not very often connected, and when they are it is as a rule done only indirectly and with a more or less unfavorable attitude. It may be noted that Booth in an article lists some synonyms for "irony" and "ironic" that he suggests should be used more often instead of these two (in his view) overused terms. One of them is "cabalistic."[12] In his book, *Against Deconstruction*, John M. Ellis accuses deconstruction of being unoriginal, as its rhetorical device is "simply the standard formula of many branches of religious mysticism."[13] Deconstruction is in its turn very often seen as an ultimately ironic interpretive device.

Ellis is certainly right when he compares deconstruction and mysticism and emphasizes the similarities. He cites Barbara Johnson, who in a discussion on Derrida claims that "Instead of a simple either/or structure, deconstruction attempts to elaborate a discourse that says *neither* 'either/or', *nor* 'both/and' nor even 'neither/nor', while at the same time not totally abandoning these logics either."[14] This initiated description of deconstruction might be compared to Matilal's equally initiated description of the mystic Nāgārjuna's "fourfold negation," which consists of "saying 'no' to the four alternatives: Is it? Is it not? Is it both? Is it neither?"[15] These categories of inclusion and exclusion are certainly the basis for deconstructive thought, they are certainly the basis for mysticism, and together they certainly form a valid map over the conceptual and normative history of irony.

One is, consequently, left with three conceptual couples: deconstruction/mysticism, deconstruction/irony, and mysticism/irony. The first two are already married, whereas the third relationship is not yet settled in fidelity. However, it does have a history, although not a very prominent one: a history that of course starts with Romanticism. During this era irony began to be appreciated as an instrument for reaching some inches beyond the ordinary boundaries of language, in a way that I believe to be analogous to the language of mysticism. The philosophical aspects of Romantic irony imply that the "real" reality is full of contraries that can be grasped only with a language that is contradictory, paradoxical, and—ironic. The theological aspects of mystical language imply that the "real" divine reality is of a nature that transcends the ordinary categories of thought and hence can be described only in terms of logical contradiction, paradox, and—this is my supplement—irony. Both irony and mysticism are thus seen as modes of understanding and interpretation that aim at reaching something that is "beyond" the deceptive stability of language, the difference being (to put it simply) that for the Romanticists irony is "realism," for the mystics it is "symbolism." Romantic irony tends to accept chaos; mysticism tends to believe in cosmos.

Friedrich Schlegel does not himself make explicit comparisons between irony and mysticism, but he sometimes mentions the word *Mystizismus*, notably in "Über die Unverständlichkeit."[16] Some of his most famous descriptions of irony might, however, have passed also as excellent descriptions of mystical language. In "Kritische Fragmente" number 108 he asserts that Socratic irony "holds and evokes a feeling of the insoluble conflict between the unconditional and the conditional, the impossibility and necessity of a complete communication."[17] Generally, Schlegel emphasizes that neither language nor the human mind ever finally reaches the chaotic world of realities. "Fragmente" number 121, in which is actually found the word *Mystik*, speaks of the conjunction, not the harmonization or the reconciliation, of conflicting thoughts.[18]

Solger is more explicit as far as the relationship between irony and mysticism is concerned, although *Mystik* is for him a very wide notion that may be compared also to allegory and symbol. In a letter he maintains that "mysticism is, if one considers the reality, the mother of irony—and if the eternal world, the child of enthusiasm or inspiration."[19] Kierkegaard must also be mentioned here. His religious ideas are based on a belief in the absurdity and irrationality of religious belief, which is often associated with the famous dictum, attributed to Tertullian, *Credo quia absurdum* [I believe because it is absurd]. Kierkegaard is here balancing on the edge of orthodox Christianity, close to pure mysticism. In his book on irony he distinguishes between "the mystical Nothing" and "the ironical Nothing," but the difference seems to be marginal. The ironist, however, runs the risk of becoming "nothingness," whereas for God "nothingness" is always much more than nothing.[20] Of the two interpretive modes irony and mysticism, he thus chooses to favor mysticism. For Kierkegaard irony is, in the end, "neither/nor," whereas mysticism is "both/and." This conceptual difference might be said to be arbitrary, but it is of course a product of what he himself calls his absurd choice of religion.

The two concepts are now and then joined in texts from the twentieth century also, although rather sporadically. Vladimir Jankélévitch, to mention a writer on irony who has had some influence, has put irony and mysticism together in rather vague terms.[21] The resemblance of irony and mysticism might, however, also be traced in the reactions to the two concepts. Both irony and mysticism are highly controversial phenomena, disputed in theory and not so seldom rejected in practice. It is interesting to note that the "denials" of God in terms of "nothingness" and "absence" have been understood to be heresy. Mysticism has thus been rejected for ethical reasons, as has irony and lying. To see something as a lie, I have argued, is to reject the implications of some words on an ethical ground—words that might as well be interpreted as ironic if one does not object to them. There is hence a parallel between the notions mysticism/heresy and irony/lying. The battles of interpretation concerning certain mystical (or heretical?) texts are in many ways parallel to the battles of interpretation concerning certain ironical (or non-ironical?) texts. Religious persons who saw themselves as mystics have been condemned for heresy; authors who interpreted themselves as ironists have been accused of lying or having sick opinions.

Yet, the comparison of mysticism and irony is valid also from the opposite perspective: both mysticism and irony have had enthusiasts and exegetes who, with varying success, have claimed that reality beyond logical categories is "One"—something that can be reached only by means of paradoxical or mystical or ironic language. Both mysticism and irony imply a critical awareness and a crossing of the border between logical and nonlogical categories of experience and language. Finally, neither irony nor mysticism comes into existence until it is interpreted as such: a "mystical" text might be read "straightforwardly" as a heretical text, an unintelligible text, or something else, and an "ironic" text might be read as anything but ironic.

The analogy between mysticism and irony must not be strained, though. Mysticism tends to demand rather overt contradictions, and perhaps one can say that the "mystical interpreter" is generally interested in what he or she believes to be the deepest realities of the world, whereas the "ironical interpreter" is generally more interested in what he or she believes to be the deepest meaning of the text. Nevertheless, the parallelism between mysticism and irony is there if one wants to see it, and, as

far as I am concerned, mysticism might very well be seen as one
of the many variants of ironic interpretation.

KABBALAH, MEISTER ECKHART, AND CELAN

If mysticism is irony, how does it look when it is found in different places? To answer this question, I will discuss first Kabbalah, then a sermon by Meister Eckhart, and finally a poem by Paul
Celan. Initially I shall direct my attention to the famous Kabbalist
Isaac Luria. Luria's cosmogonic "theory"—or perhaps it should
rather be called a "poem"—which was never written down, is indeed fascinating and might be interpreted in ways that make it a
splendid example of mysticism as irony.

The cosmogony of Isaac Luria is specific because of its terminology that opposes the standard formulas. Before Luria, God's
creation of the world was described as a progressive process
within Kabbalah. According to Luria, the creation is a regressive
process. In the first stage of creation, *zimzum* (which originally
means "concentration"), God withdraws within himself in an
inner "exile." Through this "withdrawal" he makes room for the
world. The creation of the world is thus an indirect result of a
"negative" action. The only "positive" action of God is that he
sends *yod*, the first letter in his name YHWH (the so-called *tetra-
grammaton*) into the world that is coming into being. These negative qualities of God's actions and position—his withdrawal and
his exile—are the basis for Kabbalah's description of Him as
ayin—absolute Nothingness.[22]

In his book, *Kabbalah and Criticism*, Harold Bloom describes
zimzum as a "trope-of-limitation" and points to a resemblance
to the "loss-in-meaning" or even "death-of-meaning" of poetry:
"a sense that representation cannot be achieved fully, or that
representation cannot fill the void out of which the desire-for-
poetry rises."[23] In analogy with God's negative creation of the
world according to Luria—a creation that involves both the withdrawal of the creator and the delivery of a sign, a letter—I assert
that the author delivers a text that is in fact made up of fragmentary signs that must be construed by the reader. The author himself or herself is, of course, in exile inside himself or herself. In
analogy with Kabbalah's divine, paradoxical *ayin* the author is
both "nothingness" and the Word—a "nothingness" the exile of
which is a condition for the existence of the text. Translated into
more familiar terminology, this means that the intention of the

author can never be reached. The existence of the *literary* text, the *created* text, is conditioned by the withdrawal of its creator. The author sends the letter out of which the world of meaning is created but not determined.

This is my interpretation, although it is based on Bloom's presumption that Kabbalah and the creation of literary meaning are intimately related:

> Kabbalah is a theory of *writing* . . . a writing before writing (Derrida's "trace") . . . a speech before speech . . . Kabbalah too thinks in ways not permitted by Western metaphysics, since its God is at once *Ein-Sof* and *ayin*, total presence and total absence, and all its interiors contain exteriors, while all of its effects determine its causes.[24]

So, we are back to the paradoxes and ironies of mystical and deconstructive meaning. Bloom points to the fundamental opposition between God's presence and His absence, the peculiarity of being at the same time the One and Nothing. Luria's description of God as *ayin* Bloom interprets as an irony of the simplest, rhetorical kind.[25] In Bloom's view, this irony is only the first trope in a large chain of tropes that constitutes the cabalistic cosmogony.

In Bloom's interpretation of *zimzum* we find a rewarding view of the relation between mysticism and irony. For Bloom, the cosmogony of Luria is a map of rhetoric:

> *Zimzum* is initially a rhetorical irony for the act of creation, in that it means the opposite of what it appears to "say." It says "withdrawal" and means "concentration." God withdraws from a point only to concentrate Himself upon it. The image of His absence becomes one of the greatest images ever found for His presence, a presence which is intensified by the original metaphor of *mezamzem*, His holding in of His breath.[26]

It is certainly a good thing that Bloom recognizes the importance of the concept of irony in the cabalistic context. Irony is involved also in interpretation of the most basic opposites. In this way, it is definitely ironic that something that is supposed to certainly exist is described as nothingness, and in my view it is definitely ironic that God may perform the huge task of creating the world while actually being on vacation in himself. Yet, irony seen as a more complex relation of opposites is not recognized by Bloom in *Kabbalah and Criticism*. If one wants to leave the level of rhetoric (interesting enough in itself but unsatisfactory for a wider account of the concept of irony), mystical language must be seen as something more intricate than a language that with the aid of an "image" (absence) refers to a "literal" meaning (presence). I think that a simple transformation of "nothingness" to its contrary is a next to meaningless act of interpretation. Bloom's *Kabbalah and Criticism* would have been even more intriguing had he considered the sort of irony that he mentions in another book. In *Ruin the Sacred Truths* he writes that "To represent Yahweh at all is the largest instance of such sublime irony"; an irony "in which absolutely incommensurate realities collide and cannot be resolved."[27]

Luria's God is thus more and something else than just Presence and All, I assert; He is also at the same time Absence and Nothingness. As God is beyond ordinary conception, He may be both present and absent. This interpretation is an ironic or mystical strategy to make sense of contradictive nonsense.

I have pointed out that the bulk of the learning of Isaac Luria is not available for us in original texts. Many other mystics are known only from fragmentary texts, which may make their words seem even more ironic than they would in a larger context. Thus the words of the Gnostic Basilides, according to which a non-being God creates a not-being world out of nothingness,[28] might form the basis of one of the most complex mystical ironies.

Of the many mystic authors whose texts are more fully known to us, however, I chose to comment on Meister Eckhart. As the aspects of language may be said to be foregrounded in his writings, he is perhaps the Western mystic who is most interesting for a text-oriented interpretation. Eckhart often discusses the name of God and the figurativity of language, while at the same time he uses the traditional, negative descriptive categories of mysticism. He stresses that every attempt to describe God necessarily reduces Him: the "name" is greater than "language." One can reach God only by way of making oneself empty of images, meaning that the figurativity of language reduces His essence.

Meister Eckhart's sermon "Videte qualem caritatem dedit nobis pater, ut filii dei nominemur et simus" [Behold what manner of charity the Father has bestowed upon us, that we should be called, and should be the sons of God] may illustrate into what kind of complexities the interpreter of mysticism may fall.[29] In the following, I will read this sermon from within an interpretive community that takes certain ideas of religious language and divine matters for granted. Certainly, my very choice of the text is determined by a knowledge of, an interest in, and a certain sympathy for this interpretive community. What I add to the standard observations of the community is, I think, some knowledge of irony and an inclination to fuse the interpretive strategies of mysticism and irony.

The sermon's starting point is a principle of the identity of the human and the divine. In order to be the son of God, Eckhart states, one must be of the same nature as God.[30] Yet, how does one know when one's nature, one's *wesen*, is of the right kind? Eckhart's answer is that there is "a spark of reason" in the soul where one places "the image of the soul." As I understand it, this spark (a common, mystical metaphor) guarantees correct, divine knowledge. However, the image, *daz bilde*, that may be placed in this spark seems to be opposed to "a knowledge" that belongs to "the sensual and the rational."[31] As this kind of knowledge is revealed "through simile and speech," *nâch glîchnisse und nâch rede*, it hides the true knowledge.

Thus, there seem to be two kinds of images, *bilde*—one that reveals and one that hides. Now the difficulties begin to emerge. As in Kafka's "Von den Gleichnissen," one does not know where to find a stable point. What, one may ask oneself, is in fact an image of what? This kind of question might lead the thought to poststructuralism's emphasis on the boundless referentiality of language. All signs lead only to other signs.

However, let me return to Eckhart. What kind of *bilde* does he use himself? Does his text reveal or hide the divine truth? In the sermon he explicitly "gives us a simile"—*Ich gibe ein glîchnisse*.[32] Soon after that, he takes it back, because it is a "sensual simile." Instead, he gives us another explanation, one that is "more spiritual": "in the kingdom of heaven all is in all and all is one and all is ours."[33] Now, does this simile, a typical, mystical formulation about the Oneness of everything, really belong to the "spark of reason" where the true image is placed, that is "the image of the soul," the one that reveals rather than conceals? How could one know? What argument does Eckhart offer? Is not the simile of Oneness also an image that hides?

These are questions that may be asked from "within" the sermon. Toward the end of the text, all images are categorically dismissed. *Nothing*, it is now said, that is resemblance or image may be a part of one if one wants to reach God.[34] Yet, how shall one then understand the image in the divine spark?

Even when it comes to "nothingness" Eckhart makes a distinction. The first kind of nothingness is deduced out of the principle of Oneness and the refutation of resemblance. God is One and he is not comparable to anything, at least not with the similes that hide. The only simile that does not hide seems to be the one that likens God to Oneness. Because humans are part of God (who is everything), one can only understand oneself as nothing, *niht* (which, according to my interpretation, is the only aspect of everything that language can properly express), if one wants to reach God—that is, ourselves. Pure identity expels all similarity.[35]

Now, if one were to translate the statement that pure identity expels all similarity into the language of rhetoric, it would mean that all metaphorical language blocks the road to God. However, Eckhart's language is obviously figurative. How could it not be? As I read it, it forces itself to abandon its own similarities, its metaphors, in order to reach beyond the categories of ordinary sense. When the similarities are abandoned, only their remains are left: the empty shells that do not embody any pretended knowledge. As long as one continues to read and interpret the sermon, however, these empty shells of words are also figurative, but they now work through the principle of contrariety. To be everything one must be nothing; *niht sîn.* Consequently, the mystic's way to God is the ironist's way to meaning—at least in my story.

Yet, one must not forget that there is also a second kind of nothingness in Eckhart's sermon: a much less metaphysical nothingness that reveals itself as complaint and sorrow. This nothingness I read as a metaphor for the human feelings that prevent us from reaching God: "Observe wherein the defectiveness lies! It comes from nothingness [*nihte*]. All that is of nothingness in the human beings must therefore be obliterated, because as long as the defectiveness is in you, you are not the son of God. That man complains and is full of sorrow, is all due to defectiveness."[36] The principle of similarity here strikes back. When this second kind of nothingness is annihilated in humans, one is of the same nature as God and consequently identical to Him—at least according to the way the standard interpretive strategies of Christianity are applied to "nothingness."

If one follows the interpretive track that I have set up, one finds oneself in the end left with two incompatible kinds of *bilde* and two mutually exclusive variations of *niht.* The principles of similarity and contrariety are sometimes similar, sometimes contrary. Only when one combines the interpretive strategies of "mysticism" and "orthodoxy," or "irony" and "metaphor," may preliminary meaning be reached. One must allow oneself to interpret "nothingness" as both the enemy and the ally of God. There are two concepts but only one word. Perhaps this too is ironic.

However, the interpretive problems that emerge from our reading of *niht* are still nothing compared to the fundamental problem of figurativity. On the other hand, this problem is only a problem if one demands divine control. Eckhart's and my only method of reaching any conclusion at all is by way of using language, and Eckhart's warnings against figurativity are necessarily expressed by way of figurative language. This is, however, an essential part of his mysticism, not something that undermines it. The language of his sermons does certainly not reach the divine realities, but its images can be said to illustrate rather convincingly exactly why it fails to do so—and in this indirect way it is a successful tool to reach what is not reachable. Eckhart's attempts to circumscribe God are, in another word, ironic. All meaning, and in particular mystical meaning, emerges out of difference, and difference may result in contrariety. All language is more or less figurative, and similarities cannot exist without differences. One would hardly be convinced by a language that succeeded in explaining everything by way of perfect similarity. The reason for this is that one would not be convinced by a language that does not exist.

Mysticism is the poetry of religion, it might be argued. Paul Celan's poems, it might likewise be argued, belong to the mysticism of literature. His "Psalm" from *Die Niemandsrose* [*The No One's Rose*], a book published in 1963, is a good case in point:

> Niemand knetet uns wieder aus Erde und Lehm,
> niemand bespricht unsern Staub.
> Niemand.
>
> Gelobt seist du, Niemand.
> Dir zulieb wollen
> wir blühn.
> Dir
> entgegen.
>
> Ein Nichts
> waren wir, sind wir, werden
> wir bleiben, blühend:
> die Nichts-, die
> Niemandsrose.
>
> Mit
> dem Griffel seelenhell,
> dem Staubfaden himmelswüst,
> der Krone rot

vom Purpurwort, das wir sangen
über, o über
dem Dorn.[37]

In Michael Hamburger's fine translation, the poem reads like
this:

No one moulds us again out of earth and clay,
no one conjures our dust.
No one.

Praised be your name, no one.
For your sake
we shall flower.
Towards
you.

A nothing
we were, are, shall
remain, flowering:
the nothing-, the
no one's rose.

With
our pistil soul-bright,
with our stamen heaven-ravaged,
our corolla red
with the crimson word which we sang
over, O over
the thorn.[38]

As there is no point in repeating all the intricacies of mystical and
ironical interpretation, I will give only some brief remarks that
may set the stage for further thinking.

First the titles of the book and the poem must be considered.
The words *Die Niemandsrose* are a part also of the poem, the title
of which reads "Psalm." We are thus initially confronted with
three semantic segments that may lead us in various directions:
"nothingness"/"no one," "rose," and "hymn." Nothingness is
abstract and general, "rose" is, in its denotative aspect, a sign for
a concrete flower, and "hymn" receives its most common meaning from a religious context.

Niemandsrose may be associated with the word *Niemandsland*
[no-man's-land], but if we follow the implications of the title
"Psalm" also "nothingness" and "rose" may be seen as aspects

of religious ideas. A reading of this sort is supported by the many myths of creation that may be seen as intertexts to the first line "No one moulds us again out of earth and clay." The idea that one or many gods formed the first human beings out of clay is found in religions all over the world. What the poem does is to (seemingly?) negate these myths: "No one" molds us—at least not again, *wieder.*

Other associations might be added. The history of Odysseus who manages to escape the Cyclops by way of calling himself Nobody is a potential intertext to Celan's poem, but it has not played a major role in the readings of "Psalm" that have been presented so far. Instead there are two interpretive communities, both of which belong to religious traditions, that have struggled about the meaning of this poem: one that prefers a nonmystical reading, one that wants to read it in the context of Kabbalah.[39]

In order to simplify the contours of this battle, one might say that the two interpretive communities support their readings on mainly one of two intertextual fields. The first of these consists of the Christian hymns—for example, the anonymous German hymn "Es ist ein Ros entsprungen" [There Is a Rose E'er-Blooming] from the end of the sixteenth century. This hymn is traditionally seen as a symbolic and metaphoric figuration of the newly born redeemer. Within Christianity, the rose is a common emblem for the Virgin Mary also. The other intertextual field is the bulk of mystical writings that emphasizes nothingness.[40]

In the end, the meaning of the poem is of course an open question. Is *Niemand* (who is explicitly praised) the unknown God of the Christian hymns who is described in negative figures, or is he "nothing"? Is *Niemand* an ironic description of God, or is he a nothingness that is praised ironically? Are "we" (who are also "nothing," a nothing that is yet a rose) perhaps a nothing in Eckhart's first sense—that is, a nothing that is united with God—or a nothing that is separated from Him because of our complaint and sorrow? Is the Christian hymn "Es ist ein Ros entsprungen" a constructive intertext that supports the faith of the poem, or is it an ironic intertext that transforms Celan's text to a parody? Should the words "Dir / entgegen" be interpreted so that one is understood to move *toward* or *against* "no one"? These questions may be contemplated while considering the meaning of the last stanza with its beautiful, synecdochal extension of the poem's matrix:

> With
> our pistil soul-bright,

      with our stamen heaven-ravaged,
      our corolla red
      with the crimson word which we sang
      over, O over
      the thorn.

The varying contexts can be said to help create meaning, not to determine meaning. Irony is an interpretive strategy that may be supported by arguments, but it is never definitely there, and if one sees it it never stops moving. In this respect, ironic meaning is similar to all meaning, only more apparently fugitive and implying greater complications. Irony is, after all, a "figure" of contrariety. It says no, no, and yet yes. This is divine madness: an interpretive mode that is not satisfied with what seems to be apparent in language; an interpretive mode that wants it all—both chaos and cosmos. However, verbal language is not the only language. I will now consider the divine madness of the languages of images and music as well.

7

Irony and the Arts

We mean it man.
—Sex Pistols

INTERPRETING IMAGES AND MUSIC IRONICALLY

IRONY IS BEST UNDERSTOOD AS AN INTERPRETIVE STRATEGY, I HAVE argued. It may be "placed" or "found" everywhere. To take it to extremes, virtually everything may be seen as ironic by someone in some context; and if everything may be ironic, all sorts of images and pieces of music may also be ironic. To state simply that everything may be interpreted as ironic in some sense is perfectly correct, I think, but there is more to learn about irony, the problem of intentionality, and the relations between the arts if one investigates the way ironic interpretations of images and music have been and might be performed.

In this chapter I will make a general, not too extensive survey of some of the art fields where the concept of irony has been applied. Most of these, such as the *Lied* and the film, include a verbal element. No doubt the extension of the concept of irony from verbal to visual and aural texts has occurred mainly through "direct touch" between words, images, and music. The "literary" irony seems to be contagious.

Adding a visual or aural aspect to a verbal text is in a way nothing more than adding a special kind of context. To put it another way, word, image, and music may be parts of one and the same context where verbal, visual, and aural elements influence each other's significance. All irony is "situational," I have maintained, and obviously a situation that combines or merges various sign systems is open to ironic interpretation. "Visual" and "musical" irony are notions that have become more and more accepted, and yet there is still a rather strong resistance to ironic interpretations of anything but verbal texts. For most people, if they think

135

of it, the notion of "musical irony" is especially awkward. If they
do not think, however, there is generally no problem in charac-
terizing music as ironic. Of course, the old notion of "verbal
irony" is the obstacle to irony and music: music cannot "say"
anything. However, if we do not worry much about this, or if we
think a little further, the obstacle disappears. In due course I will
pose more intricate questions concerning the nature of ironic interpretation of images and music, but for the moment one will
have to settle for the correct but perhaps not very enlightening
view that images and music may constitute or be part of situations that are interpreted ironically.

The focus of this and the following chapters will be on works
of art in a broad sense. Whatever profit one may derive from a
distinction between the fine arts and popular culture, this distinction is hardly relevant to the theory of irony. Ironic situations
may be found everywhere, and as far as the creation of irony is
concerned there is no difference in principle between, say, a situation on stage in the theater, a sequence in a rock video, and an
event in the street. It might also be noticed that over the past century it has been gradually accepted that art may be created out of
"found" objects. Some aestheticians say that art is a quality in
the eye of the beholder. Similarly, I believe, irony is a quality in
the eye of the beholder, and, like art itself, this quality may be
"found" everywhere. Both artistic situations and everyday situations may be seen as ironic—for instance, by way of being both
tragic and comic at the same time. My experience of a fat boozer
seen early in the morning in the street, wearing a T-shirt with the
text "Liquor saved me from sport" and whistling a merry tune,
certainly differs in some respects from experiences that I have
had watching a play by Shakespeare, but they are similar in many
other respects. My ironic interpretation of what I take to be conflicts of meaning and moods is one of the common denominators.

The scene in the street is in fact a good example of interart
irony. When I see the boozer and interpret the situation ironically, a multitude of sign systems as well as personal associations
and norms are activated. In reading the text on the T-shirt I construct a reversal of the nice but square statement "Sport saved
me from liquor" and perceive a conflict between the visual appearance of the large body and the word "saved." When I see the
man smiling, I remember the many good times I have had myself
when slightly intoxicated (although perhaps not so often that
early in the morning), but I also pity the man who, I guess, is not

always so cheerful. Still, the tune that he whistles makes me happy, and I am reminded that I, who probably lead a much more pleasant life than the boozer, have no reason to feel as miserable as I did a few minutes earlier. Then I wonder if all my studying and thinking that was supposed to make me happy has in fact made me gloomy, whereas the boozer, the living sign system of decay, is perhaps satisfied with his life. All these conflicts are to me ironic, and for some reason I also find it ironic that I start thinking about irony in order to get things straight. Finally I reach the conclusion that nobody will ever know much about anything.

This meeting in the street of a small town in Sweden, as well as an event in the theater, or an episode read in a book, or no matter what, is a complex situation that includes a multitude of signs and calls for a multitude of interpretive strategies. Irony is one of them, and I cannot see how the notion of intention could be of much help in determining the ironic meaning of the whole situation. In the case of my haphazard meeting with the boozer, there is no intention in any sense of the word, except for the trivial fact that the boozer, I expect, has himself chosen to wear the T-shirt. I have argued that intentionality is problematic also in rather limited verbal contexts, but when one includes visual and aural aspects in the discussion its irrelevance becomes even more apparent. One might even say that the emigration of irony to the visual arts and music "proves" the redundancy of intention. That luggage may be left behind.

Titles

When the concept of irony is used within art criticism, some sort of verbal text is generally connected to the works of art that are dealt with. One of the most common visual-verbal relations is that between an image and its title, and it is here that perhaps the majority of ironic interpretations of visual art are focused. I will consider a few examples.

In her book, *Aubrey Beardsley: Symbol, Mask and Self-Irony*, Milly Heyd argues that there is irony in the relation between a Beardsley drawing that not "even hints at a sacred icon" and its title "Icon."[1] Karen Bernard calls attention to the reiteration and at the same time the contradiction of "culturally dominant and naturalized representations of women" in Joanne Tod's paintings.[2] She finds ironic tensions in particular between titles and images, as when the painting "Self-Portrait" does not at all resemble the artist. Barry Ulanov is vaguer when he calls Paul Klee a "master of the light ironic touch" and refers to allegedly ironic titles such as "The Mocker Mocked" and "Child Consecrated to Suffering."[3]

In Linda Hutcheon's rich and exciting but theoretically vague book, *Splitting Images: Contemporary Canadian Ironies* from 1991, a considerable number of ironic readings are included. Hutcheon puts literature, painting, sculpture, photography, and installation art side by side. In most of her readings of visual works of art a verbal element is crucial for the irony, and very often it is the title that is somehow seen to be in conflict with the visual aspects.[4] Hutcheon's book *Irony's Edge*, which was published three years later, is much more theoretically oriented, although here also one finds a series of stimulating ironic readings of clashes between historical contexts, titles, and images in the visual art of Anselm Kiefer and Beauvais Lyons.[5]

Many more examples could surely be found, but the general principle remains the same: when it is felt that a title "states" something that is somehow opposed to what is depicted, or when it "suggests" something that is at odds with or not really relevant to what one actually sees, the result is called irony.[6] Within music criticism also titles are now and then interpreted ironically in relation to the "content" of the music. The interpretive strategy is here similar, although it is of course even more difficult to be precise about the way in which the verbal title opposes the music. Music is not conceptual, and it has been argued that nonformal titles of pieces of music are always arbitrary. Nevertheless, the term irony has been suggested to describe the quality of titles such as Schumann's "Time to Make a Decision" and "End of Song," titles that may be said to direct the attention to the question of "when and how to end a composition."[7] Erik Satie, one of the most popular composers in the context of irony, has perhaps gained his position as an ironist especially because of original titles like "Desiccated Embryos"—the title of some short piano pieces that succeed in coming to an end only with severe difficulty.[8]

The Lied

For the few musicologists who have written about irony and music, the Lied is a popular topic. Schumann's *Dichterliebe* in particular has been penetrated, but also songs by Schubert and some other composers have received attention. In most articles the notion of Romantic irony in literature is an important context, and it must also be noted that the majority of the articles I know of that are devoted especially to irony in Lieder center on musical settings of poems by Heine.[9] Heine is seen by many as the incarnation of an ironic author. His manner of destroying an established mood with a "sting in the tail" by the end of his poems is famous.

Although the articles on irony in Lieder differ in important aspects, many of them are good illustrations of the "contagious" nature of irony in verbal texts. A very crude model for the common line of reasoning reads like this: the text of a song is normally written before the music, and if the text is ironic the music also may well become ironic.[10] The verbal text is thus seen as authoritative in at least two ways: it was there first, and it consists of words with conventional, decodable meaning. Traits in the music that are understood to be ironic are generally said to have their counterparts in the poems. According to one interpretation of a Lied by Schumann, "sudden changes of mood or feeling" in the text correspond with "a rising chromatic line in the upper register" and "some unexpected harmonic motion."[11] In another article it is noted that the irony of Heine finds an equivalent in that the dissonant tone is three times longer than the resolving tone.[12] On the other hand, inconsistencies between words and music are sometimes highlighted.[13] An ironic *Widerspruch* [contradiction, contrast]—a popular term in the German articles—between poem and music may be found, or the phenomenon that "the same words are put to different musical phrases" may be understood to be ironic.[14] The fact that the music affects the interpretation of the text and that the performances of the Lieder are crucial for the interpretation of them is stressed surprisingly seldom.[15]

In "Romantic Irony in the Works of Robert Schumann," Heinz J. Dill's focus is not on the texts of the Lieder, but nevertheless other verbal texts are of great importance for his conception of irony: "Schumann's music is also surrounded by and embedded in a whole network of signs, so that one could almost speak of a secret language that is added to and superimposed on the purely musical language."[16] Clearly, musicologists as a rule prefer to anchor ironic interpretations of music in verbal texts. Some even maintain that verbal language is a necessary condition for irony. From a historical point of view this is perfectly understandable, but I will later argue that musical irony need not necessarily rely on words.

On the whole a wide range of terms is used to describe the allegedly ironic oppositions, terms that one recognizes from ironic
interpretations of literature. Oppositions that are understood to
be rather precise are implied by the terms *Widerspruch* and paradox, whereas somewhat vaguer oppositions are hinted at by
terms such as anomaly, abnormality, incongruity, discrepancy,
duality, exaggeration, and underemphasis. It is sometimes recognized that these oppositions are results of what is supposedly expected by the listener: that the irony emerges from a clash of
norms or conventions and what is actually, unexpectedly heard.
One scholar notes that the *Abnormität* arises compared to a
"normal" expectation of what might be heard in a Lied.[17] The
consequence of this—irony appearing and disappearing, depending on what is expected by the individual listener—is not
properly considered, however. Hence the authors of the various
articles reach sometimes very different results. As the musical
norms are only relatively stable even within the same culture and
in the same era, there can be no general agreement about when
conventions are ironically ruptured.

Visualized Dramatic Irony

The Lied may seem to be an obvious field for those musicologists who look for irony because the music here is tightly connected to words. In the visual arts also words are often linked to
images (not only through titles), but within art discourse there is
a much stronger inclination to use the concept of irony even in
interpretations of "pure" images. This may be done in numerous
ways. Milly Heyd's book on Beardsley is a representative example
of how visual irony may be conceived. This is one of the few art
books I know of that really makes use of the concept of irony.
Heyd includes few theoretical considerations, however, and her
conception of irony is rather vague.

Heyd finds many variations of oppositions in Beardsley's drawings. One might say that as a rule oppositions that are not
conventional or expected (by Heyd herself) are interpreted ironically. Often she finds that symbolic or mythological contexts are
reversed. The oppositional relations between Beardsley's drawings and, say, a myth might of course include verbal elements,
but a direct relation between text and image is not a prerequisite
for Heyd's ironic interpretations.

Perhaps the most common type of irony that Heyd discusses is
self-irony, which means that Beardsley's biographical context is

seen to be in some sort of conflict with his drawings. For Heyd irony is often an "attitude" that is attributed to Beardsley rather than to his artworks. She claims that Beardsley "is ironic" or that he is "looking at" something ironically, but she refrains from discussing Beardsley's intentions.[18] Another noteworthy variation of irony that Heyd discusses is dramatic irony. She points to a resemblance between the situations in literature that are labeled *dramatic irony* and the depicted situations in some of Beardsley's drawings where one sees "victims of dramatic irony, unaware of the nature of their situation, which we—the spectators—fully comprehend."[19] Also in the case of dramatic irony in Beardsley, verbal texts are sometimes part of the context in which Heyd finds contrasts and incongruities, and it is the "stories" told by the images that are of interest for this conception of irony—not their visual qualities.

Heyd has a very sharp eye for ironic oppositions in Beardsley. It is obviously perfectly legitimate to use the concept of irony the way she does, and I think that her interpretations of Beardsley's drawings are fascinating. The only problem is that Heyd writes as if irony were really there: in the drawings or in Beardsley himself. I submit that the irony is actually in Heyd's own eyes, and that her project is rather to convince her readers of the merits of her interpretations than to point at actual facts. Is she convincing, then? For me, she is—often. However, doubtless many spectators would not characterize Beardsley's drawings as ironic, had they not got the idea from Heyd.

Drama and Theater

Heyd maintains that dramatic irony may be visualized, or perhaps one should say that an image may be interpreted as conveying the kind of situational irony that is conventionally called *dramatic irony*. When the Romanticists wrote about irony and drama and more specifically about dramatic irony and tragic irony, however, it was primarily the verbal texts of the dramas that interested them, and irony in a drama that is read is of course not different from irony in a verbal text of whatever kind. However, when a drama is performed in the theater, a complex web of sign systems presents itself immediately. As a rule, though, this complexity is not reflected in the critical texts on irony in drama. The verbal aspects are very much in focus in contemporary criticism also. Only rarely are the ironic clashes located within the visual signs or between the verbal and visual signs.

Because many of the ancient discussions of irony focused on the physical behavior of the ironist, this lack of interest in the visual aspects of irony might be slightly surprising when seen in a historical perspective. Actually it is only a short step from the ancients' descriptions of "ironic behavior" to irony in theater. Incongruities between, say, speech and gestures or action may certainly be interpreted ironically on stage as well as in reality.[20]

Yet, it is often recognized, although rather vaguely, that irony and theater are intimately related, and not only because of the many dramatic ironies found in dramatic texts. In 1984 it was even stated that irony is "the most prevalent theatrical mode of our time."[21] Now and then the very relationship between reality and pretense, or between identification and detachment of the spectator, is seen as the ultimate irony of theater. Eli Rozik suggests that the spatial relationship between audience and actors in the classical theater is a direct parallel with this ironic tension: the spectators are at a distance from the action of the play and "look downward" at it, and the borderline between fiction and reality is literally open. In fact, Rozik states, theaters are "architectonic images" of the spectator's ironic contemplation.[22]

The space within the stage itself may also be vital for ironic interpretations. Peter N. Dunn, who believes that "irony is the characteristic of dramatic structure" (which includes an extensive "system of signifiers," not only a verbal text), focuses on the contrasting, visual effects that may emerge from theatrical space.[23] Thus a king "may stand and address his court," Dunn notes, "in exactly the place where he will be humiliated two acts later."[24] Dunn also discusses the sometimes peculiar relationship between actor and role (a visual, physical, nonverbal relationship) and gives some examples of ironic oppositions where the general theatrical conflict between reality and pretense is carried to its extreme. The most famous of these is when Rosalind in Shakespeare's *As You Like It* is dressed as a boy but tries to act like a girl. If the actor who plays Rosalind is a boy, which was the case in Shakespeare's time, the spectator actually sees a boy who acts as a girl who acts as a boy who acts like a girl.[25] Raymond J. Pentzell goes even deeper into these matters in an article in which he scrutinizes ironic incongruities between the actor, the *maschera* (the audience's "image" of the actor), and the role that he or she is acting.[26]

Ironic oppositions may apparently be found on very many levels of the theatrical complex of verbal and visual sign systems. Only a few of these have been highlighted. At one end of the scale one finds ironic interpretations of theater as such; on the other end one finds ironic interpretations of single lines and objects. As in all ironic interpretation the perceived incongruities are dependent on the interpreter's knowledge, norms, and expectations. In accordance with this, Eli Rozik states that iconic signs such as Nazi uniforms or Punk outfits may reference "cognitive-ethical" systems and thus provide a norm upon which the ironic interpretation may lean.[27] Huston Diehl demonstrates that items on stage to which symbolic values are ascribed within a certain iconographic tradition may appear in new contexts where they are interpreted as deceptive, ironic inversions of the conventions.[28] Similarly characters that belong to one dramatic tradition (where they are identified by clothes, gestures, and general behavior) may find their way to radically different traditions and then suddenly appear in an ironic light.[29] In such cases the inversion of the visual meaning is a product of an interpretation of the whole complex of signs, including verbal language. Indeed, the whole "situation" of theater makes it apparent, I would say, that all perceived ironies are situational ironies where verbal, visual, and also aural signs merge.

Music Drama and Opera

Many theatrical productions of dramas include music, and some genres are by definition a combination of drama and music: opera, music drama, musical, and so forth. As noted, most scholarly texts discussing musical irony focus on the relationship between words and music, and this is the case also with opera and related genres. The visual aspects are as a rule left out, and even the musical aspects are indeed sometimes totally neglected. Irony in opera is often simply equated with irony in the libretto, and it is not unusual that the label *irony* is put on rather vaguely described conflicts or contrasts in opera plots, sometimes combined with only very general references to the music.[30] This is a fact that again indicates the dominating status of the verbal text in relation to irony.

In opera and related genres, as in drama, irony may be found on a multitude of levels.[31] It may be circumscribed indirectly in terms of an "oxymoronic quality of the verbal, dramatic, and musical signals."[32] It may also be described explicitly in terms of what is understood to be contrasts in mood and moral value between music and text or characters: "solemn" music sounding when characters involved in "treachery" are on stage; music that contributes to "festivity" being played when "the tragic potentialities" of the plot become evident.[33] Irony may be seen in the conflict that appears when a familiar text from liturgical chants is sung to the accompaniment of a decidedly nonliturgical instrument such as the balalaika, and one may find an ironic contrast between the most "exuberant music" and the joking of the characters in an opera.[34] Music may be said to be ironic if a melody is understood to be exaggerated, excited, rapid, and generally "incongruous" with a text that expresses woe, or if a song is seen as "improperly introduced" and hence comically reveals a character to be something very different from what he or she seems to be.[35] Of course music may also reinforce the interpretation of dramatic irony—for example, by way of underscoring "a given character's false expectation, or an event that only the audience knows will never happen."[36]

Among the composers whose music has been interpreted ironically one finds Mozart. In *Così fan tutte*, it has been argued, the contrasting "tunings and moods" contribute to irony, as do conflicts between "morbid" words and unexpectedly gay music and "exaggeration of melodic contour."[37] *Così fan tutte* is actually the opera that, probably more than any other, by any composer, has tempted scholars to set the concept of irony into play.[38] *Die Zauberflöte*, however, has been more fully interpreted in terms of irony. In Joseph Thomas Malloy's dissertation "Musico-Dramatic Irony in Mozart's 'Magic Flute' " from 1985, the focus is mainly on what Malloy takes to be ironic contrasts between Mozart's music and the words of the libretto.[39] Malloy emphasizes Mozart's personality and intentions, but he also carefully analyzes the relation between text and music. Because of the dramatic weaknesses of the libretto, Malloy argues, Mozart had to write music that modifies its structure: "Music and text are, at times, saying rather different things."[40] Malloy also stresses other types of incongruities. When "our expectations of the genre" are not fulfilled, we become confused, he asserts.[41] Once he notes an "incongruity" between character and orchestral accompaniments,[42] but most often irony seems to emerge from an "unexpected shift": a sudden reversal of mood and a "change in accompaniment" may give the sung words an opposite meaning.[43] As a rule, Malloy states, "musical irony calls attention to itself by its unexpected and apparently inexplicable difference from its surroundings."[44]

In the last few pages I have quoted extensively in order to demonstrate the vocabulary at work in texts concerning irony in music, and not unexpectedly it can be noted that it is the vaguer types of notions that are generally used. Musical irony is not often circumscribed in terms of strict contradiction or even paradox. Instead the notions of contrast and incongruity are more common, as are the descriptions of sudden and unexpected changes. Again, this is of course perfectly legitimate, but it should be noted that these notions are generally used in contexts that aim at describing the verbal and musical texts themselves. Sometimes it is recognized that it is the expectations of the listener himself or herself, perhaps formed by a knowledge of certain conventions, that produce the incongruities, but as a rule they are seen as qualities of the work of art itself, which might be misleading.

In Linda Hutcheon's readings of some productions of Wagner's *Der Ring des Nibelungen*, however, the ironies in the relationships between settings and visual intertexts, between different conductors' versions of the music, between operatic conventions and specific productions of Wagner's music dramas, and between the texts and various political contexts, are seen as products of discursive communities and explicitly related to her own personal acts of interpretation. Furthermore she considers not only words and music, but also scenery, stage effects, and the acting.[45] I have earlier noted that Hutcheon's notion of intentionality is rather confusing, but her approach to irony in music drama is the one that I find most well balanced and by far most theoretically thorough.

An aspect that is generally neglected, though, is that the musical expression in sung texts is but an elaborated variation of tone and stress of the voice in speech.[46] The interpretation of irony in sung texts is thus a modern variation of the interpretation of irony in speech grounded on the theories of classical antiquity. Although it is not recognized, contemporary articles on musical irony have an approach to the concept of irony that is sometimes very close to the approach in classical treatises. There is simply no fundamental difference between irony generated by intonation, melody, and rhythm, respectively. An interesting consequence of this is that the cultural rules for encoding and decoding irony in oral communication may well become part of a work of art that includes words, gestures, and music. Of course, this does not mean that irony in song must be subject to intentional hermeneutics. Like all art, an opera or a music drama creates a "situation" that must be interpreted. One may certainly infer that a character on stage intends to be ironic, judging from *what* he or she says and *how* he or she says it or sings it, or judging from what music is accompanying the speech or song—but this is simply a part of the overall interpretation of what one sees and hears. The character's intention is a part of the work of art as one perceives it.

Dance

In considering the art of dance, one finds oneself in the same theoretical situation as was recently discussed. The gestures and movements of a dancing body may obviously be in line with the conventionally encoded ironic gestures and mimicry that were recognized already in antiquity. In the very few texts performing ironic interpretations of dance that I know of, this aspect in not hinted at, in spite of the recognized "textual" status of dance performances.[47] Instead—and this is well in accordance with the way the concept of irony is used in general—ambivalence, reversals, contrasts, and incongruities between dance and music or words, movements, dramatic action, visual attributes and their connotations, "burlesque fashions," and the norms of the society have formed the base of ironic interpretations of dance performances.[48]

Film

A field where one might expect to find rather developed theories of irony is the study of film. This is not the case, though. The frequency of the word *irony* in film discourse is no doubt very high, but the concept is almost never theoretically scrutinized. This is slightly surprising because film scholars have generally been quite eager to conceptualize their study, and I do not believe that many agree with Ong when he argues in "From Mimesis to Irony: The Distancing of Voice" that "the height of irony in the movies can probably never reach that possible in print." Ong claims that this is the case because the "voice" of the narrator is radically distanced in movies; it is "not there at all as words. . . . Vision has taken over completely from voice."[49]

Probably because of his interest in oral communication, Ong supposes that images are less likely to generate irony. A written text is related to and yet completely different from an oral message, which means that the "intentional" irony of oral communication may be part also of a written text—but in a somewhat distorted and fruitfully complex way. In a movie, on the other hand, the distancing of voice has gone too far, Ong assumes. The connection to oral communication is fundamentally broken because of the concentration on visuality, and hence the ironic potential is severely limited.

Ong's line of argument is informative. I do not believe that he is right, but he explains quite well why there might be good reason to hesitate before calling a film ironic. The historical connection between irony and oral communication is strong, and it is understandable that one may feel slightly uncomfortable with the notion of "filmic irony." On the other hand, it must be recognized that the concept of irony has been emancipated from its historical roots in a way that makes it perfectly suited for interpreting movies also. Most theories of irony that have seen the light of day in the past two hundred years apparently prepare the ground for filmic irony. If it makes sense to talk about dramatic irony and ironic situations in real life, why should it be unreasonable to talk about irony in a movie? Even the limited aspect of irony as an opposition between two mutually exclusive meanings of a few words may be realized in a movie, either in the speech of a character or in the words of a voice-over narrator.

Some theoretical work has been done in the field of film and irony, however. A handful of articles and a few book-length studies that I know of have been published. Unfortunately, the hermeneutical basis of the concept of irony is almost always taken for granted: ironies are "found" in films and are hence supposed to "be" there. Most labor has been spent on categorizing these ironies, or integrating them in the oeuvre of a specific director. Naturally, the concept of irony is sometimes used very vaguely or in many different ways within one and the same text.[50] As Thomas Elsaesser puts it, irony in cinema includes "all the strategies of displacement, distanciation, detachment—verbal, visual, structural—whereby a statement, a message, a communication, image or action may be qualified, put in question, subverted, parodied or indeed wholly negated *while preserving visible that to which it refers itself ironically*."[51] In Elsaesser's view, these "strategies" belong to the directors or the films themselves, not the beholders.

The concept of irony is also quite often used in a very general sense. Irony found in movies is not always specifically "filmic" in the sense that it is not always generated by the particularities of the film medium. Films with antiheroes, films that lack certain closure and accept complexity and plurality, films that tend toward general absurdity, and films that reverse certain narrative conventions might thus be described as ironic.[52] This is frequently done, now and then explicitly in accordance with the circumscription of irony in novels.

Irony in film may certainly also be equivalent to irony in reality. Like the world around one, a film is presented via speech, visual and aural elements, characters, actions, and situations. To write about irony in film may be simply a variation of making ironic interpretations of the more or less ordinary lives that the viewers live.[53] Similarly, irony as a worldview or a philosophy of life may be found in movies.[54] More specifically, one may certainly say that there is "self-conscious Romantic irony" or "ironic self-consciousness" in a movie.[55]

Neither does irony in film always differ much from irony in theater or opera—especially when a movie is in fact a filmed setting of a (music) drama.[56] Like an opera, a film may be said to display comic contrasts between song texts and what happens to the characters.[57] In a film one may also find disjunctions between what is narrated by a voice-over and what is represented visually, between what is told and what is shown, between word and image, or between what is represented by voice and by camera.[58] (Interestingly enough, it is almost never questioned that it must be the image that represents the "truth," the words the "false" ironic reversal.) Irony may certainly be found also in the relationship between a drama and a filmed version of it, between two filmed versions of the same drama, or between a specific film and certain genre patterns.[59] Needless to say, interpretation of irony in television builds on the same premises as the interpretation of irony in films. When watching nonfictional television programs also, one may perform ironic interpretations of what one takes to be, say, a "crossing of generic constraints" or a "tension between reportorial objectivity and the rhetoric of public argument."[60]

In his book, *The Hitchcock Romance: Love and Irony in Hitchcock's Films* from 1988, Lesley Brill focuses on the tension between romantic expectations and disappointment in Hitchcock's work, which he also takes to be a tension between the conventions of romantic narratives and their undercutting or reversal. To both these tensions, and the "destructive" part of the dualities, Brill gives the name *irony*. He describes many examples of disappointed expectations and reversed conventions of the romance—in sounds, images, and speech. The problem is only that he seems to suppose that his interpretations are facts of the filmic texts. He believes that there are "apparent opposites," but it is not clear how his observations may acquire the quality of objectivity.[61]

Brill's readings of Hitchcock's films are often very interesting, but I fail to realize how he can be so sure that "about three-quarters of Hitchcock's films have predominantly romantic tonalities and resolutions," whereas "Most of the rest are ironic."[62] I suggest that Brill confuses the irony that he creates in his fine interpretations of *Vertigo*, *Psycho*, and many other movies with the objective qualities that he thinks he sees and calls "elements" of irony.[63]

Örjan Roth-Lindberg's approach to the hermeneutics of irony is also problematic. In his dissertation published in 1995, he is eager to circumscribe what he calls "pure" filmic irony: a "contradictory" relation between two succeeding shots or within a montage.[64] Unfortunately, his presentation of his considerable theoretical work is a rather confused mixture of almost every approach to irony that has been launched. In a voluminous part of his dissertation, Roth-Lindberg distinguishes between twenty-seven categories of irony in movies—categories that he seems to regard as rather stable entities, the existence of which are superbly independent of the interpretive act of the spectator.[65]

Even in Mary Ann Doane's brilliant, pioneering dissertation, "The Dialogical Text: Filmic Irony and the Spectator" from 1979, irony is supposed to be a more or less solid quality of the filmic text. According to Doane, the meaning of a film is created by the spectator, but irony is seen as a structural trait to be interpreted, not an interpretive strategy employed by the spectator. Instead Doane writes about "the ironical texts themselves," and she regards irony as a "discursive strategy . . . a particular means of positioning the spectator"—as if irony were not a part of the "meaning" of the filmic text, only a given prerequisite for it.[66] In an article published in 1983 in which she emphasizes Freudian psychoanalysis (an aspect that dominates her dissertation also), she prefers to write about "the effect of irony upon the spectator."[67]

The ironic structures described by Doane are of diverse kinds. Generally, though, they are based on a dialogic relation between "the filmic narration" and some kind of "intertext" or on "a duality of narration."[68] Doane, for instance, writes about "a calculated and sustained misuse or over-use of certain narrative devices," "a hyperbolization of gesture, duration, and scale," and "a perverse rewriting" of a genre.[69] However, she also focuses on internal relations. Ironic interpretations may be based on "a fundamental incoherency" in an image/sound structure that is "essentially unreadable" or on "an incongruity between sound and image."[70]

Yet, these ironies are seen as actual qualities of the filmic texts, waiting for an interpretation. Consequently, the significance of the movies read by Doane is strangely "preread." The position and interpretive maneuvers of the spectator are emphasized and problematized, proceeding from the assumption that "meaning is not given but produced."[71] However, much as in Mark Jeffry Dicks's dissertation "Reading Irony," irony in itself is placed in the texts on very unclear hermeneutical grounds. Although irony is never equated with particular filmic traits, it is permitted to play the role of a positioner of the spectator, while in fact, as I see it, it is the spectator who is the positioner of irony.

As an example, Doane states that "the narration provides a particular perspective on the narrative so that it must be read, simultaneously, from two different angles."[72] This is a problematic view because both the narrative and the narration, as Doane herself stresses, are far from fixed entities. Both must, at least partly, be constructed by the spectator on the grounds of codes and individual norms and knowledge. The activity of reading "from two different angles" may thus very well be the result of an interpretive strategy that is activated before the spectator recognizes a discrepancy between narrative aspects—indeed the narrative discrepancy might be the result of an ironic reading. It is not only the narration that provides perspectives that cannot be ignored—the narration itself is always already the result of a reading, although often not recognized as such. The uniformity of certain codes and interpretive communities is so dense that one tends not to realize that no level of narration is definite.

Although Doane breaks up the theoretical fixation on monological, filmic texts and instead emphasizes ironic, dialogical texts, her very notions of irony and dialogicity are defined in relation to and heavily dependent on the notion of monologicity. The problem is that both irony and nonirony, dialogicity and monologicity, as defined by Doane, seem to be products of some sort of authority of the filmic text itself. The fundamental difference between irony and nonirony is thus generated by an equally fundamental hermeneutical similarity: it is the narration that "provides a particular perspective on the narrative so that it must be read, simultaneously, from two different angles," just as the narration in a monological text is supposed to provide a perspective on the narrative that leads to a uniform reading.

However, there is good reason to hold the view that these two perspectives are already read by the spectator. Irony is, I think, best understood as an interpretive strategy that is, or is not, activated *before* the narrative structure of a film is definitely set by the spectator. In my view, Doane's emphasis on the spectator is too limited to give an understanding of irony's way into film.

Other Areas

Ironic interpretations have of course been performed within more areas in the wide field of arts. Ceramics could be mentioned, or the relationship between illustrations and texts and between words and images in cartoons and caricatures.[73] There is, however, little value in trying to track down and rigorously systematize all thinkable ironies. There exist endless series of potential irony in our interpretations of the world and the arts. The aim of systematizing is a fallacy to which too many scholars fall victim in the belief that what one sees is what exists. Like irony, the color blue is certainly something very real, although it is impossible to say when blue stops being blue and instead becomes green or purple. I do *not* suggest that the qualities "irony" and "blue" are similar in very many respects, but I do suggest that none of them is better understood by way of building taxonomies. In categorizing all imaginable more or less blue objects—blueberries, blue cars, the sky, your mother's eyes, and so on—you gain a certain knowledge of the world, but not very much knowledge of the color in itself.

So instead of hinting at possible ways of building complex systems of irony, I will make a general observation. The majority of the texts about irony in the arts are implicitly or explicitly based on "readings" of works of art. Often the results of these readings are projected to the surface of the work of art itself, but artistic intentions are mentioned quite rarely. The praxis of interpreting irony in the arts thus shows that the conception of irony as a result of the creator's intention is not dominant, at least not in practice. On the other hand, it must be emphasized that there are very few theoretical, hermeneutical considerations in these texts. The hermeneutics of intentionality is perhaps avoided because of the difficulties involved in tracing a palpable intention in images and music, but few interpreters seem to find the idea problematic that irony is located in the verbal, visual, and aural texts themselves.

I will return to these issues later, but there is one important aspect of visual and musical irony that has been saved for a section of its own: parody.

INTERTEXTUAL IRONY AND PARODY

Muecke, the influential systematizer of irony, does not often step outside the domain of literature. In one of his books, however, he states that

> there seem to be no ways of being ironical that are specific to music, painting, landscape gardening, kinetic art, patisserie and so on. Nonrepresentative art can be ironical in perhaps only two ways: incongruities of formal properties and parodies of the clichés, mannerisms, styles, conventions, ideologies and theories of earlier artists, schools or periods.[74]

In spite of the many examples of various kinds of ironic interpretations that we have hitherto discussed, Muecke has a point in this remark, and it should be noted that also other scholars have advocated similar views.[75] I agree that musical and visual irony is not "specific," but on the other hand it is misleading to say that music and painting can be ironic in only two ways.

What Muecke calls "incongruities of formal properties" has already been touched upon and will be discussed in detail in a later chapter; here we shall focus on parody. Parody is commonly accepted to be a valid category of most art forms. As I stated before, I believe that it makes sense to regard parody as a form of intertextual irony, and as such parody is probably the most widely used conceptual tool for describing irony in nonverbal art forms like painting, architecture, and music. In her book *A Theory of Parody: The Teachings of Twentieth-Century Art Forms*, published in 1985, Hutcheon claims that the variety of possible modes of parody is in fact greater in the visual arts than in literature.[76] This might very well be true, especially if her rather wide notion of parody as "repetition with difference" is applied.[77] Hutcheon herself offers a wide range of interpretation in terms of parody of film, music, architecture, and painting. Like Muecke, Hutcheon treats parody as a species of irony: "Ironic inversion is a characteristic of all parody," she states.[78]

This is basically true, I think, but I would prefer to put it differently: parody is an ironic interpretation of an intertextual relation—between two texts (in the widest sense of the word), between a text and a genre, or between a text and a style or a convention; it is "intertextual irony" with an addition of some sort of satire or laughter. Generally, parody is associated with exaggeration of stylistic or ideological characteristics, and as in all ironic interpretation at least two interpretive maneuvers must be performed to establish parody: the interpreter must argue for the existence of some sort of conflict, which in the case of intertextual irony involves the choice of a contrasting intertext, and furthermore the interpreter must establish an ironic meaning that somehow involves laughter at a "victim" on the base of what is understood to be, for instance, an exaggeration.[79] In this stricter sense of parody, the reader, beholder, or listener is in one way or another amused at the cost of a specific work of art, an artist, a genre, a style, or a convention. If one accepts Linda Hutcheon's less common notion of parody, the element of ridicule is eliminated, and parody hence becomes equivalent to intertextual irony.

As a rule art critics use the concept of parody with more stringency than the concept of irony. Historically, irony is more alien to art criticism than parody, the latter of which is a firmly established conceptual tool within the discourse on the visual arts. Among art critics there is generally consensus on what parody is, whereas the concept of irony generates confusion. Nevertheless the terms *parody, irony, satire,* and *humor* are often mingled in a number of ways in art criticism as well as in literary criticism.

It is not unusual that parody and irony seem to melt together in a conceptual unity. This is the case, for instance, in Milly Heyd's book on Beardsley. Heyd uses the term *parody* only a few times, as when she describes a clash between a "religious atmosphere" and some "completely secular" faces.[80] In other instances, when referring to *parody* according to its common definition might very well have been appropriate, the term is not mentioned. Instead Heyd sticks to the term *irony* when she describes conflicts between drawings and specific visual intertexts or general mythological intertexts.[81] This might be seen as an indication that parody, for Heyd, is a concept that is dispensable once the general category of irony has been introduced.

Other art critics also choose not to use the term *parody* when discussing intertextual irony. In an article called "Intervention and Irony," it is argued that some specific paintings are involved in a "negation of painting history"; in another article irony is traced in "the ways in which the artistic genres of portraiture and genre painting [in Dutch painting] converge," and in yet another text it is claimed that food images of Pop artists such as Andy Warhol give ironic dimensions to the *vanitas* theme and seventeenth-century still-life painting.[82] Ironies of these kinds are no doubt intertextual, although the intertextual relations do not necessarily involve a critical distance of the sort that gives rise to laughter or degradation at the expense of the intertexts.

In his book *The Lies of Art: Max Beerbohm's Parody and Caricature*, John Felstiner, also, uses the term *parody* sparingly when dealing with the visual arts. Felstiner mobilizes the notions of parody and irony to describe Beerbohm's writings, whereas his drawings are generally characterized as caricature. Sometimes, though, the caricatures are seen as parodies as well, as when Beerbohm "drew Beardsley in the style of Beardsley."[83] The notion of style here seems to be crucial. For Felstiner, it is not parody but caricature when one laughs at a drawing that distorts the looks of a person—but when a stylistic characteristic is connected to the laughter, parody becomes involved. The looks of a person are part of a contextual field, one may say; style is part of an intertextual field.

Intertextual irony is also in focus in the only text I know of that is dedicated specifically to irony in architecture: Monique Yaari's article "Ironic Architecture: The Puzzles of Multiple (En)coding." Yaari argues for the referentiality of architecture and hence "its ironic potential." She finds ironic incongruities of architecture mainly "among several conflicting or evolving denotations or connotations, or in the *manner* in which representation occurs."[84] Yaari does not use the term *parody* very frequently, but her many ironic interpretations of buildings draw heavily on unexpected, reversed uses of stylistic and culturally encoded features. What she sees as irony in architecture is very often the kind of "intertextual irony" that most art critics would subsume under the heading of *parody*.

When it comes to the visual aspects of drama, Huston Diehl's article about the visual rhetoric of Renaissance English tragedy is informative. For Diehl ironic inversions of visual conventions are closely associated with parody.[85] He makes no distinction between the notions of irony and parody, which indicates that irony generated by conflicts between historically encoded visual signs and their "reversals" is equivalent to parody. This is certainly a reasonable contention, I would say. It is also reasonable that the notions of irony and parody are often very closely related in film criticism, too, when it comes to interpreting inversions of conventions or critical use of clichés.[86]

Music is, however, probably the artistic field that, next to literature, is most closely associated with parody. On the one hand, parody is a very well established concept within music criticism; on the other hand, it is often conceptually more distant from irony than in the case of literary criticism and art criticism. It is informative to note that in the leading musical dictionary, *The New Grove Dictionary of Music and Musicians*, the term *irony* is not listed, whereas a rather extensive article and a not insignificant bibliography are devoted to *parody*.

It must be noted, though, that parody in music is subject to a rather sharp, terminological distinction. The first sense of musical parody is a specific, historically determined technique of composition "involving the use of pre-existent material." The second, related but yet distinct sense of musical parody is a composition "generally of humorous or satirical intent in which turns of phrase or other features characteristic of another composer or type of composition are employed and made to appear ridiculous."[87] It may be noticed that Hutcheon's definition of *parody* in postmodern literature and visual art as an intertextual relation without elements of satire and laughter in fact comes very close to the first sense of musical parody—with the obvious exception that musical parody had its heyday many hundred years ago. The second sense of musical parody is of course the one that is equivalent to the normal conception of parody in the other arts.

Parody is thus the variation of irony that has been most generally acknowledged within musicology, and it has long been the subject of writings. The associations with the term *irony* were, however, very rare until a few decades ago. Parody, also in its second sense, has traditionally been identified as a genre, and as such its theoretical, hermeneutical complications have not been scrutinized. For interest in the concept of irony, it is simply not very fruitful to read the older texts on musical parody, although the existence of this bulk of literature must be noted.

I have earlier maintained that the distinction between irony and parody is of more historical than theoretical value. Parody but not irony has been seen as a genre, and the two terms have not always been very closely linked. As terms and as historical phenomena, *irony* and *parody* have lived their own, separate lives. The few attempts to distinguish *theoretically* between parody and irony in music that I know of are, however, not so well

justified. They are neither clearly outlined nor based on compre-
hensible definitions of the two notions. Delores Jerde Keahey
aims at a distinction by way of suggesting that irony is preferably
"a technique which may or may not use means identical to parody" but that has "deeper meaning" than parody: "Irony needs
the knowledge of context to achieve its effect; parody may exist
purely for its own sake, apart from any perspective. Thus techniques of parody may be used to produce an ironic effect, but not
vice versa."[88] Yet, how can parody exist without "perspective"?
Are not the "parodied" phenomena—style, tradition, or specific
works of music—parts of contexts? Unfortunately, no attempt is
made to explain what the "deeper meaning" of irony implies, although one may guess that it is the philosophical theories of
irony that lie behind the contention.

Due to its sketchiness, Keahey's aim to make a distinction
leads to confusion rather than clarification. Marius Flothuis, on
the other hand, builds on a very narrow definition of *irony* when
distinguishing between *parody* and *irony*: "Parody is the deformation of a concrete and perceptible object. . . . In irony the intonation is of decided significance," he states.[89] Both "deeper
meaning" and "intonation" are related to verbal language, and it
seems as if the aim to keep irony close to literary ideas and devices prevents both Keahey and Flothuis from seeing the very
fundamental similarity between irony and parody as theoretical
concepts.

In spite of the sometimes confused relation between irony and
parody, musicologists interested in irony also have found a
rather safe ground in the notion of parody. Musical irony requires some sort of oppositions or contraries, and when it comes
to parody these are not based on "vague" phenomena but comparatively solid things such as historical conventions and specific
works of music. Jankélévitch, who interprets both literature and
music in his book on irony, has a very clear conception of parody.
It is "the most glaring form of irony," he states; it "always apes
somebody, the 'manner' of somebody, the style of somebody."[90]
It might be added that "somebody" is not necessarily an individual author or composer; it may also be the style of an era. Jankélévitch is not always very easy to follow when he interprets music
in terms of irony, but when it comes to parody he is quite com-
prehensible.

Among the musical genres, opera is the one that most often is
associated with parody. A critical phrase such as "an ironic parody of the conventions of classical opera" is indeed representa-

tive.[91] When parody in opera is focused on, it is, however, very often the verbal aspects that are highlighted. The standard interpretation of operatic parody investigates how librettos, dramatic action, and lyrics in "serious" opera are transformed into "parodic" opera through exaggeration and distortion.[92]

However, parody of opera may certainly involve the music also. Frits Noske compares a cadence in *Così fan tutte* with the baroque hemiola cadence and finds Mozart's cadence to be "parodically disproportioned."[93] This might be called *parody of musical style*, but Noske also sees ironic transformations of *Don Giovanni* in *Così fan tutte*: "The tender 6/8 section of 'Là ci darem la mano' is parodically transformed into a march-like melody with a concluding *forte* chord."[94] This is an example of a parodic interpretation of not a whole opera but at least the relationship between two specific musical sections by the same composer. Of course a combination of characteristics in text and music may also form the ground for parodic interpretations. A song may, for instance, well become "a witty parody of the famed laments of former times" by way of a contrast between what is taken to be a "cheerful setting" and a "sorrowful lyric."[95] Clearly it is the breaking of conventions that here gives rise to parody.

Gustav Mahler is a composer who from time to time is discussed in terms of *irony* and *parody*, as when a "mock-serious mood" in his First Symphony is said to undermine the expected solemnity of a funeral march.[96] The expectations of a genre are here crucial for the parodic interpretation. In his seminal book on the classical style in music, Charles Rosen focuses on formal conventions, but he does not use the term *parody* when he writes about "the irony of Mahler . . . who employed sonata-forms with the same mock respect that he gave to his shopworn scraps of dance-tunes."[97] Also, Peter Winkler does not adopt the term *parody* when he compares a song by Randy Newman with the gospel tradition and finds Newman's variation of it "entirely ironic." The song, Winkler states, is not to be taken at face value; it "is really an *anti*-hymn."[98] All these variations of intertextual irony are very similar, and the fact that the term *parody* sometimes occurs and sometimes does not seems not to be of crucial importance.

Finally, it should perhaps be emphasized that parody, like irony in general according to my hermeneutical stance, might be seen as an interpretive strategy.[99] To begin with, it is in no way always self-evident which styles or conventions are the "correct" musical intertexts, and furthermore an alleged intertextuality is not necessarily parodic. Even if one finds a very distinct resemblance between two pieces of music, there are no secure criteria that make it possible to distinguish between a quotation—a "neutral" intertextual relationship—and a parody. In other words, even if one establishes an intertextual relationship that can be said to involve some sort of conflict, that does not necessarily imply that one feels that a specific musical work or genre becomes a victim of ridicule.

The problem of whether a passage of music is a quotation or a parody would be easily resolved, however, if the application of the terminology were objective. The notion of *quotation* is defined in terms of similarity, *parody* in terms of dissimilarity: similarity with a distinct, contrastive difference. Yet, the question "Zitat oder Parodie?" [Quotation or Parody?], as the title of a Beethoven article by Harry Goldschmidt reads, is not a question of facts as this musicologist asserts; it is rather a hermeneutical problem that is impossible to resolve because there is no formal truth.[100] The notions of *quotation* and *parody* are related in the same problematic way as *metaphor* and *irony*, and, as I have shown, the difference between *similarity* and *difference* may be surprisingly difficult to detect as traits like *similarity, contrast,* and *difference* are often created in relation to what one finds in oneself, not in the works of art. The disagreements among scholars that aim at definite objectivity in questions like "Zitat oder Parodie?" serve as evidence of the fact that there are no formal criteria that can settle such disputes definitely.

SEX PISTOLS: "GOD SAVE THE QUEEN"?

Up until now I have discussed irony and parody in some of the most important art forms. Instead of making my exemplification more extensive, I prefer now to perform a reading of a specific song in order to demonstrate some of the ironic potentials of an interartial complex involving various artistic media and "texts." In a book like this, borrowing its title from Kierkegaard, it would perhaps be suitable to write about the Madonna CD *Divine Madness.* The question of what Kierkegaard and Madonna have in common is indeed intriguing, but I hesitate to answer it. Otherwise I could have made an ironic interpretation of the Madonna video "Like a Virgin," focusing on a certain ambiguity in the notion of virginity as it is represented verbally, visually, and musically. I choose, however, to instead focus on a song performed by the punk rock group Sex Pistols—"God Save the Queen" from 1977[101]—as it gives me the opportunity to make some comparisons that I find interesting. The reading will be my own, and hence the ironies that I will find in the song and its contexts have been placed there by me, just as the contexts and intertexts have been chosen and placed within the frame of interpretation by me. I will, however, perform my reading from a platform that most readers of this book probably share, at least partly: some interpretive communities of Western society that include knowledge of its literary and musical traditions and its popular culture of today.

With its texts, music, stage performance, and mimicry, punk offers an interart perspective on irony that has hitherto not raised any scholarly interest. Punk is perhaps as far as one can get from the Metropolitan Opera or university libraries, and yet striking historical and conceptual connections can be found between punk and the highbrow cultural forms. In other words, the same interpretive strategies may successfully be employed on both opera and punk.

In a mixed-media text such as a performance of a punk song, the ironic contrasts may be found either *within* or *between* the verbal, visual, and musical sign systems. They may be intratextual in the sense that the traits that are understood to be somehow incongruous are each present in the performance, or intertextual in the sense that the incongruities are dependent upon certain intertexts that the interpreter finds relevant.

The irony of "God Save the Queen" is definitely partly intertextual, and it is not the only Sex Pistols song that uses a well-known text or melody as material for musical transformation. Their famous version of Frank Sinatra's megahit "My Way" follows the original quite closely but distorts its smoothly orchestrated melody to such a degree that the expression of both text and melody is fundamentally changed. The soft popular music turns into punk rage. One might be justified in calling the intertextual relationship between Sinatra's and the Sex Pistols' versions parodic because the original may seem rather silly compared to the hardboiled version. To do it "my way" according to the Sex Pistols seems to be something completely different from doing it "my way" according to Sinatra—in spite of the identical words.

In "God Save the Queen" only fragments of the original text are identifiable and scarcely anything of the music, but certainly enough to establish the national anthem of Great Britain, dating from the eighteenth century, as a very vital intertext.[102] The iden-

tical titles of the two songs tempt us to compare them—a comparison that instantly leads to an evident result: the extreme
clash between the solemn melody of the national anthem and
the wild monotony of the Sex Pistols' version.

A comparison of the lyrics also gives noteworthy results. In the
anthem royal government seems to be celebrated in a totally unambiguous way, whereas the text of the Sex Pistols' song is more
complicated for all its straightforwardness. The fundamental
contrast can be found in the two initial lines: "God save the
queen / The fascist regime." The first line is intertextually colored
by patriotism, religion, tradition, and hope, but it is reversed in a
brutal way by its new context. Its traditional message to the people, which may be paraphrased as "Be loyal citizens, you live in
a great nation," is ironically contradicted if one's political norms
do not include fascism. This is the main characteristic of the
song, as can be seen also in lines such as: "God save the queen /
She ain't no human being / There is no future / And England's
dreaming." The Sex Pistols give us a heretical response to the
words of the anthem that read "May she defend our laws, / And
ever give us cause / to sing with heart and voice / God save the
Queen." It is no wonder that they were banned by the British
media.

With reference to this intertextuality, "God Save the Queen,"
too, may be called a parody: a parody implying criticism not
solely of the genre of national anthems or the specific national
anthem of Britain, but also of the whole of British society. As it
is stated in a book on the national anthem, "Every British man,
woman, and child, whether in the mother country or overseas,
looks upon that tune as part of his or her personal inheri-
tance."[103] To attack the national anthem is to attack the funda-
ment of conservatism in British society: the view that the queen
and the political power *are* the people.[104] The Sex Pistols' version
of "God Save the Queen" is, incidentally, not the first variation
of the anthem that may be called a parody. In one version it is
said that "We, all your slaves, agree / To doat [sic] on Mon-
archy."[105]

A somewhat more complicated statement in the song of the
Sex Pistols is "God save the queen / We mean it man / We love
our queen." One may interpret this as an ironic denial of the potential irony of "God Save the Queen," but also as a slightly ambiguous statement meaning something like "the queen is
certainly in need of God's protection because there is a riot coming up and it will be lovely to make a mess of her." The message

of the song is, however, clear-cut within the interpretive communities of Western society: "No future no future / no future for you."

Ironic contrasts can be found also in the relationships between text and music and between text and the visual. In the context of cultural conventions the incongruities between the repeated words "God save the queen" and the musical and visual expressions are very sharp. The standard modes of behavior, tone of voice, and mimicry used in royal contexts are needless to say not in any way compatible with the uncouth music and stage performance of the Sex Pistols. When singing the overtly mocking "the fascist regime," however, music and stage behavior are in line with established musical and visual codes of delivering criticism.

The quasi-documentary film, *The Great Rock 'n' Roll Swindle*, written and directed by Julian Temple and dating from 1980, is a specific intertext of relevance. In this film the song "God Save the Queen" is performed and furthermore put into a visual context that is related to and sometimes partly identical to the clothes and record sleeves of the Sex Pistols. *The Great Rock 'n' Roll Swindle* offers an interpretation of the Sex Pistols as a phenomenon, and at the same time it is a visual intertext to their music. The film's iconography, verbal comments, and soundtrack constitute a piece of fiction in its own right, but here it is brought to attention because of its relation to the specific song "God Save the Queen."

In its most general sense *The Great Rock 'n' Roll Swindle* highlights the commercial aspects of rock music and particularly punk and the Sex Pistols. In the film it is suggested that the whole business around rock music is a swindle, a swindle that punk reacts against but at the same time takes advantage of. On the one hand, the reactions of the media and the authorities are focused in a way that gives the impression of punk as being genuinely anarchic. On the other hand, the "smartness" of the Sex Pistols and their manager Malcolm McLaren is heavily emphasized as we are continually informed of how much money they make. In this contrast the most inclusive irony of the Sex Pistols may be found. What is the "meaning" of it all? Does "God Save the Queen" represent a serious protest against the authorities of society, or is it only part of a commercial swindle? As I see it, the film encourages both interpretations and consequently provokes the spectator to find his or her own answer to the question as to whether it is really possible to attract large-scale attention to genuine protest without corrupting it.

Among the multitude of possible ironies in the film, a few others may be mentioned. The swastika is a very provocative visual icon that appears on a T-shirt several times, and because it gives associations to Nazism it might lead us to identify the attitude of the Sex Pistols with fascism. On the other hand, there is a German officer appearing at the end of the film, enthusiastically shouting *schneller!* [quicker!] when hearing the punk music, and he seems to be a rather silly caricature of a representative of the Third Reich. In fact the very names of the two most prominent band members, Sid Vicious and Johnny Rotten, may be understood to be silly, ironic exaggerations of the myth of rock rebels.

A final potential irony of the film in its entirety that I shall mention is the conflict between the repeated statement that the band "can't play" and the fact that it apparently can—although in a punky way. The film constantly states that the Sex Pistols is a swindle both ideologically and musically, but at the same time it demonstrates the considerable force of their music. From the point of view of certain standards that are recognized even within the rock genre, their music certainly stinks, but valued from different standards its aggressive expression is high-powered. Perhaps it is, after all, not a swindle.

The film *The Great Rock 'n' Roll Swindle* gives further musical and visual material in direct connection to "God Save the Queen." In the section that includes this song one initially sees a picture of the British queen with a giant safety pin added to her nose, a picture stemming from a widespread photo collage by Jamie Reid.[106] Some cuts later we hear the beginning of the Overture to Georg Friedrich Händel's *Music for the Royal Fireworks,* which is immediately followed by "God Save the Queen" performed by the Sex Pistols. First one sees the band playing on a boat on the Thames under the bridges of London, and then on stage. Shots of the band on stage, band members struggling with the police, and spectacular fireworks are put into a montage. By the end of the song the words "no future" are repeated over and over again and accompanied with an accelerating display of fireworks. What one sees and hears is a party in the middle of a disaster.

The correlation between the title of the Händel music that one hears and the fireworks that one sees is obvious, but also another musical intertext is of relevance: Händel's *Water Music,* which was written for the purpose of being played at festivities on the

Thames in 1715–1717, exactly where the Sex Pistols now play their punk song. The images of the film, the titles of the music of Händel, and the words sung by the Sex Pistols together form an intricate web of associations. The ironic reversals that may be created out of this complex are multiple. Händel and highbrow culture in association with royalty, his *Music for the Royal Fireworks*, are put in focus but are instantly reversed and replaced by the furious guitars and the antiroyalist words of the Sex Pistols, and the angry faces of the rock musicians are contrasted with magnificent fireworks over London. I see irony—definitely intertextual irony and sometimes parody. I see aggression directed toward a society that does not care for its youngsters, but also detachment and a comical fulfillment of rebellious clichés.

If one investigates the visual aspects of the performance of the Sex Pistols from a more specific point of view, it is interesting to note that many of the gestures and voice intonations used by punk artists have been connected with irony for a very long time. In his *History of Animals,* Aristotle considers eyebrows rising up toward the temples marks of the mocker and ironist.[107] Post-Quintilian rhetoric defines sarcasm, a notion that is considered a species of irony, as mocking speech that is accompanied with a specific kind of mimicry: "to show the teeth."[108] It is believed, I have already noted, that the word *sarcasm* means "biting of flesh." The classical, medieval, and Renaissance authors are aware that *pronuntiatio*—that is, intonation, tone, or gesture—can unmask irony; they hold that certain variations of it may be considered replacements for the word "not" omitted from the speaker's statement. Ironic intonation is usually described as an emphatic, bitter, mocking, or caustic tone.[109] Living in the sixteenth century, Jacopo Mazzoni draws on the Stoic satirist Persius from the first century and lists a number of potentially ironic gestures, including "a clenched fist with the middle finger outstretched; sticking out one's tongue; a grimace in which the teeth were bared; and nasal gestures like wrinkling the nose"— gestures to be made behind the victim's back.[110]

All these descriptions of the ironist, all these culturally coded images of the ironist, fit eminently into the image of the Sex Pistols. Indeed many listeners are likely to comprehend the repeated words "God save the queen" as stating the opposite merely through the aural qualities of the voice and the instruments, but the visual aspects of the punk performance are definitely in line with the auditory and may thus fortify an ironic interpretation.

Punk music and culture were extremely rebellious in many ways. Musical standards and the commercial music industry were challenged. Clothes, hairstyles, and makeup were used as visual signs of alienation, and stage behavior aimed at provoking and offending established society. The rebellion in punk is not clear-cut, I have argued, especially not as it is given form in *The Great Rock 'n' Roll Swindle*, but I believe that punk was revolutionary in at least some respects. However, even revolution has its tradition and its history. The irony of punk, and the irony of all rebellious movements, is that it falls into very traditional patterns—which does *not* make it meaningless. The tradition of rebellion is a very vital part of Western culture. Putting many other comparisons aside, it can be noted that both Christ and Socrates were considered rebels.

One could in fact argue that the punk musician is an *eiron* of our time—the *eiron* being an important figure in the early conceptualization of irony. When Socrates was initially called an *eiron*, the word was not associated with his philosophical virtues.[111] The *eiron*, I have earlier noted, was a deceiver and a mocker, one of the standard characters in Greek comedy: a cunning and sly figure who gives the impression of being an ignorant fool, but who regularly, thanks to his cleverness, triumphs in the end.

As noted, phenomena related to twisted mimicry, exaggeration, and verbal paradox have been discussed in the context of irony from the very beginning. To me, being formed by the cultural history of Western society, it is obvious that some of the characteristics of punk are best understood in relation to this discussion. The modes of expression connected with punk may be regarded as aspects of irony in a rhetorical manner (that is, saying/singing one thing literally, and at the same time implying the opposite) but also as the general mocking behavior of the *eiron*. Of course it is not reasonable to interpret all punk texts as ironic statements in a narrow, antiphrastic sense, no matter how intensely the face of Johnny Rotten is twisted—but "verbal," "rhetorical" irony is only one small part of irony—an aspect that is not possible to differentiate from other variations of irony by means of any theoretical method worth bothering with. The interpretation of the words "God save the queen" is dependent on resemblances and incongruities that can be found on infinitely many levels, as is the interpretation of the whole punk phenomenon. Irony is a creation of a mind involved in interpretation of what is seen, heard, read, and remembered. That is all, and that is more than enough to fill discussions for a lifetime.

8

The Irony of the Arts

Only silence can "affirm" ultimate negation.
—Wayne C. Booth

ART AND IRONY IN THE EYE OF THE BEHOLDER: DUCHAMP

IN THE LAST CHAPTER I INVESTIGATED VARIOUS STRATEGIES OF INTERPRE-
ting different sorts of texts and works of art ironically. Now it is
time to attempt to highlight some more radical questions: Is art
in itself ironic? Are all forms of art, as they are known, in some
sense ironic by definition? Are there specific works of art
that may be seen as ironic because of their status as "art"—or
"nonart"?

These questions have already been hinted at a few times. In
the context of ironic interpretations of drama, I noted Eli Rozik's
suggestion that the ironic relationships between reality and pretense and between the identification and detachment of the
spectator are parallels to the spatial relationship between audience and actors in the classical theater: the spectators are at a
distance from the action of the play and "look downward" at it.
The borderline between fiction and reality is literally open. Rozik
states that theaters are "architectonic images" of the spectator's
ironic contemplation.[1] Similar claims have been made for the
fundamental irony of literature and visual art dating from the last
few decades. The alleged loss of stable subjects in postmodern
literature and art has led to suggestions that all postmodern art
is "hovering" ironically. More broadly, the new art notions of the
twentieth century have opened the way for ironic interpretations
of art as such. Art, it is often suggested, is created by conventions
and attitudes; the "artistic" or "aesthetic" qualities are not properties of the "objects"—and if art is created solely in the eye of
the beholder, it might be said to be ironic that the same item or
phenomenon, depending on its "position," may both "be" and

165

"not be" art. Furthermore, the claim that it is impossible for artists to be "original" is sometimes put into relation with an ironic tension between honesty and pretense, value and worthlessness.

Ever since the beginning of the twentieth century, it has also been gradually accepted that art may be created out of "found" objects. The works of the originator of the notion "ready-made," Marcel Duchamp, are of great importance in this context. In many ways the works of Duchamp form the beginning of an aesthetic discourse that highlights the question of the fundamental irony of the arts. Duchamp's paintings and ready-mades have inspired many ironic readings, ranging from rather traditional interpretations of visual and verbal aspects (often it is Duchamp's word puns and titles that are focused on) to more far-reaching claims concerning the nature of art itself.[2] Of course different critics do not always agree on where the irony really is to be found. One critic mentions "the indifferent irony of Duchamp"; another one names the artist "this ironical iconoclast."[3] The varying ironic interpretations of Duchamp's work mirror the varying evaluations of its power and meaning.

Milly Heyd values this controversial artist highly, and she maintains that "Duchamp, who changed the basic concepts of modern art history, brought irony in the visual fields into focus."[4] Because her book is on Beardsley, not Duchamp, she does not develop this thought very much. However, it is a significant point of view, particularly if one considers the words "the basic concepts of modern art history" rather than "the visual fields." For most writers, including myself, irony in Duchamp does not primarily emerge from the visual but rather from the conceptual aspects—although one of the most important conceptual aspects is the deconstruction of the notion of "visual art."

Duchamp's own term "meta-irony" often occurs in the texts that circle around Duchamp and irony. For Albert Cook, who discusses the distance between art as it is conceived conventionally and the "artistic act" of Duchamp, it is essential.[5] The author who has written some of the most brilliant texts on Duchamp, Octavio Paz, also leans heavily on the notion of meta-irony. In *Marcel Duchamp, or The Castle of Purity,* Paz puts the "an-artistic" ready-mades in opposition to artistic objects and asserts that Duchamp's ready-mades constitute an "active criticism: a contemptuous dismissal of the work of art seated on its pedestal of adjectives." Duchamp, he suggests, "has placed in parentheses not so much art as the modern idea of the work of art. His inactivity is the natural prolongation of his criticism: it is meta-irony."[6]

The very concept of art is obviously involved here: not only the verbal and plastic aspects of the individual works and objects but also their "mental" aspects. What is art? Is this object, or that object, a work of art? To answer these questions, somehow some sort of context must be picked out as relevant. One can ascribe artistic qualities to an object or an act only if it is affirmatively compared to other objects or acts that are somehow, in some context, by some interpretive community, accepted as artistic. How is it that Paz may argue so convincingly that the works of Duchamp are profoundly ironic? He can do so because of the innumerable visual intertexts that traditionally have been categorized as art. Duchamp's works, such as his *Fountain*, which is in fact an urinal, differ profoundly from these—and yet it has been claimed very successfully that they also are works of art. It is ironic, we may say, that a urinal can be both a criticism of art and a vital part of it, and perhaps it is also ironic that both a skillfully painted picture and an "ugly" object can be accepted as works of art, and on entirely different grounds. The very concept of art holds incongruities of ironic potential, and these are penetrated by Duchamp.

To call Duchamp's work ironic in this aspect is thus an act that implicitly puts it into an intertextual field. One may then ask whether Duchamp's intertextual irony ought to be called parody. *Parody* may be defined as an ironic interpretation of an intertextual relation including some sort of satire, but it is of course an open question whether the "critique" of Duchamp is also "satire"; and whether one "laughs" or not and if so at the expense of what: art at large or only Duchamp's own art? Paz seems to think that Duchamp works "within" the field of art—his objects are "an-artistic," not "anti-artistic"—and hence his oeuvre is not seen as parodic. Some specific works, however, such as Duchamp's moustache-embellished Mona Lisa titled *L.H.O.O.Q.* (read in French, these letters sound like the sentence "She has a hot ass"), are probably more apt to attract parodic interpretations. In the case of *L.H.O.O.Q.* a very well-known visual intertext is distorted.

I will now return to Paz's text about the meta-irony of Duchamp. Meta-irony, he explains, is "an irony which destroys its own negation and, hence, returns in the affirmative." Duchamp's criticism is "two-edged," he further states: "it is criticism of myth and criticism of criticism." Paz's reason for using the term *meta-*

irony seems to be that "ordinary" irony is associated with criticism that is unambiguously directed toward a fixed target. In Paz's view, Duchamp's irony is in a sense hovering; it returns to itself and includes itself among its own victims. Paz's ironic interpretation of Duchamp is certainly complex, but it must be noted that meta-irony is basically a variation of Romantic irony. Both Schlegel and Solger have written about the intricate ironic play that may take place on a multitude of levels and that is in no way reducible to univocal critique. I have also stated that Solger is an early exponent of the view that art in itself is ironic.

It is interesting that Paz refers to Buddhism and its mystical aspects. This may be borne in mind when reading his statement that "Duchamp's silence does have something to tell us: it is not an affirmation (the metaphysical attitude) nor a negation (atheism) nor is it indifference (sceptical agnosticism). His version of the myth is not metaphysical or negative but ironic: it is criticism." Meta-ironic interpretation, according to Paz, is clearly related to postmodern ironic readings, deconstruction, and mysticism. In the chapter on mysticism I cited Barbara Johnson, who claims that "Instead of a simple either/or structure, deconstruction attempts to elaborate a discourse that says *neither* 'either/or', *nor* 'both/and' nor even 'neither/nor', while at the same time not totally abandoning these logics either," and also Bimal Krishna Matilal's description of the mystic Nāgārjuna's "fourfold negation," which consists of "saying 'no' to the four alternatives: Is it? Is it not? Is it both? Is it neither?"[7]

Both deconstruction and mysticism claim to somehow transcend ordinary, Western logics and rationality. Undoubtedly Paz is in good company when he calls Duchamp's irony "insane wisdom."[8] It is, again, irony as divine madness that haunts us.

MUSIC: EMPTY SIGNS FULL OF IRONY?

It may now again be stated that irony, in all its variations—whether it is simple or complex, whether it is located in a single sentence or in the very concept of art—always finds its way back to its core: opposition. However, the question of whether art can be said to be ironic in itself can be put more radically if music is considered. Music is the art form that is supposed to "mean" nothing, and hence it ought to come close to the "non-signifying" aspects of Duchamp's art.

Today it is a common opinion among theorists that music

without words has very little meaning that is possible to verbalize. Conventional or iconic meaning is ascribed to musical signs only within a rather limited range. This has not always been the case, though. The view that music has its own, specific kind of semiosis that radically differs from verbal semiosis has gained ground parallel to the rising popularity of instrumental music. The old *Affektenlehre* tried to formulate the laws for musical meaning on the basis of mimesis and conventionality, whereas many of the new conceptions of musical semiosis rather emphasize individual form and complexity.

In his book, *Language, Music and the Sign*, Kevin Barry shows that already in the eighteenth century a number of less known theorists considered music made up of what Barry calls "empty signs"—as opposed to the "full signs" of visual art.[9] John Neubauer, too, in *The Emancipation of Music from Language*, investigates how the *Affektenlehre*, the mimetic conception of music, was gradually abandoned at the turn of the nineteenth century. He prefers to place the definite break later than Barry and maintains that not before German Romanticism did music come to be seen as something that actually represents nothing specific—and hence has the capacity to represent the most individual and refined states of mind.[10] Mimesis also was certainly questioned earlier (notably by Diderot, Chabanon, and Kant), Neubauer states, but it was not definitely abandoned.[11]

About two hundred years ago there was thus a change in the attitude toward music in Western society. It now became possible for the listener to enjoy purely instrumental music without having a sense of being obliged to "translate" it into something verbal. Vocal music gradually lost its normative advantage, and the stage was set for an intriguing development of musical form.

Now, there is a definite resemblance between poststructuralist statements about the "unreadability" of texts and the "empty sign" theories of music. Both advocate a radically open character of semiosis. It would indeed not be misleading to say that the postmodern view of literature in many ways echoes the Romantic view of music, although the latter is definitely more concerned with formal unity. Postmodern literature, it is said, does not state anything, it only demonstrates; it has no authoritative center, and it generates meaning only with the aid of the reader. In a similar way the Romanticists came to regard music as a form of art that is not mimetic but yet has the capacity to fill the listener with boundless "meaning." It is interesting to note that literary signs were compared to the "open signs" of music already by the end of the eighteenth century. Barry demonstrates that the view of literature as being fundamentally open has very old roots.

What is of interest for us here is that the postmodern view is often identified as an ironic view, and that the "open sign" theories of music hence might be inscribed in the line of thought that also includes irony. It is of course the double status of music that might be interpreted as ironic: it has no meaning, and yet it has; and this meaning may very well differ so radically from one person to another, or from one occasion to another, that it can be said to be inherently inconsistent. The meaning of music hovers, and there is nothing one can do about it. If one carries this line of reasoning to its extremes one has to deduce that all music, if interpreted in the Romantic and post-Romantic way, is in itself ironic.

I do not think that the parallel between poststructuralist theories of literature and Romantic theories of music can be dismissed without consideration, but it is admittedly a rather extreme interpretation to conclude that all music is ironic in itself. The possibility exists, however, and that is enough to make it worth discussing.[12] In fact one may continue following the historical tracks and find even more connections. It might be called into mind that the distinction between the two notions postmodern and Romantic irony is very vague. It might also be remembered that the German Romanticists were not only the first to circumscribe the modern notions of irony, but also the first to recognize the "autonomous" meaning of instrumental meaning. Of course, this is not a coincidence. (Romantic) irony and (instrumental) music are closely connected both theoretically and historically: they share the idea/potential of boundless semiosis, and they have both been accused of undue vacillation. Instrumental music, Romantic literature, the "formalistic" views on music and literature, Romantic and postmodern notions of irony—they have all been the subject of criticism on moral grounds. It is "irresponsible," it has been argued, to accept or (even worse) support ideas of "hovering" meaning that is created by the subject rather than by a fixed community.

IRONY AND THE ART OF LISTENING: CAGE

If music may be said to be ironic in itself, the music of John Cage is certainly not an exception. Oddly enough, not much attention seems to have been paid to the topic of Cage and irony, maybe because of the famous silence of Cage. If one says nothing, it is admittedly difficult to be ironic in a rhetorical mode. Yet, irony may also be found elsewhere, and it is rather the conceptual level, where art in the manner of Duchamp finds its nourishment, that will be of interest in the next few pages.

Sometimes Duchamp and Cage are explicitly compared. It has, for instance, been noted that Cage's music has the "character" of ready-made: "in tone, harmony, rhythm, melody or counterpoint."[13] At other times the parallels are implicit but, for those familiar with the two artists, evident—as when Paz stresses the ironic, critical "silence" of Duchamp and furthermore mentions the importance of chance: "The role which chance plays in the universe of Mallarmé is the same as that which is assumed by humour and meta-irony in Duchamp"; their works are "in search of a meaning."[14] Cage, too, by the way, has been placed in relation to Mallarmé.[15]

Now, silence and chance are also well-known keywords for the study of Cage. From "empty sign" theories of music and the alleged lack of stable subjects in postmodern irony, it is but a short step to the notion of chance. Few composers, if any, are so closely associated with chance music as Cage. From the year 1951 and onward, chance is a fundamental aspect of his music. In his monograph on the composer, Paul Griffiths asserts that Cage's music at this time becomes "purposeless."[16] The literature on Cage, however, demonstrates an abundance of terms that in various ways aim at circumscribing the character of chance music. One may find everything from rather fruitless efforts to associate chance with "nonintentionality" to exciting discussions of Zen Buddhistic concepts and ideas.[17]

When trying to get a grasp on chance music, one must first of all distinguish between two fundamentally different levels: chance as an element in the act of composing and chance as an element inscribed in the very score, and hence connected to the choice of the musicians. For some reason, though, this is almost never done.[18] Far too many scholars, I think, are interested in the act of composing. How the music is composed is of course interesting from a creative point of view, but scarcely from a musical point of view. The fact that Cage has allowed himself to be governed by chance is actually not very noteworthy. Artists have been guided by chance in all times, consciously or unconsciously, although not as systematically as Cage.

In my opinion, it is not until one investigates the completed work that the element of chance (which might then perhaps preferably be called "indeterminacy") becomes of vital interest.[19] In many of Cage's works it is possible for the performers to combine segments from different pieces, and from *Fontana Mix* (1958) and onward chance is often inscribed in the scores. It is when one investigates the relation between score and performance, and between different performances, that irony announces itself—at least in my eyes and ears. Music may possibly be said to be ironic in itself, but this general irony acquires sharper contours when Cage's chance music is considered: the more "chance" is allowed to determine the sound of the music, the more the "subjective" center is dissolved. When most of the musical parameters are governed by chance (meaning the different choices of the musicians), the "center," the "subject," or the "stability" of the work vanishes. Of course, "someone" has written the score, but that is the same "someone" who is hidden behind and beyond the actual allegedly postmodern text.

My point is that there is an important difference in degree between the experience of "conventional music" on the one hand and "chance music" and other related music on the other hand. I feel confident that few people sharing my interpretive communities will disagree with me on that. "Conventional" music has certainly no concrete "subject" comparable to what can be found in literary texts, but one may construe the "shadow" of a subject, meaning that one feels that the music is some kind of "proposal." Chance music, I would say, erases this "shadow." What is left is the "shadow" of the eraser.

According to this highly metaphoric interpretation of mine, there is a "hollow" space in chance music that may be perceived ironically. If one simply listens to a piece of chance music once, without considering the score, there is probably nothing in it that makes it more ironic than other music. The chaotic effect that may emerge from chance music might be associated with lack of subjectivity, but not necessarily so. The important thing is that one and the same piece of chance music actually is, in itself and by itself, always different. All music sounds different on different occasions, but chance music varies in a more radical way. When the "same" music may actually sound in many very "different" or perhaps even "opposite" ways, the ironic "space" is clearly wider than when a conventional, "identical" piece of music is interpreted in various ways.

I admit that I have used a lot of quotation marks recently, but let me now try to be a little more concrete. Some of Cage's scores are difficult or impossible to read in a linear way, which is to say that the conventional axis of time is annulled. In these pieces there is a latent possibility for "before" and "after" to change places from one performance to another.[20] If "before" is seen as the opposite of "after," these reversals might very well be interpreted as ironic in a rather conventional way. In Concert for Piano and Orchestra (1957–1958), one finds another remarkable trait: numbers ranging from one to sixty-four mark the intensity of sound for various tones, but it is the performer who is supposed to choose whether it is the high or the low number that indicates maximum intensity.[21] Two performances of the same piece may consequently "negate" each other as far as the intensity of sound is concerned—negate each other ironically, one might say.

I have said enough about Cage and chance. The other aspect to be discussed here is silence. The connection between silence and irony is not very far-fetched. Litotes has been seen as a mode of irony for ages, and the distance from litotes to silence is short. For Jankélévitch, who discusses litotes as an important form of irony in literature and music, silence is an extreme ironic understatement.[22] Booth, too, in a section of his book where Beckett is in focus, connects irony and silence. "The very effort at ultimate negation," he states, is "ironically trapped in its own inconsistencies, a truth the recognition of which seems to be leading Beckett into a more and more laconic pose. Only silence can 'affirm' ultimate negation."[23]

John Cage, on the other hand, uses not a few words on the subject in his book Silence.[24] What interests one here, though, is first of all his famous piece of music 4'33" (1952), which consists of three movements of massive silence. The difference between this piece and the second quietest piece of music that I know of, Ligeti's Trois bagatelles—the first section of which consists of only one tone, the two others of pauses—is noteworthy. The difference between nothing and something is in fact enormous.

Margaret Leng Tan has made a very fruitful interpretation of Cage's piece. She puts it in relation to the philosophy of Zen and its paradoxes. The form of Cage's piece is empty, Tan submits, and yet it is not; it is freed of intention and yet full of intention: "And so, we come to the Zen state of 'no-mindedness' where, in becoming purposeless, the doing occurs ('it' happens) beyond the need of a controlling or reflecting intelligence." With a reference to the well-known Zen-koan "How does it sound to clap just one hand?" Tan summarizes: "And so, in John Cage's perform-

ance without means, we hear at last the sound of one hand clap-
ping."[25]

Tan does not lean on the concept of irony in her interpretation,
but she could very well have done so. Zen is a relevant starting
point for discussing Cage and silence, but I believe that one
might just as well consider other forms of religious mysticism.[26]
Paz, we noted, refers to Buddhism and its mystical aspects in his
discussion of meta-irony in Duchamp. Jankélévitch not only
mentions silence in his book on irony, he also briefly connects
irony and mysticism.[27] For mysticism God is nothing and everything at the same time, He is both total absence and full presence. Similarly, one might maintain, 4'33" is "nothing" and yet
"everything." There is no music in it, and yet every imaginable
music, sounds of all kinds, may penetrate its silence. Its significance is without limits, but at the same time it is extremely limited by its lack of limits.

It is thus possible to perform an ironic interpretation of 4'33"
that is very broad and in fact includes even the very concept of
art. Cage's "artistic" piece is—nothing. Is art then "nothing"? Of
course art is nothing—interpretation is everything; and yet . . .
However, one should comfort oneself with a more tangible situational irony: the audience that expects to be entertained by music
but is led by the nose—or the informed audience that expects to
hear nothing and suddenly discovers the musical qualities of silence. So, what is the problem? Nothing is the problem. Is that
not ironic?

9

The Spatial Metaphors of Irony

Thinking calls for images, and images contain thought.
—Rudolf Arnheim

THE TREASON OF IMAGES

IN THE WORLD BEFORE ROMANTICISM THE WORD CONSTELLATION "IRONIC art" would probably have been considered more or less unintelligible. As I have shown, though, the expansion of the concept of irony performed by Schlegel and others, based on the so-called Socratic irony, made it possible to understand not only linguistic phenomena in terms of irony but also "situations," "state of affairs," and in fact even the very conditions of human life. Becker rightly notes that the application of the word *irony* to the field of visual arts "depends heavily upon the development of the word in the nineteenth century."[1] One may thus notice that the notion of irony has also become increasingly important in the discourse on visual art during the past two hundred years. A few years ago it was even suggested that "the virus of 'irony' had swept across the artworld in the last twenty years"—but also that "its heyday has past."[2]

There is no doubt that changes have occurred in the artistic modes of expression that can justify the immense popularity of irony in the past few decades, but it seems as if the notion of irony became popular also in its own right. As seen, poststructuralist thinking and deconstruction are clearly related to irony, and the boom of irony in the art world is perhaps not even mainly a question of new artistic developments, but rather of new interpretive strategies. Irony is about seeing, listening, reading, thinking, and interpreting, and the discourse on art that makes use of the notion of irony is often focused on art that is visual in a rather traditional way—traditional in the sense that it exists as objects: pictures painted on a canvas.

175

The ironic interpretations of visual art that have been dealt with hitherto in this book have had a clear bias toward verbal and linguistic aspects. The visual has been treated as an aspect that should be confronted with verbal language to gain ironic potential. In Paz's conceptual, intertextual reading of Duchamp in terms of meta-irony, not much attention was paid to visuality even as a subordinate factor. However, attempts have been made to discuss irony also as a more genuinely visual phenomenon, and this chapter will mainly focus on visual, "intratextual" irony in this narrower sense: irony in art that does not primarily rely on verbal factors such as titles.

As might be expected, visual art and artists are quite often characterized as ironic in a very vague and general sense. As in literature, irony may be conceived to be "a type of view" or some sort of "attitude" colored by "distance" that hovers over the creation of art.[3] This kind of ironic interpretation, sometimes made with references to Schlegel, is not only subjective, as is all ironic interpretation, but also indeterminate in the sense that it is difficult to argue for or against the case in point. However, there are a few critics and scholars who have tried to pin down more precise characteristics of allegedly ironic, visual art. Muecke, as noted, mentions "incongruities of formal properties" as a possibility for art and music to become ironic.[4] This proposition is reasonable enough but not very elaborated, and of course it always remains to be shown where these incongruities are to be found and why they should be called ironic.

The one painting that, according to my knowledge, has been most thoroughly scrutinized with the aid of irony and related notions is Velázquez's *Las meninas*, completed in 1656. In his discussion of meta-irony in Duchamp's *The Bride Stripped Bare by Her Bachelors, Even*, Paz finds a parallel to this very famous painting. It constitutes, Paz states, a self-sufficient world: "Nor is there any need of spectators because the work itself includes them."[5] John R. Searle interprets *Las meninas* in terms of paradox and ambiguity. He argues that the problem with this picture, so elaborately composed with a mirror revealing who occupies "our" (the spectators') position, is that it depicts the view of the model, not the artist. It has "all the eyemarks of classical illusionist painting," Searle states, "but it cannot be made consistent with these axioms."[6] Ann Hurley, too, emphasizes "the illusion that both model and spectator occupy the same, again incompatible, space," but she also rightly notes that the mirror, oddly enough, "reflects nothing from the painted room in which it

hangs," which is not very realistic.[7] Hurley's terminology includes the notion of both paradox and irony.

In the discussions on *Las meninas*, the main focus has been
on its formal aspects, but the problem of form merges with the
problem of fictionality, a favorite topic for ironic interpretations
of literature. This has inevitably led to comparisons with the conventions of pictorial representation: whether one wants it or not,
intratextual perspectives call for intertextual perspectives. Yet, if
one leaves *Las meninas*, the importance of the social context of
artistic production is stressed at least as often as the problem of
fictionality, and irony is hence seen as generated by conflicts between attitudes and political norms.[8] When the aspect of external
referentiality is focused on, the resulting irony may be said to be
more "extratextual" than "intratextual," but of course also formalistic (rhetorical or semiotic) analyses of irony in images rely
on various contexts. As a rule, knowledge available within certain
cultural communities is presupposed. The properties of images
that Geneviève Dolle describes in terms of *écart* [distance, gap],
contradiction, and *ironie* are thus not really visual traits, but
properties derived from the cultural context.[9] Needless to say,
formalistic analysis is basically nothing but systematized interpretation. This is explicitly admitted in Groupe μ's semiotically
oriented text "Ironique et iconique." Iconic irony, the group
maintains, is always a result of a meeting with another, heavily
coded semiotic system. They mention the Gestalt theory and emphasize that iconic irony arises in the interpretation of the beholder as a result of contextual frames: "the iconic cannot be
ironic in itself."[10]

Many aspects imply that this is a correct statement, but one
may discuss whether there is a difference between the visual and
the verbal when it comes to being "ironic in itself." In order to
do so, I will now turn to surrealism, the movement in art history
that, together with Dada, has probably most often been attached
to irony. Writing about Beardsley, Milly Heyd associates surrealism with irony, and Searle compares *Las meninas* to "surrealism
and cubism that are paradoxical from the standpoint of classical
pictorial representation."[11] In his famous book, *The Grotesque in
Art and Literature*, Wolfgang Kayser connects the grotesque, surrealism, and, to a certain extent, irony. Their common ground is
the fusion of incompatibilities, Kayser asserts.[12] Judi Freeman
discusses many of the titles of Duchamp, Picabia, and Miró in
terms of irony in her essay "Layers of Meaning: The Multiple
Readings of Dada and Surrealist Word-Images," and John C.

Welchman does not hesitate to claim that in Dada "(almost) everything is already ironic."[13] Katz-Freiman states that "Of all the avant-garde movements of the twentieth century, it was Surrealism that totally immersed itself in the dark realms of black humor, irony and absurd."[14]

René Magritte is especially mentioned by Katz-Freiman, and probably no other artist has been subject to more ironic interpretations than he has. In the only dissertation on irony in the visual arts that I know of, William August Becker gives Magritte a prominent place. On the other hand, however, irony is a far from universal tool for understanding his paintings.

Naturally, some writers on Magritte use the concept of irony in its most vague and general sense as some sort of artistic "distance,"[15] but it is more common to find the word *irony* connected to descriptions of certain paintings or specific motifs of Magritte. As might be expected, the many sibling concepts of irony are often almost indistinguishable from or used more or less as synonyms for irony. In an article dealing with Magritte and Poe, Renée Riese Hubert proposes several ironic readings of paintings by Magritte, and the concept of irony is used in close association with parody, paradox, ambiguity, and polyvalence.[16] Fred Miller Robinson, too, compares Magritte and Poe and connects the notions of contradiction and the comic to irony.[17] In an essay, I myself have argued for ironic interpretations of some of Magritte's paintings and furthermore discussed the vague borderlines between the notions of antithesis, contrast, contradiction, paradox, and irony.[18]

It is also common to discuss contradiction and paradox in Magritte's paintings without mentioning irony, as does Ralf Schiebler, among others.[19] One critic claims of a painting that it "embodies a visible paradox," and another one states that many of Magritte's paintings "explore the tensions and contradictions between linguistic signs and visual images."[20] In one article, contradiction and *le mystère* are discussed—and even mysticism has been mentioned as an aspect of Magritte's art.[21]

Many of these various interpretations follow the pattern of emphasizing verbal elements. Not only the fanciful titles of Magritte's paintings are of interest. There are also many paintings with words inscribed in them: words that often tend to highlight the very phenomenon of visual and verbal representation. By far the best known of these paintings is *La trahison des images* [*The Treason of Images*], completed in 1929. It depicts, in a very realistic way, a pipe; but below the image of the pipe there is a neatly formed inscription telling us that "Ceci n'est pas une pipe" [This is not a pipe].

It is obvious that it is possible to apply several interpretive strategies to a painting like this. The one that for most people probably announces itself first—simply because it is an interpretation that is inherent in the normal codes of reading, representation, and language use—is that there is a "contradiction of image by text."[22] One sees a pipe, and yet the text says that it is not a pipe. On the level of generally accepted conventions, one may furthermore conclude that this contradictive painting expresses a lie, that it is a joke, or that it is simply nonsense.

The almost universally accepted language convention that allows one to interpret *La trahison des images* in this way is that the expression "X is Y" may be an ellipsis of "X is a representation of Y." This is a convention that is reinforced every time one looks in an illustrated book or journal. It would undoubtedly be unbearably irritating if every text accompanying, for instance, photos always stated that the image is a *representation* of this or that actress or minister. You might say that the copula "is" is a kind of metonymical glue: to place some words stating that *this* "is" a pipe very close to a representation of a pipe is normally equivalent to stating that *the representation* of the pipe "resembles" a pipe.

These are facts that everyone knows without having to consider them, but one also knows that the text in Magritte's painting reads "This is not a pipe." Nevertheless, one may choose to take this statement literally. If one puts parentheses around the implied words "a representation of," the statement "This is not a pipe" suddenly appears to be perfectly true and not the least contradictory. Many writers on Magritte have quite rightly concluded that "the painted image is not a pipe, but a representation."[23] Seen from this point of view, the words "This is a pipe" would be mendacious if written in Magritte's painting.

This reading "resolves the problem" and "makes sense" of *La trahison des images*, but on the other hand it introduces a problem that is located not so much in the painting itself as in the world of language and images at large: images are "traitors," as the title suggests; they "are" not what they pretend to be. Writing about *La trahison des images*, Suzanne Rodin Pucci states that "the codes of reading and viewing at first glance appear to sustain each other in a traditional hierarchy of representation, while actually they are introduced to undo a time-honored felicitous collaboration."[24] Many others have scrutinized the intricate problems of representation and referentiality to which Magritte's painting gives rise.[25]

It might, however, be argued that the contention that "This is not a pipe" is simply true is a rather flat reading, as it might be argued that the painting in itself is quite poor. However, one may continue interpreting *La trahison des images* and find even more ambiguities of a linguistic and philosophical nature. One may call in Saussure and penetrate the arbitrariness of language, or discuss the painting the way Foucault does, focusing on the many ambiguities in the assertion "This is not a pipe." Does the word "This" refer to the image of the pipe, to the word "This" itself or to the whole sentence "This is not a pipe"?[26] Otherwise, one may—like Rudolf Arnheim, who is vainly looking for symbolic or allegorical meaning—conclude that "Unfortunately a pipe is all it is."[27]

Finally, one may choose the interpretive strategy of irony. Jonathan Weil follows the track of Foucault and asks how one is supposed to know for sure to what words refer. "This," the word itself, is certainly not identical to a pipe, neither the word nor the object, and the image of the pipe is of course not a real pipe. The painting is, Weil states, "magnificently ironic."[28] Becker is of the opinion that *La trahison des images* "has minimal presence as a painting" and that it takes us very close to "verbal irony."[29] Magritte's image certainly looks like a pipe, wherefore the assertion "This is not a pipe" might be interpreted as, among other things, an ironic assertion.

La trahison des images thus displays traits that have been seen as incongruous and even contradictive. However, the incongruities have been found on different levels, and they have been regarded as more or less important. Due to the differences between the notions of ambiguity, opposition, and contradiction, which are after all not identical, differing ironic interpretations have been put forward. Becker settles for the rather simple sort of irony that springs from what he sees as a contradiction of almost genuinely verbal nature, whereas Weil penetrates many sorts of opposition and does not feel content with irony of any lower dignity than "magnificent."

The interpretations of *La trahison des images* are a case in point for the vague, perhaps even nonexistent borderline between irony in verbal texts and irony in images. The connections between the two semiotic systems are clearly strong enough to allow one to "read" them together, and consequently also to create ironic meaning that one would "place" in the "space" between word and image and in the contextual "space" of conventions that surrounds the decoding of both words and images. One is again faced with the practical impossibility of distinguishing between what has been called "verbal" and "situational" irony.

It should then be clear to see that the historical emergence of "visual irony" is a natural, unavoidable consequence of the development of the concept of irony. There is no definite difference between verbal and visual semiosis, and crucial notions such as opposition and incongruity are distinct enough to do their service in the act of ironic interpretation, but vague enough to be able to cross the border between the verbal and visual domains. The fact that surrealism and Magritte have rather frequently been the focus of ironic interpretation is partly explained by the principle of closeness. Verbal language is conceptual, and surrealism and Magritte have also been interpreted very much in conceptual terms. Becker, who wrote a dissertation on irony in the visual arts, states that he has selected in Magritte "an artist whose work, I feel, stands as that of an ironist in the most obvious sense."[30] He stresses the conceptual character of Magritte's images, the most obvious reason for which is the fact that his art may be said to be situated somewhere "between" literature and visual art.

On the whole it is really amazing how much has been written about Magritte from an intellectual, philosophical, or linguistic point of view. Becker, however, thinks that Magritte's work is ironic also "in a much deeper sense"; his images are not simply verbal ironies transformed to images, Becker maintains.[31] When it comes to describing the "deeper sense" in which he finds Magritte ironic, Becker is not very explicit, however, but he mentions phenomena that involve opposites and that in my opinion definitely tend toward mental categories of interpretation: "the tension of the mystery, the unsolvable riddle, the enigma, the psychological contradiction."[32]

In a rewarding article, R. Jongen emphasizes the inclination to conceptualize surrealistic images and become involved in "an intense rhetorical activity."[33] He points out that it is not the visual items represented in the paintings that in themselves decide how to conceptualize the images, but the viewer. This is, although Jongen does not discuss irony, a very important point. As is known, it is often far from obvious which term is the best for describing a certain phenomenon in a text, a painting, or a piece of music. Jongen discusses the notions of metaphor and metonymy, but of course irony is also part of the viewer's "conceptual hypotheses."[34] Often one may simultaneously "read" Magritte's paintings, I claim, in terms of similarity (metaphor), closeness (metonymy), and difference (irony).

Groupe μ, one remembers, claims that visual (what they prefer to call iconic) irony arises in the interpretation of the beholder as a result of his or her contextual frames: "the iconic cannot be ironic in itself." This is true, I have already asserted: contexts, codes, and norms are always the heart of the matter. Yet, it is important to emphasize that visual irony is neither more nor less dependent on contexts than irony in verbal texts. In spite of the more overtly conceptual character of verbal language, the interpretive maneuvers in the reading of literature include the same sort of contextualization as the reading of visual art. The existence of a logical contradiction in language does not automatically lead to the existence of irony. The nonexistence of logical contradictions in images also does not lead to the nonexistence of visual irony. Irony is a mode of seeing, and the glasses one needs for finding irony in images are no stronger than those the literary critic needs. Neither the verbal nor the visual can be ironic in itself.

Nevertheless, it must be remembered that *doxa*—that is, "meaning"—is present in a weaker sense in the visual arts. In literature, it is true, one can often distinguish fairly well between, for instance, contrast, antithesis, and contradiction or paradox, but in the visual arts and, indeed, in music this is more difficult. Images, not even the "conceptual" paintings of Magritte, cannot actually "state" or "propose" anything. In his discussion of *La trahison des images*, Foucault opposes the inclination to talk about a "contradiction" between words and image in this painting: "Contradiction could exist only between two statements, or within one and the same statement," he states.[35] If Foucault is right—and I think he is, if one is to hold on to the strict logical claims of the notion of contradiction—it naturally follows that contradictions cannot exist in any sort of images. When, for instance, Cook writes à propos Duchamp that "A contradiction obtains between the visual and the verbal,"[36] the use of the term *contradiction* might be said to be unfortunate.

However, this does not mean that irony does not belong to the conceptual frames of Magritte or Duchamp. There is no basic difference between ironic interpretations of literature and visual art. One might say that the conceptual richness of verbal language is an advantage when circumscribing irony, but on the other hand it could be argued that the relative conceptual stringency of verbal language is deceptive for ironic interpretation. Irony is not to be identified with its related concepts. It is not primarily "in" the verbal or visual texts, and it is not even "in" the contradictions and incongruities; it is in the attitude of the interpreter. Hence a perceived, vague "opposition" justifies an ironic interpretation as well as a verbal, logical contradiction.

Another crucial notion that has been connected to irony from the very beginning is "negation." The expression "to negate something" is not as strong as "to contradict something," but the relationship is clear. Doane maintains that "irony must be supported by a medium which is capable of signifying negation or contradiction. The iconic sign, by itself, is unable to do so."[37] Again, I would say that the stress on *by itself* is slightly misleading, and it is not uncontroversial to state that images lack the capacity of expressing negation. W. J. T. Mitchell observes that pictorial representation can be defined as a subset of the linguistic system, a "language which is incapable of expressing negation"; but he maintains that "sheer sensory perception" is the only image that lacks this capacity.[38]

This seems to be an acceptable contention, because as soon as images are related to a context—that is, as soon as the visual signs are related to the codes of perception and the norms of the beholder—negations may appear indirectly (without the verbal signs "no" or "not" being physically present). All meaning is given shape in the act of interpretation, and it is an obvious fact that one understands many images as being fraught with conflicts and incongruities in their internal or external relations. In interpreting images, the decision to call these conflicts "contradictions," "negations," or something else is of course not entirely unimportant or uninteresting, but it is not, I believe, decisive for the existence or nonexistence of irony. Roth-Lindberg, who interprets paintings by Hals and Goya in terms of irony, therefore has good reason for starting out from the contention that the visual structures of images may express negations and oppositions.[39] In practice this simply means that images may be understood to express negations when put into a contextual, perhaps conceptual framework.

I have argued extensively for the contention that irony is preferably to be seen as an interpretive strategy on the part of the perceiver. All interpretive strategies are a result of, among other factors, the way one *thinks* about what one perceives. That readers of art and literature do think when they interpret should perhaps not be necessary to emphasize (the need for pointing out that people who interpret differently *do not* think is probably more urgent), but I believe that it is worthwhile to consider some mental aspects of the interpretive processes involved in the forming of ironic meaning. For that reason I will again focus on some of the most crucial terms that have been linked to ironic interpretations: contradiction, contrast, opposition, incongruity, and so forth. These terms are, I will argue, spatial metaphors that are in no way limited to the verbal area.

IRONY AND SPATIALITY

W. J. T. Mitchell, among others, has argued for the importance of spatial thinking and structuring in our reading of literary texts. When readers conceptualize what they read, they tend to think in terms of space. Spatial terms used to describe literature are certainly in a way metaphoric, but Mitchell claims—rightly, I think—that "every act of knowledge involves a metaphoric leap."[40]

In his book *Visual Thinking* from 1969, and also in later articles, Rudolf Arnheim develops his thesis that "thinking is impossible without recourse to perceptual images."[41] In Arnheim's view, thinking and perception cannot be separated, and he stresses the inescapable interaction between "direct perception," "stored experience," and "imagination." Perception in the broader sense, he states, "must include mental imagery and its relation to direct sensory observation."[42]

Arnheim bases his arguments on several psychological studies, and one of his aims is to blur the age-old distinction between perception and thinking. He demonstrates that not only does one process images mentally already "before" or "at the same time" as one perceives them, but also that that part of one's thinking that does not immediately spring from perception is nevertheless "shaped" by visual categories. Seeing is thinking, and thinking is seeing. "Thinking calls for images, and images contain thought."[43] In practice, it is impossible to separate the two notions of "seeing" and "thinking" if one takes them broadly, which is indicated by, among other factors, the very strong inclination of teachers and scholars to visualize ideas. Yet, "perceptual and pictorial shapes are not only translations of thought products," Arnheim emphasizes, they are "the very flesh and blood of thinking itself."[44]

The word "thinking" is used as a term applicable in both art and science, and he does not hesitate to discuss perceiving and thinking in terms of both aesthetic and conceptual categories. The conceptual is visual and, conversely, the visual is conceptual. Arnheim sees the world of visual art as an important but not significantly different part of the perceived world. Looking at images is both seeing and thinking, reading books is both thinking and seeing.

Arnheim maintains that it is in "the perception of shape" that "the beginnings of concept formation" lie; concepts are not "handled in empty space."[45] One has mental images of both objects and concepts, and the visual nature of a concept "is not different in principle from pictorial representation in drawing and painting."[46] If I understand Arnheim right, he believes that a visualization of a theoretical concept has basically the same character of iconicity as a visual representation of a physical object. This is possibly true, I would say, although of course difficult to definitely prove—or disprove. The idea that abstract thinking was originally formed after the patterns of, or as an aspect of, visual perception is reasonable enough, but of course the processes in the human brain have at least partly developed to such a degree that iconicity is perhaps not always the best term to describe the relation between the "inner" thought and its "outer" representation. It is, however, hard to deny that visuality is always in some respect an important aspect of thinking and concept formation. How many of the words used in only these last sentences do not in fact denote visual "representations," "images," or "metaphors" of ideas? Let me mention only the most obvious ones: basically, character, formed, patterns, aspect, partly, degree, relation, between, inner, outer, formation.

If it is true, as Mitchell and others have claimed, that all knowledge involves "a metaphoric leap," it is certainly not meaningful to lay too much stress on the question of whether the visuality of concepts is "factual" or "figural." In fact, Arnheim hovers between these two modes of describing the relationship between thoughts and their representations. "Some visualizations of theoretical concepts can be described as routine metaphors," he asserts, but he also discusses the figurative quality of *all* theoretical speech.[47] Yet the term "figurative" seems to mean at least two different things, and this crucial ambiguity might be said to deconstruct the ideas of Arnheim. Figurative means both "not literal" and "consisting of visual figures that exist literally." The question to be answered is thus whether the literally figurative language is literal or figurative.

Perhaps Arnheim's project may be said to be to argue for the literal existence of those images that are often understood as "merely metaphors." Yet, the distinction is difficult to uphold for at least two reasons, and these difficulties might actually support Arnheim's ideas. The first reason is that both "literal" and "metaphorical" visual representations are based on the principle of iconicity. If one follows Peirce, the metaphor is a variation of the icon generated through some sort of parallelism. The second and related reason is that visual representations are not possible to divide into those figures that "really" look like and those that only "somehow," through some sort of parallelism, look like an object or a concept. Iconicity is simply not an unambiguous phenomenon.

A further complication that is not really considered by Arnheim is that the mental representations of concepts are not necessarily "literal," "metaphorical," or something in between. Rather than saying that all knowledge involves "a metaphoric leap," as Mitchell proposes, I would say that all knowledge involves a figurative leap. The figurativity of mental representations may also be of a noniconic, nonmetaphoric kind, being based on the principle of closeness: metonymy. Closeness is in a way, one might argue, a visual quality, but it is not an iconic quality. As the notion of visuality might easily be confused with or reduced to iconicity, I prefer to use the notion of spatiality that embraces both metaphoric iconicity and metonymic closeness more smoothly than the notion of visuality.

Nevertheless, I think that Arnheim has a very important point when he refuses to accept that visual representations in images and language are nothing more than "routine metaphors." Concepts that are described in terms of visuality are *in themselves* visual, or spatial. As an example, Arnheim mentions the notion of "depth of thought," which is obviously derived from physical depth. However, what is more, Arnheim maintains, "depth is not merely a convenient metaphor to describe the mental phenomenon but the only possible way of even conceiving of that notion." Human thinking "cannot go beyond the patterns suppliable by the human senses."[48]

This makes sense, and I think that Arnheim is right. There is only one problem: "literal" figurativity also always "looks" as if it were figurative, and it is perhaps impossible to prove that there are nonmetaphoric (nonfigurative) iconic relations between concepts and their representations. How could one see the difference? It is probably true that thinking cannot go "beyond" the human senses, but "where" does "beyond" "begin"? Trapped in the visual patterns of thinking, it is difficult to imagine a language having the capacity of expressing nonvisual thinking—or is it rather so that we are trapped in the figurative patterns of language, and therefore find it impossible to describe nonvisual thinking?

There are consequently some problems connected to Arnheim's ideas. He may not be entirely right—but for my line of argument in the following it suffices that he is partly right. Thinking is about "seeing," I submit, and this "seeing" is in one respect very literal, but it also often includes displacements and distortions that give it qualities that one tends to call metonymical or metaphorical. A metonymy is based on closeness—not identity. A metaphor is based on similarity—not identity. If not taken literally, the notion of "depth of thought" might be interpreted as both a metaphor and a metonymy. Because one does not know how a deep thought "really" looks, it is difficult to say whether the verbal representation of it is "close" or "similar," "associative" or "formal."

When one thinks about concepts, it is hence extremely difficult to tell whether one will "see" them or "visualize" them "exactly" as they are or "approximately" as they are—because they do not exist but in the thinking itself. Due to this uncertainty I prefer to discuss in terms of figurativity when it comes to concepts that are represented verbally, well aware that figurativity is perhaps all we have. Verbal representations of concepts might thus be called spatial metaphors. I think that the term *spatial metaphor* is appropriate although it somehow obscures the fact that concepts might also be represented metonymically. After all, the word "metaphoric" is often used as a synonym for "figurative."

It should again be noted that I prefer the notion of spatial instead of visual, not least because I presume that people who were born blind certainly have the capacity to think in spite of their lack of visual experience of the world. Blind people experience the world very much in terms of spatiality. The notion of spatiality is furthermore to be preferred because it may also include the sensations given by other senses. Thinking is certainly not connected only to seeing, but also to touching, feeling, moving, hearing, smelling, and tasting.

Among the many concepts that are best understood as spatial metaphors, some have to do with problems related to the organization of space. Space might be seen as a three-dimensional structure, and ordinarily spatial metaphors visualize certain relations between "items" within this structure. Sometimes, though, there is not "space enough" for these "items," and "collisions" occur. Arnheim notes that "properties of physical objects and actions are applied without hesitation to non-physical ones by people all over the earth . . . a clash of opinions is depicted in the same way as a crash of cars."[49]

This leads back to irony. In my view, irony can be seen as not only one of the main tropes or figures, but even as one of the basic principles of thinking. Interpreting ironically, I have argued extensively, is a question of interpreting what takes place around one. Indeed, irony is a strategy of interpreting what one *sees* in the world, and to *see* things and events in the world, or to *see* the world itself, means that one both perceives and thinks at the same time. One interprets things not *after* having perceived them, but perceives things *as* one interprets them. Irony is simply one out of many modes or strategies of seeing, and the space of ironic vision includes more or less solid "items" that "collide," "strive to occupy the same place," or are actually "placed at the very same spatial spot."

This proposition of mine needs some support, I guess, and I find it in the many notions that through history have followed the concept of irony as inescapable shadows. In interpretive practice, irony (in speech, texts, images, and music) is always circumscribed with the aid of terms such as *opposition, paradox, contrast,* and *incongruity.* All these terms are spatial metaphors, as I will soon try to show. They express spatial relations that are clearly "seen" or "felt" by the interpreter of irony in literature, which explains why irony has been "found" also in images: spatial relations are certainly one of the most important aspects of visual art, and naturally these visual spatial relations may be similar to the spatial relations seen or perceived in irony in verbal language. Hence there need not be any fundamental difference between interpreting verbal texts and images in terms of irony. Already Cicero and Quintilian *saw* the "morphological" similarities between an ironic statement and a certain type of discourse, or even the attitude prevailing throughout a whole life, and after the German Romanticists' re-recognition of Socratic irony, the blinkers that prevented people from seeing irony also in images were finally removed.

I thus assert that one can "see" irony in both literature and visual art, and that one sees it in a sense that is less metaphorical than is usually recognized. From this it follows that the concept of irony is in its essence also a mental image. Originally, if for the sake of simplicity one assumes that irony "started" as anti-phrasis, irony was visual also in the simple sense that it was de-fined as simultaneously hearing one thing (words) and seeing other things (gestures and mimicry) that through convention in-dicate the opposite. The mind of the perceiver is thus invaded by two "signals" that are in conflict because they try to occupy the same "place" in mental space. One of the signals is originally ver-bal, the other one visual, but when they meet in the mind they have become compatible enough to be perceived as incompati-ble. This is an "intermediate" situation that is more or less in ac-cordance with how one may perceive a conflict when one sees Magritte's depiction of a pipe and reads the words attached to it. Nowadays, when it is accepted to presume that the words of literature have been freed from their context of production, words still express concepts that have visual character, but one sees these concepts only with one's inner eyes.

Visuality, or spatiality, is thus a very important aspect of com-prehension of language. When one "creates" meaning, one "forms" meaning that can be "seen" in mental images or "felt" in mental entities. In my view (a fitting metaphor that is perhaps not a metaphor), the creation of ironic meaning is a mental act that involves the forming of "clashing" entities that are related to each other along a rather simple "line," on a more complex "surface," or in an even more complicated "space." Perhaps one might even add time as a fourth dimension, which would mean that an ironic clash might also involve two incompatible entities "changing places." This sort of irony could then be seen as a spa-tial relationship that is transformed in time.

It seems to me that the most obvious method for seeking the spatial roots of ironic interpretation is to investigate the etymol-ogy of the words that are connected to irony. The etymology of the word *irony* itself is unknown, as already noted, although one approach has been that the Greek word *eironeia* may stem from *iron* [opposite] and *onoma* [term].[50] When it comes to *contradic-tion, antiphrasis,* and *antithesis,* the etymology is clearer. *Dictionis* (Latin) means "utterance," *phrasis* (Greek) means ap-proximately "expression," and *thesis* (Greek) means "arrange-ment" (of statements). These are terms that are rather closely associated with verbal language, but the prefixes emphasize the spatial "order" of the "verbal items." One of the meanings of *contra* (Latin) is "on the opposite side," and *anti* (Greek) means in particular "against."

Contradiction, antiphrasis, and *antithesis* are notions that are mainly associated with the interpretation of irony within limited texts. Most critics hesitate to use them in interpreting larger contexts. They are, as I see them, clearly linear, describing the relationship between two poles of verbal meaning. In order to visualize their character, one would probably draw something like two arrows pointing toward each other. The three notions are not identical, but their visual shapes are quite simple and quite similar. In the context of the narrower definitions of *irony*, these notions are the most "correct" because they are explicitly connected to verbal language and indicate some sort of *either/or* situation—especially *contradiction* and *antiphrasis*. Nevertheless, they have a spatial, albeit rather simple linear character.

These rather "strict" terms are, however, not commonly used in ironic interpretation of literature, and of course they are even more rare in interpretations of nonverbal texts. Instead, irony, even irony in literature, is generally associated with notions that are not directly connected to verbality. Two of these are contrariety and opposition. These very common notions, also, are representatives of a primarily linear mode of thinking, I would say, although freed from the linguistic aspects of contradiction, antiphrasis, and antithesis. *Contra*, as already noted, may mean "on the opposite side," and *oppositio* (late Latin) means, approximately, "a movement against" or "a position against." *Oppositio* stems from the word *ponere* (Latin) meaning "to put." The mental images of contrariety and opposition are, I submit, in accordance with these etymologies: one sees "items" that are put near the two extremes of a line or on the two sides of a border, or one sees "items" that move toward each other on a straight line.

Ambiguity and paradox are two notions that are situated within the domain of verbal language and yet have an even more pronounced character of spatiality. These notions, I claim, are primarily seen as surfaces, as "webs" of relations between meanings. *Ambiguitas* is Latin and means "doubt." It is thus not explicitly connected to spatiality, but the notion of doubt suggests a multitude of possible, interrelated alternatives from which one chooses as when one chooses roads or paths. Ambiguity is meaning that emerges from the same "place" but is "directed toward" or "located at" different "places," which makes us feel doubt. *Paradoxos* is Greek and means literally "against the public opinion." The term is a combination of two words: *para*, meaning among other words "against," "at the side of," and *doxa*, meaning "meaning" or "rumor." The firmly established meaning of paradox, though, is that it is a contradiction that somehow "makes sense," which for me evokes the figure of a triangle: the line of the contradiction completed with two lines that emerge from the two opposites and unite in the third "point of truth" situated beside the two opposites. Paradox might also be visualized as two different "objects of meaning" occupying the same space and together forming a third figure.

Notions connected to irony that evoke mental images of surfaces or space are, I believe, contrast, incongruity, and conflict. The word *contrast* comes from *contra*, which means, as stated, "on the opposite side," but the meaning of *contrast* is much vaguer and broader than, for instance, the meaning of *contradiction*. In my view, the "opposite sides" of a contrast are to be found on a field or in a space rather than on a line.

Incongruity also is generally connected to mental images that are two- or three-dimensional. If a contrast is formed by items that "look very different" and perhaps even "seem to repel each other" when juxtaposed, an incongruity is visualized as items the forms of which do not fit together, like two or more jigsaw pieces that belong to different puzzles. In Latin, *congruere* means "to coincide" in time or in space, and it might be noted that in plane geometry "congruent figures" are of the same size and shape. Needless to say, the addition of the negative prefix *in-* inverts the meaning to "not to coincide."

The Latin word from which *conflict* is derived, *conflictus*, means "collision." One may remember that Arnheim mentioned the two words "clash" and "crash" when arguing for the close relationship between the two worlds of concepts and objects. The word "collision" is also a good case in point for the intimate connections between the visual qualities of mental and physical phenomena. Collisions occur between both objects and ideas, and to paraphrase Arnheim one might say that to state that there is a conflict between two ideas or concepts or that they collide is not "merely" to open the way to metaphoric interpretation; it is also to state something that cannot be put in other words. It cannot be put in words that are "less metaphoric."

The notion of conflict is closely associated with human behavior. A conflict in its most radical sense is a battle between armed people, something that very literally takes place in both space and time and has considerable consequences. In a way, then, "conflict" might be said to be the most general (and also the vaguest) notion that is commonly used to circumscribe irony. It is perhaps also the notion that is spatial in the most pronounced and obvious way. Also, a battle between conflicting meanings or concepts takes place, as one visualizes it, as it is created in one's thinking, in both space and time.

It must be emphasized that the experience of space seems also to be a fact for those interpreters who prefer to stick to the conceptualizations of irony as something that emerges from intentions or the "texts" themselves. Not only are the binary oppositions—for instance, in a contradiction—of a spatial nature, but also notions such as incongruity, conflict, and opposition that are often used in pseudo-objective ways are fundamentally spatial. There is certainly a considerable difference between the binary, linear, linguistic phenomenon of contradiction and the four-dimensional, anthropomorphic phenomenon of conflict, but they are nevertheless related in being spatial metaphors for irony.

Of course, all this has very much to do with "structure," a notion that is fundamental for the description and interpretation not only of literature, painting, music, and film, to mention only a few categories of art, but of almost everything in this world. The extreme popularity of the notion of structure in most areas of human investigation indicates that Arnheim's theory of the fundamentally visual character of human thinking is very plausible. Structure is the organization of space, and spatiality is an aspect of the perception of all the senses.

Although it is rather obvious, it must be stressed that the spatial creation of irony is difficult to describe in a very strict manner because it "takes place" in a mental universe of images: images that hold "conflicts" of rather different nature. It is no wonder then that so many terms have been used to circumscribe irony, and no wonder that it is virtually impossible to make satisfying taxonomies of irony. The morphology of spatial conflicts is endless.

Finally the importance of the notion of spatial metaphor for the interpretation of irony in images must also be restated. The point is that if one accepts the view that irony in literature is actually *best* understood as an interpretive strategy that relies heavily on spatial thinking, it becomes clear why ironic interpretations of visual art have become increasingly popular and subject to fewer and fewer reservations. Spatiality has always been an important aspect of ironic communication and interpretation, I assert, and the more the strictly verbal and linguistic definitions of irony have been backgrounded in both theory and interpretive practice, the more the "natural" affinity between irony and spatiality has surfaced—and the more the "natural" affinity between irony and the visual has become visible. This is not only because one actually *sees* most so-called works of art, but also because one *thinks* of them in spatial categories that are in principle identical to the spatial categories with the aid of which one thinks about literary texts and verbal language in general.

SPACY MAGRITTE

The conclusion in the last section was that spatiality in visual art is a quality of both the physical object and the mental conceptualization of it: the perception and the thinking. Consequently it may be concluded that the spatial metaphors of ironic interpretations can be "applied" to all sorts of images. Furthermore, images are only one of the many phenomena in the world that are perceived, comprehended, and conceptualized with the aid of spatial thinking.

However, there are some images that hold an exceptional position in terms of irony—namely, those that represent a spatial universe that does not make sense as a "real" spatial universe. All images must be interpreted in order to mean something, of course, but there is a certain kind of images that definitely tend to be seen as "impossible": images that follow certain conventions of realistic depiction and yet violate them. The result is that they bring about a "clash of seeing" within the interpretive communities that accept pictorial devices such as the illusion of perspective and the representation of three dimensions on a flat surface.

Two artists that very clearly tend to evoke this sort of "clash of seeing" are Maurits Escher and Oscar Reutersvärd. The latter of these explicitly calls his images "impossible figures" and the famous images of Escher are generally considered deceptive for the eye. Images like these, it might be maintained, are more apt than others to be interpreted ironically because the spatial metaphors of irony in them find spatial "equivalences" that are very "close" to the pictorial surface. For those spectators who are equipped with a set of ironic metaphors and who belong to the kind of interpretive communities that I recently described, the irony is literally there to be *seen*. The spatial conflicts take place in what is understood to be "the image itself." It might be mentioned that the cover illustration of Booth's book *A Rhetoric of Irony* is such a "pseudo-geometrical" figure: a figure that is impossible to make sense of according to the established codes of represented space. Muecke's most prominent example in his brief discussion of visual irony is also an "impossible" image: a man engaged in the process of drawing himself.[51]

In fact no image is ever seen "in itself," of course, but there is nevertheless a certain difference between seeing irony in the misrepresentation of space and seeing irony in the "inner" conceptual relations of an image. One of my reasons for concluding this is that the reluctance to interpret images in terms of irony has been weakened during the century of modernism and postmodernism, a century during which also the old codes of representing "realistic" space have been partly annulled. Tendencies to "flatten" the images could be noticed already by the end of the nineteenth century in artists such as Gauguin and Cézanne, but it is in modernism that the representation of space is finally stood on its head. Cubism might be mentioned, of course, but again the importance of surrealism must be emphasized. I think that the tendency to interpret surrealistic images ironically is closely connected to the specific representation of space in surrealism. I have noted that surrealism is often understood in terms of conceptuality—and concepts are spatial. One explanation of the eagerness for connecting Magritte and conceptuality is of course his abundant use of verbal language in his paintings; another is his original representations of spatiality.

In surrealism, and especially in Magritte, one is apt to see morphological and spatial incongruities in the very concrete sense that I described above, incongruities that draw attention to the artistic medium in itself and hence also highlight a meta-perspective. Many critics have written about irony in Magritte without being very specific, and even more critics have written about the awkward spatiality in his paintings without connecting it to irony. Some, however, have seen both irony and spatial conflicts in Magritte (in one of his paintings he "offers two spaces instead of one," Hubert argues), but without connecting the two phenomena.[52] The possibility of seeing the spatial conflicts in Magritte as "equivalents" to the many spatial metaphors associated with irony should not be ignored, however. It opens up a new path for understanding why and how irony, surrealism, and Magritte cling to each other so firmly. Many of Magritte's paintings may simply be seen as depicting a spatiality that is incongruous: it is not possible to choose a manner of seeing that "resolves" the conflicts that emerge from the clash between the conventions of spatial representation and the devices of Magritte—as one sometimes finds it impossible to "make sense" of a verbal text and hence feels directed to the spatial metaphors of irony. In both cases one deals with visual "figures" that are "placed" in some sort of "opposition" and yet are part of "the same" space.

On a more general level, one of the most striking devices of surrealism consists of the juxtaposing of items that are incongruous or sharply contrasting from the point of view of, I believe, many interpretive communities. Yet, what is an incongruity? An exponent of New Criticism would probably say that even what is apprehended to be the harshest of incongruities could always be harmonized in one way or another, whereas a representative of poststructuralism would doubtless maintain that many incongruities remain intact and insoluble. Again, it is the strategy of the interpreter, his or her mode of *seeing*, that determines the results.

Perhaps particularly in surrealism a certain aspect of incongruities and contrasts may be emphasized, however. A juxtaposition that might at first seem to be merely perplexing may be interpreted as a transformation of the language of dreams, mingled with displacements, compressions, and hidden affinities. Seemingly unrelated items might, if interpreted as signs from the unconscious, reveal themselves as aspects of one and the same phenomenon. This is a good example of how the interpretive construction of similarities and potentially ironic contraries is a result of a meeting between a visual text and the norms and contexts supplied by the reader. Items and events that are "incongruous" and "incomprehensible" in the spatial setting of reality may be interpreted as wholly "congruous" and "explicable" in the spatial setting of a dream. As everyone knows, the character of time and space in dreams is often completely different from how it is perceived when one is awake. In dreams people and objects are transformed and can be seen as two or more persons or items at the same time, and the chronology often reminds one more of a modern novel than the experience of reality. Freud notes that dreams feel themselves at liberty "to represent any element by its wishful contrary" and compares this phenomenon to the philologist Karl Abel's interesting discovery that in the oldest languages known to us "there are a fair number of words with two meanings, one of which is the exact opposite of the other."[53]

The task of deciding which images are "congruous" or "incongruous," "harmonic" or filled with "conflicts," and "nonironic" or "ironic" is thus a risky one. Even if everyone sees the same paintings by Magritte, everyone sees them differently as everyone thinks differently: mental images differ. Again this does not mean that it is meaningless to interpret. By way of interpreting works of art and interpreting interpretations of work of art, one learns a great deal about both *how* art can be seen in different ways and *why* the spatial images of it differ between individuals and interpretive communities. Interpretations consequently tell things worth knowing about both art and people.

Suzi Gablik is an influential critic who has tried to say something that is generally valid for Magritte regarding contrasts and incongruities. She asserts that the painting entitled *Affinités électives* [*Elective Affinities*], probably painted in 1936 and depicting a huge egg in a cage, is an early example of a new period in Magritte's work. In his early work, Gablik maintains, Magritte was chiefly interested in contrasts, and in his later work he emphasized affinities.[54] Gablik is certainly aware of the simplification inherent in this division into two periods, but it nevertheless indicates what I see as two opposite tendencies in the interpretation of Magritte's paintings rather than in the images themselves: some of them are said to deal with contrasts that are not so easily interpreted as hidden affinities, whereas some—such as the painting of the egg in the cage—are said to link contrasts together by way of fairly simple associations.

Instead of arguing for or against the interpretive strategies chosen by the critics of Magritte, I will conclude this chapter by way of looking at some paintings by Magritte and suggest some ways of getting a grip on irony and spatiality. His oeuvre embodies many variations of spatial transformations and arrangements, some of which are perfectly possible to imagine as a "realistic" although very unusual state of affairs—such as depicted objects that are partly a bottle, partly a carrot (*L'explication* [*The Explanation*], 1952), or partly a fish, partly a woman (*L'invention collective* [*Collective Invention*], 1935). Confronted with these two paintings, it is perhaps more likely that one will interpret the latter in terms of irony, I submit, because it can be seen as a spatial inversion of the image of a mermaid. Magritte's "mermaid" that has the legs of a woman and the head of a fish might be said to form an intertextual irony.

One of Magritte's paintings, *La bataille de l'Argonne* [*The Battle of the Argonne*] from 1959, depicts a huge rock hovering side by side with a cloud over a landscape. The rock and the cloud are about the same size, but apart from that their characteristics differ: the cloud is white and seems to be soft, the rock is colored and angular. This painting can be understood to be a realistic image, if one takes it for granted that the rock is captured by the artist on its way to the ground. However, if one insists on seeing the painting according to the codes of realism, one must conclude that the rock is obviously much too cool to be a meteor, and the pictorial devices in general give the impression of a non-moving rock. The spatial arrangement is in itself fully possible, but the laws of nature seem to be violated within the "realistic" spatiality. Yet, how does one *see* these depicted objects? Does the similarity between the rock and the cloud, for instance, form a metaphor for spiritual balance? Is the representation of a heavy, weightless rock an ironic image of the unbearable burdens of life that in spite of everything one manages to uphold? Is it perhaps possible to see both these relations, the similarity and the contrary, and hold on to both interpretations at the same time? It all depends on the focus, the norms, and the interpretive strategies of the beholder.

Many of Magritte's paintings have a meta-perspective. They depict paintings on easels that "cover" the landscape behind the canvas and yet display a painted surface that seems to be identical to what is covered. Of course, it is impossible to "know" what would "really" be seen behind one of these depicted canvases, because all that exist are the painted canvases of Magritte that invite us to think about the codes of representation. Again, these paintings may be seen to be fully in accordance with the codes of realism—and yet they tease the spatial thinking of the beholder. One possibility is indeed to choose to see the depicted canvases as displaying images of space that ironically invert or distort the "real," invisible spaces "behind" the depicted canvases. However, this is, of course, one out of many possible interpretive strategies.

At least one of Magritte's paintings may be seen as also including time in its spatial world. In *Les travaux d'Alexandre* [*The Labors of Alexander*] from 1950, one sees an axe that has been tied to the ground by a root of a tree that is cut down. If one chooses to see the painting as visually realistic and the axe as the tool that actually cut down the tree, one has to conclude that either the tree has continued to grow as a stub (the tree's revenge on the axe!), or that the axe did its job *after* it got stuck under the root (the axe's revenge on the tree!). In the latter case one is faced with incongruous time that is as impossible to conceive as are some of the spatial traits in Magritte's world.

The paintings that I have hitherto discussed are all possible to interpret within the codes of realism. However, Magritte has also

painted images in which the represented space holds a visual incongruity that is definitely incompatible with the real world.
Some of Magritte's paintings are likely to cause confusion because what one sees in them, if one tries to decode the images as
representations of three-dimensionality, is simply impossible to
imagine as spatial reality. In one painting (*La bonne aventure*
[*Good Fortune*], 1939) the "foreground" has the contours of
buildings, but its "surface" is depicted as a dark, starry sky with
a moon while the "background" is depicted as a somewhat
lighter sky at sunset or dawn. This scenery is certainly impossible
to imagine as a part of reality. One may see it as a dream landscape or as an ironic inversion of "private space" and "outer
space." In another painting (*Le blanc-seing* [*The Blank Signa-
ture*], 1965) one sees a depiction of a horse that partly "disappears" behind the leaves in the "background" rather than behind
the trees in the "foreground." "Spatially," A. M. Hammacher
states, "the rider and the woods become an absurdity."[55]

A variation of the spatial duality foreground/background is the
duality indoors/outdoors. *L'éloge de la dialectique* [*In Praise of
Dialectics*] from 1937 depicts a window and parts of a facade seen
from the outside. The window is open, but the room inside shows
no signs of private life—instead one sees another facade with one
door and five closed windows. The painting may be perceived as
perfectly realistic, but only if one takes it for granted that the big-
ger house contains an overgrown doll's house. Knowledge of toy
design and codes of representation may tempt one to think just
a little bit more, though, and then a conflict between inside and
outside emerges. Any Peeping-Tom expectations one may have
had are sorely disappointed when one sees nothing of interest
in the room, just another boring housefront. Spectators become
involved in what might be described as an ironic situation when
the expected inside turns out to be another outside.

However, also the visual aspects of the painting may be interpreted in terms of irony, as the picture can be said to demonstrate that the inside *is* the outside. An image merely representing inside and outside juxtaposed in a striking but utterly realistic
way would no doubt be antithetical, but Magritte's painting can
take us further. As I see it, the inside and the outside are forced
together into a conceptual conflict. The inside *is* the inside *and*
at the same time the outside. This irony is not fundamentally different from the ironic situation of the spectator; it is only placed
at a different level of the relationship between painting and interpreter.

Needless to say, this ironic interpretation involves a stress on the aspect of contrariety. If, on the other hand, the aspect of similarity is emphasized, the reversed, antithetic connection between inside and outside may be interpreted as a metaphor for the lack of privacy in modern society or, conversely, for the hollow nature of humanity. Irony and metaphor are thus closely related in the visual arts, as they are in literature, when it comes to interpretive practice and the visual objects in which they are "seen." The "items" in our mental space of thinking may be arranged in ways that make either their similarities or their differences "visible." This, however, does not mean that the concepts of irony and metaphor are in themselves similar or conditioned by each other, as is suggested in a thesis by Wendy Dawe.[56]

I will refrain from drawing elaborate parallels between irony, divine madness, and being "spacy." Instead I will propose some further reading for those who are interested in investigating a literary spatiality that, according to my judgment, is not without its parallels with the visual spatiality of Magritte. It is found in Jorge Luis Borges's short story "Las ruinas circulares" [The Circular Ruins]. This is an exquisite little tale about a man who tries to create a son by way of dreaming him into reality. In the end, when he has finally succeeded after many years of intense efforts, he believes that he will die, but instead he realizes that he is himself a creation of some unknown creator. He understands, as the final words of the short story state, that he exists only in a dream: "With relief, with humiliation, with terror, he realized that he, too, was but appearance, that another man was dreaming him."[57]

Some comparisons between the world of Magritte and Borges's short story may evidently be made. "Las ruinas circulares" is a story that easily lends itself to meta-fictional interpretations. It is about creation, deceptive resemblance, representation, and illusion. It blurs the border between reality and dream in a manner that may call forth the famous words of Shakespeare's Prospero: "We are such stuff / As dreams are made on."[58] Finally, it is in particular a tale that may be read as a story about the impossible and yet possible (within the frame of the story) junction of a multitude of spaces: the spaces of reality and the spaces of dreams. The irony of "Las ruinas circulares," as I see it, consists of its double exposure of what happens in the two incompatible "realities" of the story: the man's reality and the story's reality, and in its paradoxically intermingled dreams: the man's dreams and the dream that the man is part of.

Although Borges's short story is perceived through a different medium, the interpretive strategy of irony that it might be read through does not differ from the methods by which one creates irony in images. With the aid of spatial metaphors, one can both "read" and "see" irony, in both literature and the visual arts.

10

Musical Meaning, Irony, and Value

Madness diagnosed in a sonata seemed to him as mysterious
a thing as the madness of a dog or the madness of a horse.
—Marcel Proust

MUSIC AND MEANING

Having reached this far in the book, readers know that musical
irony is most often seen as a result of a clash between meanings
that stem from verbal texts. Frits Noske's remark that "in order
to contradict, music must first adopt a meaning" is representative of this view. The "meaning" of music is not in the music itself, Noske believes, and hence musical irony is not really a
musical phenomenon.[1] However, I will narrow down the issue in
this final chapter: what would it mean to say that there is musical
irony that is not at all related to verbal texts? Of course it is never
possible to completely isolate music from its contexts, but the
question is nevertheless legitimate. Does truly *musical* irony
exist, and, if so, what is it?

To be able to answer these questions, one must focus on so-
called pure music, by which is meant music that excludes all
sorts of verbal texts except a formal title and standard indications
in the score. In the chapter "The Irony of the Arts," I discussed
Cage and irony from the perspective of the concept of art. Now it
is time to penetrate the ontology of music, and more specifically
its relation to human experience and the outside world. Is there
musical meaning or not, and, if so, what is it?

This seems to be a crucial question for all discussions concerning musical irony. Nevertheless it may be avoided. In musicological contexts the word *irony* is sometimes used as a vague
synonym for humor or light moods. This is of course perfectly
legitimate, but the risk is that this sort of word usage creates
more confusion than clarity. The writings of Jankélévitch are a

201

case in point. He characterizes Gabriel Fauré as an *ironiste* but does not say much that is specific about Fauré's music.[2] Regarding Debussy and Satie, he is a little more explicit, although he confines himself to giving us a few hints. Jankélévitch maintains that the irony of these two composers consists of "the refusal to develop, the pirouette, the war against serious modulations."[3] Irony has also been attributed to composers such as Prokofiev, Stravinsky, Schoenberg, and Bartók, but not always with very strict terminology. Barry Ulanov does not bother much with explaining the musical irony in the works of these composers. For himself it is obvious that there are "subtle flashes of irony," but the reader of his article does not become very enlightened.[4]

To me it seems as if both Jankélévitch and Ulanov avoid more detailed attempts to circumscribe musical irony simply because they find no relations between their experience of the music and its "formal" or "logical" characteristics. Writing about irony in music connected to narrative texts is "tricky enough," Hutcheon comments: "In the case of instrumental music, the difficulties in attributing irony would seem even more problematic."[5] Irony is madness, readers have learned, and perhaps one can say that the issue of irony in music is analogous to the issue of madness in music. In Proust's famous novel *In Search of Lost Time*, Swann thinks that pure music, *une œuvre de musique pure*, "contains none of the logical sequences whose deformation in language is a proof of madness; madness diagnosed in a sonata seemed to him as mysterious a thing as the madness of a dog or the madness of a horse, although that in fact may be observed."[6] For many people, irony in music is something utterly mysterious, just as mysterious as madness in music. The reason is clear: a pure musical work has no *rapports logiques* in itself. If there are no "logical sequences," there are no logical sequences to annul—and hence no *folie*, no madness or irony.

Not a few scholars who have discussed the issue of musical irony are clearly against the notion because of a reluctance to think about music in terms of meaning. Writing about Robert Schumann, Walter Gieseler maintains that "it is completely impossible to express irony and madness in music."[7] In "Erik Satie and the Music of Irony," Rudhyar D. Chennevière states that irony is "purely intellectual," whereas "music is not intellectual in its essence." In Chennevière's view the word constellation "ironic music" is simply nonsense. Satie's music needs words to become ironic.[8] Among those who do not simply reject the notion of musical irony without discussion, one also finds Catherine Kerbrat-Orecchioni. She does not see how irony in music could be possible. With the exception of parodic quoting, she states, irony does not belong to music and abstract painting.[9]

Yet, what is so very specific about parodic quoting? If intertextual, musical incongruities can be found and called ironic, why not intratextual incongruities? The fact that Kerbrat-Orecchioni accepts an "exception" when it comes to irony in music indicates that there is something wrong in her contention. Her use of the notion of "trope" is furthermore clearly delimiting because the notion in itself excludes nonverbal phenomena, whereas the concept of irony has long ago grown out of this much too tight garment.

Muecke, too, mentions parody as one of the few instances of ironic music, but he is more open to intratextual aspects of art and music. Yet, he asserts that "It is difficult, though not impossible, for some arts to be ironical." Music is one of these arts, and the problem is that "non-representational arts do not even refer to anything." Musical sounds, Muecke states, "are as unironical as mathematical theorems or scientific hypotheses."[10] He is of the opinion that, compared to the graphic arts, it is very unlikely that music would be ironic. What nevertheless makes it *possible* for music to be ironic is that it is yet "in a sense" a language.[11]

There is a slight inconsistency in Muecke's view, I think. On the one hand he states that music is definitely nonrepresentational and therefore incapable of being ironic, and on the other hand he holds that music is some sort of language that sometimes, although very rarely, might be ironic. His vacillation is understandable, and also very symptomatic of perhaps the most common view of irony and music: irony is a reversal of "meaning," and music does not "mean" anything—from which follows the conclusion that there is by definition no ironic music.

To understand how musical irony still seems to be something that exists in the mind of many listeners and critics, these two premises—that irony is a reversal of "meaning" and that music does not "mean" anything—must be scrutinized. I have already argued extensively against the definitions of *irony* that narrow it down to strict reversals of meaning, and I think that it would be possible to circumscribe musical irony even with the contention that music does not mean anything. Even in literature, ironic oppositions and incongruities are far from always related to the linguistic traits of language or the logical meaning of texts. Nevertheless I find it rewarding to question the second premise also, because it will give us an opportunity eventually to see more nuances in the various ironic interpretations of music that have been suggested by scholars and critics.

One is thus confronted with the very central and apparently never-ending question concerning meaning and representation in music.[12] First of all it must be stated that the meaning of music, if it exists, must doubtless be of a different and "weaker" character than the meaning of verbal language and even images. All agree that the capacity of refined, rational intersubjective communication is immensely greater in verbal language than in music. Verbal language has a superb ability to connect between widely varying areas. "Like the visual," Hutcheon states, "the aural has different and perhaps more limited abilities to suggest (and means to convey) context than does the verbal."[13] Of course, this is why it is common to circumscribe musical meaning as a result of an interpretation that includes both music and verbal language. Lawrence Kramer thus postulates that musical "representation" (a rather "strong" instance of musical meaning) is only possible with the help of a "designator"—for example, "texts for vocal setting; titles, programs, and epigraphs."[14]

Yet, again, it is the music itself that is of interest right now. In an earlier chapter I considered the opinion that music basically consists of "empty signs": that its meaning is definitely not determinable. This view formed the ground for an interpretation of music as ironic in its essence in a very wide sense. However, there is also another, at least as important line of thought in the history of the aesthetics of music. Many of the treatises on music hold the opinion that music does have some sort of meaning, although the opinions vary on how stable and definite this meaning is.

As within most aesthetic fields the terminology regarding musical meaning is complex and sometimes confused, but there seems to be a tendency to take it for granted that musical meaning has rather little to do with reason. Instead, musical meaning is generally connected to the "signification" or "representation" of emotions, passions, and moods. In *Esthetics of Music*, Carl Dahlhaus reminds us that "The idea that music's goal was to represent and arouse affections is a commonplace, rooted as deeply in history as the opposing thesis that music is sounding mathematics."[15] He follows this idea from the *Affekt* theories, via the eighteenth-century aesthetics of imitation, *mimesis*, and the theory that tones are universally understood, "natural," not conventional signs of feelings, to the theories of expression.[16]

In his book *The Emancipation of Music from Language*, John

Neubauer, too, gives a critical survey of this aesthetic field. *Affekt* theorists of the seventeenth and eighteenth centuries, he concludes, "attempted to assign emotional value to the basic musical materials and forms, including intervals, keys, styles, meters, and rhythms, but they disagreed on the most fundamental definitions and categorizations."[17] Fast music, for instance, was a category that included not only happiness, but anger as well. Neubauer also discusses the conventional methods of representing affects, the so-called musical rhetoric, which is a limited but not insignificant aspect of musical meaning.[18] Romanticism, he states, "was a death knell for rhetoric but required only adaptation from affect theories."[19]

Neubauer's theory is that the shift from "musical representation in the seventeenth and early eighteenth century to what came to be called musical expression in the later eighteenth century is in no way a movement away from mimesis," but rather "a move toward greater verisimilitude in representation, for composers were now asked to portray finely shaded, individualized, and personal emotions instead of stock affects."[20] That music was gradually emancipated from language did not mean that its meaning, its capacity to copy and evoke feelings and passions, was questioned, but that it came to be understood and described differently and more on its own terms; freed from connections to the meter, accent, prosody, and syntax of verbal language.

If Neubauer is right, it means that the idea of music carrying meaning is even more widespread than thought, and that the "empty sign" theories are of only marginal interest. Whether that is true, I cannot tell. What I *can* tell is that musical meaning is almost always related to feelings, passions, moods, and emotions,[21] and that the borderline between "emotive meaning" and "nonmeaning" is rather diffuse. How definite must the emotive import of a piece of music be to qualify for the epithet "meaning"? That seems to be a very crucial question.

Eduard Hanslick is the musicologist who has given the most famous and also the most misunderstood answer to this question. In his sharp and witty book, *Vom Musikalisch-schönen* [*On the Musically Beautiful*] from 1854, he attacks those theories that advocate the primacy of feelings in music.[22] In itself, music is nothing but form, Hanslick asserts. When people listen to music they feel emotions, but those emotions are not part of the music, and neither are the emotions aroused by poetry and paintings part of the verbal and visual texts. Hanslick definitely does not believe that the emotional reactions are unimportant; the point is that they are relatively subjective and not part of the music it-self. As a matter of fact the same piece of music causes widely differing reactions in different listeners, and hence it is impossi-ble to maintain that the music in itself "represents" or "embod-ies" specific feelings.

Hanslick does not at all deny that motions of harmony and melody are somehow analogous to what might be called the dy-namics of emotions, but he concludes that these analogies are so ambiguous that it is impossible to uphold a real connection. Music is an *unbestimmte Sprache* [indefinite speech] and is hence not capable of representing *Begriffe* [concepts], from which it follows that music is not capable of representing *be-stimmte Gefühle* [definite feelings]: "the definiteness of feelings lies precisely in their conceptual essence."[23] He distinguishes be-tween the physical appearance and the intellectual "content" of feelings. Agitated wrath and agitated love have the same "dy-namics," and yet the two feelings differ widely. Music represents dynamic qualities, not intellectual qualities.

Hanslick thus opposes the most common view of musical meaning: that it is related to feelings and emotions. "How, then, can we designate something as what an art represents, when the very dubious and ambiguous elements of that art themselves are perpetually subject to debate?," he asks rhetorically.[24] In its es-sence, music is nothing but form, he asserts, *Tönend bewegte Formen* [tonally moving forms].[25] His attitude toward mathemat-ics and music is, on the other hand, somewhat ambivalent.

Hanslick's views have been immensely influential, and like all influential writers he has been said to have opinions that he does not hold. The popular image of Hanslick is that he is someone who rejects all emotive import of music, which he certainly does not—he only concludes that it is not part of the music itself.

Almost a century after *Vom Musikalisch-schönen*, Susanne K. Langer published a book that also was to become very influential: *Philosophy in a New Key*, in which there is a chapter called "On Significance in Music." Langer does not belong to the "formal-ist" school of Hanslick—on the contrary. She argues that music indeed has "meaning," and that this "emotional content" of music is expressed symbolically: "Music is not the cause or the cure of feelings, but their *logical expression*."[26] She connects to Schopenhauer's attempt "to interpret music as a symbol of the irrational aspect of mental life, the Will."[27] Music is not self-ex-pression, she emphasizes, but *"formulation and representation of emotions, moods, mental tensions and resolutions—a 'logical* picture' of sentient, responsive life, a source of insight, not a plea for sympathy."[28]

For Langer, music is not a language, and she does not believe that music has semantic properties. It has no literal meaning, she states; rather it is "a presentational symbol."[29] Therefore she does not feel entirely comfortable with the notion of meaning. Instead she stresses what she takes to be the well-established fact that "musical structures logically resemble certain dynamic patterns of human experience . . . patterns of motion and rest, of tension and release, of agreement and disagreement, preparation, fulfilment, excitation, sudden change, etc."[30] She is well aware of the run-of-the-mill argument against musical "meaning" that one and the same piece of music may be interpreted as conveying widely different moods, and her answer is that music simply does not work in the same way as verbal language. To emphasize the incapacity of music to express distinct moods and hence conclude that it has no meaning is a fallacy, Langer believes. The verbal notions by which we rubricate emotions are not universal, and there is no reason to believe that the verbal categorization of moods is the only valid one. The "meaning" of music, its "expressiveness," lies in its capacity to give symbolic form to emotions that are out of reach of language: "*music articulates forms which language cannot set forth,*" she states. "Because the forms of human feeling are much more congruent with musical forms than with the forms of language, music can *reveal* the nature of feelings with a detail and truth that language cannot approach."[31]

In all its simplicity, this argument to me seems to be very plausible. Yet, I cannot escape the feeling that the problem of coming to an agreement on the question of musical meaning is very much a terminological issue. The notion of "meaning" is undoubtedly problematic, and often scholars and critics who seem to be in complete disagreement are simply not willing to accept each other's terminology—when in fact their ideas are intimately related. Langer, for instance, criticizes Hanslick harshly, in spite of the obvious similarity of their ideas. Both emphasize the importance of musical forms and their correspondence with the dynamics of emotions, and they even agree upon the fact that there are no clear-cut relations between musical forms and specific moods. As I have noted, Hanslick objects to the idea that music "is" or "embodies" moods, and Langer also states that "*what music can actually reflect is only the morphology of feeling.*"[32]

Likewise, it is important to both of them to stress the exclusiveness of music.

Still their conclusions differ. Hanslick, who directed his polemic against earlier theories that tried to subsume music under language, states that there is no meaning in music (it is merely "tonally moving forms"), whereas Langer, for whom the notion of meaning is much more flexible, is willing to find "meaning" in music—although not in the sense that the *Affektenlehre* suggested.[33] It might be noted that in *Feeling and Form*, a book in which Langer develops her ideas of musical significance to include all of the arts, her terminology has changed slightly. She now rejects the notion of meaning and instead proposes "vital import."[34] Perhaps Hanslick would have accepted this terminology. The musicologist Leonard B. Meyer, on the other hand, whose influential ideas will be discussed later, holds on to the notion of meaning in *Emotion and Meaning in Music*, a book published in 1956, a few years after *Feeling and Form*. His conception of musical meaning does not differ much from Langer's, but he emphasizes that music "cannot stipulate the causal connection" between the presented experiences.[35]

Finally the more recent writings of Peter Kivy must be mentioned. In his book, *The Corded Shell: Reflections on Musical Expression*, he maintains that music must be explained by both a "contour" theory and a "convention" theory, which means that musical expressiveness is a result of both musical qualities and extramusical conventions.[36] His "contour" theory has much in common with Langer's ideas, although their terminologies differ significantly. Kivy has his historical starting point in Johann Mattheson's *Der vollkommene Capellmeister* from 1739, where the author, according to Kivy, sets forth the theory that music "in its structure, bears a resemblance to the 'emotive life.' "[37]

Kivy's concern is to show that music *is expressive of* emotions and moods.[38] It is not a question of subjectivity, he argues, to characterize music in terms of, for instance, sorrow and gaiety. Music may be an "emotive icon."[39] Hence, he stresses the relations of similarity between musical and emotive forms—as Langer and Hanslick, among others, have done before him. Kivy manages to show convincingly that these relations do exist, but the weakness of his argument is that he confines himself to discussing rather crude opposites of moods and emotions. Although he happily admits that a great deal of music is ambiguous in terms of the particular mood it is expressive of, he seems to be quite satisfied with being able to distinguish between sadness and joy: "That is the kind and degree of agreement required for the theory of musical expressiveness to be presented here."[40]

Unfortunately this makes Kivy's arguments related to "intrinsic" musical moods rather weak. As far as I can see, his "contour" theory cannot cope with Hanslick's remark that agitated wrath and agitated love have the same "dynamics" and yet differ widely. In this respect Langer's theory is more plausible, although her terminology is more outdated than Kivy's.

To sum up, it is clear that history shows a great variety of theories that try to define the meaning of music. It is true that one often looks in vain for agreement, but it is also true that the two opposite positions, the "formalist" theories and the "emotive meaning" theories, in many respects resemble each other. From a pragmatic point of view one might simply observe the fact that meaning *is* constantly being attributed to music. Everyone "emplots" music, as John Neubauer states.[41] Instrumental music cannot narrate in the same sense as literature or film does, but it offers the opportunity to emplot it. One does, albeit in widely different ways, and with the help of widely differing contexts. Carolyn Abbate advocates the view that music is not narrative, but nevertheless "possesses moments of narration"; without having narrative content it "makes distinctive sounds when it is speaking (singing) *in a narrative mode.*"[42] Abbate does not give the epithet *meaning* to the "multiple disjunctions" that mark the "narrating voice," but obviously her argumentation aims at circumscribing musical traits that are in some way meaningful. [43] Yet, the meaning cannot be described in terms of content or emotions. Rather, it is the *motion* of music that allows one to interpret it as narrating something that is in itself unknown.

What surprises me is that the area of "ambiguity" and "uncertainty" in musical meaning, an area that is certainly universally recognized, is quite often avoided: it is seen as a problem rather than an asset. Either the ambiguity of meaning is taken as evidence for the nonexistence of true meaning, or it is seen as less determinate and hence less interesting (but not necessarily "bad") meaning. Langer is wise enough to emphasize the specific power of musical meaning that is indeterminate from the point of view of verbal language, but if music is otherwise being praised it is rather the "lack" than the "ambiguity" or "uncertainty" of meaning to which homage is being paid. Jean-Jacques Nattiez, however, also emphasizes that verbalization of musical meaning is not the same as musical meaning (as the paraphrase of a poem is not the same as the meaning of that poem, it might be added). Above all, he reminds readers, "we must not confuse music's meaning, properly speaking, with *translation* of that meaning"; it cannot be defined "solely as a reflection of some *linguistic* meaning."[44]

Before putting an end to this section, I will reformulate what I wrote in the last paragraph. There are, I think, two solutions to the apparently problematic fact that people often cannot agree upon which mood a piece of music is expressive of. Either one can say that music *is* sometimes expressive of moods that are ambiguous, specifically musical, double—or ironic—or one can say that music in itself is *not* expressive of any moods at all, as moods really can exist only one at a time (at least if they are incompatible). I am not sure that the last contention is tenable, but neither am I sure that it really matters which of the two theoretical solutions is chosen. The problem for Hanslick "was not the existence or non-existence of emotional traits in music," Dahlhaus remarks, "but their definiteness or indefiniteness."[45] This distinction is certainly important, but it is perhaps even more important to remember that all questions concerning definiteness and indefiniteness in the end boil down to a question of the way one interprets music. It might simply be misleading to try to describe music in objective terms.

Nevertheless it is an empirical fact that some music—for instance, the music of Shostakovich—is much more controversial than other music when it comes to attributing precise moods to it. This indicates that there do exist musical traits that give rise to rather distinct, recognizable uncertainties—at least within certain interpretive communities. Once these pronounced uncertainties of meaning have been discovered—or, to put it differently, once these widely differing interpretations have been recognized—irony comes knocking at the door.

MUSICAL CONTRASTS AND HUMOR

Thus it seems as if a majority of those who have scrutinized the issue are of the opinion that music has meaning—if one defines meaning in a not too narrow way. It is not easy to agree exactly on the nature of this meaning, but clearly it has appeared to be "solid" enough (for some people) to form the basis of ironic interpretations. The historical reality that lies behind this book, and in particular this chapter, is that the concept of irony has become more and more common in musical discourse. This is a fact that one has to deal with, whether one believes that the meaning of music is comparable to the meaning of literature or not.

If one sticks to a definition of irony that involves some sort of conflict of meaning (not necessarily strict reversals), it is self-evident that music must have "meaning" if it is to be ironic: without meaning there can be no ironically twisted meaning. When one reads texts about musical irony, at least three things become clear. First, music is certainly understood to be full of meaning; second, the issue of the nature of this meaning is being avoided; and third, the terminology describing the conflicts of musical meaning varies within the same range as does the terminology connected with literary and visual irony. It is slightly surprising that the term *contradiction* is fairly common in spite of the fact that musical meaning cannot be literally contradictive. It is known that pure contradiction or strict opposition is present only rarely even in verbal irony, which in my view makes the notion of contradiction almost redundant within musicology. Contradiction is not required for irony in literature, and it would be absurd to require it for musical irony.

However, it is even more common to use the much vaguer and more subjective notions of contrast and incongruity when interpreting music. Musical contrasts are sometimes described in rather technical terms, but more often they are seen as clashes of emotions and moods.[46] Musical contrasts are as a rule simply equivalent to contrasts of musical "meaning."

The notion of contrast is, of course, one of the basic, structural notions within the whole field of aesthetic studies, and it is in no way exclusively delimited to the field of irony. One of the chapters in Calvin S. Brown's classic study *Music and Literature: A Comparison of the Arts* is called "Balance and Contrast," but the concept of irony is not considered.[47] Contrast and incongruity do not necessarily imply irony, but irony always implies some sort of contrast or incongruity. Notions like these seem to be unavoidable when it comes to circumscribing musical irony also.

However, as already noted, it is not always recognized that it is the music itself that is capable of harboring ironic contrasts or incongruities. Peter Jost, writing about irony in some of Brahms's songs, sees incongruities between the poems and their musical settings, but he emphatically objects to the notion of pure musical irony.[48] Yet, if there can be incongruities between words and music, why not within the music itself? If the musical meaning is "strong" enough to be at odds with the verbal meaning, why cannot the musical meaning be "strong" enough to be incongruous in itself? That I do not understand. As soon as one accepts that music has the capacity of "modifying" the meaning of a literary text, one must also accept that it has the capacity of modifying its own meaning. The same conclusion can be drawn from Joseph Thomas Malloy's remark in his discussion on Mozart's irony that "Music and text are, at times, saying rather different things."[49] If music has the capacity of "saying" things that are "different" from what words say, it must also have the capacity of saying various things that are different from each other.

This view is actually accepted already in the earliest article on musical irony of which I know. In "Die Ironie in der Musik: Ein Beitrag zur Aesthetik der Musik" from 1881, Max Schasler discusses contrasts between music and text, but he is first and foremost interested in incongruities within the music itself: "where melodies become ironized by melodies."[50] Although his hermeneutical method is based on intentionality, he in fact interprets pieces of music rather freely and concludes that what the music "obviously" displays must be the (conscious or unconscious) intention of the composer. Schasler discusses Beethoven, Mozart, and some other composers, and he finds irony in, for instance, a "contradiction between the introduction and the main music" in a piece of music.[51] He frequently uses the term *Widerspruch*, and, according to Schasler, it is moods and feelings that are "contradicted." In some music, he states, one finds a "contradiction to a given emotional content."[52]

In a discussion on Beethoven, Hans Mersmann, too, is of the opinion that music may be able to "simultaneously say contradictory things," which makes it outstanding among the arts.[53] He does not use the term *irony* for this simultaneity of opposites, though. For Ernst Lert, on the other hand, the term *irony* is relevant in his interpretation of Mozart, although he states that irony demands contrast and that in music "idea and expression" can only be congruent. Yet, Mozart found the formula for musical irony, Lert asserts: "the musical litotes."[54]

It is clear that the conceptual web that includes irony, contradiction, contrast, incongruity, meaning, mood, and so forth is woven in a very intricate way and that only small differences in the definitions of these concepts cause conflicts between musicologists that are not very easy to disentangle. Furthermore, irony is not a concept that is definitely determined by certain conditions. For instance, it would have been more "natural" if Mersmann, who believes that music has the capacity of expressing contradictions, had adopted the concept of irony, and if Lert, who believes that idea and expression are always identical in music, had avoided it. Yet, as noted, the situation turned out the other way around. The creation of irony is a result not only of conceptual prerequisites, but also of interpretive strategies and subjective, normative conditions.

Nevertheless, contrasts and incongruities are what almost all writers on musical irony find in the music. When the notion of contradiction is being used, it must be understood as a synonym for *sharp contrast* or *opposition,* although the term *Widerspruch* gives stronger associations to determinate meaning than does the term *contrast*—which might be a reason for using it in spite of its inaccuracy. The way the notions of contradiction, contrariety, and contrast are actually being used, it is impossible to keep them distinct from each other. Sometimes one and the same writer uses them in several different ways, as for instance Jankélévitch. In *L'Ironie* he states that irony does not express "something else" but "the opposite of what it feels."[55] In *La musique et l'ineffable,* he writes about the ironic Satie and states that "sometimes music expresses not exactly 'the opposite' but 'something else.' "[56] Yet, perhaps terminology is not the most important issue for Jankélévitch. The point is that he hears contrasts in the music: contrasts of motion and mood. About a piece of music by Debussy, it is significantly said that "the heavy becomes airy, whereas the light dances the ridiculous steps of the elephant."[57] I have noted that Muecke, on the other hand, for whom terminology is much more important, mentions "incongruities of formal properties" as a possibility for music to become ironic.[58]

The ironic contrasts of music have thus been attributed to both its mood and its form. However, is it possible to make such a distinction between "content" and "form"? In theory it is; in practice, no. The history of the efforts to circumscribe the meaning of music clearly demonstrates, I think, that the vital qualities of music are at the same time form and content, and that there is no way of really distinguishing between ironic contrasts of form, meaning, and mood.

Discussing contrasts and irony in music, it is necessary to say a few words also about humor. The two terms are often used in conjunction in texts on music, and sometimes they are treated as synonyms.[59] From a conceptual point of view, irony and humor are overlapping. In an earlier chapter, I discussed the general resemblances between the two notions, and these resemblances hold within musicology also. In Zofia Lissa's *Aufsätze zur Musikästhetik,* to take a prominent example, *Komik* is defined in a way that is explicitly close to many aspects of irony. Not surprisingly, the notions of *Inkongruenz* and *Kontrast* are important to Lissa, although she is of the opinion that there cannot be true irony, *wirkliche Ironie*, in music without words.[60]

By tradition the notion of humor is much more closely connected to music than is irony, undoubtedly as it originates not from the realm of verbal communication but from medical observations concerning the alleged benefits of certain body fluids. Comparatively little has been written on irony and music, but quite a lot on humor and music.[61] In the chapter to which I recently referred, the similarity between the notions of humor and irony in German Romanticism was highlighted, and it is in Romanticism that one finds the first traces of thinking about music in terms of irony. In a dialogue by E. T. A. Hoffmann from 1821, the question is asked: "But has music the power to express the comic in all its nuances?" The answer given is yes: "there may lie in music the expression of the most entertaining irony."[62]

Schasler, who perhaps published the first article on musical irony, connects irony and humor, and also in the later writings on musical irony it is almost a rule to at least mention the notion of humor. Marius Flothuis discusses humor, parody, and irony in music and notes that an important element in humor is that "what the listener expects, does not occur."[63] In the article "Chopins Witz und Ironie," Stefan Szuman describes musical irony in a similar way as "an abandoning of the agenda."[64] Again, Kant's definition of the comic comes to mind: "Laughter is an emotion derived from the sudden transformation of a tensed expectation into nothing."[65] This, if anything, includes a strong contrast. Laurie-Jeanne Lister, too, follows this path. In her book, *Humor as a Concept in Music*, she defines "absolute humor" as "a play with or distortion of the expectations set up by the music."[66] She wisely stresses that a prerequisite for humor of this kind is that the listener has acquaintance with the musical style in which the piece is written. Lister also mentions some "techniques" for creating humor in music that one will recognize from the discourse on irony: exaggeration, clumsiness, parody, and incongruity.

However, it was in German Romanticism that irony and humor first came to be connected in a way that would eventually lead to some of the most important efforts to circumscribe musical irony. It is now time to follow the cues that lead from humor to Romantic irony.

ROMANTIC IRONY AND SPATIALITY

I have earlier noted that the heart of Romantic irony lies in a conjunction of opposites: *both/and* is the formula for Romantic irony rather than the classical *either/or*. For Schlegel, an ironic text is paradoxical and dialectic in its entirety. Like the world itself, it embodies a multitude of sharply contrasting or even mutually exclusive phenomena that cannot be neatly ordered.

Bernhard Appel, among others, has stressed the difficulties involved in trying to distinguish between Romantic *Humor* and Romantic *Ironie*. Neither before nor after German Romanticism have the notions of irony and humor been more closely associated, and in the context of Romanticism the choice of terms might seem almost arbitrary. From a historical point of view, though, it is clearly humor that has been most intimately connected to music. Appel rightly states that *Humor* is comparatively as important for musical Romanticism as the concept of irony is for literary Romanticism.[67] In *Humor als Formkonzept in der Musik Gustav Mahlers*, Mirjam Schadendorf emphasizes the importance of Jean Paul, whose notion of humor obviously has strong resemblances to Schlegel's notion of irony.[68] For *Musikalischer Humor*, she states, "the disintegrating aspects of the work" are decisive.[69] Musical humor is *ein Formkonzept* that is characterized by both strong contrasts and a peculiar lack of progression.[70] Schadendorf also describes musical humor as "a sharp instrument that builds a short-lived world only to immediately destroy it."[71] The resemblance to Romantic irony is clear to see. Jankélévitch, too, who is primarily interested in irony, gives us a hint of this connection between irony, music, and Romanticism. Writing about Schumann and Ravel, he asserts that irony is associated with "the Romantic 'spleen'—that is the synthesis of dissonances and the fusion of contrasts."[72]

However, it was Rey M. Longyear who in 1970 published the first article in which the topic of Romantic irony and music was properly dealt with: "Beethoven and Romantic Irony."[73] The article is very informative, and it has come to be one of the most quoted texts on musical irony. One of its merits is that Longyear is eager to really analyze the music of Beethoven and distinctly describe the traits in the music that are relevant to the ironic interpretation. It is also important that the emphasis is placed so distinctly on each musical work as a whole. Apparently it is much easier to find musical irony if one looks for it in the relationship between different parts of a complete piece of music rather than

in isolated passages or in a vague conception of its general "attitude."

Longyear's method is of course not new, but it is important
that musical irony is explicitly freed from the narrow implications of rhetorical irony. Rhetorical irony consists of a clash of
opposite meanings that stem from the same words in a text,
whereas Romantic irony consists of a clash of meanings that exist
on equal terms in the entirety of a text. As is known, the distinction between these two variations of irony is certainly not clear-
cut, but it highlights an important shift of emphasis in the history
of the concept of irony, and it seems as if the notion of Romantic
irony is generally more appropriate to the interpretation of music
than the notion of rhetorical irony.

I think that the importance of Longyear's article is indisputable. Some objections must be raised, however: objections that
work on a rather nearsighted but nonetheless highly relevant
level. The question is what Longyear actually does when deciding
which pieces of music are ironic. Let us take a look at his description of the second movement of Beethoven's String Quartet, op.
59, no. 1. It is said to contain passages in the "wrong key," an
"abrupt interruption," a "humorously sudden modulation," an
"irregular resolution," a "sudden tonal shift," "surprisingly unexpected irregular modulations emphasized by silences," "an
unpredictable return to the tonic," and an "exaggerated pathos"
that is "ironically concluded."[74] Yet, how can one decide between
what is an unexpected incongruity and a logical, unified development? Partly it is a question of whether one is listening to the
music for the first time or listening to it with preknowledge of the
piece itself and its genre; partly it is a question of whether one
belongs or does not belong to the interpretive community of skil-
ful musicologists—but primarily, I assert, the unexpected incongruities are results of interpretations involving a subjective use of
a wide range of key terms that are given the impression of being
more or less objective.

I definitely do not say that Longyear's ironic interpretation of
Beethoven's string quartet is wrong, only that the music "in itself" is neither ironic nor unironic, neither incongruous nor unified. Longyear's ironic interpretations of several pieces by
Beethoven are valid, I think, but in no way final. If one accepts
the relevance of Romantic irony, the general validity of music
analysis based on very initiated knowledge of the style of a composer and an era, and Longyear's own conclusions regarding the
music's deviations from what he takes to be the musical

norms—if so, his arguments are convincing and congruent. That is perhaps all one can ask of an interpretation.

Yet, these premises are no doubt subjective. The contrasts that Longyear hears are, I repeat, a result of certain expectations that he has, and these expectations are formed by a knowledge of and a conception of a certain style and how it "ought" to sound. Furthermore, the decisive step from hearing contrasts and deviations to labeling them "ironic" is a result of a choice of a certain context, not of necessity. Longyear's ironic interpretation is a strategy, just as all interpretations are results of choices and strategies. The only thing that is wrong is that Longyear's text gives the impression of describing a musical truth.

It might be interesting to compare Longyear's interpretive strategy to Leonard B. Meyer's influential ideas in *Emotion and Meaning in Music*. Meyer's theory is that *all* musical meaning is a result of the fulfillment of or deviations from expectations. "Embodied musical meaning is," he states, "a product of expectation."[75] Often one feels that music is ambiguous, and that it might continue in several different ways, but nevertheless one has expectations—if one is at all familiar with the style.[76] One of Meyer's basic hypotheses is that affect is aroused when an expectation activated by the music "is temporarily inhibited or permanently blocked."[77] For Meyer, reason and emotion are not opposites. Thinking and feeling are "different manifestations of a single psychological process."[78] Meyer thus proposes a psychological solution to the age-old problem of what musical meaning really is: it includes both affective and intellectual experience, and the two are complementary—not mutually exclusive: "Whether a piece of music gives rise to affective experience or to intellectual experience depends upon the disposition and training of the listener."[79] Perhaps, then, Longyear's conception of irony and his response to Beethoven is primarily intellectual, even though he also uses a few expressions such as "exaggerated pathos." It is definitely a product of a very trained listener.

I think that Meyer's theory of musical meaning is basically correct. Listening to and ascribing meaning to music is to a high degree a matter of having expectations fulfilled, modified, or frustrated. Yet, the theory's strength is also its weakness: the generality. It says so much about music that it threatens to say very little. However, it has its specific interest in this context. In short, if one combines Meyer's and Longyear's approaches to music, one gets the perhaps awkward result that the bulk of all music to which one ascribes meaning is also ironic. If all deviations from

expectations give rise to meaning, and if all deviations from expectations give rise to irony, only meaning that stems from perfect fulfillment of expectations is not ironic. If one does not
accept that, one will naturally have to modify the criteria and
perhaps say that irony can be said to come into being only when
the deviations are significant enough—and then, of course, one
is once again necessarily back on an even more subjective level.
Who decides which deviations are prominent enough to be
ironic? The individual listener does.

Yet, again, perhaps all music *is* ironic? I have already discussed
that conclusion, and although most people for quite good reason
would reject it, it might be rewarding to compare it to the ideas
put forth by the literary scholar Cleanth Brooks. In spite of the
fact that literature and music are often acknowledged to be unified in the aspect of temporality, they are as a rule seen as opposites, and it is interesting to note that the concept of irony seems
to have the capacity to bridge most alleged differences between
the two art forms. In fact Meyer's theory of musical meaning is
very similar to Brooks's notion of irony. Brooks, one should remember, maintains that every part of a text is constantly modified by its other parts and that "irony is the most general term
that we have for the kind of qualification which the various elements in a context receive from the context"; it is "our most general term for indicating that recognition of incongruities."[80]
Perhaps, then, the construction of meaning in music does not
after all differ very much from the construction of meaning in literature. Perhaps irony is a concept that is as valid in music as it
is in literature.

However, one must not forget Longyear. His approach has
been influential, but naturally objections have been raised.
Longyear performed his interpretation of Beethoven's music,
and there are many other musicologists who have had different
opinions regarding the interpretation of this great composer. For
many, it has been a necessity to state that Longyear is more or
less wrong, and that they themselves have the right keys to Beethoven. In his dissertation on irony in Mozart, Joseph Thomas
Malloy adopts Longyear's ideas of Romantic irony in music, but
criticizes his interpretations of Beethoven for being not entirely
correct. Malloy seems to believe that irony is a completely objective phenomenon, the existence of which it is possible to determine once and for all if only one has sufficient knowledge.[81] His
own method of finding irony in Beethoven and Mozart does not,
however, differ very much from Longyear's. Mozart's "purely

musical irony" in a piano concerto is, for instance, said to be "expressed in the abrupt shift in texture and the ostensibly problematical nature of the formal development section."[82] What Malloy does is to interpret the music in terms of contrasts and incongruities and then to conclude—sometimes on the basis of what he believes to be "intentional" evidence—that it is ironic. That his conception of musical contrasts, incongruities, and ironies is a result of an interpretive strategy, chosen by Malloy himself, does not occur to him. Malloy believes that Longyear finds ironies that exist only as illusions, whereas all ironies that he himself finds exist in the real, objective world.

Jean-Pierre Barricelli, too, adopts Longyear's ideas and criticizes his "subjective" manner of circumscribing irony. Barricelli accepts the existence of Romantic irony in music, but he believes that "the composer's ironic *intent*" is a necessary qualifier.[83] He does not at all discuss *how* this intent is to be found, but obviously he himself is in possession of the magic formula that opens the gates to the composers' hidden intentions. Barricelli does not hesitate to determine the existence of Romantic irony in a good number of musical works without explaining on what grounds his conclusions rest. One simply learns that the irony is "surely" there.[84] To be honest, I cannot see the point of applying the notion of intent if it is as hollow as in Barricelli's text. When discussing a piece by Ravel, he says that "the intention here may have been only marginally ironical," which is almost exactly the same, I argue, as saying "I do not know exactly how to interpret this piece of music"—but covered under a pseudo-objective shield.[85] Barricelli's ironic interpretations are neither more nor less convincing than Longyear's and Malloy's, but his method of arguing is poor.

There are a few more rewarding studies of Romantic irony in music, notably Mark Evan Bonds's "Haydn, Laurence Sterne, and the Origins of Musical Irony."[86] Bonds follows the path set out by Longyear, and he does it for a special reason. It is relevant to connect irony and music, he believes, but "it is highly questionable whether nonprogrammatic instrumental music is capable of sustaining irony, at least in the traditional sense of 'saying one thing and meaning another'. The concept of 'meaning' in absolute music is far too vague to provide the kind of referential basis that is essential for this kind of irony to make its effect."[87] Romantic irony, on the other hand, is a notion that is more congruent with music, Bonds assumes—and I think that he is basically right.

Bonds, too, depends on notions such as contrast and incongruity when interpreting Haydn's music in terms of irony. In the last chapter, I advocated the idea that irony is always circumscribed with the aid of notions that, like these two, are best understood as spatial metaphors. The idea was put forth in the context of visual art, but I think that it might be sustained also by the context of music. Spatial thinking is important for the way one comprehends music as well. Visuality is a prominent aspect of spatiality, but thinking is certainly not connected only with seeing, but also with, for instance, feeling, moving, and hearing.

The more the strictly verbal and linguistic definitions of irony have been backgrounded by theorists and in interpretive practice, I have argued, the more the "natural" affinity between irony and spatiality has surfaced. The shift from rhetorical irony to Romantic irony involves an increased emphasis on contextuality and hence also on spatiality. Rhetorical irony works primarily on the paradigmatic axis of language, whereas Romantic irony may be said to be a syntagmatic phenomenon; it is a phenomenon of "extension."

If irony is almost always dependent on spatial metaphors, and if important aspects of our comprehension of music are spatial, this might explain why and how the concept of irony has invaded musical discourse. I think that both of these two premises are valid. "Ever since antiquity," Dahlhaus notes, "it was the concept of motion that provided a connection between music and affection or ethos."[88] Dahlhaus mentions some common metaphors used by aestheticians in describing "psychic motion": stretching and contraction, rising and falling. As one can move only within space, these terms are no doubt spatial metaphors that might very well be put in relation to the spatial metaphors of irony. If the "psychic motion" in a piece of music consists, for instance, of one rising motion and one falling motion, and if these two motions are perceived to be "incongruous," it makes sense to make an ironic interpretation of the music.

It is important to note the close conceptual relation between motion and emotion. Both those who believe that music represents emotions, feelings, or moods and those who believe that it consists of forms think basically in terms of motion. Although they draw different conclusions, both Hanslick and Langer, as noted, focus on musical form. Furthermore, their terminologies for describing it are closely related—and clearly of a spatial nature. One might consequently tentatively conclude that musical space as perceived consists of both motions and emotions, and that they are two aspects of one and the same idea: musical form.

Victor Zuckerkandl is a scholar who has specifically stressed that music is a fundamentally spatial phenomenon. In the way he describes it, musical space is certainly not completely identical with the three-dimensional world of items. It goes without saying that sounds do not have shapes that are analogous to circles or cubes, for instance. Yet, music nonetheless consists of tones and sounds that are clearly distinguishable and related to each other not only via the flow of time.[89] Like Arnheim, Zuckerkandl leans on psychological investigations, but it is clear that his ideas are not uncontroversial. The problem is, of course, to be found in the very concept of space. What *is* space? If one defines it very narrowly as the world of three dimensions that one can see and touch, music is definitely not spatial. However, if space is defined as to include also the psychological world of perception and comprehension, music is definitely spatial—as are indeed very many other phenomena.

It is, however, important to realize that language itself sets the limits for understanding what music really is, and that language unavoidably directs one toward spatial notions. It appears, Zuckerkandl concludes, "that we cannot even talk about these phenomena [of music] except with words that, whether latently or patently, have a *spatial* meaning."[90] One way of describing this situation is to say that language sets the limits for one's "intellectual" understanding of music. Another way is to say that, thanks to the metaphorical qualities of language, one may understand at least a little of what music is and how it is perceived.

Zuckerkandl's view is echoed by Robert P. Morgan in his article "Musical Time/Musical Space," in which he stresses that "it would seem to be impossible to talk about music at all without invoking spatial notions of one kind or another."[91] In Morgan's view, music embodies relationships that are, in a sense, "independent of time"—relationships that exist "in *abstracto*."[92] The quality of "volume" that one feels in music is perhaps the most prominent example of what Langer calls the "virtual space" of music.[93] In Morgan's words, it stems from "the fact that two or more distinct musical events—whether individual tones, chord complexes, or entire phrases—can occur simultaneously without mixing into a fundamentally new and different substance."[94] Apart from a linear axis, music has also "width" that allows the coexistence of musical events "side by side."

The experience of contrasting or incongruous moods and emotions in music might thus be described as contrasting or incongruous volumes and motions: motions that cause "clashes" or even "crashes." When one feels or thinks that the abstract, virtual space of music embodies fundamental conflicts, these conflicts (that are of both a formal and an emotional nature) are potentially ironic. Further conflicts in our comprehension of musical works might stem from the phenomenon that the "same form" in music may correspond to very different emotions, as has been pointed out by the critics of the *Affektenlehre*. In those cases musical space has "four dimensions." If one feels that a piece of music holds two different moods at the same time, the conflict is in fact of a paradigmatic rather than a syntagmatic nature. The possibly resulting irony is not strictly rhetorical, however, because the different moods are neither explicit nor implicit.

It is clear that by now I have moved the discussion of irony quite a long way from where it usually takes place. Perhaps it might seem as if a spatial metaphor in musical discourse is not exactly the place where one expects to find doors that open the way to irony—but again one must remember that ironic interpretations of literature also have, as a matter of fact, for a long time been fostered by rather abstract contrasts, conflicts, and incongruities. From a historic point of view, the spatial metaphors of irony stem from the interpretation of verbal communication and literature. In a classic study of irony in literature, such as Alan Reynolds Thompson's *The Dry Mock: A Study of Irony in Drama*, the ironic dimensions are found, for instance, in the intertwining of tragedy and comedy. One of the chapters of the book is called "Emotions that Clash."[95] To interpret conflicts of emotions and moods in music in terms of irony is clearly not something that is at odds with how the concept of irony has been and is being used in literary studies influenced by the notion of Romantic irony.

Again, one might refer to Eduard Hanslick. Some of his ideas are also relevant to the notion of spatiality in music. One remembers that Arnheim stresses the impossibility of separating perception and thinking. To see is to think, and to think is to see. Hanslick believes that a multitude of *Geistesprocessen* [processes of the mind] are involved when one listens to music, but that they are impossible to separate in practice: "Art first of all puts something beautiful before us. It is not by means of feeling [*Gefühl*] that we become aware of beauty, but by means of the imagination [*Phantasie*] as the activity of pure contemplation [*Schauen*]."[96] This activity of the *Phantasie* seems to correspond to what today is called interpretation; it is an activity that combines *Gefühl* and *Verstand*, Hanslick states: "Certainly with regard to beauty, imagining is not mere contemplating [*Schauen*], but contemplating with active understanding [*Verstand*], i.e., conceiving and judging. Of course these processes occur so swiftly that we are unaware of them and are deceived into thinking that what, in truth, depends on several intermediate processes [*Geistesprocessen*] occurs immediately." [97]

It is interesting to note that Hanslick uses the word *Anschauung* when it comes to the process of interpreting music, the way one uses *Phantasie* when listening to music. Music is chiefly form, Hanslick emphasizes over and over again, and the visual metaphor according to which we "see" [*schauen*] these forms seems to be unavoidable for Hanslick too. As I interpret his text, the *Phantasie* is an activity that involves the perception of musical sounds and the instant transformation of them into spatial forms. "Perception" and "transformation" cannot be separated, though. As language offers no alternative terms by whose aid one would be able to describe the interpretive process more accurately, *Anschauung* is not *only* a metaphor: "The word *contemplation* [*Anschauung*] has long since been extended to include all sense appearances and not merely the visual," Hanslick notes, and "it serves very well for what we do when we listen attentively to the sequence of tonal forms that is music." He continues: "Imagination [*Phantasie*], moreover, is by no means an isolated domain; it draws its vital impulse from our sensation and rapidly transmits our sensations to intellect [*Verstand*] and feeling [*Gefühl*]." [98]

So, it is all obviously intimately interconnected. It is a sad fact that many dichotomies, such as reason versus feeling, that are set up by science to help one grasp the world at the same time delimit one's understanding of the complex reality. One is consequently obliged to deconstruct these dichotomies: to deny the difference between reason and feeling, and yet uphold it; to have a system and yet not have a system.

But Hanslick chose his stance. Music can represent only *das Dynamische* in itself, not the specific feelings: "It can reproduce the motion [*Bewegung*] of a physical process according to the prevailing momentum: fast, slow, strong, weak, rising, falling." [99] Again, one can conclude that whether one prefers to describe music in terms of emotion or in terms of form, one is forced to use spatial notions—be they metaphoric or not. This Hanslick also realized. There is a "well-grounded analogy" between movement in time and movement in room, he asserts. [100] He also

adopts the very common comparison between music and architecture.[101]

Yet, how is it that architecture and sculpture are so rarely interpreted in terms of irony? They are, after all, the most spatial art
forms of all. Perhaps this is the very problem: their space is so
real that it leaves very little room for abstract, virtual space. The
space of buildings and sculptures is always already "possible"
and "congruent," which might close one's eyes for ironic incongruities in their virtual space. However, the ironies are undoubtedly there, if one wishes to see them.

SHOSTAKOVICH AND THE QUEST FOR INTENTIONS

By now it is time to pick up a thread that became visible now
and then in the last section of this chapter: the problem of intentionality. In the beginning of the book I concluded that there is
no way of proving which hermeneutical stance is the right one:
the hermeneutics of orality, which leans on intentionality, or the
hermeneutics of textuality, which does not. However, I also argued that the hermeneutics of orality involves many problems,
especially in relation to irony. Tracing intentions behind literary
texts is no easy task, and it is no less problematic when interpreting images and music. Intentions are almost always connected to
verbal statements, and the tendency is that the more "formal"
one's own views on art or music are, the less inclined one is to be
interested in the artist's or the composer's intentions. Hanslick,
for instance, who believed that it is impossible for music to represent specific emotions, is clearly against intentionality.[102]

I do not think, however, that the relevance of intentions is necessarily dependent on what view one has of representation and
meaning in the arts. It is entirely a result of which hermeneutical
stance is chosen. The intentional hermeneutics is not wrong
(how could it be?), but it is my opinion that it is *better* not to lean
on it when dealing with irony in noncommunicative situations. I
will now once again argue for this stance of mine, and I will do it
by way of interpreting the ironic interpretations of Dmitry Shostakovich's music.

Marshall Brown has suggested that irony is an "inescapable"
characteristic of early modernist music.[103] Although it is quite
easy to avoid irony if one wishes, it is definitely true that early
modernism has been in focus for many writers on musical irony.
Mozart and Beethoven keep company with Mahler and Shosta-

kovich in the literature on humor and irony in music. It might be disputed whether Mahler really belongs to modernism, but similarities between Mahler and Shostakovich are often adduced.

For many reasons Shostakovich is one of the most controversial composers of the twentieth century. At times the debate around his person and his music has been rather heated. He has been a much too influential and popular composer to be left alone, and so his life and opinions have attracted as much attention as his music. Yet, he has also been subject to widely varying evaluations. Humor and irony are controversial characteristics of music that often produce disapproval, and in reading about Shostakovich (and Mahler) one constantly comes across such words as *grotesque, burlesque, macabre, comical, sarcasm, parody, mockery, caricature, satire, incongruity,* and—*irony.*[104]

Shostakovich lived and worked in the Soviet Union, and until his death in 1975 he was generally appreciated as, on the whole, a faithful representative of the communist ideology, both as a person and as an artist. This image became severely questioned in *Testimony: The Memoirs of Dmitri Shostakovich,* published in 1979 and allegedly representing the authentic words of the composer himself. In his introduction to this much-debated book, the editor, Solomon Volkov, calls Shostakovich a *yurodivy,* a person who conveys new ideals "through a screen of mockery, sarcasm, and foolishness."[105] Not only the composer himself but also the people close to him, Volkov asserts, recognized him as such. The *yurodivy* is apparently a variation of the *eiron,* and the difference between a serious upholder of political ideology and a mocking court jester is admittedly palpable.

This double image is interesting in itself, but it is perhaps even more interesting that Shostakovich's music has proved to have the capacity to support the two opposite interpretations of its creator and his alleged messages to the public. This is most clearly seen in the various, sometimes antagonistic interpretations of Shostakovich's Fifth Symphony from 1937. This symphony is one of the composer's most loved and also most debated works. According to Volkov, Shostakovich himself believed that everyone who liked his Fifth Symphony also understood what Stalin was actually doing in the Soviet Union.[106] The rejoicing in the finale of the symphony is said to be forced: "It's as if someone were beating you with a stick and saying, 'your business is rejoicing, your business is rejoicing' and you rise, shakily, and go marching off muttering, 'Our business is rejoicing, our business is rejoicing.' "[107]

This is the alleged intention of the composer, but is it true? How could one know? First of all it is far from sure that Volkov's account of Shostakovich's words is correct. However, I will postulate that it is. Then one must face the fact that the words were uttered a very long time after the symphony was written, at a time when Shostakovich was not "the same" person as several decades earlier. Even if one assumes that it later came to be his own interpretation of the music, it is uncertain whether the description of forced rejoicing was really the composer's original intention—and if the notion of intention is to be meaningful it must correlate with the conception of the work. Otherwise, is it reasonable to call the composer's later interpretations his "intentions"? If so, and if one believes in the normative force of intentions, one must accept either that a piece of music has many meanings decided by the composer or that its meaning becomes fixed the day he happens to die.

Shostakovich's alleged description of the Fifth Symphony is not a bad interpretation of the music, although I cannot see how it could be considered in any way final. The notion of forced rejoicing fits my ears pretty well, and it has gained ground. Mstislav Rostropovich has remarked that "anyone who thinks the finale is glorification is an idiot."[108] Needless to say, this is his very personal opinion, although shared by others in slightly more subtle forms. A few years after the publication of Volkov's book, Michael Oliver wrote about the same finale in a review of a recording with Bernard Haitink and the Concertgebouw Orchestra. Oliver asserts that "the triumph of the coda seems hollow, its exultation bitterly false—and the symphony gains in stature thereby."[109] He likes Haitink's interpretation very much, and he describes the symphony in terms of irony.

Christopher Norris reacted against Oliver's interpretation and its accompanying evaluation. With an answer to Oliver's review, Norris initiated a debate in *Gramophone.* He wrote that a favorite device of Western commentators on Shostakovich is "to domesticate otherwise disturbing or subversive texts by discovering subtle ironies at work, thus allowing them to 'mean' more or less whatever the critic would wish upon them."[110] In Norris's view, critics tend to forget that Shostakovich himself was inclined to feel "Socialist Optimism."

This is an interesting example of the ambiguous relation between form and feeling that illuminates the force of the critique of the *Affektenlehre.* The same piece of music seems to have the capacity of being interpreted as indicating both false rejoicing and true optimism. According to the review the exultation is false, which furthermore suggests that the music somehow holds two mutually exclusive moods at the same time: it *sounds like* exultation but it *is* not. It seems as if only very small nuances discerned in the listening are enough for a reversal of the meaning of the music. Of course one must not forget that there are two layers of interpretation: from score to sounding music, and from sounding music to "meaning."

I believe that Norris is definitely right when he points to the fact that it is always possible to discover "subtle ironies at work" wherever one wishes, and he is most certainly right when he stresses the political and ideological implications of ironic and nonironic interpretations. The weakness of Norris's stance is that it is equally as easy for an interpreter to be blind to subtle ironies as it is to discover them. In his reply to Oliver, Norris implies that there is a true meaning, but his image of Shostakovich the man is no more stable than Volkov's image.

What Oliver does in his review is to argue in terms of artistic value, although it is true that such an argument *might* lead to political conclusions—which is proved by Norris's objections. Of course, Oliver's view that an emphasis on ironic double meaning in Shostakovich's Fifth Symphony makes it better artistically is not definite, but he does not in any way claim to have access to the truth. Norris, on the other hand, gives the impression of believing that he knows what Shostakovich actually thought and felt and what his music as a matter of facts means, but he has no arguments as far as the artistic value is concerned.

Norris's views are, however, much more sophisticated when put forth in a lengthier format. Earlier the same year that Oliver's review appeared in *Gramophone,* 1982, Christopher Norris had published the book *Shostakovich: The Man and his Music,* edited by and with two contributions written by himself. In the introduction to this volume, Norris questions the authenticity of Volkov's book and its claim to faithfully give voice to Shostakovich's own ideas and feelings. In this less polemic situation, Norris also emphasizes "the irreducibility of music to any clear-cut programmatic meaning."[111]

When reading Norris's "Shostakovich: Politics and Musical Language," it becomes obvious that he does not at all believe that there is a single, pro-Soviet meaning in Shostakovich's music. On the contrary, Norris here argues *for* an ironic interpretation of Shostakovich. Considering his harsh words about discovering "subtle ironies," it might seem strange that Norris himself even tries to distinguish Shostakovich's "subdued *structural* irony" from his "indulged romantic irony."[112] When he describes the so-called structural irony in terms of "cryptic understatement and defensive irony" (as one remembers, both litotes and hyperbole belong to the standard repertoire of terms associated with irony), it is certainly difficult to realize the huge difference between his and Oliver's stances, especially as he even sees the much-debated finale of the Fifth Symphony as crudely transforming ideas from the earlier movements: "a process of more-or-less conscious deformation which reflects ironically on the music's idealistic programme."[113] Earlier in the same article he wishes to reject the interpretation of the finale according to which the rejoicing is forced, but his only argument against it is that "it squares so perfectly with what a Western ideologue would want to say."[114] Considering how the words are put later in the article, it seems as if his own interpretation is not completely at odds with what he calls Western ideology.

Obviously, Norris's stance is somewhat ambivalent, or perhaps it would be better to say that his conception of irony is ambivalent. His distinction between Romantic and structural irony is explained very scantily, and I think that it is difficult to uphold in the long run. If one wants to engage in distinctions, it is more important to here distinguish between *either/or*-irony and *both/and*-irony. I believe that it is through this distinction that one is able to see the most important difference between Oliver's and Norris's positions. Oliver seems to interpret the finale of the Fifth Symphony according to something that resembles the standard of rhetorical irony: the music says *rejoice!*—but means/implies *despair!* Norris, on the other hand, finally reaches the conclusion that the music says both *rejoice!* and *despair!*, although he sometimes gives the impression of believing that the music says *and* means *rejoice!*. The *both/and*-irony might seem to be the more sophisticated, and in a way it comes closest to one kind of truth: that the musical meaning is not definite until it has been created in an interpretive act of an individual listener. Hence, the music "means" potentially everything, even though it is clear to see that all interpretations of the finale circle "strong" feelings. It might even be maintained that for some persons joy is such an utterly false feeling that all joy *is* despair. In the end, however, the *either/or*-irony is of course as valid an interpretation as the *both/and*-irony.

The weakness of Norris's article is, I think, that he argues on the base of intentionality. The way they are circumscribed by

Norris, Shostakovich's intentions are redundant simply because he cannot find them—and he knows that he cannot. Norris asserts that the composer's intentions are ambiguous, and for me that is the same as acknowledging their nonexistence or nonaccessibility. However, Norris, perhaps because of the heavy burden of intentionalism in earlier Shostakovich research, wishes the hovering mind of the composer to bear evidence of the hovering meaning of his music. Understanding Shostakovich, Norris states, "is often a matter of sensing this conflict between musical impulse and various kinds of extra-musical imperative." Yet, the relation between life and work is "difficult to interpret," he also states: intentions are "at best an ambiguous matter."[115] Why bother, then, if the quest for intentions, even for ambiguous intentions, does not lead to anything but increased confusion?

Norris concludes by stating that the documentary and musical record "is too full of puzzles and downright contradictions" to admit of any "pure-minded faith," and he calls in Bakhtin's description of a polyphony of "muted, ambivalent voices" to explain Shostakovich's "subversive irony."[116] I have no objections to Bakhtin's relevance—but do we really need the so-called intentions of Shostakovich to reach this conclusion? I do not think so. Norris interprets the music itself as being full of "downright contradictions," and the documentary record does not modify this interpretation. As a matter of fact, Norris's article demonstrates superbly the irrelevance of intentional evidence when it comes to interpreting music ironically. It is no more possible to confirm that the composer's intentions are ambiguous than it is to confirm that they are definitely pro- or anti-Soviet. It is perhaps only more likely that they are ambiguous, and that does not take us very far.

If one simplifies it slightly, one thus has three different opinions regarding Shostakovich's political beliefs and musical intentions. Much of the music criticism in the Soviet Union, and also the musicologist Robert Stradling, think that he was a true Communist and that his music is not subversive.[117] It is sometimes "formalistic," yes, but with no hidden messages. In Volkov's view, Shostakovich was not a Communist, and his music is clearly double-edged and subversive. Norris is the most prominent representative of the middle stance: Shostakovich's political position was contradictive and ambiguous, and so is his music: sometimes subversive and ironic, sometimes not.

However, much more can be said about Shostakovich and irony. It sneaks in here, there, and everywhere. Although not very inclined to find irony in Shostakovich's Fifth Symphony, or in any of his other symphonies for that matter, Robert Dearling cannot help wondering, as Shostakovich "builds the Symphony towards its mighty climax, whether his tongue was in his cheek."[118] In spite of that, Dearling believes that the symphony has "an immensely healthy assurance and optimism." He calls a theme in the finale "belligerently optimistic," and the final section of this last movement is characterized as "affirmative."[119]

Certainly, the Fifth Symphony is often seen as an affirmative, pro-Soviet, fundamentally unironic piece of music. In the article "Shostakovich's Fifth Symphony: A Soviet Artist's Reply . . . ?", J. Daniel Huband notes that the symphony has been acclaimed as "a model of Socialist Realism" (a notion demanding firm belief in music's capacity to represent not only emotions but also historic reality),[120] in particular because of its so-called "heroic finale."[121] Yet, if the metronome markings of the composer were to be followed, Huband remarks, it would not sound heroic at all. Again, one must not forget that interpretation of music is generally twofold. What most people interpret is music already interpreted by musicians.

Huband also mentions the very often quoted words "a Soviet artist's creative reply to justified criticism," Shostakovich's own view of the Fifth Symphony according to many reports. The quotation has often been taken as the proof of an "anti-ironic" intention of Shostakovich—although its origin has been questioned. Huband points to the fact that it is not clear whether those are the exact words of the composer, and that only small differences in the word constellation might lead to contrary interpretations.

It is certainly worth considering that this "intention" must itself be interpreted before it can be used to interpret the music. What is, for instance, a "creative reply"? Is it something that *follows* the doctrine of Socialist realism, or something that *modifies* it? If so, in what way does it modify it? Trying to answer these questions, one is already back into the interpretation of the music itself, leaving the stable hermeneutics of intentionality far behind. To be sure, Shostakovich's utterance might be seen as an irony in itself; an utterance meaning "a Soviet artist's creative reply to unjustified criticism," or "an individualist artist's disguised denial of official taste."

So, what does one have? Two alleged intentions that are at odds: the one seemingly implying that the symphony is a face-value celebration of Soviet optimism ("a Soviet artist's creative reply . . ."), the other seemingly implying that it is an ironic, subversive criticism of that very same society ("your business is rejoicing . . ."). These are two alleged intentions that in themselves mean very little if not being interpreted in one direction or another.

Trying to stabilize the meaning of music, one undoubtedly becomes involved in maneuvers that are not at all stable themselves. Unfortunately, "reality" is not always more fixed than musical sounds. Is it perhaps time to acknowledge the importance of the listener in the interpretation of music?

Peter J. Rabinowitz has taken a step in that direction. In a very interesting article about the advantages of employing literary "reader criticism" in music criticism, he discusses the finale of Shostakovich's Fifth Symphony as a case in point for the problem of musical referentiality. The march in this movement, he argues, is "fictional." He finds some indications in what he takes to be the music itself, such as an "extreme" shift of key and some oddities in instrumentation and form, but "the central point of the movement lies in the listener's presumed reactions, not to the music itself, which could well be unambiguously 'positive,' but to the fictional circumstances it evokes." [122] It is therefore likely, Rabinowitz assumes, that the rejoicing finale actually demonstrates fictional joy. Put in its social context, the march is of a kind that is "most likely to be heard at a large public spectacle glorifying the state."[123] The march might thus be listened to as a reference to historic reality, and from the point of view of the music "itself" this external reference is fictional; it is not a part of its "own" mood, what it "says."

Rabinowitz's arguments are very well balanced, and it is interesting that he declares himself unable to actually "*hear* the music the way that I feel I should."[124] This peculiar problem is due to his belief that it is the composer's intentions that determine the meaning of the music: the way it "should" be heard. The consequences of his declared interest in reader criticism are hence very limited. Rabinowitz's music listener is more an effect of the composer's intentions and the music than a genuine interpreter. It is "the listener's presumed reactions" that are of theoretical interest for him—and of course a "presumed" reaction is presumed by the composer, in this case Shostakovich.[125] In spite of his search for an alternative approach to music criticism, one finds Rabinowitz looking for Shostakovich's intentions: intentions that are of course never found. Rabinowitz can only state what he believes them to be. Yet, he is oddly convinced that "the music is indeed a negative apotheosis" and that contrary interpretations of it are an "apparent misunderstanding."[126]

This clash between a declared interest in the receiver and a genuine interest in the artist is not, by the way, unique. Much art criticism from the last few decades is dedicated to proving that one artist or another *intends* his or her work to be created by the spectator. Quite often one is also taught which method is the *best* if one wishes to behold the art in full freedom, and how the artist in question manages to determine this interpretive freedom.

Finally, the latest extensive text concerning meaning, politics, and irony in Shostakovich must be scrutinized. In his book from 1991, *The New Shostakovich*, Ian MacDonald uses the concept of irony quite often. His hermeneutics is based on Shostakovich's intentions, and he deals principally with factual, political, and historical contexts. According to MacDonald, there is correct meaning and there is inappropriate meaning, the latter of which is characterized as "a sort of self-hypnotic dream."[127]

Like so many others, however, MacDonald equates the composer's intentions with his own interpretations, while pretending that the intentions are part of the objective truth of the world. Writing about the slow movement in the Fifth Symphony, he states that "so transparent is its intention that close description is unnecessary."[128] Of course, MacDonald is not dreaming. As far as the finale is concerned, he adopts Shostakovich's alleged intention as presented in Volkov's book. It is, MacDonald says, "difficult to disagree with him."[129] From MacDonald's point of view, it is not only difficult to disagree, I would say that it is impossible. There is a correct meaning, and MacDonald knows what it looks like. In fact, he knows it so well that "description is unnecessary."

I must admit to developing grave misgivings when MacDonald claims that there is one single meaning in Shostakovich's music, and that any listener who is not aware of the composer's intentions, or of the political and historical circumstances surrounding the conception of the music, inevitably misinterprets it. If the intentional hermeneutics proposed by MacDonald were valid, listeners would all run the risk of hearing and loving Shostakovich's music in a constant state of total misinterpretation. MacDonald believes that this is the case, and that is "arguably the most grotesque cultural scandal of our time."[130] This is indeed an ironic situation.

In his influential book, *Validity in Interpretation*, E. D. Hirsch declares that "consensus can be reached by mastering the relevant evidence."[131] As far as I can see, though, the hermeneutics of intentionalism does not lead to clarification, but rather to irresolvable oppositions. The debate goes on, and unfortunately the qualities of Shostakovich's music tend to disappear behind the argumentation centered on his person. It is a cliché to say that music talks to us in terms beyond specific political language, but to me it is a true cliché. Even within this nonpolitical, musical world, however, ambiguities and ironies may dwell. Whether irony is good or bad, its existence or nonexistence cannot be determined even with the aid of an intentionalistic hermeneutics. No matter what hermeneutical strategy one chooses, one must always interpret.

Shostakovich has thus been thoroughly scrutinized, and yet the confusion concerning his intentions has mounted. Indirectly, however, this increased confusion might lead to an increased awareness of the richness of his music, and irony seems to be a potent part of its meaning as it has been construed by widely differing interpreters. Mock-heroism or heroism, irony or not irony, that seems to be the crucial question—and not a few listeners vote for irony.[132]

In the beginning of this chapter I discussed the notion of musical meaning mainly as an intrinsic quality. The discussions around Shostakovich's music make it clear that hearing musical meaning is also a matter of attributing specific historic meaning to music. This is indeed a perfectly legitimate business, but, contrary to what might be expected, it is sometimes even more fallacious than trying to interpret the music "in itself." Relating music to history or biography does *not* make its meaning more stable, it only gives it a different character: a character that is closer to literary meaning but still no more determined. The ambiguities will always remain, contrary, for instance, to what MacDonald claims in his new and "definitive" version of Shostakovich. Whether one places the emotive categories "joy" and "despair" in a subjective, general context, or in the context of the Soviet society, they will remain the results of interpretation.

The last few pages have also made it clear that irony in music need not necessarily be circumscribed within the paradigm of Romantic irony. Most often, surely, it is suggested that the ironic coexistence of opposite emotions and moods in music is "linear." *First,* one is confronted with one mood, and *then* with a fundamentally different one. However, some ironic interpretations of the finale in Shostakovich's Fifth Symphony claim that the music is in some sense both happy and sad at the same time, with the analogy of how the word *happy* might be ironically interpreted as meaning sad in a certain text—or perhaps both happy and sad.

Before putting an end to this discussion, I must emphasize that my dismissal of intentionalism and historical contexts is not a general dismissal. I find it futile to try to determine, or even "narrow down" the (non-)ironic meaning of music, but historical studies always have values in themselves. Of course, everyone is curious about how it "actually" was. Personally, I guess that Volkov and MacDonald are right, at large, when it comes to giving an account of Shostakovich as a *yurodivy* in the Soviet Union, but that does not settle the argument about the meaning of his music—not even the historical meaning. Historical meaning is actually historical *meanings*. There are doubtless historical truths, such as the fact that the regime of Stalin killed and suppressed millions of people, but one has no definite access to how these factual truths are being construed by different people, if they are known at all. It is not known what are the subconscious responses or what conclusions are drawn at different times and how all this affects the personal moods, beliefs, and attitudes toward political, religious, and existential issues. Often people do not really know it themselves, and often it all exists beyond the realm of words. That is why one has no access to intentions. That is also why one finds it necessary to write and listen to music.

What about the music of Shostakovich? I, too, hear irony in the finale of the Fifth Symphony. I hear forced rejoicing and dark despair, but I also hear hope and, toward the end, some sort of victory. Yet, as soon as I try to hear it *either* as optimistic *or* pessimistic, *either* for *or* against the Soviet ideology, the music loses its force. That is the way I react, and I think that the urge to find intentional meaning in music as a rule narrows down the scale of expressiveness. After all, as Langer reminds us, the meaning of music, its capacity to represent forms of highly complex feelings, bursts the conceptual framework of verbal language. Shostakovich's Fifth Symphony seems to be a musical work that, more than many others, challenges the imperialism of language.

GOOD MUSIC, BAD MUSIC, OR IRONIC MUSIC?

In the year 1967 these wise words of Dahlhaus got into print: "Some important works—Mahler's symphonies and even Bruckner's—are characterized by inconsistencies and discontinuities, and to deny their existence would be a false defence; rather, a usable theory of criticism ought to do justice to these characteristics. Categories like ambivalence, paradox, ambiguity, and irony, which have long been at home in literary criticism, ought to be so in music esthetics too." The problems of "esthetic judgement," Dahlhaus states, begin "after a well-founded decision as to whether a particular discrepancy represents a fault or can be justified as a paradox." One has on the one hand "the complementary contrast that even classicistic esthetics reckons as a part of its own repertory," and on the other hand "the incoherent juxtaposition of parts that marks bad music."[133]

I do not believe, as Dahlhaus seems to, that "inconsistencies and discontinuities" are objective qualities of music, and I do not believe that it is very easy to agree upon how to distinguish between contrasts and incoherencies—not even after a very long time of thought—but Dahlhaus's implied observation about the *interpretive* role of the critic and the importance of his or her "esthetic judgement" is very important. He realizes the growing need for musicologists to consider notions such as irony and reconsider notions like contrast and incoherence, and he clearly sees the connection between these notions and the evaluation of music.

The relation between irony and value has been a controversy for thousands of years. Most of the time the objective existence or nonexistence of irony in specific texts has been taken for granted, and the question has been whether irony is good or bad in itself. Is it the Devil's vehicle for chaos, or is it allied to God's superior madness? It has been despised as some sort of lie, and it has been praised to convey the highest wisdom. Kierkegaard, one remembers, is fundamentally ambiguous in a very symptomatic way when it comes to evaluating irony. It fascinates him and it gives rise to some lyrical descriptions—and yet it is dismissed as nothingness.

Already in one of the earliest examples of discussions on irony in music that I have found, some passages in Alexandre Oulibicheff's *Beethoven: Ses critiques et ses glossateurs* from 1857, irony and value are explicitly connected. Writing about Beethoven's Seventh Symphony, Oulibicheff mentions "the most bitter irony. Beethoven forgot that sarcasm is impossible in music"![134] Oulibicheff does not like the finale and complains that "Beethoven wanted to write musical satires." Apparently, Oulibicheff states, "Beethoven's intention was ironic in this finale." The critic thinks that the movement is full of platitudes, which is called *humor* by the fanatics; but a platitude remains a platitude "in the ear of men of taste," he concludes.[135]

Irony may thus be judged as good or bad in itself. In interpretive practice one often first evaluates the artistic work intuitively, and then, depending on the conception and evaluation of irony, one determines the ironic dimensions. Of course, one's attitude toward irony may be changed through the experience of reading a novel, for instance, but I think that it is far more common that one's conception of irony governs the determination of its existence than the other way around. However, first of all comes one's instinctive evaluation of the work: a response that is certainly always a mixture of personal, emotive bents and intellectual prefigurations.

One way of explaining the interaction of evaluation and ironic interpretation is to see it from a narratological point of view. In literature, one distinguishes between the implied author and the narrator. Reading a narrative, one sometimes feels that the narrator is "unreliable" or at least distinct from the implied author. The narrator makes statements that one understands to be at odds with what the narrative as such implies. Conversely, one may feel that there is a discrepancy between the narratee and the implied reader; that the narrator actually addresses some sort of "naive" reader who is part of the narrative's construction but that it is implied that the words of the narrator be interpreted differently. One way of construing irony in literature is to focus on such discrepancies between narrative levels. Sometimes this is labeled structural irony.

The implied author and the implied reader are far from stable entities. Actually, they are constructions created by the reader; constructions that often, but not always, are made by the majority of readers within the same interpretive communities. When reading Dickens, for instance, most readers find it impossible to avoid seeing ironic incongruities between narrative levels in remarks such as "the tender mercies of churchwardens and overseers," as one sees Oliver being brutally mistreated.

In music also it is sometimes reasonable to see discrepancies between "narrative levels." Although it is not possible to formalize the narrative levels of music as distinctly as in literature, the mechanisms of ironic interpretation are the same. Music, too, can and has been "read" as ironic on the basis of apprehended "incongruities" between what it "says" and what it "implies." In literature, the implied author is a construction of the reader, and of course the "implied composer" of music is also a construction of the listener. The "implied composer" stands for what one takes to be the "norms" of the music. Consequently, there may emerge a clash between the music as it is actually heard and the music as it is believed to be seen by the "implied composer." If one likes the music even if it embodies "bad" elements, the existence of which is justified, one also feels that there is a distance within the music itself—and irony is a reasonable term for describing this distance. If, on the other hand, one does not like the music because of its "bad" elements, one feels that there is no distance between the "implied composer" and the "musical narrator"—and hence there is no irony. The music is simply poor. If, however, one does not fancy irony at all, all music embodying what one takes to be "bad" elements is wrecked beyond rescue, no matter what distances might be traced in it. One may even call what one takes to be poor music ironic if one finds that its incongruities, like irony in itself, are an aesthetic or moral failure. That was the stance adopted by Oulibicheff, who had no mercy for Beethoven's ironic platitudes.

Again, the reception of Shostakovich is a good case in point. Many commentators agree that his music is (as Kivy would put it) expressive of emotions that are somehow inconsistent, incongruous, or sharply contrasting. Yet, they cannot agree on the value of these incongruities. Even trained musicologists betray signs of unsteadiness when evaluating, for instance, some of the finales of Shostakovich's symphonies. Clearly, there are parts of his music that do not fit well into acknowledged ways of comprehending a musical work as a whole. Some critics praise it for being effectively contrastive, ironic, and complex; some blame it for being full of incongruities and disparate elements.

Form and emotion are intimately interwoven, and to blame music for its formal ruptures is often not very different from blaming it for displaying sharply differing moods. According to Norris, the opera *Lady Macbeth of the Mtensk Region* was condemned by *Pravda* for, among other things, the incoherence of its musical language.[136] Dearling thinks that Shostakovich's Sixth Symphony is the least satisfying due to "its world of varied, apparently disassociated, moods."[137] Again, the differing evaluations of the finale of the Fifth Symphony are illustrative. Many feel that its optimism is forced, and consequently also "flawed."[138] However, if one interprets what one takes to be forced optimism in terms of irony, the evaluation may be reversed. This is the case for Oliver and MacDonald. According to MacDonald, irony is good—if not in itself because of its distancing capacity of undermining Soviet propaganda. Ambiguity, on the other hand, is definitely bad in MacDonald's eyes, and that goes for irony, too, if it does not follow the principle *either/or*. Norris, on the other hand, is sometimes distinctly allergic to ironic interpretations of the model *either/or*, especially when he believes that they are a comfortable escape from a more complex and truthful stance. Sometimes, however, he finds the concept of irony valuable. His interpretation of the finale of the Fifth Symphony is appraisive, and his advocacy of Bakhtin is in line with this interest in "many-voiced" discourse.

The next most appreciated and discussed Shostakovich symphony, after the Fifth, is probably the Tenth. Like much of Shostakovich's music, this symphony has been considered to have a meaning of a concrete and political nature. Volkov discusses Shostakovich's music as if it were full of meaning of a very definite kind. The second movement of the Tenth Symphony, for instance, is called a "musical portrait" of Stalin.[139] Gregory Karl and Jenefer Robinson, on the other hand, do not primarily lean on external evidence when maintaining that music in general may express "cognitively complex emotions." As a case in point, they analyze the Tenth's third movement and conclude that parts of it express hope, although the symphony as a whole is "a largely pessimistic work."[140] Karl and Robinson do not discuss the concept of irony, but their willingness to accept the existence of complex emotions in the music of Shostakovich points toward the same line of thought that is involved in ironic interpretations: music may "say" things that are contrasting or incongruous.

Ian MacDonald, of course, discusses the Tenth Symphony in terms of irony,[141] but it is David Fanning who has written the most extensive study of it. He analyzes the symphony in a rather formal way, but he also interprets the music in terms of rhetoric, eloquence, and statements.[142] His attitude toward intentionality is somewhat ambivalent, and he feels obliged to declare that his interpretation of the last movement is the most personal one. It is no coincidence, I think, that Fanning is most eager to see ironies in the finale. He knows that the ironies he hears cannot be found in the score.

Fanning supplies some illuminating examples of what he sees as internal conflicts in the symphony, and these conflicts are given ironic interpretations. Irony is in its turn circumscribed in terms of expectations and surprising or failed fulfillments. He writes about hope that "peters out into the void," "the extreme discrepancy in character of certain transformations," "disjunction between gesture and immediate context," and "sorrowful" themes that are transformed into "cheerful" ones.[143] This is a terminology with which one is by now very familiar.

What is important in this context, is that Fanning approaches the music from a normative angle. His starting point in the book is "the widely held view that the Tenth is Shostakovich's finest symphony, possibly even his finest work," and perhaps his most important interpretive tool for explaining this high evaluation is irony.[144] Fanning is naturally well aware that the finales of Shostakovich's symphonies have been strongly criticized in the West for their supposed banality, hollowness, or exhaustion. Writing in 1988, he rightly remarks that the willingness to see them as ironic has increased in recent years.[145] Hand in hand with these new, ironic interpretations an aesthetic revaluation has followed.

I do not think that it is necessary to exemplify further. It is clear enough that the normative dimensions are intimately interwoven with the interpretive and descriptive dimensions. There are several questions that are impossible to disentangle, no matter how skilled a musicologist one is. Is the music annoyingly incongruous or suggestively complex? Is it fragmented or unified? Are its elements poorly integrated or effectively contrastive? Is it ironic?

No matter how one answers these questions, the answers are connected to the question of whether the music is supposed to be good or bad, and I am convinced that statements about the music itself more often than not are products of evaluations. Few scholars, I believe, are able to first analyze and then evaluate music—or art, literature, film, or dance. Often the alleged formal descriptions build upon subjective, aesthetic norms. To put it simply, those who for some reason like Shostakovich's music and approve of irony, as I myself do, call it ironic; those who do not call it a failure.

In the final chapter of his book on Shostakovich, Fanning stresses something that has become apparent in the course of this book: it is "no more possible to prove the existence of irony in music than to define the parameters of an ironic 'Oh, yes' in literature. Timing, context and cultural conventions, some would say ideology, too, all contribute to the instinct which may lead us to impute such meaning."[146] I would like to emphasize that contexts, norms, and ideas belonging to the interpreter himself or herself are not the least crucial factors in this respect. Whether one reads texts, looks at images, or listens to music, irony primarily exists in the reader, the spectator, or the listener. Ironic interpretation is a strategy that helps one come to terms with the understanding and evaluation of apprehended contrasts, para-doxes, incongruities, conflicts, and contradictions that would otherwise be considered meaningless, puzzling, or irritating. Irony in itself does not exist outside one's head. All one has—and that is not too bad—is a large set of spatial metaphors that help one to grasp the peculiar nature or ironic experience.

Nachspiel

Which gods will be capable of rescuing us from all these
ironies?

—Friedrich Schlegel

ABOUT TWO HUNDRED YEARS AGO, FRIEDRICH SCHLEGEL WROTE "ÜBER DIE
Unverständlichkeit," a short text in which he penetrates the
irony of irony. Schlegel clearly realized that there is no way to
fence in irony; that it is impossible to put an end to it by way of
rules or definitions. It might very well invade our discourse completely. He saw a scenario where "irony becomes wild and escapes all control." This is a fascinating but also threatening
scenario: "Irony is definitely no laughing matter. Its aftermath
can be incredibly long."[1]

Readers now know that he was right, from a historical point of
view also. Irony has gone wild. It has invaded the discourse on
images and music. It has long been known and accepted that
irony is a phenomenon that includes clashes of emotions and
meanings found on many different levels of the literary texts.
Now it is possible to conclude that irony is an even more widespread phenomenon than hitherto accepted by the majority of
scholars and laypersons, and that it might possibly become a part
of every existing sign system. This book has given only a few examples of this expansion, limited to the world of artistic expression, but I believe that the understanding of irony as it has been
sketched here is generally valid.

I have tried to show that the interpretation of irony, or better
the ironic interpretation, may be performed according to either
of two hermeneutical stances: the oral model or the literary
model. Depending on which model one chooses to apply, the interpretations may vary considerably. This is the situation also for
interpretation in general. In fact, I think that many interpretive
battles and disagreements about the meaning of verbal, visual,
and aural texts are caused by a not always clearly recognized hovering between these two hermeneutical stances. However, differ-

ing ironic interpretations are extreme in a way that makes them
serve well as illuminating examples of the general predicaments
of all interpretation. When it comes to choosing between not
only nuances of meaning, but also between mutually exclusive
meanings, one simply cannot ignore the problem any longer. By
trying to understand how irony works, one also tries to understand how all interpretation works.

Not much has been said about the communicative aspect of
irony in this book—the fact that irony, as everyone knows, *may
be* both "intended" and successfully "understood" within interpretive communities. Over and over again I have argued for the
advantages of treating irony as an interpretive strategy, but I have
done so not because I want to deny the existence of functioning,
ironic communication, or the fact that some texts are more
readily seen as ironic, but because I believe that the notion of
interpretive strategy is necessary for one's understanding of irony's way from the oral to the textual, visual, and aural domains:
from the rhetorical to the situational. I do not think that the em-
bracing of irony as a spatial metaphor and an interpretive strategy radically changes the whole business of circumscribing irony
in specific texts, images, or pieces of music—but I do think that
it can help avoid quite a lot of confusion and misguided attempts
to find a truth that has to be sought for elsewhere. There are no
textual, visual, or aural traits that are ironic in themselves, only
traits that may be seen as incongruous, and hence—if it makes
sense—interpreted in terms of irony.

The fact that irony has gone wild cuts both ways. Many people
no doubt regret what they believe to be a loss of terminological
stringency, whereas others—including me—welcome the tearing
down of false boundaries between concepts and art forms. Instead of taming the wild beast of irony, I think it is better to learn
to live with it as it has turned out to be. It is wild but wise.

Divine Madness is a book on interart issues. Two stories have
been told. One is a story of how literary conceptualization has
conquered the fields of the other arts. The other is a story of how
literary conceptualization, conversely, has been successively rel-
ativized. The most important thing to learn from the success of
the concept of irony within art and music criticism is, I believe,
not that images and pieces of music may be interpreted after the
model of literary criticism, but that, when the crunch comes, the
interpretation of literature is actually no less relative and subjective than the interpretation of images and music. All three fields
have had their advocates for objectivity and subjectivity, but the

commonly held view is that literature, when it comes to aspects that really matter—moods, feelings, and ideas—is much more determinate than the art form that has been seen as literature's opposite in this respect: music.

I do not think that this is quite true. The fact that it is often possible to say much more about specified moods, feelings, and ideas in literature without leaving the area of a certain intersubjective, verbal stability has been confused with the illusive conception that the overall interpretation of literature is a much safer business than the interpretation of images and music. After all, one might think, literature consists of words, and everyone knows the meaning of words. The phenomenon of irony, however, is the extreme variation of interpretive strategies that makes it more clear than ever that the meaning of literary works—like the meaning of paintings, films, operas, ballets, songs, sonatas, and sculptures—is never evidently there to be seen and picked up. The problem of irony, I repeat, concentrates and highlights all the problems of interpretation; it is the hermeneutical touchstone *par préférence*. I hope to have demonstrated that, when it comes to ironic interpretation, the differences between the various fields of art are marginal. Irony "in" language is no more "in" it than it is "in" images and music. With the aid of verbal language, one can discuss and describe irony, but irony "in" language is a creation of one's interpretation, as is all irony. *The fact that one can verbally paraphrase what one takes to be ironic incongruities in language does not make its existence more real or palpable. The stability created by the identity of language and meta-language in literary interpretation is illusive.*

Indeed, the most important terms in the discourse on the arts are definitely not objective when it comes to really using them. Even though it is often possible to agree upon what certain terms stand for, or ought to stand for (one may always postulate an ahistoric, objective definition), it is an entirely different issue to agree upon when these terms, or the notions that they refer to, are relevant to the description and interpretation of specific works of art. Although possible to distinguish in theory, the basic dichotomies similarity/difference, unity/incongruity, simplicity/complexity, and metaphor/irony are far from always possible to disentangle in interpretive practice. Irony and metaphor are related, I have argued, not in spite of their opposite positions in the rhetorical system, but because of them. Together with a wide range of other notions, they are primarily interpretive strategies rather than formal categories: interpretive strategies that may

mold literary texts, images, and musical pieces into very different—or similar—phenomena.

Hence, one always employs terminology in more or less pronounced subjective ways when analyzing and comparing works
of art. Response and interpretation are almost always the heart
of the matter, much more often than one perhaps realizes—and
to accept subjectivism as a necessary part of interpretation is to
accept also relativism. Relativism, however, is a philosophically
rather vague term. Unfortunately (or perhaps fortunately), even
relativism is relative. The disagreements on what relativism in interpretation really is are highlighted in an issue of the *Journal of
Aesthetics and Art Criticism* from 1995 in which Joseph Margolis,
Stephen Davies, and Robert Stecker all agree that they do not
agree.[2] I will, however, confine myself to making a reference to
these three articles and declare that it seems to me as if Margolis
is the one of the three who has the most profound insight into
what interpreting works of art is all about.

My opinion is that all interpretation is not only related to varying contexts, but that it *necessarily* takes form in more or less subjective contexts. The results of interpretation are consequently
always more or less relative, and that is a good thing. Otherwise,
interpretation would be a boring business; what is more important, it would be a business without the capacity of saying anything worth saying about the world. Creations that do not move
die. The meaning of *Hamlet* has moved constantly for hundreds
of years like two pairs of feet engaged in an Argentinean tango,
and the play is still more alive than ever. Interpretation is life,
and life changes. Only matter that has reached absolute zero is
absolutely immobile, and at that temperature it is also absolutely
dead.

That does not mean, however, that there is no truth at all or
that all truth is relative. In my view, interpretations can never
make *general* claims to be true. Interpretations may be "true"
only—relatively. There are facts about the world that are true and
stable, be it that Shostakovich's Tenth Symphony consists of four
movements or that the Nazis murdered millions of Jews. No ironies can do away with those facts. Yet, when it comes to *interpreting* these facts, these truths, there is no definite stability. Even if
one agrees that Shostakovich's symphonic form is rather traditional or that the Holocaust is one of the worst things that have
occurred in the history of humankind, one can never agree on
what these facts really *mean*—what their "true" meaning is—as

they can be placed in so many various contexts. For art it is furthermore more important to be "plausible" than to be "true."

Is all this madness? I am not so sure. The beast of irony is wild but wise. If ironic interpretation is madness, it is divine madness.

In a famous article, Roman Jakobson has suggested that two types of the speech defect known as aphasia have their equivalents in the tropes metaphor and metonymy. Metaphor operates on the paradigmatic axis of language, the axis of selection, and metonymy on the syntagmatic axis, the axis of combination. Jakobson asserts that similarity and contiguity are the two major structural relations of language and that they not only become visible in aphasic disturbances—they also form the core of poetry and prose respectively.[3]

It might be suggested (without any scientific claims) that schizophrenia has its equivalent in irony. Schizophrenia is a mental disturbance primarily characterized by split personality. Being schizophrenic is not, most people believe, a good thing. Nor is irony a good thing, quite a lot of people say. However, there are many cultures where being mad is a sign of having direct contact with the divine powers, and Kierkegaard, who tried to be an enemy of irony, called it divine madness. For Schlegel and other Romanticists, irony is superior knowledge and genuine understanding of the infinite complexity of one's life and the world in which one lives.

Like aphasia, irony can be divided into two variations—variations that are only two aspects of the same phenomenon. If one clings to the established terminology and allows oneself to slightly simplify its implications, one might say that verbal/rhetorical irony works on the paradigmatic axis of language, situational/Romantic irony on the syntagmatic axis. One thus has a Siamese twin pair of holy fools. In one of them, two souls fight each other continuously. In the other, a succession of hostile souls have the command, one at a time. Yet, it is only a game—a game of life and death.

Notes

Prolegomena

The Gospel according to John, in *The Revised English Bible* (Oxford and Cambridge: Oxford University Press and Cambridge University Press, 1989), The New Testament, 79.

1. See above.
2. "l'ironie, c'est le visage même du diable." Quoted in D. C. Muecke, "Images of Irony," *Poetics Today* 4 (1983): 404.

Chapter 1: History

"definierbar ist nur das, was keine Geschichte hat." Friedrich Nietzsche, *Zur Genealogie der Moral*, in *Werke in drei Bänden* 2, 2d ed., ed. Karl Schlechta (München: Carl Hanser Verlag, 1960), 820.

1. Dilwyn Knox, *Ironia: Medieval and Renaissance Ideas on Irony* (Leiden: E. J. Brill, 1989), 11. Cf. J. A. K. Thomson, *Irony: An Historical Introduction* (Cambridge: Harvard University Press, 1927), 1–4.
2. Dilwyn Knox, *Ironia*, 140; Norman Knox, *The Word Irony and its Context, 1500–1755* (Durham, N.C.: Duke University Press, 1961), 4.
3. G. G. Sedgewick, *Of Irony: Especially in Drama* (Toronto: University of Toronto Press, 1935), 8–9.
4. Ibid., 112–13.
5. Otto Ribbeck, "Ueber den Begriff des εἴρων," *Rheinisches Museum für Philologie* neue Folge 31 (1876): 381–87.
6. Ribbeck, "Ueber den Begriff des εἴρων," 387–88; Sedgewick, *Of Irony*, 10; Dilwyn Knox, *Ironia*, 127.
7. Leif Bergson, "Eiron und Eironeia," *Hermes* 99 (1971): 412–13, 415.
8. Wilhelm Büchner, "Über den Begriff der Eironeia," *Hermes* 76 (1941): 340, 353–54, 358; Bergson, "Eiron und Eironeia," 416–17, 420.
9. Gregory Vlastos, *Socrates: Ironist and Moral Philosopher* (Cambridge: Cambridge University Press, 1991), 23–29; Joseph A. Dane, *The Critical Mythology of Irony* (Athens and London: University of Georgia Press, 1991), 29; Ribbeck, "Ueber den Begriff des εἴρων," 389; Sedgewick, *Of Irony*, 14–15.
10. St. Thomas Aquinas, "Question CXIII: Of Irony," in *Summa Theologica*, 2d ed., trans. fathers of the English Dominican Province (London: Burns Oates & Washbourne, 1935), 114.
11. Dilwyn Knox, *Ironia*, 97–98.
12. Ibid., 124–27.

13. Norman Knox, *The Word Irony and its Context, 1500–1755*, 7–16, 181, 185–86.

14. Søren Kierkegaard, *Om Begrebet Ironi: Med stadigt Hensyn til Socrates*, in *Samlede Værker* 1, 4th ed., eds. A. B. Drachmann, J. L. Heiberg, and H. O. Lange (Copenhagen: Gyldendal, 1991), 288.

15. Raymond Immerwahr, "Romantic Irony and Romantic Arabesque Prior to Romanticism," *German Quarterly* 42 (1969).

16. Lilian R. Furst, *Fictions of Romantic Irony in European Narrative, 1760–1857* (London and Basingstoke: Macmillan, 1984), 29–30.

17. "im Ganzen und überall." Friedrich Schlegel, "Kritische Fragmente" ("Lyceums-Fragmente"), in *Kritische Friedrich-Schlegel-Ausgabe* 2, eds. Ernst Behler and Hans Eichner (München, Paderborn, and Wien: Verlag Ferdinand Schöningh, 1967), 152.

18. "Ironie ist klares Bewußtsein der ewigen Agilität, des unendlich vollen Chaos." Schlegel, "Ideen," in *Kritische Friedrich-Schlegel-Ausgabe* 2, 263.

19. "In ihr soll alles Scherz und alles Ernst sein, alles treuherzig offen, und alles tief verstellt."; "der Unmöglichkeit und Notwendigkeit einer vollständigen Mitteilung." Schlegel, "Kritische Fragmente" ("Lyceums-Fragmente"), in *Kritische Friedrich-Schlegel-Ausgabe* 2, 160.

20. Ernst Behler, "The Theory of Irony in German Romanticism," in *Romantic Irony*, ed. Frederick Garber (Budapest: Akadémiai Kiadó, 1988), 56–62.

21. Ingrid Strohschneider-Kohrs, *Die Romantische Ironie in Theorie und Gestaltung* (Tübingen: Max Niemeyer Verlag, 1960), 162–85; Behler, "The Theory of Irony in German Romanticism," in *Romantic Irony*, ed. Garber, 65–66.

22. Karl Wilhelm Ferdinand Solger, *Erwin: Vier Gespräche über das Schöne und die Kunst*, ed. Wolfhart Henckmann (München: Wilhelm Fink Verlag, 1971); Strohschneider-Kohrs, *Die Romantische Ironie in Theorie und Gestaltung*, 195; Behler, "The Theory of Irony in German Romanticism," in *Romantic Irony*, ed. Garber, 69–76; Dane, *The Critical Mythology of Irony*, 98.

23. G. W. F. Hegel, *The Philosophy of Fine Art* 1, trans. F. P. B. Osmaston (New York: Hacker Art Books, 1975), 93. The original phrasing is: "unendliche absolute Negativität." Quoted in Strohschneider-Kohrs, *Die Romantische Ironie in Theorie und Gestaltung*, 215.

24. Quoted in Ernst Behler, *Irony and the Discourse of Modernity* (Seattle and London: University of Washington Press, 1990), 90. Cf. Behler, "The Theory of Irony in German Romanticism," in *Romantic Irony*, ed. Garber, 47, 78.

25. Uwe Japp, *Theorie der Ironie* (Frankfurt am Main: Vittorio Klostermann, 1983), 133–46, 192–227; Behler, "The Theory of Irony in German Romanticism," in *Romantic Irony*, ed. Garber, 64.

26. "dens hele Totalitet." Kierkegaard, *Samlede Værker* 1, 136, 270.

27. "en Dialektik, der i idelig Bevægelse stedse vaager over, at Spørgsmaalet ikke besnæres i en tilfældig Opfattelse, der aldrig trættet altid er rede til at gjøre Problemet flot, naar det er sat paa Grund, kort sagt, der altid veed at holde Problemet svævende, og netop heri og herved vil løse det." Ibid., 162.

28. Ibid., 164–65.

29. Ibid., 261–62, 270, 276, 280.

30. Ibid., 326.

31. "*Ironien* i hele sin guddommelige *Uendelighed*, der slet Intet lader bestaae"; "uendelige Frihed." Ibid., 96, 198, 280, 326, 221.

32. Ibid., 64.

33. "sund og glad og let." Ibid., 328–29.

34. *"uendelig tvetydig."* Ibid., 242.

35. Connop Thirlwall, "On the Irony of Sophocles," in *Remains: Literary and Theological* 3, ed. J. J. Stewart Perowne (London: Daldy, Isbister & Co., 1878), 3.

36. Ernst Behler, *Klassische Ironie, Romantische Ironie, Tragische Ironie: Zum Ursprung dieser Begriffe* (Darmstadt: Wissenschaftliche Buchgesellschaft, 1972), 134–54; Dane, *The Critical Mythology of Irony*, 122–25.

37. Thirlwall, *Remains*, 27, 55.

38. Ibid., 44.

39. Thirlwall, *Remains*, 15; Dane, *The Critical Mythology of Irony*, 130–32.

40. I. A. Richards, *Principles of Literary Criticism* (London and New York: Kegan Paul, Trench, Trubner & Co., and Harcourt, Brace & Co., 1925), 242, 250–53.

41. Cleanth Brooks, *The Well Wrought Urn: Studies in the Structure of Poetry*, 2d ed. (San Diego, New York, and London: Harcourt Brace Jovanovich, 1975); "Irony and 'Ironic' Poetry," *College English* 9 (1948); "Irony as a Principle of Structure," in *Literary Opinion in America*, 3d ed., ed. M. D. Zabel (New York and Evanston: Harper & Row, 1962). Cf. Cleanth Brooks and Robert Penn Warren, *Understanding Fiction* (New York: Appleton-Century-Crofts, 1943), xvi–xix.

42. Brooks, *The Well Wrought Urn*, 209–10.

43. Ibid., 195–96.

44. Ibid., 13–14, 17, 93–94, 102, 110–13, 125–26, 139–40, 159, 189.

45. Daniel O'Hara, review of Jacques Derrida, *Grammatology*, *Journal of Aesthetics and Art Criticism* 36 (1977): 361–65; Ihab Hassan, "Pluralism in Postmodern Perspective," *Critical Inquiry* 12 (1986): 506; Behler, *Irony and the Discourse of Modernity*, 36, 100–110.

46. Paul de Man, *Allegories of Reading: Figural Language in Rousseau, Nietzsche, Rilke, and Proust* (New Haven and London: Yale University Press, 1979), 301.

47. Paul de Man, *Romanticism and Contemporary Criticism: The Gauss Seminar and Other Papers*, eds. E. S. Burt, Kevin Newmark, and Andrzej Warminski (Baltimore and London: Johns Hopkins University Press, 1993), 111, 116.

48. Paul de Man, *Blindness and Insight: Essays in the Rhetoric of Contemporary Criticism*, 2d ed. (Minneapolis: University of Minnesota Press, 1983), 223–24; Brooks, "Irony as a Principle of Structure," 735–37.

49. Alan Wilde, *Horizons of Assent: Modernism, Postmodernism, and the Ironic Imagination* (Baltimore and London: Johns Hopkins University Press, 1981), 7, 10, 44, 129, 131.

50. See the chapter "The Theory of Romantic Poetry" in Ernst Behler, *German Romantic Literary Theory* (Cambridge: Cambridge University Press, 1993).

51. See Anne K. Mellor, *English Romantic Irony* (Cambridge and London: Harvard University Press, 1980), 5, 22–23; "On Romantic Irony, Symbolism and Allegory," *Criticism* 21 (1979): 218, 229. Cf. Gary J. Handwerk, *Irony and Ethics in Narrative: From Schlegel to Lacan* (New Haven and London: Yale University Press, 1985); and Ernst Behler, *Ironie und literarische Moderne* (Paderborn: Ferdinand Schöningh, 1997). Behler's book is an extensive volume that reached me when the manuscript of this book was almost completed.

52. Nietzsche, *Werke in drei Bänden* 2, 820.

53. Kim Sichel, *From Icon to Irony: German and American Industrial Photography*, with additional essays by Judith Bookbinder and John Stomberg (Seattle and London: University of Washington Press, 1995).

54. Richard Rorty, *Contingency, Irony, and Solidarity* (Cambridge: Cambridge University Press, 1989), xv.

55. Tamasin Doe, *Patrick Cox: Wit, Irony and Footwear* (London: Thames and Hudson, 1998).

56. William August Becker, "Concepts of Irony with Special Reference to Applications in the Visual Arts" (Ph.D. diss., Columbia University, New York, 1970), 2.

57. "Mit der Ironie ist durchaus nicht zu scherzen." Schlegel, "Über die Unverständlichkeit," in *Kritische Friedrich-Schlegel-Ausgabe* 2, 370.

58. "et guddommeligt Vanvid." Kierkegaard, *Samlede Værker* 1, 276.

CHAPTER 2: IRONY AND THE PROBLEM OF INTENTIONALISM

Plato, *Phaedrus*, trans. R. Hackforth, in *The Collected Dialogues of Plato Including the Letters*, eds. Edith Hamilton and Huntington Cairns (New York: Bollingen Foundation and Pantheon Books, 1961), 521.

1. See above.

2. Walter J. Ong, "From Mimesis to Irony: The Distancing of Voice," in *The Horizon of Literature*, ed. Paul Hernadi (Lincoln and London: University of Nebraska Press, 1982), 17.

3. Dilwyn Knox, *Ironia*, 58–77.

4. D. C. Muecke, *Irony and the Ironic*, 2d ed. of *Irony* (London and New York: Methuen, 1982), 19.

5. Ong, "From Mimesis to Irony," 27.

6. "Wenn Er auch keine Absichten hatte, so hat doch seine Poesie und die eigentliche Verfasserin derselben, die Natur, Absicht." Schlegel, "Fragmente" ("Athenäums-Fragmente"), in *Kritische Friedrich-Schlegel-Ausgabe* 2, 173.

7. "wenn die Ironie wild wird, und sich gar nicht mehr regieren läßt." Schlegel, "Über die Unverständlichkeit," in *Kritische Friedrich-Schlegel-Ausgabe* 2, 369.

8. "alt Sligt er ikke i Naturen, men *det ironiske Subject* seer det deri." Kierkegaard, *Samlede Værker* 1, 270.

9. W. K. Wimsatt and Monroe C. Beardsley, "The Intentional Fallacy," in W. K. Wimsatt, *The Verbal Icon: Studies in the Meaning of Poetry* (Lexington: University of Kentucky Press, 1954), 3–4.

10. Brooks, *The Well Wrought Urn*, 209.

11. Brooks, "Irony and 'Ironic' Poetry," 234.

12. Brooks, *The Well Wrought Urn*, 209.

13. Dane, *The Critical Mythology of Irony*, 154.

14. Daniel O. Nathan, "Irony and the Artist's Intentions," *British Journal of Aesthetics* 22 (1982): 252, 254.

15. D. C. Muecke, *The Compass of Irony* (London: Methuen, 1969), 14.

16. Ibid., 29–30, 53.

17. Ibid., 56–57.

18. Muecke, *Irony and the Ironic*, 43–44.

19. Ibid., 46, 100–101.

20. Wayne C. Booth, *A Rhetoric of Irony* (Chicago and London: University of Chicago Press, 1974), 3–7, 91, 120–34.

21. Ibid., 11–12, 120, 133, 166.

22. Susan Suleiman, "Interpreting Ironies," *Diacritics* 6.2 (1976): 16.

23. Wayne C. Booth, "The Empire of Irony," *Georgia Review* 37 (1983): 724, 726. Cf. Japp, *Theorie der Ironie*, 47, 55, 57.

24. Göran Hermerén, "Intention and Interpretation in Literary Criticism," *New Literary History* 7 (1975): 73–74.

25. P. D. Juhl, *Interpretation: An Essay in the Philosophy of Literary Criticism* (Princeton, New Jersey: Princeton University Press, 1980), 47, 58–65.

26. Furst, *Fictions of Romantic Irony in European Narrative, 1760–1857*, 21.

27. The same is true for this line of reasoning in Mary Sirridge, "Artistic Intention and Critical Prerogative," *British Journal of Aesthetics* 18 (1978): 150.

28. David J. Amante, "The Theory of Ironic Speech Acts," *Poetics Today* 2.2 (1981): 83.

29. Norbert Groeben and Brigitte Scheele, *Produktion und Rezeption von Ironie: Pragmalinguistische Beschreibung und psycholinguistische Erklärungshypothesen* (Tübingen: Gunter Narr Verlag, 1984); Norbert Groeben, Hanne Seemann, and Arno Drinkmann, *Produktion und Rezeption von Ironie. Band II: Empirische Untersuchungen zu Bedingungen und Wirkungen ironischer Sprechakte* (Tübingen: Gunter Narr Verlag, 1985).

30. William E. Tolhurst, "On What a Text Is and How It Means," *British Journal of Aesthetics* 19 (1979): 14.

31. Paul A. Bové, *Destructive Poetics: Heidegger and Modern American Poetry* (New York: Columbia University Press, 1980), 103. Cf. Pierre-Louis Vaillancourt, "Sémiologie de l'ironie: L'exemple Ducharme," *Voix et images* 7 (1982).

32. Stanley Fish, "Short People Got No Reason to Live: Reading Irony," in *Doing What Comes Naturally: Change, Rhetoric, and the Practice of Theory in Literary and Legal Studies* (Durham, N.C., and London: Duke University Press, 1989), 180.

33. Fish, *Doing What Comes Naturally*, 187–96. Cf. the critique of Booth's distinction between stable and unstable ironies in Mark Jeffry Dicks, "Reading Irony" (Ph.D. diss., University of California, Santa Cruz, 1985), 17–22.

34. Cf. Suleiman's discussion on Hirsch and Booth, "Interpreting Ironies," 17, 20.

35. Dane, *The Critical Mythology of Irony*, 8.

36. Linda Hutcheon, *Irony's Edge: The Theory and Politics of Irony* (London and New York: Routledge, 1994), 10–11, 116–24.

37. Different notions of "meaning" are listed in Juhl, *Interpretation*, 4–9.

38. Hermerén, "Intention and Interpretation in Literary Criticism," 60, 63, 65, 81.

39. Frank Stringfellow, *The Meaning of Irony: A Psychoanalytic Investigation* (Albany: State University of New York Press, 1994), 1–30.

40. Wimsatt and Beardsley, "The Intentional Fallacy," 3–6.

41. Marike Finlay, "Perspectives of Irony and Irony of Perspectives: A Review," *Canadian Journal of Research in Semiotics* 5.3 (1978): 43.

42. E. D. Hirsch, *Validity in Interpretation* (New Haven and London: Yale University Press, 1967), 183; Wendell V. Harris, *Interpretive Acts: In Search of Meaning* (Oxford: Clarendon Press, 1988), 61.

43. W. B. Yeats, "Among School Children," in *The Collected Poems of W. B. Yeats*, 2d ed. (London: Macmillan, 1950), 245.

CHAPTER 3: CLASSIFICATIONS OF IRONY

"Es ist gleich tödlich für den Geist, ein System zu haben, und keins zu haben. Er wird sich also wohl entschließen müssen, beides zu verbinden." Schlegel,

"Fragmente" ("Athenäums-Fragmente"), in *Kritische Friedrich-Schlegel-Ausgabe* 2, 173.

1. Thirlwall, *Remains*, 1.
2. Ibid., 3.
3. Wayne C. Booth, *The Rhetoric of Fiction*, 2d ed. (London: Penguin Books, 1991).
4. Thirlwall, *Remains*, 2.
5. Sedgewick, *Of Irony*, 43.
6. Booth, *A Rhetoric of Irony*, 63.
7. Japp, *Theorie der Ironie*, 37.
8. Booth, "The Empire of Irony," 723.
9. Dane, *The Critical Mythology of Irony*, 6.
10. Ibid., 4.
11. Behler, *Klassische Ironie, Romantische Ironie, Tragische Ironie*, 134–42.
12. Thirlwall, *Remains*, 1.
13. Leon Satterfield, "Toward a Poetics of the Ironic Sign," in *Semiotic Themes*, ed. Richard T. De George (Lawrence: University of Kansas Publications, 1981), 158.
14. Booth, "The Empire of Irony," 723.
15. Muecke, *The Compass of Irony*, 42, 99; Muecke, *Irony and the Ironic*, 56, 63.
16. Ibid., 56–57; Ibid., 42–44.

CHAPTER 4: THE CREATION OF IRONY

Elleström, *Divine Madness*, 58.

1. Dilwyn Knox, *Ironia*, 58–77.
2. Ibid., 71–77.
3. Quoted in Norman Knox, *The Word Irony and its Context, 1500–1755*, 147.
4. Ibid., 155.
5. Hutcheon, *Irony's Edge*, 159.
6. Rainer Warning, "Irony and the 'Order of Discourse' in Flaubert," trans. Michael Morton, *New Literary History* 13 (1981): 257.
7. Muecke, *The Compass of Irony*, 52–60. Cf. the critique in Dicks, "Reading Irony," 19–22.
8. D. C. Muecke, "Irony Markers," *Poetics* 7 (1978): 374.
9. The term "psychorhetorical" is coined in David S. Kaufer, "Understanding Ironic Communication," *Journal of Pragmatics* 5 (1981).
10. See Barbara Godard, "Modalities of the Edge: Towards a Semiotics of Irony: The Case of Mavis Gallant," *Essays on Canadian Writing* issue 42 (1990).
11. See for instance Yael S. Feldman, "How Does a Convention Mean? A Semiotic Reading of Agnon's Bilingual Key-Irony in *A Guest for the Night*," *Hebrew Union College Annual* 56 (1985).
12. Charles S. Peirce, "Logic as Semiotic: The Theory of Signs," in *Semiotics: An Introductory Anthology*, 2d ed., ed. Robert E. Innis (London: Hutchinson, 1986), 5.
13. Ibid., 10.
14. Ibid., 12.
15. Ibid.

16. Marike Finlay, *The Romantic Irony of Semiotics: Friedrich Schlegel and the Crisis of Representation* (Berlin, New York, and Amsterdam: Mouton de Gruyter, 1988), 1. Cf. 7–8, 62, 95, 113, 120, 184–85, 194, 215, 222–23, 271–72.

17. Booth, *A Rhetoric of Irony*, 52–53.

18. Ibid., 53–76.

19. Stanley Fish, *Is There a Text in This Class? The Authority of Interpretive Communities* (Cambridge and London: Harvard University Press, 1980), 13–17, 167–80, 268–99, 303–21.

20. Hutcheon, *Irony's Edge*, 89–115.

21. Fish, *Is There a Text in This Class?*, 171–72.

22. Charles Dickens, *Oliver Twist*, ed. Kathleen Tillotson (Oxford: Clarendon Press, 1966), 2.

23. Ibid., 3.

24. Fish, *Doing What Comes Naturally*, 182–83.

25. Ibid., 195.

26. Booth, *A Rhetoric of Irony*, 99–100.

27. Dickens, *Oliver Twist*, 3–4.

28. See, for instance, Harvey Peter Sucksmith, *The Narrative Art of Charles Dickens: The Rhetoric of Sympathy and Irony in His Novels* (Oxford: Clarendon Press, 1970), 140–76.

29. Fish, *Doing What Comes Naturally*, 194.

30. Dilwyn Knox, *Ironia*, 39–40.

31. Cf. Marike Finlay who chooses not to use the term *situational irony* because "any attempt to describe the world is of necessity mediated by words," *The Romantic Irony of Semiotics*, 93. Once the distinction between verbal irony and situational irony is questioned, the choice of term is, as I see it, arbitrary.

32. Erasmus of Rotterdam, *Praise of Folly and Letter to Martin Dorp*, ed. A. H. T. Levi, trans. Betty Radice (London: Penguin Books, 1971). Excerpts below are reprinted by permission of the copyright holders.

33. See, for instance, Zoja Pavlovskis, *The Praise of Folly: Structure and Irony* (Leiden: E. J. Brill, 1983), 70–71, 195. Pavlovskis's aim is to read *Praise of Folly* as coherently as possible. He succeeds quite well—because he equates his own, brilliant ironic interpretations with the alleged norms of Erasmus and his text.

34. See Pavlovskis, *The Praise of Folly*, 2–3, for references.

35. Booth, *A Rhetoric of Irony*, 38, 43–44.

36. Erasmus, *Praise of Folly and Letter to Martin Dorp*, 59.

37. Ibid., 66.

38. Ibid., 69.

39. Ibid., 93.

40. Ibid., 99.

41. Ibid., 111.

42. Ibid., 77.

43. Ibid., 105, 116.

44. Ibid., 87.

45. Ibid., 88–89.

46. Ibid., 147.

47. Ibid., 121.

48. Ibid., 155.

49. Ibid., 164.

50. Ibid., 167.

51. Ibid., 183.

52. Ibid., 201.
53. Ibid., 208.

Chapter 5: Irony, Obliqueness, and Incongruities

Rudolf Arnheim, *Visual Thinking* (Berkeley and Los Angeles: University of California Press, 1969), 182.
1. Dilwyn Knox, *Ironia*, 38.
2. Ibid., 44.
3. C. Jan Swearingen, *Rhetoric and Irony: Western Literacy and Western Lies* (New York and Oxford: Oxford University Press, 1991), 4–5, 130–31, 210–11, 224–34.
4. Dane, *The Critical Mythology of Irony*, 46–47.
5. Norman Knox, *The Word Irony and its Context, 1500–1755*, 12.
6. Dilwyn Knox, *Ironia*, 51–55; Vlastos, *Socrates*, 27.
7. Muecke, *Irony and the Ironic*, 35.
8. "nous admettrons en conséquence qu'interpréter un texte, c'est tenter de reconstituer par conjecture l'intention sémantico-pragmatique ayant présidé à l'encodage; et que *le sens d'une séquence peut être défini comme ce que le récepteur . . . parvient hypothétiquement à reconstruire de l'intention signifiante.*" Catherine Kerbrat-Orecchioni, "L'ironie comme trope," *Poétique* 41 (1980): 114.
9. Hutcheon, *Irony's Edge*, 118.
10. Dilwyn Knox, *Ironia*, 172.
11. Ibid., 170–77.
12. See, for instance, Northrop Frye's discussions of the ironic as both a tragic and a comic fictional mode, in *Anatomy of Criticism: Four Essays* (Princeton: Princeton University Press, 1957), 40–49.
13. Dilwyn Knox, *Ironia*, 33–36.
14. "Das Lachen ist ein Affekt aus der plötzlichen Verwandlung einer gespannten Erwartung in nichts." Immanuel Kant, *Werke in sechs Bänden. Band V: Kritik der Urteilskraft und Schriften zur Naturphilosophie*, ed. Wilhelm Weischedel (Wiesbaden: Insel-Verlag, 1957), 437.
15. Strohschneider-Kohrs, *Die Romantische Ironie in Theorie und Gestaltung*, 147–54; Behler, "The Theory of Irony in German Romanticism," in *Romantic Irony*, ed. Garber, 67–69.
16. Marcella Tarozzi Goldsmith, *Nonrepresentational Forms of the Comic: Humor, Irony, and Jokes* (New York: Peter Lang, 1991), 22, 29, 32.
17. The terms *humor* and *irony* are very often juxtaposed in book titles, for instance. One example is Allan J. Ryan, *The Trickster Shift: Humour and Irony in Contemporary Native Art* (Vancouver, Toronto, and Seattle: UBC Press and University of Washington Press, 1999).
18. "trop cruelle pour être vraiment comique"; "finalement sérieuse." Vladimir Jankélévitch, *L'ironie* (Paris: Librairie Félix Alcan, 1936), 1, 136.
19. Candace D. Lang, *Irony/Humor: Critical Paradigms* (Baltimore and London: Johns Hopkins University Press, 1988), 7, 45.
20. Behler, *Klassische Ironie, Romantische Ironie, Tragische Ironie*, 85–103, 117–18.
21. "des racines communes." René Schaerer, "Le mécanisme de l'ironie

dans ses rapports avec la dialectique," *Revue de métaphysique et de morale* 48 (1941): 196.

22. Beda Allemann, *Ironie und Dichtung*, 2d ed. (Pfullingen: Günther Neske, 1969), 73–74; Immerwahr, "Romantic Irony and Romantic Arabesque Prior to Romanticism," 673, 683; Mellor, *English Romantic Irony*, 18–19; Patricia Stanley, "Hoffmann's *Phantasiestücke in Callots Manier* in Light of Friedrich Schlegel's Theory of the Arabesque," *German Studies Review* 8 (1985); Gerald Gillespie, "Romantic Irony and the Grotesque," in *Romantic Irony*, ed. Garber. See also Marianne Shapiro, "The Status of Irony," *Stanford Literature Review* 2 (1985): 15–16.

23. Donald Rice and Peter Schofer, *Rhetorical Poetics: Theory and Practice of Figural and Symbolic Reading in Modern French Literature* (Madison: University of Wisconsin Press, 1983), 19–87.

24. Booth, *A Rhetoric of Irony*, 22–24; Rice and Schofer, *Rhetorical Poetics*, 31.

25. See Claes Entzenberg, *Metaphor as a Mode of Interpretation: An Essay on Interactional and Contextual Sense-Making Processes, Metaphorology, and Verbal Arts* (Uppsala: Uppsala University, Department of Aesthetics, 1998).

26. Booth, *A Rhetoric of Irony*, 22.

27. Norman Knox, *The Word Irony and its Context, 1500–1755*, 11, 36–37; Booth, *A Rhetoric of Irony*, 24–25.

28. Norman Knox, *The Word Irony and its Context, 1500–1755*, 6, 10; K. S. Campbell, "Irony Medieval and Modern and the Allegory of Rhetoric," *Allegorica* 4 (1979); Dane, *The Critical Mythology of Irony*, 49–50, 53, 64.

29. Jankélévitch, *L'ironie*, 33, 44; Hutcheon, *Irony's Edge*, 65.

30. Dilwyn Knox, *Ironia*, 44.

31. de Man, *Blindness and Insight*, 226, 228.

32. Ibid., 209, 222.

33. Quoted in Sedgewick, *Of Irony*, 10. Cf. Ribbeck, "Ueber den Begriff des εἴρων," 388; Dilwyn Knox, *Ironia*, 111.

34. Dilwyn Knox, *Ironia*, 127.

35. Norman Knox, *The Word Irony and its Context, 1500–1755*, 15, 79–82.

36. Muecke, *The Compass of Irony*, 78.

37. Linda Hutcheon, *A Theory of Parody: The Teachings of Twentieth-Century Art Forms* (New York and London: Methuen, 1985), 11, 37.

38. Dilwyn Knox, *Ironia*, 73.

39. Dane, *The Critical Mythology of Irony*, 66.

40. See, for instance, Shlomith Rimmon, *The Concept of Ambiguity: The Example of James* (Chicago and London: University of Chicago Press, 1977), 15, 25.

41. William Empson, *Seven Types of Ambiguity*, 2d ed. (London: Hogarth Press, 1984), 38–47.

42. Brooks, *The Well Wrought Urn*, 125–26, 175, 195–96.

43. Muecke, *Irony and the Ironic*, 100–101.

44. Hutcheon, *Irony's Edge*, 66.

45. Mikhail M. Bakhtin, "Discourse in the Novel," in *The Dialogic Imagination*, ed. Michael Holquist, trans. Caryl Emerson and Michael Holquist (Austin: University of Texas Press, 1981), 259–422.

46. Ibid., 330, 328.

47. Ibid., 262.

48. Ibid., 274, 299, 303–304, 317–20, 322–23, 335, 353, 371, 374, 402, 416. Cf. especially Mary Ann Doane, "The Dialogical Text: Filmic Irony and the Spectator" (Ph.D. diss., University of Iowa, 1979).

49. Bakhtin, *The Dialogic Imagination*, 275.

50. Ibid., 361–63.

51. Dilwyn Knox, *Ironia*, 140.

52. Rice and Schofer, *Rhetorical Poetics*, 31, 82.

53. Of course, this is the case also in oral communication. See Katharina Barbe, *Irony in Context* (Amsterdam and Philadelphia: John Benjamins Publishing Co., 1995).

54. Dilwyn Knox, *Ironia*, 19.

55. Ibid., 19–37.

56. Ibid., 28.

57. Ibid., 29–37.

58. Ibid., 149.

59. "Die Ironie ist ein Versuch zur Versprachlichung der Welt in Form einer gleichzeitigen Gegenrede." Japp, *Theorie der Ironie*, 327.

60. See Strohschneider-Kohrs, *Die Romantische Ironie in Theorie und Gestaltung*, 22.

61. "Ironie ist die Form des Paradoxen. Paradox ist alles, was zugleich gut und groß ist." Schlegel, "Kritische Fragmente" ("Lyceums-Fragmente"), in *Kritische Friedrich-Schlegel-Ausgabe* 2, 153.

62. Brooks, *The Well Wrought Urn*, 8, cf. 17–18, 125–26, 175–77, 195–96, 209–10.

63. Wilde, *Horizons of Assent*, 21.

64. Plato, *Apology*, trans. Hugh Tredennick, in *The Collected Dialogues of Plato Including the Letters*, 7–8.

65. "Forsaavidt er det altsaa *paa eengang Alvor* med hans Uvidenhed og *dog atter ikke Alvor*, og *paa denne Spidse* maa man fastholde Socrates." Kierkegaard, *Samlede Værker* 1, 282.

66. Vlastos, *Socrates*, 32.

67. David S. Kaufer, "Irony, Interpretive Form, and the Theory of Meaning," *Poetics Today* 4 (1983): 456, 458.

68. Dilwyn Knox, *Ironia*, 31; Norman Knox, *The Word Irony and its Context, 1500–1755*, 10; Dane, *The Critical Mythology of Irony*, 49.

69. Dane, *The Critical Mythology of Irony*, 51.

70. Furst, *Fictions of Romantic Irony in European Narrative, 1760–1857*, 12.

71. Hutcheon, *Irony's Edge*, 12.

72. Philippe Hamon, "Analyser l'ironie," in *Discours et pouvoir*, ed. Ross Chambers (Ann Arbor: Department of Romance Languages, University of Michigan, 1982), 169.

73. Dicks, "Reading Irony," 42, 49–79.

74. Muecke, *The Compass of Irony*, 19–29; D. C. Muecke, *Irony* (London: Methuen, 1970), 32.

75. Booth, *A Rhetoric of Irony*, 109.

76. Jonathan Culler, *Flaubert: The Uses of Uncertainty*, rev. ed. (Ithaca and London: Cornell University Press, 1985), 188.

77. Cf. Lars Elleström, *Vårt hjärtas vilt lysande skrift: Om Karl Vennbergs lyrik* (Lund: Lund University Press, 1992), 119. Dicks, "Reading Irony," 80–167, distinguishes between four modes of reading irony that partly cover the three categories here proposed: "sarcastic," "orientational," "levitational," and "resignational." For Dicks, though, irony is not in itself an interpretive reading; irony may be read in different ways, but it is already "there."

78. Hutcheon, *Irony's Edge*, 56.

79. Ibid., 37.
80. See Alan Reynolds Thompson, *The Dry Mock: A Study of Irony in Drama* (Berkeley and Los Angeles: University of California Press, 1948), 225.
81. "die Durchschnittsbildung eines Europäers"; "Trinker von Fach." Franz Kafka, "Ein Bericht für eine Akademie," in *Das Erzählerische Werk I: Erzählungen Aphorismen Brief an den Vater*, ed. Klaus Hermsdorf (Berlin: Rütten & Loening, 1983), 238, 237.
82. Cf. Lawrence O. Frye, "Word Play: Irony's Way to Freedom in Kafka's *Ein Bericht für eine Akademie*," *Deutsche Vierteljahrsschrift für Literaturwissenschaft und Geistesgeschichte* 55 (1981).
83. Franz Kafka, "Von den Gleichnissen," in *Das Erzählerische Werk I*, 372–73.
84. Franz Kafka, "On Parables," trans. Willa and Edwin Muir, in *Parables* (New York: Schocken Books, 1947), 11. Reprinted by permission of the copyright holders.

CHAPTER 6: IRONY AND MYSTICISM

"Gelobt seist du, Niemand." Paul Celan, *Gedichte in zwei Bänden* 1 (Frankfurt am Main: Suhrkamp Verlag, 1975), 225; *Selected Poems*, 2d ed., trans. Michael Hamburger (Harmondsworth: Penguin Books, 1990), 175.
1. Cf. Jankélévitch, *L'ironie*, 72.
2. W. T. Stace, *Mysticism and Philosophy* (London: Macmillan, 1961), 94.
3. Steven T. Katz, "Mystical Speech and Mystical Meaning," in *Mysticism and Language*, ed. Steven T. Katz (New York and Oxford: Oxford University Press, 1992), 15.
4. Ibid., 25, 33.
5. Stace, *Mysticism and Philosophy*, 270–71.
6. Ibid, 303–306.
7. Shira Wolosky, *Language Mysticism: The Negative Way of Language in Eliot, Beckett, and Celan* (Stanford, Calif.: Stanford University Press, 1995).
8. Stace, *Mysticism and Philosophy*, 202.
9. Stephen H. Phillips, "Mystic Analogizing and the 'Peculiarly Mystical,' " in *Mysticism and Language*, ed. Katz, 131.
10. Bimal Krishna Matilal, "Mysticism and Ineffability: Some Issues of Logic and Language," in *Mysticism and Language*, ed. Katz, 155.
11. See Edwin M. Good, *Irony in the Old Testament*, 2d ed. (Sheffield: Almond Press, 1981).
12. Booth, "The Empire of Irony," 722.
13. John M. Ellis, *Against Deconstruction* (Princeton: Princeton University Press, 1989), 7.
14. Ibid., 6.
15. Matilal, "Mysticism and Ineffability," in *Mysticism and Language*, ed. Katz, 155.
16. Schlegel, "Über die Unverständlichkeit," in *Kritische Friedrich-Schlegel-Ausgabe* 2, 364.
17. "Sie enthält und erregt ein Gefühl von dem unauflöslichen Widerstreit des Unbedingten und des Bedingten, der Unmöglichkeit und Notwendigkeit einer vollständigen Mitteilung." Schlegel, "Kritische Fragmente" ("Lyceums-Fragmente"), in *Kritische Friedrich-Schlegel-Ausgabe* 2, 160.

18. Schlegel, "Fragmente" ("Athenäums-Fragmente"), in *Kritische Friedrich-Schlegel-Ausgabe* 2, 184.

19. "Die Mystik ist, wenn sie nach der Wirklichkeit hinschaut, die Mutter der Ironie,—wenn nach der ewigen Welt, das Kind der Begeisterung oder Inspiration." Karl Wilhelm Ferdinand Solger, *Solger's nachgelassene Schriften und Briefwechsel* 1, eds. Ludwig Tieck and Friedrich von Raumer (Leipzig: F. A. Brockhaus, 1826), 689.

20. "det mystiske Intet"; "det ironiske Intet." Kierkegaard, *Samlede Værker* 1, 273, 293. Cf. Birgit Baldwin, "Irony, that 'Little, Invisible Personage': A Reading of Kierkegaard's Ghosts," *MLN* 104 (1989): 1133–35.

21. Jankélévitch, *L'ironie*, 40, 64.

22. Gershom G. Scholem, *Major Trends in Jewish Mysticism*, 3d ed. (London: Thames and Hudson, 1955), 251–86; Gershom G. Scholem, *Kabbalah* (Jerusalem: Keter Publishing House, 1974), 128–35; Harold Bloom, *Kabbalah and Criticism*, 2d ed. (New York: Continuum, 1984), 38–43.

23. Bloom, *Kabbalah and Criticism*, 74.

24. Ibid., 52–53.

25. Ibid., 26.

26. Ibid., 74.

27. Harold Bloom, *Ruin the Sacred Truths: Poetry and Belief from the Bible to the Present* (Cambridge and London: Harvard University Press, 1989), 4.

28. Robert Haardt, *Die Gnosis: Wesen und Zeugnisse* (Salzburg: Otto Müller Verlag, 1967), 44.

29. Meister Eckhart, *Die deutschen Werke: Predigten Dritter Band*, ed. Josef Quint (Stuttgart: Verlag W. Kohlhammer, 1976).

30. "solt dû sîn der sun gotes, des enmaht dû niht gesîn, niuwan dû enhabest denne daz selbe wesen gotes, daz dâ hât der sun gotes." Ibid., 313.

31. "ein vünkelîn der redelicheit"; "daz bilde der sêle"; "ein bekennen"; "daz sinnelîche und verstentlîche." Ibid., 315–16.

32. Ibid., 317.

33. "lîplîcher glîchnisse"; "noch geistlîcher"; "in dem rîche der himel al in al ist und al ein und al unser." Ibid., 319.

34. Ibid., 323–24.

35. Ibid., 322.

36. "Merke, waz gebreste ist! Der ist von nihte. Dar umbe: waz der nihtes ist in dem menschen, daz muoz getilget werden; wan, als lange der gebreste in dir ist, sô enbist dû niht der sun gotes. Daz der mensche klaget und leidic ist, daz ist allez von gebresten." Ibid., 324.

37. Celan, *Gedichte in zwei Bänden* 1, 225. Reprinted by permission of the copyright holders.

38. Celan, *Selected Poems*, 175. Reprinted by permission of Michael Hamburger.

39. Wolosky, *Language Mysticism*, 256–63.

40. See Arnold Stadler, *Das Buch der Psalmen und die deutschsprachige Lyrik des 20. Jahrhunderts: Zu den Psalmen im Werk Bertolt Brechts und Paul Celans* (Köln and Wien: Böhlau Verlag, 1989), 155–60; Gerd Heinz-Mohr and Volker Sommer, *Die Rose: Entfaltung eines Symbols* (München: Eugen Diederichs Verlag, 1988), 201–202; Dietlind Meinecke, *Wort und Name bei Paul Celan: Zur Widerruflichkeit des Gedichts* (Bad Homburg v. d. H., Berlin, and Zürich: Verlag Gehlen, 1970), 195–97.

CHAPTER 7: IRONY AND THE ARTS

Sex Pistols, "God Save the Queen."

1. Milly Heyd, *Aubrey Beardsley: Symbol, Mask and Self-Irony* (New York, Bern, and Frankfurt am Main: Peter Lang, 1986), 113.

2. Karen Bernard, "Ironing Out the Differences: Female Iconography in the Paintings of Joanne Tod," in *Double Talking: Essays on Verbal and Visual Ironies in Canadian Contemporary Art and Literature*, ed. Linda Hutcheon (Toronto: ECW Press, 1992), 135.

3. Barry Ulanov, "The Art of Irony," *Union Seminary Quarterly Review* 35 (1980): 258.

4. Linda Hutcheon, *Splitting Images: Contemporary Canadian Ironies* (Toronto, Oxford, and New York: Oxford University Press, 1991), 8, 21, 25, 27, 84–85, 101–108, 151.

5. Hutcheon, *Irony's Edge*, 106–15, 166–75.

6. See, for instance, Richard Martin, "Tale and Transgression: The Art of Timothy Woodman," *Arts Magazine* 59 (May 1985): 137; Julie Beddoes, "The Writing on the Wall: The Ironies in and of Lothar Baumgarten's 'Monument for the Native Peoples of Ontario, 1984–85,' " in *Double Talking*, ed. Hutcheon.

7. "Zum Beschluss"; "Ende vom Lied." Heinz J. Dill, "Romantic Irony in the Works of Robert Schumann," *Musical Quarterly* 73 (1989): 193.

8. "Embryons Desséchés." Ulanov, "The Art of Irony," 259.

9. Among others Gernot Gruber, "Romantische Ironie in den Heine-Liedern?," in *Schubert-Kongreß Wien 1978: Bericht*, ed. Otto Brusatti (Graz: Akademische Druck- u. Verlagsanstalt, 1979); Charles S. Brauner, "Irony in the Heine Lieder of Schubert and Schumann," *Musical Quarterly* 67 (1981); Ingeborg Pfingsten, "Musikalische Ironie 'im wunderschönen Monat Mai' von Schumann?," *Musica* 41 (1987); Wolf Rosenberg, "Paradox, Doppelbödigkeit und Ironie in der 'Dichterliebe,' " *Dissonanz/Dissonance* 15 (February 1988); Douglass Seaton, "Interpreting Schubert's Heine Songs," *Music Review* 53 (1992).

10. See Peter Jost, "Brahms und die romantische Ironie: Zu den 'Romanzen aus L. Tieck's Magelone' op. 33," *Archiv für Musikwissenschaft* 47 (1990): 29–30; Marius Flothuis, "Einige Betrachtungen über den Humor in der Musik," *Österreichische Musik-Zeitschrift* 38 (1983): 692–93; Albrecht Dümling, " 'Ganz einzig in ihrer Art . . . ': Ironie und Realismus in Hugo Wolfs *Alten Weisen* nach Gottfried Keller," *Musik-Konzepte* issue 75 Hugo Wolf (1992): 103–5; Patrick Dinslage, "Traum, Phantasmagorie und Ironie in den Heine-Liedern Robert Schumanns, dargestellt an *Mein Wagen rollet langsam* op. 142/4," in *Schumann und seine Dichter*, ed. Matthias Wendt (Mainz: Schott, 1993), 41; Jon W. Finson, "The Intentional Tourist: Romantic Irony in the Eichendorff *Liederkreis* of Robert Schumann," in *Schumann and his World*, ed. R. Larry Todd (Princeton: Princeton University Press, 1994).

11. Brauner, "Irony in the Heine Lieder of Schubert and Schumann," 274–75.

12. Rosenberg, "Paradox, Doppelbödigkeit und Ironie in der 'Dichterliebe,' " 9.

13. See Edward T. Cone, *The Composer's Voice* (Berkeley, Los Angeles, and London: University of California Press, 1974), 39–40; Edward T. Cone, "Poet's Love or Composer's Love?," in *Music and Text: Critical Inquiries*, ed. Steven Paul Scher (Cambridge: Cambridge University Press, 1992), 191; Berthold Höck-

ner, "Spricht der Dichter oder der Tondichter? Die multiple *persona* und Robert Schumanns *Liederkreis* op. 24," in *Schumann und seine Dichter*, ed. Wendt, 30.

14. Susanne K. Langer, *Feeling and Form: A Theory of Art Developed From Philosophy in a New Key* (London: Routledge & Kegan Paul, 1953), 156. Cf. Gruber, "Romantische Ironie in den Heine-Liedern?," 326–27; Pfingsten, "Musikalische Ironie 'im wunderschönen Monat Mai' von Schumann?"; Jost, "Brahms und die romantische Ironie"; Marcel Brion, *Schumann and the Romantic Age*, trans. Geoffrey Sainsbury (London: Collins, 1956), 229.

15. See, however, Brauner, "Irony in the Heine Lieder of Schubert and Schumann"; Rosenberg, "Paradox, Doppelbödigkeit und Ironie in der 'Dichterliebe.'"

16. Dill, "Romantic Irony in the Works of Robert Schumann," 176.

17. "im Vergleich zu einer 'normalen' Liederwartung." Gruber, "Romantische Ironie in den Heine-Liedern?," 328. Cf. Brauner, "Irony in the Heine Lieder of Schubert and Schumann."

18. Heyd, *Aubrey Beardsley*, 17, 26, 40, 50, 68, 73, 78–79, 85, 103, 114, 128–129, 210, 221.

19. Ibid., 13, cf. 20, 37–38, 48–49, 74, 80–81.

20. See Eli Rozik, "Theatrical Irony," *Theatre Research International* 11.2 (1986): 134–35.

21. Elinor Fuchs, "Is There Life After Irony?," *Village Voice* 29 (3 January 1984): 77.

22. Rozik, "Theatrical Irony," 149. Cf. Bertrand Rougé, "L'ironie, ou la double représentation," *Lendemains* issue 50 (1988): 36–37. Muecke emphasises the "verticality" of images of irony in "Images of Irony."

23. Peter N. Dunn, "Irony as Structure in the Drama," *Bulletin of Hispanic Studies* 61 (1984): 317.

24. Ibid., 324.

25. Ibid., 318–19.

26. Raymond J. Pentzell, "Actor, *Maschera*, and Role: An Approach to Irony in Performance," *Comparative Drama* 16 (1982).

27. Rozik, "Theatrical Irony," 141.

28. Huston Diehl, "Inversion, Parody, and Irony: The Visual Rhetoric of Renaissance English Tragedy," *Studies in English Literature 1500–1900* 22 (1982).

29. Pentzell, "Actor, *Maschera*, and Role," 203.

30. Wiley Feinstein, "Dorinda as Ariostean Narrator in Handel's *Orlando*," *Italica* 64 (1987); Frank Vulpi, "Irony in Verdi's *Rigoletto*," *Opera Journal* 21.4 (1988); Rodney Milnes, "Degrees of Irony," *About the House* 7.2 (1984): 51–52.

31. See Betty Sue Diener, "Irony in Mozart's Operas" (Ph.D. diss., Columbia University, New York, 1992), 32–33, 386–92.

32. J. Peter Dyson, "Ironic Dualities in *Das Rheingold*," *Current Musicology* 43 (1987): 37. Cf. Walter Bernhart, "Prekäre angewandte Opernästhetik: Audens 'sekundäre Welt' und Hans Werner Henzes *Elegie für junge Liebende*," in *The Semantics of the Musico-Literary Genres: Method and Analysis*, ed. Walter Bernhart (Tübingen: Gunter Narr Verlag, 1994), 243–44.

33. John H. Long, *Shakespeare's Use of Music: The Histories and Tragedies* (Gainesville: University of Florida Press, 1971), 18, 22–23, 26, 45–46, 215–16, 264–65.

34. Carolyn Roberts Finlay, "Operatic Translation and Shostakovich: *The Nose*," *Comparative Literature* 35 (1983): 203; Susan Greene, "Comedy and Puccini's Operas," *Opera Quarterly* 2.3 (1984): 105.

35. Linda Phyllis Austern, "Sweet Meats with Sour Sauce: The Genesis of Musical Irony in English Drama after 1600," *Journal of Musicology* 4 (1986): 482, 478, 484.

36. Ibid., 486. Cf. Frits Noske, *The Signifier and the Signified: Studies in the Operas of Mozart and Verdi* (The Hague: Martinus Nijhoff, 1977), 100–120; Audrey Davidson, "Romanticism and Irony in Beethovens's *Fidelio*," in *Substance and Manner: Studies in Music and the Other Arts* (St. Paul, Minn.: Hiawatha Press, 1977); Edward Forman, "Musique et quiproquo: L'ironie dans les intermèdes musicaux," *Littératures Classiques* 21 (1994); Julia Liebscher, "Mythos und Verfremdung: Musikalische Ironie als Mittel der Distanzierung in *Oedipus Rex* von Igor Strawinsky," in *Altes im neuen*, eds. Bernd Edelmann and Manfred Hermann Schmid (Tutzing: Hans Schneider, 1995).

37. Susanne Vill, "Das psychologische Experiment in de Laclos' *Les Liaisons Dangereuses* und in Mozarts *Così fan tutte*: Zur Frage von Rationalismus und Ironie in Mozarts Musiktheater," in *Aufklärungen: Studien zur deutsch-französischen Musikgeschichte im 18. Jahrhundert: Einflüsse und Wirkungen* 2, eds. Wolfgang Birtel and Christoph-Hellmut Mahling (Heidelberg: Carl Winter Universitätsverlag, 1986), 133; Delores Jerde Keahey, "Così fan tutte: Parody or irony?," in *Paul A. Pisk: Essays in His Honor*, ed. John Glowacki (Austin: College of Fine Arts, University of Texas, 1966), 120, 130.

38. See Hermann Abert, *W. A. Mozart* (Leipzig: Breitkopf & Härtel, 1921), 655, 657, 664, 673; Ernst Lert, *Mozart auf dem Theater* (Berlin: Schuster & Loeffler, 1918), 410–26; Diener, "Irony in Mozart's Operas," 194–237; Scott Burnham, "Mozart's *felix culpa*: Così fan tutte and the Irony of Beauty," *Musical Quarterly* 78 (1994).

39. Joseph Thomas Malloy, "Musico-Dramatic Irony in Mozart's 'Magic Flute' " (Ph.D. diss., University of Virginia, 1985). Cf. Attila Csampai, "Das Geheimnis der 'Zauberflöte' oder Die Folgen der Aufklärung," in Wolfgang Amadeus Mozart, *Die Zauberflöte: Texte, Materialen, Kommentare*, eds. Attila Csampai and Dietmar Holland (Reinbek bei Hamburg: Rowohlt, 1982), 28–30.

40. Malloy, "Musico-Dramatic Irony in Mozart's 'Magic Flute,' " 89.

41. Ibid., 92.

42. Ibid., 125.

43. Ibid., 93, 99, 113–14, 133.

44. Ibid., 154.

45. Hutcheon, *Irony's Edge*, 131–40, 159–66.

46. The correlation is, however, noted in Diener, "Irony in Mozart's Operas," 238–50.

47. Mark Franko, *Dance as Text: Ideologies of the Baroque Body* (Cambridge: Cambridge University Press, 1993).

48. Franko, *Dance as Text*, 3, 5, 45, 65, 69, 81, 94, 103–104, 106, 112, 126. Cf. Susan Leigh Foster, *Reading Dancing: Bodies and Subjects in Contemporary American Dance* (Berkeley, Los Angeles, and London: University of California Press, 1986), 32–41, 234–35.

49. Ong, "From Mimesis to Irony," 33.

50. See, for instance, Christian Comanzo, "*Sunset Boulevard* or the Coding of Irony," in *Hollywood: Réflexions sur l'écran*, ed. Daniel Royot (Aix-en-Provence: Université de Provence, 1984); Frederick Garber, "Fabulating Jazz," in *Representing Jazz*, ed. Krin Gabbard (Durham, N.C., and London: Duke University Press, 1995).

51. Thomas Elsaesser, "Editorial: The Cinema of Irony," *Monogram* issue 5 (1975): 1. Cf. Erik Hedling, *Lindsay Anderson: Maverick Film-Maker* (London and Washington: Cassell, 1998), 73–76.

52. Yvette Biró, "Pathos and Irony in East European Films," and František Daniel, "The Czech Difference," both in *Politics, Art and Commitment in the East European Cinema*, ed. David W. Paul (London and Basingstoke: Macmillan, 1983).

53. This is the case, I think, in Beatrice Stiglitz, "A Joke of Destiny: Irony and Paradox in Italian Film: Bellocchio, Scola, Wertmuller," in *National Traditions in Motion Pictures*, ed. Douglas Radcliff-Umstead (Kent, Ohio: Kent State University, 1985).

54. Julie Christensen, "The Films of Eldar Shengelaya: From Subtle Humor to Biting Satire," in *Inside Soviet Film Satire: Laughter with a Lash*, ed. Andrew Horton (Cambridge: Cambridge University Press, 1993).

55. Svetlana Boym, "Perestroika of Kitsch: Sergei Soloviev's *Black Rose, Red Rose*," in *Inside Soviet Film Satire*, ed. Horton, 125, 131.

56. Pamela Robertson, "Structural Irony in *Mildred Pierce*, or How Mildred Lost Her Tongue," *Cinema Journal* 30 (1990). Cf. Malloy, "Musico-Dramatic Irony in Mozart's 'Magic Flute,' " 17–19.

57. C. Morris, "Woody Allen's Comic Irony," *Literature/Film Quarterly* 15 (1987): 178–80.

58. Eric Smoodin, "The Image and the Voice in the Film with Spoken Narration," *Quarterly Review of Film Studies* 8 (Fall 1983); Sarah Kozloff, *Invisible Storytellers: Voice-Over Narration in American Fiction Film* (Berkeley, Los Angeles, and London: University of California Press, 1988), 102–26.

59. See Hutcheon, *Irony's Edge*, 67–88; Morris, "Woody Allen's Comic Irony."

60. Thomas Rosteck, "Irony, Argument, and Reportage in Television Documentary: *See It Now* versus Senator McCarthy," *Quarterly Journal of Speech* 75 (1989): 285, 287.

61. Lesley Brill, *The Hitchcock Romance: Love and Irony in Hitchcock's Films* (Princeton, New Jersey: Princeton University Press, 1988), 163.

62. Ibid., 196.

63. Ibid., 200.

64. Örjan Roth-Lindberg, *Skuggan av ett leende: Om filmisk ironi och den ironiska berättelsen* (Stockholm: T. Fischer & Co., 1995), 158–65, 172.

65. Ibid., 166–370.

66. Doane, "The Dialogical Text," 168, 8.

67. Mary Ann Doane, "The Film's Time and the Spectator's 'Space,' " in *Cinema and Language*, eds. Stephen Heath and Patricia Mellencamp (Frederick, Md.: University Publications of America, 1983), 40.

68. Doane, "The Dialogical Text," 9–10, 83, 291.

69. Ibid., 231, 260, 262.

70. Ibid., 157, 183.

71. Ibid., 300.

72. Ibid., 97–98.

73. See Donald Brackett, "The Ironic Ceramics of Richard Milette," *American Ceramics* 12.4 (1996); Ray Morris, "Irony in Political Cartoons," in *Essays in Canadian Irony* 1, ed. Linda Hutcheon (North York, Ont., Canada: Robarts Centre for Canadian Studies, 1988); John Felstiner, *The Lies of Art: Max Beerbohm's Parody and Caricature* (London: Victor Gollancz, 1973), 118, 128.

74. Muecke, *Irony and the Ironic*, 2–3. Cf. Muecke, *The Compass of Irony*, 78–79; Muecke, *Irony*, 4–7.

75. Hutcheon, *Irony's Edge*, 155; Kerbrat-Orecchioni, "L'ironie comme trope," 113.

76. Hutcheon, *A Theory of Parody*, 31.

77. Ibid., 32.

78. Ibid., 6.

79. This interpretive process is discussed, although the term *irony* is not being used, in Benjamin Buchloh, "Parody and Appropriation in Francis Picabia, Pop, and Sigmar Polke," *Artforum* 20 (March 1982).

80. Heyd, *Aubrey Beardsley*, 75, 224.

81. Ibid., 116, 124, 126, 150, 192.

82. Dan Nadaner, "Intervention and Irony," *Vanguard* 13 (September 1984): 14; David R. Smith, "Irony and Civility: Notes on the Convergence of Genre and Portraiture in Seventeenth-Century Dutch Painting," *Art Bulletin* 69 (1987): 408; Donna Gustafson, "Food and Death: *Vanitas* in Pop Art," *Arts Magazine* 60 (February1986).

83. Felstiner, *The Lies of Art*, 137.

84. Monique Yaari, "Ironic Architecture: The Puzzles of Multiple (En)coding," *Restant* 18 (1990): 347, 356. Cf. Max Schasler, "Die Ironie in der Musik: Ein Beitrag zur Aesthetik der Musik," *Zeitschrift für Musik* 77 (1881): 386–87.

85. Diehl, "Inversion, Parody, and Irony," 202, 204, 209.

86. As in Barbara Godard, " 'The Empire of the Status Quo': To the Second Degree," in *Essays in Canadian Irony* 3, ed. Hutcheon, 51–52.

87. Michael Tilmouth, "Parody," in *The New Grove Dictionary of Music and Musicians* 14, ed. Stanley Sadie (London: Macmillan, 1980), 238–39.

88. Keahey, "Così fan tutte," 116.

89. "Parodie ist die Deformation eines konkreten und erkennbaren Objekts. . . . Bei der Ironie ist die Intonation von entscheidender Bedeutung." Flothuis, "Einige Betrachtungen über den Humor in der Musik," 692.

90. "la forme la plus voyante de l'ironie . . . la parodie singe toujours *quelqu'un*, la 'manière' de quelqu'un, le style de quelqu'un." Jankélévitch, *L'ironie*, 53.

91. Carolyn Roberts Finlay, "Operatic Translation and Shostakovich: *The Nose*," 207.

92. See Valleria Belt Grannis, *Dramatic Parody in Eighteenth Century France* (New York: Institute of French Studies, 1931), 111–45; Frank W. Lindsay, *Dramatic Parody by Marionettes in Eighteenth Century Paris* (New York: King's Crown Press, 1946), 46–121.

93. Noske, *The Signifier and the Signified*, 99. Cf. Abert, *W. A. Mozart*, 655, 658–59.

94. Noske, *The Signifier and the Signified*, 101.

95. Austern, "Sweet Meats with Sour Sauce," 478.

96. Zoltan Roman, "Connotative Irony in Mahler's *Todenmarsch in 'Callots Manier,*' " *Musical Quarterly* 59 (1973): 213.

97. Charles Rosen, *The Classical Style: Haydn, Mozart, Beethoven*, rev. ed. (London and Boston: Faber and Faber, 1976), 460.

98. Peter Winkler, "Randy Newman's Americana," *Popular Music* 7.1 (1987): 10.

99. Cf. Ingrid Monson, "Doubleness and Jazz Improvisation: Irony, Parody, and Ethnomusicology," *Critical Inquiry* 20 (1994): 291.

100. Harry Goldschmidt, "Zitat oder Parodie?," *Beiträge zur Musikwissenschaft* 12 (1970).

101. Their second single (Virgin Records); music and lyrics by Jones, Matlock, Cook, and Rotten.

102. Many versions of the text exist. See chap. 12 in Percy A. Scholes, *God Save the Queen! The History and Romance of the World's First National Anthem* (London, New York, and Toronto: Oxford University Press, 1954).

103. Ibid., v.

104. On "God Save the Queen" and the context of contemporary British society, see Greil Marcus, *Lipstick Traces: A Secret History of the Twentieth Century* (London: Secker & Warburg, 1989), 10–14. Circumstances around and the reactions to "God Save the Queen" are described in Jon Savage, *England's Dreaming: Sex Pistols and Punk Rock* (London and Boston: Faber and Faber, 1991), 353–67.

105. Scholes, *God Save The Queen!*, 165.

106. See Marcus, *Lipstick Traces*, 32.

107. See Ernst Behler, *German Romantic Literary Theory*, 145.

108. Norman Knox, *The Word Irony and its Context, 1500–1755*, 6.

109. Dilwyn Knox, *Ironia*, 58, 68–69.

110. Ibid., 59–61.

111. Sedgewick, *Of Irony*, 112–13.

Chapter 8: The Irony of the Arts

Booth, *A Rhetoric of Irony*, 262.

1. Rozik, "Theatrical Irony," 149.

2. For a discussion of the word puns, see Ulf Linde, "MARiée CELibataire," in Walter Hopps, Ulf Linde, and Arturo Schwarz, *Marcel Duchamp: Ready-Mades, etc. (1913–1964)* (Paris: Terrain Vague, 1964); Charles A. Cramer, "Duchamp from Syntax to Bride: Sa Langue dans sa Joue," *Word & Image* 13 (1997).

3. Tami Katz-Freiman, "Antipathos: Black Humor, Irony and Cynicism in Contemporary Israeli Art," in *Antipathos: Black Humor, Irony and Cynicism in Contemporary Israeli Art* (Jerusalem: Israel Museum, 1993), 47. "este iconoclasta irónico." Mary Farakos, "Octavio Paz y Marcel Duchamp: Crítica moderna para un artista moderno," *Cuadernos Hispanoamericanos* issue 410 (1984): 79.

4. Heyd, *Aubrey Beardsley*, 226.

5. Albert Cook, "The 'Meta-Irony' of Marcel Duchamp," *Journal of Aesthetics and Art Criticism* 44 (1986): 268.

6. Octavio Paz, *Marcel Duchamp, or The Castle of Purity*, trans. Donald Gardner (London: Cape Goliard Press, 1970) (unpaginated). An extended version of the essay is printed (together with the essay "* Water Writes Always in * Plural," in which Paz also to some extent uses the notion of meta-irony) in Octavio Paz, *Marcel Duchamp: Appearance Stripped Bare*, trans. Rachel Phillips and Donald Gardner (New York: Arcade Publishing, 1990). The quotations are from the unpaginated edition.

7. Johnson quoted in Ellis, *Against Deconstruction*, 6; Matilal, "Mysticism and Ineffability," 155.

8. Paz, *Marcel Duchamp, or The Castle of Purity* (unpaginated); Paz, *Marcel Duchamp*, 90.

9. Kevin Barry, *Language, Music and the Sign: A Study in Aesthetics, Poetics and Poetic Practice from Collins to Coleridge* (Cambridge: Cambridge University Press, 1987).

10. John Neubauer, *The Emancipation of Music from Language: Departure from Mimesis in Eighteenth-Century Aesthetics* (New Haven and London: Yale University Press, 1986), 193–210.

11. Ibid., 109–14, 169–72, 182–92.

12. See Hans-Joachim Bracht, "Schumanns 'Papillons' und die Ästhetik der Frühromantik," *Archiv für Musikwissenschaft* 50 (1993): 76–77.

13. "Klang, Harmonie, Rhythmus, Melodie oder Kontrapunkt." Clytus Gottwald, "John Cage und Marcel Duchamp," *Musik-Konzepte* Sonderband John Cage (1978): 135.

14. Paz, *Marcel Duchamp, or The Castle of Purity* (unpaginated).

15. Eric de Visscher, "Die Künstlergruppe 'Les Incohérents' und die Vorgeschichte zu 4'33''," in *John Cage: Anarchic Harmony*, eds. Stefan Schädler and Walter Zimmermann (Mainz: Schott, 1992), 72.

16. Paul Griffiths, *Cage* (London: Oxford University Press, 1981), 1, 24.

17. Tom Johnson, "Intentionality and Nonintentionality in the Performance of Music by John Cage," *Bucknell Review* John Cage at Seventy-Five (1989); Margaret Leng Tan, " 'Taking a Nap, I Pound the Rice': Eastern Influences on John Cage," *Bucknell Review* John Cage at Seventy-Five (1989).

18. The distinction is made, however, in James Pritchett, "Understanding John Cage's Chance Music: An Analytical Approach," *Bucknell Review* John Cage at Seventy-Five (1989). Unfortunately, Pritchett is here mainly interested in chance in the compositional stage.

19. See James Pritchett, *The Music of John Cage* (Cambridge: Cambridge University Press, 1993), 105–9.

20. Cf. Per Wahlsten, ". . . några rader om John Cage," in *Tonsättarens val: Texter om svensk musikalisk modernism och postmodernism*, ed. Björn Billing (Stockholm: Edition Reimers, 1993); Heinz-Klaus Metzger, "Anarchie durch Negation der Zeit oder Probe einer Lektion wider die Moral," *Musik-Konzepte* Sonderband John Cage (1978).

21. See Griffiths, *Cage*, 34; Pritchett, *The Music of John Cage*, 70–73.

22. Jankélévitch, *L'ironie*, 86.

23. Booth, *A Rhetoric of Irony*, 262.

24. John Cage, *Silence* (London: Calder and Boyars, 1968).

25. Tan, " 'Taking a Nap, I Pound the Rice,' " 50.

26. Cf. the discussion on Eckhart in Pritchett, *The Music of John Cage*, 45–47.

27. Jankélévitch, *L'ironie*, 40, 64.

CHAPTER 9: THE SPATIAL METAPHORS OF IRONY

Arnheim, *Visual Thinking*, 254.

1. Becker, "Concepts of Irony with Special Reference to Applications in the Visual Arts," 7.

2. Tony Godfrey in *Chance Choice and Irony*, ed. Colin Crumplin (London and Southampton: Todd Gallery and John Hansard Gallery, 1994), 9, 61. Cf. Laura Cottingham, "The Feminine De-Mystique: Gender, Power, Irony, and Aestheticized Feminism in '80s Art," *Flash Art* issue 147 (1989); John Peter Nils-

son, "Swedish Art: From Irony to the Sublime & Back Again," *Flash Art* issue 157 (1991); Halldór Björn Runolfsson, "Intimacy, Austerity and Irony: Eight Icelandic Artists in the Late Eighties," *Flash Art* issue 157 (1991).

3. Ulanov, "The Art of Irony"; Katz-Freiman, "Antipathos: Black Humor, Irony and Cynicism in Contemporary Israeli Art," 50; Wendy Dawe, "Visual Metaphor and the Ironic Glance: The Interaction Between Artist and Viewer (Ph.D. diss., Birmingham Polytechnic, Birmingham, England, 1991); Neal Benezra, "A Study in Irony: Modigliani's *Jacques and Berthe Lipchitz*," *Museum Studies* 12 (1986); Christiane Hertel, "Irony, Dream, and Kitsch: Max Klinger's *Paraphrase of the Finding of a Glove* and German Modernism," *Art Bulletin* 74 (1992).

4. Muecke, *Irony and the Ironic*, 2.

5. Paz, *Marcel Duchamp, or The Castle of Purity* (unpaginated).

6. John R. Searle, "*Las Meninas* and the Paradoxes of Pictorial Representation," in *The Language of Images*, ed. W. J. T. Mitchell (Chicago and London: University of Chicago Press, 1980), 253.

7. Ann Hurley, "The Elided Self: Witty Dis-Locations in Velázquez and Donne," *Journal of Aesthetics and Art Criticism* 44 (1986): 358.

8. See Andrew Solomon, *The Irony Tower: Soviet Artists in a Time of Glasnost* (New York: Alfred A. Knopf, 1991).

9. Geneviève Dolle, "Éléments pour l'analyse rhétorique d'une image," *Revue d'esthétique* 32 (1979): 243–44.

10. "l'iconique ne peut être ironique en soi." Groupe μ, "Ironique et iconique," *Poétique* 36 (1978): 436.

11. Heyd, *Aubrey Beardsley*, 222–23; Searle, "*Las Meninas* and the Paradoxes of Pictorial Representation," 247. See also two books that came to my knowledge when *Divine Madness* was almost competed: Ursula Lindau, *Max Ernst und die Romantik: Unendliches Spiel mit Witz und Ironie* (Köln: Wienand, 1997); Ulrich Heimann, *Picassos Kubismus und die Ironie* (München: Wilhelm Fink Verlag, 1998).

12. Wolfgang Kayser, *The Grotesque in Art and Literature*, trans. Ulrich Weisstein (Bloomington: Indiana University Press, 1963), 120, 161, 168–78. Cf. Muecke, *The Compass of Irony*, 29.

13. Judi Freeman, *The Dada & Surrealist Word-Image*, with a contribution by John C. Welchman (Cambridge and London: MIT Press and Los Angeles County Museum of Art, 1989), 21, 36, 42, 73. Cf. Beatrix Nobis, "Kurt Schwitters: *Merz*, le fragment et l'ironie romantique," *Cahiers du Musée national d'art moderne* issue 51 (1995).

14. Katz-Freiman, "Antipathos: Black Humor, Irony and Cynicism in Contemporary Israeli Art," 47.

15. See Eric Pil, "Deceptive Similarities in a Paradoxical Oeuvre," and Marie-Pascale Gildemyn, "Marcel Broodthaers and Irony," both in *Irony by Vision*, ed. Jan Hoet (Tokyo: Watari-Um, 1991); Cees de Boer, "Foucault et Magritte, ou Le mystère éclipsé," trans. Marie-Claire Cécilia, in *L'interprétation détourné*, ed. Leo H. Hoek (Amsterdam and Atlanta: Rodopi, 1990); Dawe, "Visual Metaphor and the Ironic Glance," 203, 236.

16. Renée Riese Hubert, "The Other Wordly Landscapes of E. A. Poe and René Magritte," *Sub-Stance* issue 21 (1978).

17. Fred Miller Robinson, "The Wizard Proprieties of Poe and Magritte," *Word & Image* 3 (1987). See also Fred Miller Robinson, "The History and Significance of the Bowler Hat: Chaplin, Laurel and Hardy, Beckett, Magritte and Kundera," *TriQuarterly* issue 66 (1986): 193.

18. Lars Elleström, "Some Notes on Irony in the Visual Arts and Music: The Examples of Magritte and Shostakovich," *Word & Image* 12 (1996).

19. Ralf Schiebler, "Das Oppositionsprinzip bei Magritte," *Zeitschrift für Ästhetik und allgemeine Kunstwissenschaft* 27 (1981).

20. Georges Roque, "Magritte's Words and Images," *Visible Language* 23 (1989): 231; Leslie Ortquist, "Magritte's Captivity in Robbe-Grillet's *La Belle Captive*: The Subjugation of the Image by the Word," *Visible Language* 23 (1989): 251.

21. Jacques Meuris, "Magritte: Le mystère, le réel, et la connaissance," *Colóquio-Artes* issue 86 (1990); de Boer, "Foucault et Magritte," 53.

22. Emma Kafalenos, "Image and Narrativity: Robbe-Grillet's *La Belle Captive*," *Visible Language* 23 (1989): 381.

23. Pil, "Deceptive Similarities in a Paradoxical Oeuvre," 42. Cf. Laurie Edson, "Disrupting Conventions: Verbal-Visual Objects in Francis Ponge and René Magritte," *L'esprit créateur* 24.2 (1984): 29.

24. Suzanne Rodin Pucci, " '*Ceci n'est pas* . . . ': Negative Framing in Diderot and Magritte," *Mosaic* 20.3 (1987): 5.

25. See, for instance, Uwe M. Schneede, *René Magritte: Leben und Werk* (Köln: Verlag M. DuMont Schauberg, 1973), 34–46; Petra von Morstein, "Magritte: Artistic and Conceptual Representation," *Journal of Aesthetics and Art Criticism* 41 (1982); Edson, "Disrupting Conventions."

26. Michel Foucault, *This Is Not a Pipe*, ed. and trans. James Harkness (Berkeley, Los Angeles, and London: University of California Press, 1983), 26–31.

27. Arnheim, *Visual Thinking*, 141.

28. Jonathan Weil, "The Role of Ambiguity in the Arts," *Et cetera* 43 (Spring 1986): 87–88.

29. Becker, "Concepts of Irony with Special Reference to Applications in the Visual Arts," 72.

30. Ibid., 68.

31. Ibid., 153.

32. Ibid., 85.

33. "une intense activité rhétorique." R. Jongen, "L'affolement métaphorique et métonymique dans l'image magrittienne," *Anthropo-Logiques* 2 (1989): 187.

34. "hypothèses conceptuelles." Ibid., 198.

35. Foucault, *This is Not a Pipe*, 19.

36. Cook, "The 'Meta-Irony' of Marcel Duchamp," 265.

37. Doane, "The Dialogical Text," 135.

38. W. J. T. Mitchell, "Spatial Form in Literature: Toward a General Theory," in *The Language of Images*, ed. Mitchell, 296. Mitchell opposes the ideas of Kenneth Burke in *Language as Symbolic Action* from 1968.

39. Roth-Lindberg, *Skuggan av ett leende*, 147–58.

40. Mitchell, "Spatial Form in Literature," in *The Language of Images*, ed. Mitchell, 286. See also Joseph Frank, "Spatial Form in Modern Literature," in *Criticism: The Foundations of Modern Literary Judgment*, eds. Mark Schorer, Josephine Miles, and Gordon McKenzie (New York: Harcourt, Brace and Co., 1948).

41. Rudolf Arnheim, "A Plea for Visual Thinking," in *The Language of Images*, ed. Mitchell, 176.

42. Arnheim, *Visual Thinking*, 294, 80.

43. Ibid., 254.

44. Ibid., 134.

45. Ibid., 27, 111.

46. Ibid., 253.

47. Ibid., 112.

48. Ibid., 232–33.

49. Ibid., 117.

50. Dilwyn Knox, *Ironia*, 11.

51. Muecke, *The Compass of Irony*, 167–169.

52. Hubert, "The Other Wordly Landscapes of E. A. Poe and René Magritte," 77. Cf. Jeremy Strick, "Notes on Some Instances of Irony in Modern Pastoral," in *The Pastoral Landscape*, ed. John Dixon Hunt (Hanover and London: University Press of New England, 1992), 202–3.

53. Sigmund Freud, "The Antithetical Meaning of Primal Words," in *Writings on Art and Literature*, ed. James Strachey, trans. Angela Harris (Stanford, Calif.: Stanford University Press, 1997), 94–95. Cf. "The 'Uncanny,' " in ibid., 199–201.

54. Suzi Gablik, *Magritte* (London: Thames and Hudson, 1970), 102–5.

55. A. M. Hammacher, *René Magritte*, trans. James Brockway (New York: Abradale Press, 1995), 158.

56. Dawe uses the word *metaphor* for figurativity in general and the word *irony* for distance, from which of course it follows that "metaphor is an ironic trope." Dawe, "Visual Metaphor and the Ironic Glance," 227.

57. "Con alivio, con humillación, con terror, comprendió que él también era una apariencia, que otro estaba soñándolo." Jorge Luis Borges, *Collected Fictions*, trans. Andrew Hurley (London: Allen Lane, 1999), 100; *Obras Completas* 1 (Barcelona: Emecé editores, 1989), 455.

58. *The Tempest*, act 4, scene 1.

Chapter 10: Musical Meaning, Irony, and Value

"la folie reconnue dans une sonate lui paraissait quelque chose d'aussi mystérieux que la folie d'une chienne, la folie d'un cheval." Marcel Proust, *À la recherche du temps perdu* 1 (Paris: Gallimard, 1987), 211.

1. Noske, *The Signifier and the Signified*, 102.

2. Jankélévitch, *L'ironie*, 75–76, 81, 91, 132–33.

3. "le refus de développer, la pirouette, la guerre aux sérieuses modulations." Jankélévitch, *L'ironie*, 92.

4. Ulanov, "The Art of Irony," 259.

5. Hutcheon, *Irony's Edge*, 141.

6. "une œuvre de musique pure ne contenant aucun des rapports logiques dont l'altération dans le langage dénonce la folie, la folie reconnue dans une sonate lui paraissait quelque chose d'aussi mystérieux que la folie d'une chienne, la folie d'un cheval, qui pourtant s'observent en effet." Proust, *À la recherche du temps perdu* 1, 211.

7. "Ironie und Wahnsinn in musik auszudrücken, ist wohl ganz unmöglich." Walter Gieseler, "Schumanns frühe Klavierwerke im Spiegel der Literarischen Romantik," in *Robert Schumann: Universalgeist der Romantik*, eds. Julius Alf and Joseph A. Kruse (Düsseldorf: Droste Verlag, 1981), 85.

8. Rudhyar D. Chennevière, "Erik Satie and the Music of Irony," trans. Frederick H. Martens, *Musical Quarterly* 5 (1919): 473–76.

9. Kerbrat-Orecchioni, "L'ironie comme trope," 113.

10. Muecke, *Irony*, 4.

11. Ibid., 6.

12. For a systematic and enlightening discussion of this topic, see Jean-Jacques Nattiez, *Music and Discourse: Toward a Semiology of Music*, trans. Carolyn Abbate (Princeton: Princeton University Press, 1990), 8–10, 102–29.

13. Hutcheon, *Irony's Edge*, 155.

14. Lawrence Kramer, "Music and Representation: The Instance of Haydn's *Creation*," in *Music and Text*, ed. Scher, 140.

15. Carl Dahlhaus, *Esthetics of Music*, trans. William W. Austin (Cambridge: Cambridge University Press, 1982), 17.

16. Ibid., 20–24.

17. Neubauer, *The Emancipation of Music from Language*, 52.

18. Ibid., 22–41.

19. Ibid., 45.

20. Ibid., 7, cf. 75, 150–57, 167.

21. For a discussion of these notions, see the chapter "Emotion and Mood in Music" in Laurie-Jeanne Lister, *Humor as a Concept in Music: A Theoretical Study of Expression in Music, the Concept of Humor and Humor in Music with an Analytical Example—W. A. Mozart, Ein Musikalischer Spaß, KV 522* (Frankfurt am Main: Peter Lang, 1994).

22. Eduard Hanslick, *Vom Musikalisch-schönen: Ein Beitrag zur Revision der Ästhetik der Tonkunst* (Darmstadt: Wissenschaftliche Buchgesellschaft, 1965); *On the Musically Beautiful: A Contribution towards the Revision of the Aesthetics of Music*, ed. and trans. Geoffrey Payzant (Indianapolis, Ind.: Hackett Publishing Co., 1986).

23. "Die *Bestimmtheit* der Gefühle ruht ja gerade in deren begrifflichem Kern." Ibid., 14; 9.

24. "Wie mag man nun dasjenige als das von einer Kunst *Dargestellte* bezeichnen, welches, das ungewisseste, vieldeutigste Element derselben, einem ewigen Streit unterworfen ist?." Ibid., 20; 14.

25. Ibid., 32; 29.

26. Susanne K. Langer, *Philosophy in a New Key: A Study in the Symbolism of Reason, Rite, and Art*, 3d ed. (Cambridge and London: Harvard University Press, 1957), 218.

27. Ibid., 219.

28. Ibid., 222.

29. Ibid., 232.

30. Ibid., 226, 228.

31. Ibid., 233, 235.

32. Ibid., 238. Cf. Langer, *Feeling and Form*, 374.

33. Langer, *Philosophy in a New Key*, 244.

34. Langer, *Feeling and Form*, 31–32.

35. Leonard B. Meyer, *Emotion and Meaning in Music* (Chicago and London: University of Chicago Press, 1956), 272.

36. Peter Kivy, *The Corded Shell: Reflections on Musical Expression* (Princeton: Princeton University Press, 1980), 77.

37. Ibid., 39.

38. Ibid., 15.

39. Ibid., 53.

40. Ibid., 48, cf. 107–11.

41. John Neubauer, "Tales of Hoffmann and Others: On Narrativizations of Instrumental Music," in *Interart Poetics: Essays on the Interrelations of the Arts and Media*, eds. Ulla-Britta Lagerroth, Hans Lund, and Erik Hedling (Amsterdam and Atlanta: Rodopi, 1997).

42. Carolyn Abbate, *Unsung Voices: Opera and Musical Narrative in the Nineteenth Century* (Princeton: Princeton University Press, 1991), 29, 27.

43. Ibid., 19.

44. Nattiez, *Music and Discourse*, 124, 9.

45. Dahlhaus, *Esthetics of Music*, 50.

46. See, for instance, Jeanpaul Goergen, "Dada: Musik der Ironie und Provokation," *Neue Zeitschrift für Musik* 155.3 (1994).

47. Calvin S. Brown, *Music and Literature: A Comparison of the Arts*, 2d ed. (Hanover and London: University Press of New England, 1987), 114–26.

48. "Inkongruenzen zwischen Dichtung und Vertonung." Jost, "Brahms und die romantische Ironie," 60.

49. Malloy, "Musico-Dramatic Irony in Mozart's 'Magic Flute,' " 89. Cf. Angelus Seipt, "Gesagt—gesungen—gemeint: über Ironie in der Oper," in *Kunst Kommunikation Kultur*, ed. Walter Nutz (Frankfurt am Main: Peter Lang, 1989), 267–70.

50. "wo Melodien durch Melodien selbst ironisirt werden." Schasler, "Die Ironie in der Musik," 406.

51. "Widerspruch zwischen der Einleitung und der Hauptmusik." Ibid., 398.

52. "Widerspruch gegen einen gegebenen Empfindungsinhalt." Ibid., 397.

53. "gleichzeitig Gegensätzliches auszusagen." Hans Mersmann, "Versuch einer musikalischen Wertästhetik," *Zeitschrift für Musikwissenschaft* 17 (1935): 40.

54. "Idee und Ausdruck"; "die musikalische Litotes." Lert, *Mozart auf dem Theater*, 414.

55. "autre chose"; "le contraire de ce qu'elle ressent." Jankélévitch, *L'ironie*, 49.

56. "Parfois la musique exprime non point 'le contraire,' mais 'autre chose.' " Vladimir Jankélévitch, *La musique et l'ineffable* (Paris: Librairie Armand Colin, 1961), 63.

57. "le lourd devient aérien, tandis que le léger danse le pas bouffon de l'éléphant." Jankélévitch, *L'ironie*, 84, cf. 90–91.

58. Muecke, *Irony and the Ironic*, 2.

59. See, for instance, Greene, "Comedy and Puccini's Operas"; Pierre Larderet, "Humour, ironie, satire, parodie dans la musique française des XVIIe et XVIIIe siècles," in *Aspects de la musique baroque et classique à Lyon et en France*, ed. Daniel Paquette (Lyon: Editions à coeur joie and Presses universitaires de Lyon, 1989).

60. Zofia Lissa, *Aufsätze zur Musikästhetik: Eine Auswahl* (Berlin: Henschelverlag, 1969), 126.

61. For bibliographies on this topic, see Bernhard Appel, "R. Schumanns Humoreske für Klavier op. 20: Zum musikalischen Humor in der ersten Hälfte des 19. Jahrhunderts unter besonderer Berücksichtigung des Formproblems" (Ph.D. diss., Universität des Saarlandes, Saarbrücken, 1981), 369–73; Mirjam Schadendorf, *Humor als Formkonzept in der Musik Gustav Mahlers* (Stuttgart and Weimar: Verlag J. B. Metzler, 1995), 6–14.

62. E. T. A. Hoffmann, "The Poet and the Composer," from *Die Serapions-Brüder*, trans. Oliver Strunk, in *Source Readings in Music History: From Classical Antiquity through the Romantic Era*, ed. Oliver Strunk (New York: W. W. Norton & Co., 1950), 792.

63. "Was der Hörer erwartet, tritt nicht ein." Flothuis, "Einige Betrachtungen über den Humor in der Musik," 688.

64. "ein übergehen zur Tagesordnung." Stefan Szuman, "Chopins Witz und Ironie," *Kulturprobleme des neuen Polen* issue 2 (1952): 7.

65. "Das Lachen ist ein Affekt aus der plötzlichen Verwandlung einer gespannten Erwartung in nichts." Kant, *Werke in sechs Bänden. Band V*, 437.

66. Lister, *Humor as a Concept in Music*, 79.

67. Appel, "R. Schumanns Humoreske für Klavier op. 20," 84–85.

68. Schadendorf, *Humor als Formkonzept in der Musik Gustav Mahlers*, 6–14, 28–34, 39–59. Cf. Constantin Floros, "Tragische Ironie und Ambivalenz bei Mahler," *Musik-Konzepte* Sonderband Gustav Mahler (1989); Manfred Angerer, "Ironisierung der Konvention und humoristische Totalität: über die ersten Takte von Gustav Mahlers IV. Symphonie," in *Vergleichend-systematische Musikwissenschaft*, eds. Elisabeth Th. Hilscher and Theophil Antonicek (Tutzing: Hans Schneider, 1994).

69. "die desintegrativen Aspekte des Werkes." Schadendorf, *Humor als Formkonzept in der Musik Gustav Mahlers*, 98.

70. "ein Formkonzept . . . welches von starken Gegensätzen einerseits, von einer eigentümlichen Statik andererseits, dort als Entwicklungslosigkeit bezeichnet, gekennzeichnet ist." Ibid., 168.

71. "ein Instrument von ätzender Schärfe, das eine kurzlebige Welt aufbaut, um diese augenblicklich wieder zu zerstören." Ibid., 271.

72. "le 'spleen' romantique—c'est la synthèse des dissonances et la fusion des contrastes." Jankélévitch, *L'ironie*, 114.

73. Rey M. Longyear, "Beethoven and Romantic Irony," *Musical Quarterly* 56 (1970). Cf. Patricia Herzog, "The Practical Wisdom of Beethoven's Diabelli Variations," *Musical Quarterly* 79 (1995).

74. Longyear, "Beethoven and Romantic Irony," 658–63.

75. Meyer, *Emotion and Meaning in Music*, 35. Cf. Leonard B. Meyer, "Meaning in Music and Information Theory," in *Music, the Arts, and Ideas: Patterns and Predictions in Twentieth-Century Culture* (Chicago and London: University of Chicago Press, 1967).

76. Meyer, *Emotion and Meaning in Music*, 51–60.

77. Ibid., 31.

78. Ibid., 39.

79. Ibid., 40.

80. Brooks, *The Well Wrought Urn*, 209–10.

81. Malloy, "Musico-Dramatic Irony in Mozart's 'Magic Flute,' " 48–66, 142, 151.

82. Ibid., 62–63.

83. Jean-Pierre Barricelli, "Romantic Irony in Music," in *Melopoiesis: Approaches to the Study of Literature and Music* (New York and London: New York University Press, 1988), 156. The essay is reprinted as "Musical Forms of Romantic Irony," in *Romantic Irony*, ed. Garber.

84. Ibid., 161.

85. Ibid., 165.

86. Mark Evan Bonds, "Haydn, Laurence Sterne, and the Origins of Musical

Irony," *Journal of the American Musicological Society* 44 (1991). Cf. Pierre Larderet, "Humour, ironie, satire, grotesque . . . : Étude de quelques aspects et procédés du comique musical" (Ph.D. diss., Université de Lyon, Saint-Etienne, 1981), 307–23; Ronald Woodley, "Strategies of Irony in Prokofiev's Violin Sonata in F minor Op. 80," in *The Practice of Performance: Studies in Musical Interpretation*, ed. John Rink (Cambridge: Cambridge University Press, 1995); Christine Moraal, "Romantische Ironie in Robert Schumanns 'Nachtstücken,' op. 23," *Archiv für Musikwissenschaft* 54 (1997). See also Dill, "Romantic Irony in the Works of Robert Schumann"; Bracht, "Schumanns 'Papillons' und die Ästhetik der Frühromantik"; Finson, "The Intentional Tourist"; Jost, "Brahms und die romantische Ironie."

87. Bonds, "Haydn, Laurence Sterne, and the Origins of Musical Irony," 67.

88. Dahlhaus, *Esthetics of Music*, 19.

89. Victor Zuckerkandl, *Sound and Symbol: Music and the External World*, trans. Willard R. Trask (New York: Bollingen Foundation and Pantheon Books, 1956), 267–377.

90. Ibid., 267.

91. Robert P. Morgan, "Musical Time/Musical Space," in *The Language of Images*, ed. Mitchell, 259.

92. Ibid., 262.

93. Langer, *Feeling and Form*, 117.

94. Morgan, "Musical Time/Musical Space," 260.

95. Thompson, *The Dry Mock*, 15–48.

96. "Das Organ, womit das Schöne aufgenommen wird, ist nicht das Gefühl, sondern die *Phantasie*, als die Thätigkeit des reinen Schauens." Hanslick, *Vom Musikalisch-schönen*, 4; *On the Musically Beautiful*, 4.

97. "Freilich ist die Phantasie gegenüber dem Schönen nicht blos ein *Schauen*, sondern ein Schauen mit *Verstand*, d. i. Vorstellen und Urtheilen, letzteres natürlich mit solcher Schnelligkeit, daß die einzelnen Vorgänge uns gar nicht zum Bewußtsein kommen, und die Täuschung entsteht, es geschehe *unmittelbar*, was doch in Wahrheit von vielfach vermittelnden Geistesprocessen abhängt." Ibid., 5; 4.

98. "Das Wort 'Anschauung', längst von den Gesichtsvorstellungen auf alle Sinneserscheinungen übertragen, entspricht überdies trefflich dem Acte des aufmerksamen Hörens, welches ja in einem successiven Betrachten der Tonformen besteht. Die Phantasie ist naturlich kein abgeschlossenes Gebiet: so wie sie ihren Lebensfunken aus den Sinnesempfindungen zog, sendet sie wiederum ihre Radien schnell an die Thätigkeit des Verstandes und des Gefühls aus." Ibid., 5; 4.

99. "Sie vermag die Bewegung eines psychischen Vorganges nach den Momenten: schnell, langsam, stark, schwach, steigernd, fallend nachzubilden." Ibid., 16; 11.

100. "wohlbegründete Analogie." Ibid., 24; 20.

101. Ibid., 6–7, 56; 5–6, 48.

102. Ibid., 55–56; 47–48.

103. Marshall Brown, "Origins of Modernism: Musical Structures and Narrative Forms," in *Music and Text*, ed. Scher, 88.

104. See, for instance, Reed Merrill, "The Grotesque in Music: Shostakovich's *Nose*," *Russian Literature Triquarterly* 23 (1990); Calum MacDonald, "The Anti-Formalist 'Rayok'—Learners Start Here!," *Tempo* 173 (June 1990): 23; Carolyn Roberts Finlay, "Operatic Translation and Shostakovich: *The Nose*," 203, 207;

Ulanov, "The Art of Irony," 259–60; Elleström, "Some Notes on Irony in the Visual Arts and Music."

105. Solomon Volkov, "Introduction," in *Testimony: The Memoirs of Dmitri Shostakovich*, as related to and ed. Solomon Volkov, trans. Antonina W. Bouis (London: Hamish Hamilton, 1979), xxi. For an overview of the debate, see Ian MacDonald, *The New Shostakovich* (Oxford: Oxford University Press, 1991), 1–15.

106. *Testimony*, ed. Volkov, 102.

107. Ibid., 140.

108. Quoted in Ian MacDonald, *The New Shostakovich*, 6.

109. Michael Oliver [M.E.O.], review of Decca record SXDL7551, *Gramophone* 60 (1982): 723.

110. Christopher Norris, "Ambiguous Shostakovich," *Gramophone* 60 (1983): 892.

111. Christopher Norris, "Introduction," in *Shostakovich: The Man and His Music*, ed. Christopher Norris (London: Lawrence and Wishart, 1982), 10.

112. Christopher Norris, "Shostakovich: Politics and Musical Language," in *Shostakovich*, ed. Norris, 181.

113. Ibid., 182.

114. Ibid., 176.

115. Ibid., 175, 165, 176.

116. Ibid., 186, 185.

117. Robert Stradling, "Shostakovich and the Soviet System, 1925–1975," in *Shostakovich*, ed. Norris.

118. Robert Dearling, "The First Twelve Symphonies: Portrait of the Artist as Citizen-Composer," in *Shostakovich*, ed. Norris, 61.

119. Ibid., 59–61.

120. See Steven Paul Scher, " 'O Wort, du Wort, das mir fehlt!' Der Realismusbegriff in der Musik," in *Literatur und Musik: Ein Handbuch zur Theorie und Praxis eines komparatistischen Grenzgebietes*, ed. Steven Paul Scher (Berlin: Erich Schmidt Verlag, 1984), 95–96.

121. J. Daniel Huband, "Shostakovich's Fifth Symphony: A Soviet Artist's Reply . . . ?," *Tempo* 173 (June 1990): 15.

122. Peter J. Rabinowitz, "Circumstantial Evidence: Musical Analysis and Theories of Reading," *Mosaic* 18.4 Music and Literature (1985): 165–66.

123. Ibid., 166.

124. Ibid., 167.

125. Ibid., 166.

126. Ibid., 164.

127. Ian MacDonald, *The New Shostakovich*, 15. See also the critique in Christopher Norris, "Shostakovich and Cold War Cultural Politics: A Review Essay," *Southern Humanities Review* 25 (1991), and Ian MacDonald's reply "Common Sense about Shostakovich: Breaking the 'Hermeneutic Circle,' " *Southern Humanities Review* 26 (1992).

128. Ian MacDonald, *The New Shostakovich*, 131.

129. Ibid., 132.

130. Ibid., 258.

131. Hirsch, *Validity in Interpretation*, xi.

132. See, for instance, Wolfgang Osthoff, "Symphonien beim Ende des Zweiten Weltkriegs: Strawinsky—Frommel—Schostakowitsch," *Acta musicologica* 60 (1988): 87–91.

133. Dahlhaus, *Esthetics of Music*, 94–95.

134. "la plus amère ironie. Beethoven oubliait que le sarcasme est impossible en musique." Alexandre Oulibicheff, *Beethoven: Ses critiques et ses glossateurs* (Leipzig and Paris: F. A. Brockhaus and Jules Gavelot, 1857), 226.

135. "Beethoven voulait écrire des satires en musique"; "l'intention de Beethoven, dans ce finale, était ironique"; "à l'oreille des hommes de goût." Ibid., 236–37.

136. Norris, "Shostakovich," in *Shostakovich*, ed. Norris, 180.

137. Dearling, "The First Twelve Symphonies," in *Shostakovich*, ed. Norris, 63.

138. See Ian MacDonald, *The New Shostakovich*, 5.

139. Volkov, "Introduction," in *Testimony*, ed. Volkov, xxxi.

140. Gregory Karl and Jenefer Robinson, "Shostakovich's Tenth Symphony and the Musical Expression of Cognitively Complex Emotions," *Journal of Aesthetics and Art Criticism* 53 (1995): 406.

141. Ian MacDonald, *The New Shostakovich*, 207.

142. David Fanning, *The Breath of the Symphonist: Shostakovich's Tenth* (London: Royal Musical Association, 1988), 7, 9, 29, 71.

143. Ibid., 54, 60, 71

144. Ibid., 3.

145. Ibid., 58.

146. Ibid., 73.

NACHSPIEL

"Welche Götter werden uns von allen diesen Ironien erretten können?" Schlegel, "Über die Unverständlichkeit," in *Kritische Friedrich-Schlegel-Ausgabe* 2, 369.

1. "die Ironie wild wird, und sich gar nicht mehr regieren läßt"; "Mit der Ironie ist durchaus nicht zu scherzen. Sie kann unglaublich lange nachwirken." Ibid., 369–70.

2. Joseph Margolis, "Plain Talk about Interpretation on a Relativistic Model"; Stephen Davies, "Relativism in Interpretation"; Robert Stecker, "Relativism about Interpretation," *Journal of Aesthetics and Art Criticism* 53 (1995).

3. Roman Jakobson, "Two Aspects of Language and Two Types of Aphasic Disturbances," in Roman Jakobson, *On Language*, eds. Linda R. Waugh and Monique Monville-Burston (Cambridge and London: Harvard University Press, 1990).

Bibliography

Abbate, Carolyn. *Unsung Voices: Opera and Musical Narrative in the Nineteenth Century.* Princeton: Princeton University Press, 1991.

Abert, Hermann. *W. A. Mozart.* Leipzig: Breitkopf & Härtel, 1921.

Allemann, Beda. *Ironie und Dichtung.* 2d ed. Pfullingen: Günther Neske, 1969.

Amante, David J. "The Theory of Ironic Speech Acts." *Poetics Today* 2.2 (1981): 77–96.

Angerer, Manfred. "Ironisierung der Konvention und humoristische Totalität: über die ersten Takte von Gustav Mahlers IV. Symphonie." In *Vergleichend-systematische Musikwissenschaft,* edited by Elisabeth Th. Hilscher and Theophil Antonicek, 561–82. Tutzing: Hans Schneider, 1994.

Appel, Bernhard. "R. Schumanns Humoreske für Klavier op. 20: Zum musikalischen Humor in der ersten Hälfte des 19. Jahrhunderts unter besonderer Berücksichtigung des Formproblems." Ph.D. diss., Universität des Saarlandes, Saarbrücken, 1981.

Arnheim, Rudolf. *Visual Thinking.* Berkeley and Los Angeles: University of California Press, 1969.

Austern, Linda Phyllis. "Sweet Meats with Sour Sauce: The Genesis of Musical Irony in English Drama after 1600." *Journal of Musicology* 4 (1986): 472–90.

Bakhtin, Mikhail M. *The Dialogic Imagination: Four Essays.* Edited by Michael Holquist and translated by Caryl Emerson and Michael Holquist. Austin: University of Texas Press, 1981.

Baldwin, Birgit. "Irony, that 'Little, Invisible Personage': A Reading of Kierkegaard's Ghosts." *MLN* 104 (1989): 1124–41.

Barbe, Katharina. *Irony in Context.* Amsterdam and Philadelphia: John Benjamins Publishing Co., 1995.

Barricelli, Jean-Pierre. *Melopoiesis: Approaches to the Study of Literature and Music.* New York and London: New York University Press, 1988.

Barry, Kevin. *Language, Music and the Sign: A Study in Aesthetics, Poetics and Poetic Practice from Collins to Coleridge.* Cambridge: Cambridge University Press, 1987.

Becker, William August. "Concepts of Irony with Special Reference to Applications in the Visual Arts." Ph.D. diss., Columbia University, New York, 1970.

Behler, Ernst. *Klassische Ironie, Romantische Ironie, Tragische Ironie: Zum Ursprung dieser Begriffe.* Darmstadt: Wissenschaftliche Buchgesellschaft, 1972.

———. *Irony and the Discourse of Modernity.* Seattle and London: University of Washington Press, 1990.

———. *German Romantic Literary Theory.* Cambridge: Cambridge University Press, 1993.

274

———. *Ironie und literarische Moderne.* Paderborn: Ferdinand Schöningh, 1997.

Benezra, Neal. "A Study in Irony: Modigliani's *Jacques and Berthe Lipchitz.*" *Museum Studies* 12 (1986): 189–99.

Bergson, Leif. "Eiron und Eironeia." *Hermes* 99 (1971): 409–22.

Bernhart, Walter. "Prekäre angewandte Opernästhetik: Audens 'sekundäre Welt' und Hans Werner Henzes *Elegie für junge Liebende.*" In *The Semantics of the Musico-Literary Genres: Method and Analysis,* edited by Walter Bernhart, 233–46. Tübingen: Gunter Narr Verlag, 1994.

Bloom, Harold. *Kabbalah and Criticism.* 2d ed. New York: Continuum, 1984.

———. *Ruin the Sacred Truths: Poetry and Belief from the Bible to the Present.* Cambridge and London: Harvard University Press, 1989.

Bonds, Mark Evan. "Haydn, Laurence Sterne, and the Origins of Musical Irony." *Journal of the American Musicological Society* 44 (1991): 57–91.

Booth, Wayne C. *A Rhetoric of Irony.* Chicago and London: University of Chicago Press, 1974.

———. "The Empire of Irony." *Georgia Review* 37 (1983): 719–37.

———. *The Rhetoric of Fiction.* 2d ed. London: Penguin Books, 1991.

Borges, Jorge Luis. *Obras completas* 1. Barcelona: Emecé editores, 1989.

———. *Collected Fictions.* Translated by Andrew Hurley. London: Allen Lane, 1999.

Bové, Paul A. *Destructive Poetics: Heidegger and Modern American Poetry.* New York: Columbia University Press, 1980.

Bracht, Hans-Joachim. "Schumanns 'Papillons' und die Ästhetik der Frühromantik." *Archiv für Musikwissenschaft* 50 (1993): 71–84.

Brackett, Donald. "The Ironic Ceramics of Richard Milette." *American Ceramics* 12.4 (1996): 15–21.

Brauner, Charles S. "Irony in the Heine Lieder of Schubert and Schumann." *Musical Quarterly* 67 (1981): 261–81.

Brill, Lesley. *The Hitchcock Romance: Love and Irony in Hitchcock's Films.* Princeton: Princeton University Press, 1988.

Brion, Marcel. *Schumann and the Romantic Age.* Translated by Geoffrey Sainsbury. London: Collins, 1956.

Brooks, Cleanth. "Irony and 'Ironic' Poetry." *College English* 9 (1948): 231–37.

———. "Irony as a Principle of Structure." In *Literary Opinion in America.* 3d ed., edited by M. D. Zabel, 729–41. New York and Evanston: Harper & Row, 1962.

———. *The Well Wrought Urn: Studies in the Structure of Poetry.* 2d ed. San Diego, New York, and London: Harcourt Brace Jovanovich, 1975.

Brooks, Cleanth, and Robert Penn Warren. *Understanding Fiction.* New York: Appleton-Century-Crofts, 1943.

Brown, Calvin S. *Music and Literature: A Comparison of the Arts.* 2d ed. Hanover and London: University Press of New England, 1987.

Buchloh, Benjamin. "Parody and Appropriation in Francis Picabia, Pop, and Sigmar Polke." *Artforum* 20 (March 1982): 28–34.

Büchner, Wilhelm. "Über den Begriff der Eironeia." *Hermes* 76 (1941): 339–58.

Burnham, Scott. "Mozart's *felix culpa*: *Così fan tutte* and the Irony of Beauty." *Musical Quarterly* 78 (1994): 77–98.

Cage, John. *Silence*. London: Calder and Boyars, 1968.

Campbell, K. S. "Irony Medieval and Modern and the Allegory of Rhetoric." *Allegorica* 4 (1979): 291–300.

Celan, Paul. *Gedichte in zwei Bänden* 1. Frankfurt am Main: Suhrkamp Verlag, 1975.

———. *Selected Poems*. 2d ed. Translated by Michael Hamburger. Harmondsworth: Penguin Books, 1990.

Chennevière, Rudhyar D. "Erik Satie and the Music of Irony." Translated by Frederick H. Martens. *Musical Quarterly* 5 (1919): 469–78.

Comanzo, Christian. "*Sunset Boulevard* or the Coding of Irony." In *Hollywood: Réflexions sur l'écran*, edited by Daniel Royot, 105–28. Aix-en-Provence: Université de Provence, 1984.

Cone, Edward T. *The Composer's Voice*. Berkeley, Los Angeles, and London: University of California Press, 1974.

Cook, Albert. "The 'Meta-Irony' of Marcel Duchamp." *Journal of Aesthetics and Art Criticism* 44 (1986): 263–70.

Cottingham, Laura. "The Feminine De-Mystique: Gender, Power, Irony, and Aestheticized Feminism in '80s Art." *Flash Art* issue 147 (1989): 91–95.

Cramer, Charles A. "Duchamp from Syntax to Bride: Sa Langue dans sa Joue." *Word & Image* 13 (1997): 279–303.

Crumplin, Colin, ed. *Chance Choice and Irony*. London and Southampton: Todd Gallery and John Hansard Gallery, 1994.

Csampai, Attila. "Das Geheimnis der 'Zauberflöte' oder Die Folgen der Aufklärung." In Wolfgang Amadeus Mozart, *Die Zauberflöte: Texte, Materialen, Kommentare*, edited by Attila Csampai and Dietmar Holland, 9–40. Reinbek bei Hamburg: Rowohlt, 1982.

Culler, Jonathan. *Flaubert: The Uses of Uncertainty*. Rev. ed. Ithaca and London: Cornell University Press, 1985.

Dahlhaus, Carl. *Esthetics of Music*. Translated by William W. Austin. Cambridge: Cambridge University Press, 1982.

Dane, Joseph A. *The Critical Mythology of Irony*. Athens and London: University of Georgia Press, 1991.

Davidson, Audrey. *Substance and Manner: Studies in Music and the Other Arts*. St. Paul, Minn.: Hiawatha Press, 1977.

Davies, Stephen. "Relativism in Interpretation." *Journal of Aesthetics and Art Criticism* 53 (1995): 8–13.

Dawe, Wendy. "Visual Metaphor and the Ironic Glance: The Interaction Between Artist and Viewer. Ph.D. diss., Birmingham Polytechnic, Birmingham, England, 1991.

de Boer, Cees. "Foucault et Magritte, ou Le mystère éclipsé." Translated by Marie-Claire Cécilia. In *L'interprétation détourné*, edited by Leo H. Hoek, 37–55. Amsterdam and Atlanta: Rodopi, 1990.

de Man, Paul. *Allegories of Reading: Figural Language in Rousseau, Nietzsche, Rilke, and Proust*. New Haven and London: Yale University Press, 1979.

———. *Blindness and Insight: Essays in the Rhetoric of Contemporary Criticism.* 2d ed. Minneapolis: University of Minnesota Press, 1983.

———. *Romanticism and Contemporary Criticism: The Gauss Seminar and Other Papers.* Edited by E. S. Burt, Kevin Newmark, and Andrzej Warminski. Baltimore and London: Johns Hopkins University Press, 1993.

de Visscher, Eric. "Die Künstlergruppe 'Les Incohérents' und die Vorgeschichte zu 4'33"." In *John Cage: Anarchic Harmony,* edited by Stefan Schädler and Walter Zimmermann, 71–77. Mainz: Schott, 1992.

Dickens, Charles. *Oliver Twist.* Edited by Kathleen Tillotson. Oxford: Clarendon Press, 1966.

Dicks, Mark Jeffry. "Reading Irony." Ph.D. diss., University of California, Santa Cruz, 1985.

Diehl, Huston. "Inversion, Parody, and Irony: The Visual Rhetoric of Renaissance English Tragedy." *Studies in English Literature 1500–1900* 22 (1982): 197–209.

Diener, Betty Sue. "Irony in Mozart's Operas." Ph.D. diss., Columbia University, New York, 1992.

Dill, Heinz J. "Romantic Irony in the Works of Robert Schumann." *Musical Quarterly* 73 (1989): 172–95.

Doane, Mary Ann. "The Dialogical Text: Filmic Irony and the Spectator." Ph.D. diss., University of Iowa, 1979.

———. "The Film's Time and the Spectator's 'Space.' " In *Cinema and Language,* edited by Stephen Heath and Patricia Mellencamp, 35–49. Frederick, Md.: University Publications of America, 1983.

Doe, Tamasin. *Patrick Cox: Wit, Irony and Footwear.* London: Thames and Hudson, 1998.

Dolle, Geneviève. "Éléments pour l'analyse rhétorique d'une image." *Revue d'esthétique* 32 (1979): 234–53.

Dümling, Albrecht. " 'Ganz einzig in ihrer Art . . . ': Ironie und Realismus in Hugo Wolfs *Alten Weisen* nach Gottfried Keller." *Musik-Konzepte* issue 75 Hugo Wolf (1992): 102–15.

Dunn, Peter N. "Irony as Structure in the Drama." *Bulletin of Hispanic Studies* 61 (1984): 317–25.

Dyson, J. Peter. "Ironic Dualities in *Das Rheingold.*" *Current Musicology* 43 (1987): 33–50.

Eckhart, Meister. *Die deutschen Werke: Predigten Dritter Band.* Edited by Josef Quint. Stuttgart: Verlag W. Kohlhammer, 1976.

Edson, Laurie. "Disrupting Conventions: Verbal-Visual Objects in Francis Ponge and René Magritte." *L'esprit créateur* 24.2 (1984): 23–35.

Elleström, Lars. *Vårt hjärtas vilt lysande skrift: Om Karl Vennbergs lyrik.* Lund: Lund University Press, 1992.

———. "Some Notes on Irony in the Visual Arts and Music: The Examples of Magritte and Shostakovich." *Word & Image* 12 (1996): 197–208.

Ellis, John M. *Against Deconstruction.* Princeton: Princeton University Press, 1989.

Elsaesser, Thomas. "Editorial: The Cinema of Irony." *Monogram* issue 5 (1975): 1–2.

Empson, William. *Seven Types of Ambiguity*. 2d ed. London: Hogarth Press, 1984.

Entzenberg, Claes. *Metaphor as a Mode of Interpretation: An Essay on Interactional and Contextual Sense-Making Processes, Metaphorology, and Verbal Arts*. Uppsala: Uppsala University, Department of Aesthetics, 1998.

Erasmus of Rotterdam. *Praise of Folly and Letter to Martin Dorp*. Edited by A. H. T. Levi and translated by Betty Radice. London: Penguin Books, 1971.

Fanning, David. *The Breath of the Symphonist: Shostakovich's Tenth*. London: Royal Musical Association, 1988.

Farakos, Mary. "Octavio Paz y Marcel Duchamp: Crítica moderna para un artista moderno." *Cuadernos Hispanoamericanos* issue 410 (1984): 79–96.

Feinstein, Wiley. "Dorinda as Ariostean Narrator in Handel's *Orlando*." *Italica* 64 (1987): 561–71.

Feldman, Yael S. "How Does a Convention Mean? A Semiotic Reading of Agnon's Bilingual Key-Irony in *A Guest for the Night*." *Hebrew Union College Annual* 56 (1985): 251–69.

Felstiner, John. *The Lies of Art: Max Beerbohm's Parody and Caricature*. London: Victor Gollancz, 1973.

Finlay, Carolyn Roberts. "Operatic Translation and Shostakovich: *The Nose*." *Comparative Literature* 35 (1983): 195–214.

Finlay, Marike. "Perspectives of Irony and Irony of Perspectives: A Review." *Canadian Journal of Research in Semiotics* 5.3 (1978): 31–50.

———. *The Romantic Irony of Semiotics: Friedrich Schlegel and the Crisis of Representation*. Berlin, New York, and Amsterdam: Mouton de Gruyter, 1988.

Finson, Jon W. "The Intentional Tourist: Romantic Irony in the Eichendorff *Liederkreis* of Robert Schumann." In *Schumann and his World*, edited by R. Larry Todd, 156–70. Princeton: Princeton University Press, 1994.

Fish, Stanley. *Is There a Text in This Class? The Authority of Interpretive Communities*. Cambridge and London: Harvard University Press, 1980.

———. *Doing What Comes Naturally: Change, Rhetoric, and the Practice of Theory in Literary and Legal Studies*. Durham, N.C., and London: Duke University Press, 1989.

Floros, Constantin. "Tragische Ironie und Ambivalenz bei Mahler." *Musik-Konzepte* Sonderband Gustav Mahler (1989): 213–20.

Flothuis, Marius. "Einige Betrachtungen über den Humor in der Musik." *Österreichische Musik-Zeitschrift* 38 (1983): 688–95.

Forman, Edward. "Musique et quiproquo: L'ironie dans les intermèdes musicaux." *Littératures Classiques* 21 (1994): 45–57.

Foster, Susan Leigh. *Reading Dancing: Bodies and Subjects in Contemporary American Dance*. Berkeley, Los Angeles, and London: University of California Press, 1986.

Foucault, Michel. *This Is Not a Pipe*. Edited and translated by James Harkness. Berkeley, Los Angeles, and London: University of California Press, 1983.

Frank, Joseph. "Spatial Form in Modern Literature." In *Criticism: The Foundations of Modern Literary Judgment*, edited by Mark Schorer, Josephine Miles, and Gordon McKenzie, 379–92. New York: Harcourt, Brace and Co., 1948.

Franko, Mark. *Dance as Text: Ideologies of the Baroque Body*. Cambridge: Cambridge University Press, 1993.

Freeman, Judi. *The Dada & Surrealist Word-Image*. With a contribution by John C. Welchman. Cambridge and London: MIT Press and Los Angeles County Museum of Art, 1989.

Freud, Sigmund. *Writings on Art and Literature*. Edited by James Strachey and translated by Angela Harris. Stanford, Calif.: Stanford University Press, 1997.

Frye, Lawrence O. "Word Play: Irony's Way to Freedom in Kafka's *Ein Bericht für eine Akademie*." *Deutsche Vierteljahrsschrift für Literaturwissenschaft und Geistesgeschichte* 55 (1981): 457–75.

Frye, Northrop. *Anatomy of Criticism: Four Essays*. Princeton: Princeton University Press, 1957.

Fuchs, Elinor. "Is There Life After Irony?." *Village Voice* 29 (3 January 1984): 77–78.

Furst, Lilian R. *Fictions of Romantic Irony in European Narrative, 1760–1857*. London and Basingstoke: Macmillan, 1984.

Gablik, Suzi. *Magritte*. London: Thames and Hudson, 1970.

Garber, Frederick. "Fabulating Jazz." In *Representing Jazz*, edited by Krin Gabbard, 70–103. Durham, N.C., and London: Duke University Press, 1995.

———, ed. *Romantic Irony*. Budapest: Akadémiai Kiadó, 1988.

Gieseler, Walter. "Schumanns frühe Klavierwerke im Spiegel der Literarischen Romantik." In *Robert Schumann: Universalgeist der Romantik*, edited by Julius Alf and Joseph A. Kruse, 62–87. Düsseldorf: Droste Verlag, 1981.

Godard, Barbara. "Modalities of the Edge: Towards a Semiotics of Irony: The Case of Mavis Gallant." *Essays on Canadian Writing* issue 42 (1990): 72–101.

Goergen, Jeanpaul. "Dada: Musik der Ironie und Provokation." *Neue Zeitschrift für Musik* 155.3 (1994), 4–13.

Goldschmidt, Harry. "Zitat oder Parodie?." *Beiträge zur Musikwissenschaft* 12 (1970): 171–98.

Goldsmith, Marcella Tarozzi. *Nonrepresentational Forms of the Comic: Humor, Irony, and Jokes*. New York: Peter Lang, 1991.

Good, Edwin M. *Irony in the Old Testament*. 2d ed. Sheffield: Almond Press, 1981.

Gottwald, Clytus. "John Cage und Marcel Duchamp." *Musik-Konzepte* Sonderband John Cage (1978): 132–46.

Grannis, Valleria Belt. *Dramatic Parody in Eighteenth Century France*. New York: Institute of French Studies, 1931.

Greene, Susan. "Comedy and Puccini's Operas." *Opera Quarterly* 2.3 (1984): 102–13.

Griffiths, Paul. *Cage*. London: Oxford University Press, 1981.

Groeben, Norbert, and Brigitte Scheele. *Produktion und Rezeption von Ironie: Pragmalinguistische Beschreibung und psycholinguistische Erklärungshypothesen*. Tübingen: Gunter Narr Verlag, 1984.

Groeben, Norbert, Hanne Seemann, and Arno Drinkmann. *Produktion und Rezeption von Ironie. Band II: Empirische Untersuchungen zu Bedingungen und Wirkungen ironischer Sprechakte*. Tübingen: Gunter Narr Verlag, 1985.

Groupe μ. "Ironique et iconique." *Poétique* 36 (1978): 427–42.

Gruber, Gernot. "Romantische Ironie in den Heine-Liedern?" In *Schubert-Kon-*

greß Wien 1978: Bericht, edited by Otto Brusatti, 321–34. Graz: Akademische Druck- u. Verlagsanstalt, 1979.

Gustafson, Donna. "Food and Death: *Vanitas* in Pop Art." *Arts Magazine* 60 (February 1986): 90–93.

Haardt, Robert. *Die Gnosis: Wesen und Zeugnisse.* Salzburg: Otto Müller Verlag, 1967.

Hammacher, A. M. *René Magritte.* Translated by James Brockway. New York: Abradale Press, 1995.

Hamon, Philippe. "Analyser l'ironie." In *Discours et pouvoir,* edited by Ross Chambers, 165–75. Ann Arbor: Department of Romance Languages, University of Michigan, 1982.

Handwerk, Gary J. *Irony and Ethics in Narrative: From Schlegel to Lacan.* New Haven and London: Yale University Press, 1985.

Hanslick, Eduard. *Vom Musikalisch-schönen: Ein Beitrag zur Revision der Ästhetik der Tonkunst.* Darmstadt: Wissenschaftliche Buchgesellschaft, 1965.

———. *On the Musically Beautiful: A Contribution towards the Revision of the Aesthetics of Music.* Edited and translated by Geoffrey Payzant. Indianapolis, Ind.: Hackett Publishing Co., 1986.

Harris, Wendell V. *Interpretive Acts: In Search of Meaning.* Oxford: Clarendon Press, 1988.

Hassan, Ihab. "Pluralism in Postmodern Perspective." *Critical Inquiry* 12 (1986): 503–20.

Hedling, Erik. *Lindsay Anderson: Maverick Film-Maker.* London and Washington: Cassell, 1998.

Hegel, G. W. F. *The Philosophy of Fine Art* 1. Translated by F. P. B. Osmaston. New York: Hacker Art Books, 1975.

Heimann, Ulrich. *Picassos Kubismus und die Ironie.* München: Wilhelm Fink Verlag, 1998.

Heinz-Mohr, Gerd, and Volker Sommer. *Die Rose: Entfaltung eines Symbols.* München: Eugen Diederichs Verlag, 1988.

Hermerén, Göran. "Intention and Interpretation in Literary Criticism." *New Literary History* 7 (1975): 57–82.

Hertel, Christiane. "Irony, Dream, and Kitsch: Max Klinger's *Paraphrase of the Finding of a Glove* and German Modernism." *Art Bulletin* 74 (1992): 91–114.

Herzog, Patricia. "The Practical Wisdom of Beethoven's Diabelli Variations." *Musical Quarterly* 79 (1995): 35–54.

Heyd, Milly. *Aubrey Beardsley: Symbol, Mask and Self-Irony.* New York, Bern, and Frankfurt am Main: Peter Lang, 1986.

Hirsch, E. D. *Validity in Interpretation.* New Haven and London: Yale University Press, 1967.

Hoet, Jan, ed. *Irony by Vision.* Tokyo: Watari-Um, 1991.

Hoffmann, E. T. A. "The Poet and the Composer." From *Die Serapions-Brüder.* Translated by Oliver Strunk. In *Source Readings in Music History: From Classical Antiquity through the Romantic Era,* edited by Oliver Strunk, 782–97. New York: W. W. Norton & Co., 1950.

Horton, Andrew, ed. *Inside Soviet Film Satire: Laughter with a Lash.* Cambridge: Cambridge University Press, 1993.

Huband, J. Daniel. "Shostakovich's Fifth Symphony: A Soviet Artist's Reply . . . ?." *Tempo* 173 (June 1990): 11–16.

Hubert, Renée Riese. "The Other Wordly Landscapes of E. A. Poe and René Magritte." *Sub-Stance* issue 21 (1978): 69–78.

Hurley, Ann. "The Elided Self: Witty Dis-Locations in Velázquez and Donne." *Journal of Aesthetics and Art Criticism* 44 (1986): 357–69.

Hutcheon, Linda. *A Theory of Parody: The Teachings of Twentieth-Century Art Forms.* New York and London: Methuen, 1985.

———. *Splitting Images: Contemporary Canadian Ironies.* Toronto, Oxford, and New York: Oxford University Press, 1991.

———. *Irony's Edge: The Theory and Politics of Irony.* London and New York: Routledge, 1994.

———, ed. *Essays in Canadian Irony* 1–3. North York, Ont., Canada: Robarts Centre for Canadian Studies, 1988–89.

———, ed. *Double Talking: Essays on Verbal and Visual Ironies in Canadian Contemporary Art and Literature.* Toronto: ECW Press, 1992.

Immerwahr, Raymond. "Romantic Irony and Romantic Arabesque Prior to Romanticism." *German Quarterly* 42 (1969): 665–85.

Jakobson, Roman. *On Language.* Edited by Linda R. Waugh and Monique Monville-Burston. Cambridge and London: Harvard University Press, 1990.

Jankélévitch, Vladimir. *L'ironie.* Paris: Librairie Félix Alcan, 1936.

———. *La musique et l'ineffable.* Paris: Librairie Armand Colin, 1961.

Japp, Uwe. *Theorie der Ironie.* Frankfurt am Main: Vittorio Klostermann, 1983.

Johnson, Tom. "Intentionality and Nonintentionality in the Performance of Music by John Cage." *Bucknell Review* John Cage at Seventy-Five (1989): 262–269.

Jongen, R. "L'affolement métaphorique et métonymique dans l'image magrittienne." *Anthropo-Logiques* 2 (1989): 187–206.

Jost, Peter. "Brahms und die romantische Ironie: Zu den 'Romanzen aus L. Tieck's Magelone' op. 33." *Archiv für Musikwissenschaft* 47 (1990): 27–61.

Juhl, P. D. *Interpretation: An Essay in the Philosophy of Literary Criticism.* Princeton: Princeton University Press, 1980.

Kafalenos, Emma. "Image and Narrativity: Robbe-Grillet's *La Belle Captive.*" *Visible Language* 23 (1989): 375–92.

Kafka, Franz. *Parables.* New York: Schocken Books, 1947.

———. *Das Erzählerische Werk I: Erzählungen Aphorismen Brief an den Vater.* Edited by Klaus Hermsdorf. Berlin: Rütten & Loening, 1983.

Kant, Immanuel. *Werke in sechs Bänden. Band V: Kritik der Urteilskraft und Schriften zur Naturphilosophie.* Edited by Wilhelm Weischedel. Wiesbaden: Insel-Verlag, 1957.

Karl, Gregory, and Jenefer Robinson. "Shostakovich's Tenth Symphony and the Musical Expression of Cognitively Complex Emotions." *Journal of Aesthetics and Art Criticism* 53 (1995): 401–15.

Katz, Steven T., ed. *Mysticism and Language.* New York and Oxford: Oxford University Press, 1992.

Katz-Freiman, Tami. "Antipathos: Black Humor, Irony and Cynicism in Contemporary Israeli Art." In *Antipathos: Black Humor, Irony and Cynicism in*

Contemporary Israeli Art, 53–46 (reversed pagination). Jerusalem: Israel Museum, 1993.

Kaufer, David S. "Understanding Ironic Communication." *Journal of Pragmatics* 5 (1981): 495–510.

———. "Irony, Interpretive Form, and the Theory of Meaning." *Poetics Today* 4 (1983): 451–64.

Kayser, Wolfgang. *The Grotesque in Art and Literature*. Translated by Ulrich Weisstein. Bloomington: Indiana University Press, 1963.

Keahey, Delores Jerde. "Così fan tutte: Parody or Irony?." In *Paul A. Pisk: Essays in His Honor*, edited by John Glowacki, 116–30. Austin: College of Fine Arts, University of Texas, 1966.

Kerbrat-Orecchioni, Catherine. "L'ironie comme trope." *Poétique* 41 (1980): 108–27.

Kierkegaard, Søren. *Samlede Værker* 1. 4th ed. Edited by A. B. Drachmann, J. L. Heiberg, and H. O. Lange. Copenhagen: Gyldendal, 1991.

Kivy, Peter. *The Corded Shell: Reflections on Musical Expression*. Princeton: Princeton University Press, 1980.

Knox, Dilwyn. *Ironia: Medieval and Renaissance Ideas on Irony*. Leiden: E. J. Brill, 1989.

Knox, Norman. *The Word Irony and its Context, 1500–1755*. Durham, N.C.: Duke University Press, 1961.

Kozloff, Sarah. *Invisible Storytellers: Voice-Over Narration in American Fiction Film*. Berkeley, Los Angeles, and London: University of California Press, 1988.

Lang, Candace D. *Irony/Humor: Critical Paradigms*. Baltimore and London: Johns Hopkins University Press, 1988.

Langer, Susanne K. *Feeling and Form: A Theory of Art Developed From Philosophy in a New Key*. London: Routledge & Kegan Paul, 1953.

———. *Philosophy in a New Key: A Study in the Symbolism of Reason, Rite, and Art*. 3d ed. Cambridge and London: Harvard University Press, 1957.

Larderet, Pierre. "Humour, ironie, satire, grotesque . . . : Étude de quelques aspects et procédés du comique musical." Ph.D. diss., Université de Lyon, Saint-Etienne, 1981.

———. "Humour, ironie, satire, parodie dans la musique française des XVIIᵉ et XVIIIᵉ siècles." In *Aspects de la musique baroque et classique à Lyon et en France*, edited by Daniel Paquette, 125–34. Lyon: Editions à coeur joie and Presses universitaires de Lyon, 1989.

Lert, Ernst. *Mozart auf dem Theater*. Berlin: Schuster & Loeffler, 1918.

Liebscher, Julia. "Mythos und Verfremdung: Musikalische Ironie als Mittel der Distanzierung in *Oedipus Rex* von Igor Strawinsky." In *Altes im neuen*, edited by Bernd Edelmann and Manfred Hermann Schmid, 345–57. Tutzing: Hans Schneider, 1995.

Lindau, Ursula. *Max Ernst und die Romantik: Unendliches Spiel mit Witz und Ironie*. Köln: Wienand, 1997.

Linde, Ulf. "MARiée CELibataire." In Walter Hopps, Ulf Linde, and Arturo Schwarz, *Marcel Duchamp: Ready-Mades, etc. (1913–1964)*, 39–68. Paris: Terrain Vague, 1964.

Lindsay, Frank W. *Dramatic Parody by Marionettes in Eighteenth Century Paris*. New York: King's Crown Press, 1946.

Lissa, Zofia. *Aufsätze zur Musikästhetik: Eine Auswahl.* Berlin: Henschelverlag, 1969.

Lister, Laurie-Jeanne. *Humor as a Concept in Music: A Theoretical Study of Expression in Music, the Concept of Humor and Humor in Music with an Analytical Example—W. A. Mozart, Ein Musikalischer Spaß, KV 522.* Frankfurt am Main: Peter Lang, 1994.

Long, John H. *Shakespeare's Use of Music: The Histories and Tragedies.* Gainesville: University of Florida Press, 1971.

Longyear, Rey M. "Beethoven and Romantic Irony." *Musical Quarterly* 56 (1970): 647–64.

MacDonald, Calum. "The Anti-Formalist 'Rayok'—Learners Start Here!." *Tempo* 173 (June 1990): 23–30.

MacDonald, Ian. *The New Shostakovich.* Oxford: Oxford University Press, 1991.

———. "Common Sense about Shostakovich: Breaking the 'Hermeneutic Circle.'" *Southern Humanities Review* 26 (1992): 153–67.

Malloy, Joseph Thomas. "Musico-Dramatic Irony in Mozart's 'Magic Flute.'" Ph.D. diss., University of Virginia, 1985.

Marcus, Greil. *Lipstick Traces: A Secret History of the Twentieth Century.* London: Secker & Warburg, 1989.

Margolis, Joseph. "Plain Talk about Interpretation on a Relativistic Model." *Journal of Aesthetics and Art Criticism* 53 (1995): 1–7.

Martin, Richard. "Tale and Transgression: The Art of Timothy Woodman." *Arts Magazine* 59 (May 1985): 135–37.

Meinecke, Dietlind. *Wort und Name bei Paul Celan: Zur Widerruflichkeit des Gedichts.* Bad Homburg v. d. H., Berlin, and Zürich: Verlag Gehlen, 1970.

Mellor, Anne K. "On Romantic Irony, Symbolism and Allegory." *Criticism* 21 (1979): 217–29.

———. *English Romantic Irony.* Cambridge and London: Harvard University Press, 1980.

Merrill, Reed. "The Grotesque in Music: Shostakovich's *Nose.*" *Russian Literature Triquarterly* 23 (1990): 303–14.

Mersmann, Hans. "Versuch einer musikalischen Wertästhetik." *Zeitschrift für Musikwissenschaft* 17 (1935): 33–47.

Metzger, Heinz-Klaus. "Anarchie durch Negation der Zeit oder Probe einer Lektion wider die Moral." *Musik-Konzepte* Sonderband John Cage (1978): 147–54.

Meuris, Jacques. "Magritte: Le mystère, le réel, et la connaissance." *Colóquio-Artes* issue 86 (1990): 30–39.

Meyer, Leonard B. *Emotion and Meaning in Music.* Chicago and London: University of Chicago Press, 1956.

———. *Music, the Arts, and Ideas: Patterns and Predictions in Twentieth-Century Culture.* Chicago and London: University of Chicago Press, 1967.

Milnes, Rodney. "Degrees of Irony." *About the House* 7.2 (1984): 51–52.

Mitchell, W. J. T., ed. *The Language of Images.* Chicago and London: University of Chicago Press, 1980.

Monson, Ingrid. "Doubleness and Jazz Improvisation: Irony, Parody, and Ethnomusicology." *Critical Inquiry* 20 (1994): 283–313.

Moraal, Christine. "Romantische Ironie in Robert Schumanns 'Nachtstücken,' op. 23." *Archiv für Musikwissenschaft* 54 (1997): 68–83.

Morris, C. "Woody Allen's Comic Irony." *Literature/Film Quarterly* 15 (1987): 175–80.

Muecke, D. C. *The Compass of Irony.* London: Methuen, 1969.

———. *Irony.* London: Methuen, 1970.

———. "Irony Markers." *Poetics* 7 (1978): 363–75.

———. *Irony and the Ironic* (2d ed. of *Irony*). London and New York: Methuen, 1982.

———. "Images of Irony." *Poetics Today* 4 (1983): 399–413.

Nadaner, Dan. "Intervention and Irony." *Vanguard* 13 (September 1984): 13–14.

Nathan, Daniel O. "Irony and the Artist's Intentions." *British Journal of Aesthetics* 22 (1982): 245–56.

Nattiez, Jean-Jacques. *Music and Discourse: Toward a Semiology of Music.* Translated by Carolyn Abbate. Princeton: Princeton University Press, 1990.

Neubauer, John. *The Emancipation of Music from Language: Departure from Mimesis in Eighteenth-Century Aesthetics.* New Haven and London: Yale University Press, 1986.

———. "Tales of Hoffmann and Others: On Narrativizations of Instrumental Music." In *Interart Poetics: Essays on the Interrelations of the Arts and Media,* edited by Ulla-Britta Lagerroth, Hans Lund, and Erik Hedling, 117–36. Amsterdam and Atlanta: Rodopi, 1997.

Nietzsche, Friedrich. *Werke in drei Bänden* 2. 2d ed. Edited by Karl Schlechta. München: Carl Hanser Verlag, 1960.

Nilsson, John Peter. "Swedish Art: From Irony to the Sublime & Back Again." *Flash Art* issue 157 (1991): 105–7.

Nobis, Beatrix. "Kurt Schwitters: *Merz,* le fragment et l'ironie romantique." *Cahiers du Musée national d'art moderne* issue 51 (1995): 65–79.

Norris, Christopher. "Ambiguous Shostakovich." *Gramophone* 60 (1983): 892.

———. "Shostakovich and Cold War Cultural Politics: A Review Essay." *Southern Humanities Review* 25 (1991): 54–77.

———, ed. *Shostakovich: The Man and His Music.* London: Lawrence and Wishart, 1982.

Noske, Frits. *The Signifier and the Signified: Studies in the Operas of Mozart and Verdi.* The Hague: Martinus Nijhoff, 1977.

O'Hara, Daniel. Review of Jacques Derrida, *Grammatology. Journal of Aesthetics and Art Criticism* 36 (1977): 361–65.

Oliver, Michael [M. E. O.]. Review of Decca record SXDL7551. *Gramophone* 60 (1982): 723.

Ong, Walter J. "From Mimesis to Irony: The Distancing of Voice." In *The Horizon of Literature,* edited by Paul Hernadi, 11–42. Lincoln and London: University of Nebraska Press, 1982.

Ortquist, Leslie. "Magritte's Captivity in Robbe-Grillet's *La Belle Captive*: The Subjugation of the Image by the Word." *Visible Language* 23 (1989): 239–53.

Osthoff, Wolfgang. "Symphonien beim Ende des Zweiten Weltkriegs: Strawinsky—Frommel—Schostakowitsch." *Acta musicologica* 60 (1988): 62–104.

Oulibicheff, Alexandre. *Beethoven: Ses critiques et ses glossateurs*. Leipzig and Paris: F. A. Brockhaus and Jules Gavelot, 1857.

Paul, David W., ed. *Politics, Art and Commitment in the East European Cinema*. London and Basingstoke: Macmillan, 1983.

Pavlovskis, Zoja. *The Praise of Folly: Structure and Irony*. Leiden: E. J. Brill, 1983.

Paz, Octavio. *Marcel Duchamp, or The Castle of Purity*. Translated by Donald Gardner. London: Cape Goliard Press, 1970.

———. *Marcel Duchamp: Appearance Stripped Bare*. Translated by Rachel Phillips and Donald Gardner. New York: Arcade Publishing, 1990.

Peirce, Charles S. "Logic as Semiotic: The Theory of Signs." In *Semiotics: An Introductory Anthology*, 2d ed., edited by Robert E. Innis, 4–23. London: Hutchinson, 1986.

Pentzell, Raymond J. "Actor, *Maschera*, and Role: An Approach to Irony in Performance." *Comparative Drama* 16 (1982): 201–26.

Pfingsten, Ingeborg. "Musikalische Ironie 'im wunderschönen Monat Mai' von Schumann?." *Musica* 41 (1987): 524–27.

Plato. *The Collected Dialogues of Plato Including the Letters*. Edited by Edith Hamilton and Huntington Cairns. New York: Bollingen Foundation and Pantheon Books, 1961.

Pritchett, James. "Understanding John Cage's Chance Music: An Analytical Approach." *Bucknell Review* John Cage at Seventy-Five (1989): 249–61.

———. *The Music of John Cage*. Cambridge: Cambridge University Press, 1993.

Proust, Marcel. *À la recherche du temps perdu* 1. Paris: Gallimard, 1987.

Rabinowitz, Peter J. "Circumstantial Evidence: Musical Analysis and Theories of Reading." *Mosaic* 18.4 Music and Literature (1985): 159–73.

The Revised English Bible. Oxford and Cambridge: Oxford University Press and Cambridge University Press, 1989.

Ribbeck, Otto. "Ueber den Begriff des εἴρων." *Rheinisches Museum für Philologie* neue Folge 31 (1876): 381–400.

Rice, Donald, and Peter Schofer. *Rhetorical Poetics: Theory and Practice of Figural and Symbolic Reading in Modern French Literature*. Madison: University of Wisconsin Press, 1983.

Richards, I. A. *Principles of Literary Criticism*. London and New York: Kegan Paul, Trench, Trubner & Co., and Harcourt, Brace & Co., 1925.

Rimmon, Shlomith. *The Concept of Ambiguity: The Example of James*. Chicago and London: University of Chicago Press, 1977.

Robertson, Pamela. "Structural Irony in *Mildred Pierce*, or How Mildred Lost Her Tongue." *Cinema Journal* 30 (1990): 42–54.

Robinson, Fred Miller. "The History and Significance of the Bowler Hat: Chaplin, Laurel and Hardy, Beckett, Magritte and Kundera." *TriQuarterly* issue 66 (1986): 173–200.

———. "The Wizard Proprieties of Poe and Magritte." *Word & Image* 3 (1987): 156–61.

Rodin Pucci, Suzanne. " '*Ceci n'est pas . . .* ': Negative Framing in Diderot and Magritte." *Mosaic* 20.3 (1987): 1–14.

Roman, Zoltan. "Connotative Irony in Mahler's *Todenmarsch in 'Callots Manier.*' " *Musical Quarterly* 59 (1973): 207–22.

Roque, Georges. "Magritte's Words and Images." *Visible Language* 23 (1989): 221–37.

Rorty, Richard. *Contingency, Irony, and Solidarity.* Cambridge: Cambridge University Press, 1989.

Rosen, Charles. *The Classical Style: Haydn, Mozart, Beethoven.* Rev. ed. London and Boston: Faber and Faber, 1976.

Rosenberg, Wolf. "Paradox, Doppelbödigkeit und Ironie in der 'Dichterliebe.' " *Dissonanz/Dissonance* 15 (February 1988): 8–12.

Rosteck, Thomas. "Irony, Argument, and Reportage in Television Documentary: *See It Now* Versus Senator McCarthy." *Quarterly Journal of Speech* 75 (1989): 277–98.

Roth-Lindberg, Örjan. *Skuggan av ett leende: Om filmisk ironi och den ironiska berättelsen.* Stockholm: T. Fischer & Co., 1995.

Rougé, Bertrand. "L'ironie, ou la double représentation." *Lendemains* issue 50 (1988): 34–40.

Rozik, Eli. "Theatrical Irony." *Theatre Research International* 11.2 (1986): 132–51.

Runolfsson, Halldór Björn. "Intimacy, Austerity and Irony: Eight Icelandic Artists in the Late Eighties." *Flash Art* issue 157 (1991): 108–11.

Ryan, Allan J. *The Trickster Shift: Humour and Irony in Contemporary Native Art.* Vancouver, Toronto, and Seattle: UBC Press and University of Washington Press, 1999.

Satterfield, Leon. "Toward a Poetics of the Ironic Sign." In *Semiotic Themes,* edited by Richard T. De George, 149–64. Lawrence: University of Kansas Publications, 1981.

Savage, Jon. *England's Dreaming: Sex Pistols and Punk Rock.* London and Boston: Faber and Faber, 1991.

Schadendorf, Mirjam. *Humor als Formkonzept in der Musik Gustav Mahlers.* Stuttgart and Weimar: Verlag J. B. Metzler, 1995.

Schaerer, René. "Le mécanisme de l'ironie dans ses rapports avec la dialectique." *Revue de métaphysique et de morale* 48 (1941): 181–209.

Schasler, Max. "Die Ironie in der Musik: Ein Beitrag zur Aesthetik der Musik." *Zeitschrift für Musik* 77 (1881): 385–87, 397–99, 405–7.

Scher, Steven Paul. " 'O Wort, du Wort, das mir fehlt!' Der Realismusbegriff in der Musik." In *Literatur und Musik: Ein Handbuch zur Theorie und Praxis eines komparatistischen Grenzgebietes,* edited by Steven Paul Scher, 84–99. Berlin: Erich Schmidt Verlag, 1984.

———, ed. *Music and Text: Critical Inquiries.* Cambridge: Cambridge University Press, 1992.

Schiebler, Ralf. "Das Oppositionsprinzip bei Magritte." *Zeitschrift für Ästhetik und allgemeine Kunstwissenschaft* 27 (1981): 74–83.

Schlegel, Friedrich. *Kritische Friedrich-Schlegel-Ausgabe* 2. Edited by Ernst Behler and Hans Eichner. München, Paderborn, and Wien: Verlag Ferdinand Schöningh, 1967.

Schneede, Uwe M. *René Magritte: Leben und Werk.* Köln: Verlag M. DuMont Schauberg, 1973.

Scholem, Gershom G. *Major Trends in Jewish Mysticism.* 3d ed. London: Thames and Hudson, 1955.

———. *Kabbalah.* Jerusalem: Keter Publishing House, 1974.

Scholes, Percy A. *God Save the Queen! The History and Romance of the World's First National Anthem.* London, New York, and Toronto: Oxford University Press, 1954.

Seaton, Douglass. "Interpreting Schubert's Heine Songs." *Music Review* 53 (1992): 85–99.

Sedgewick, G. G. *Of Irony: Especially in Drama.* Toronto: University of Toronto Press, 1935.

Seipt, Angelus. "Gesagt—gesungen—gemeint: über Ironie in der Oper." In *Kunst Kommunikation Kultur,* edited by Walter Nutz, 267–77. Frankfurt am Main: Peter Lang, 1989.

Shapiro, Marianne. "The Status of Irony." *Stanford Literature Review* 2 (1985): 5–26.

Sichel, Kim. *From Icon to Irony: German and American Industrial Photography.* With additional essays by Judith Bookbinder and John Stomberg. Seattle and London: University of Washington Press, 1995.

Sirridge, Mary. "Artistic Intention and Critical Prerogative." *British Journal of Aesthetics* 18 (1978): 137–54.

Smith, David R. "Irony and Civility: Notes on the Convergence of Genre and Portraiture in Seventeenth-Century Dutch Painting." *Art Bulletin* 69 (1987): 407–430.

Smoodin, Eric. "The Image and the Voice in the Film with Spoken Narration." *Quarterly Review of Film Studies* 8 (Fall 1983): 19–32.

Solger, Karl Wilhelm Ferdinand. *Solger's nachgelassene Schriften und Briefwechsel* 1. Edited by Ludwig Tieck and Friedrich von Raumer. Leipzig: F. A. Brockhaus, 1826.

———. *Erwin: Vier Gespräche über das Schöne und die Kunst.* Edited by Wolfhart Henckmann. München: Wilhelm Fink Verlag, 1971.

Solomon, Andrew. *The Irony Tower: Soviet Artists in a Time of Glasnost.* New York: Alfred A. Knopf, 1991.

Stace, W. T. *Mysticism and Philosophy.* London: Macmillan, 1961.

Stadler, Arnold. *Das Buch der Psalmen und die deutschsprachige Lyrik des 20. Jahrhunderts: Zu den Psalmen im Werk Bertolt Brechts und Paul Celans.* Köln and Wien: Böhlau Verlag, 1989.

Stanley, Patricia. "Hoffmann's *Phantasiestücke in Callots Manier* in Light of Friedrich Schlegel's Theory of the Arabesque." *German Studies Review* 8 (1985): 399–419.

Stecker, Robert. "Relativism about Interpretation." *Journal of Aesthetics and Art Criticism* 53 (1995): 14–18.

Stiglitz, Beatrice. "A Joke of Destiny: Irony and Paradox in Italian Film: Bellocchio, Scola, Wertmuller." In *National Traditions in Motion Pictures,* edited by Douglas Radcliff-Umstead, 38–42. Kent, Ohio: Kent State University, 1985.

Strick, Jeremy. "Notes on Some Instances of Irony in Modern Pastoral." In *The Pastoral Landscape,* edited by John Dixon Hunt, 197–207. Hanover and London: University Press of New England, 1992.

Stringfellow, Frank. *The Meaning of Irony: A Psychoanalytic Investigation.* Albany: State University of New York Press, 1994.

288 BIBLIOGRAPHY

Strohschneider-Kohrs, Ingrid. *Die Romantische Ironie in Theorie und Gestaltung*. Tübingen: Max Niemeyer Verlag, 1960.

Sucksmith, Harvey Peter. *The Narrative Art of Charles Dickens: The Rhetoric of Sympathy and Irony in His Novels*. Oxford: Clarendon Press, 1970.

Suleiman, Susan. "Interpreting Ironies." *Diacritics* 6.2 (1976): 15–21.

Swearingen, C. Jan. *Rhetoric and Irony: Western Literacy and Western Lies*. New York and Oxford: Oxford University Press, 1991.

Szuman, Stefan. "Chopins Witz und Ironie." *Kulturprobleme des neuen Polen* issue 2 (1952): 3–7.

Tan, Margaret Leng. " 'Taking a Nap, I Pound the Rice': Eastern Influences on John Cage." *Bucknell Review* John Cage at Seventy-Five (1989): 34–57.

Thirlwall, Connop. *Remains: Literary and Theological* 3. Edited by J. J. Stewart Perowne. London: Daldy, Isbister & Co., 1878.

Thomas Aquinas, St. *Summa Theologica*. 2d ed. Translated by fathers of the English Dominican Province. London: Burns Oates & Washbourne, 1935.

Thompson, Alan Reynolds. *The Dry Mock: A Study of Irony in Drama*. Berkeley and Los Angeles: University of California Press, 1948.

Thomson, J. A. K. *Irony: An Historical Introduction*. Cambridge: Harvard University Press, 1927.

Tilmouth, Michael. "Parody." In *The New Grove Dictionary of Music and Musicians* 14, edited by Stanley Sadie, 238–40. London: Macmillan, 1980.

Tolhurst, William E. "On What a Text Is and How It Means." *British Journal of Aesthetics* 19 (1979): 3–14.

Ulanov, Barry. "The Art of Irony." *Union Seminary Quarterly Review* 35 (1980): 255–65.

Vaillancourt, Pierre-Louis. "Sémiologie de l'ironie: L'exemple Ducharme." *Voix et images* 7 (1982): 513–22.

Vill, Susanne. "Das psychologische Experiment in de Laclos' *Les Liaisons Dangereuses* und in Mozarts *Così fan tutte*: Zur Frage von Rationalismus und Ironie in Mozarts Musiktheater." In *Aufklärungen: Studien zur deutschfranzösischen Musikgeschichte im 18. Jahrhundert: Einflüsse und Wirkungen* 2, edited by Wolfgang Birtel and Christoph-Hellmut Mahling, 132–42. Heidelberg: Carl Winter Universitätsverlag, 1986.

Vlastos, Gregory. *Socrates: Ironist and Moral Philosopher*. Cambridge: Cambridge University Press, 1991.

Volkov, Solomon, ed. *Testimony: The Memoirs of Dmitri Shostakovich*. As related to and edited by Solomon Volkov. Translated by Antonina W. Bouis. London: Hamish Hamilton, 1979.

von Morstein, Petra. "Magritte: Artistic and Conceptual Representation." *Journal of Aesthetics and Art Criticism* 41 (1982): 369–74.

Vulpi, Frank. "Irony in Verdi's *Rigoletto*." *Opera Journal* 21.4 (1988): 21–31.

Wahlsten, Per. ". . . några rader om John Cage." In *Tonsättarens val: Texter om svensk musikalisk modernism och postmodernism*, edited by Björn Billing, 127–50. Stockholm: Edition Reimers, 1993.

Warning, Rainer. "Irony and the 'Order of Discourse' in Flaubert." Translated by Michael Morton. *New Literary History* 13 (1981): 253–86.

Weil, Jonathan. "The Role of Ambiguity in the Arts." *Et cetera* 43 (Spring 1986): 83–89.

Wendt, Matthias, ed. *Schumann und seine Dichter.* Mainz: Schott, 1993.

Wilde, Alan. *Horizons of Assent: Modernism, Postmodernism, and the Ironic Imagination.* Baltimore and London: Johns Hopkins University Press, 1981.

Wimsatt, W. K., and Monroe C. Beardsley. "The Intentional Fallacy." In W. K. Wimsatt, *The Verbal Icon: Studies in the Meaning of Poetry,* 3–18. Lexington: University of Kentucky Press, 1954.

Winkler, Peter. "Randy Newman's Americana." *Popular Music* 7.1 (1987): 1–26.

Wolosky, Shira. *Language Mysticism: The Negative Way of Language in Eliot, Beckett, and Celan.* Stanford, Calif.: Stanford University Press, 1995.

Woodley, Ronald. "Strategies of Irony in Prokofiev's Violin Sonata in F minor Op. 80." In *The Practice of Performance: Studies in Musical Interpretation,* edited by John Rink, 170–93. Cambridge: Cambridge University Press, 1995.

Yaari, Monique. "Ironic Architecture: The Puzzles of Multiple (En)coding." *Restant* 18 (1990): 335–84.

Yeats, W. B. *The Collected Poems of W. B. Yeats.* 2d ed. London: Macmillan, 1950.

Zuckerkandl, Victor. *Sound and Symbol: Music and the External World.* Translated by Willard R. Trask. New York: Bollingen Foundation and Pantheon Books, 1956.

Index

290

naissance, 17; and Romantic irony, 18, 19, 21–22, 109; and Schlegel, 18, 19, 109, 124; and situational irony, 52; and structural irony, 52, 109; and verbal irony, 109. *See also* dialectics and irony
Solger, Karl Wilhelm Ferdinand, 20, 22, 23, 85, 93, 124, 168
Sophists, 86
Sophocles, 22, 52–53
spatial metaphors of irony: ambiguity, 190; *antiphrasis,* 189–90; antithesis, 189–90; Arnheim and, 184–87; conflict, 189, 191–92; contradiction, 189–90; contrariety, 190; contrast, 188, 191, 195, 196, 220; and experience of space, 192; figurativity and, 185–86, 187; incongruity, 188, 191, 194–96, 220; interpretation of clashing images, 193; irony as mental image, 188–89; Magritte and, 194–99; and metonymy, 186, 187; opposition, 188, 190; and organization of space, 187–88; paradox, 188, 190; perception and thinking, 184–87, 188; and "structure," 192; verbal representations of, 187, 188–89; and visual art, 184–87, 188–89, 192–93
spatiality: and architecture, 224; Arnheim and, 184–87; as aspect of ironic interpretation, 192–93; clashing of meanings, conflict in space, 189, 191, 193–94, 221–22; and concept of space, 221; and etymology of word irony, 189–90; and "impossible" images, 193–94; and language, 189; literary spatiality, 199–200; Magritte and, 194–99; and modernism, 194; music and motion, 220, 221–22; musical emotions and moods, 220, 221–24; musical form, 220–21, 223; musical irony, 220–24; musical space, 221–22; and organization of space, 187–88; perception and thinking, 184–87, 188; and postmodernism, 194; and Romantic irony, 215–24; and sculpture, 224; spatial dualities, 198–99; and "structure," 192; and surrealism, 194–99; verbal representations of, 187, 188–89; and visual works of art,

89, 175–84, 184–93, 194–99. *See also* spatial metaphors of irony
speech act theories of irony, 39–40
Splitting Images: Contemporary Canadian Ironies (Hutcheon), 138
Stace, W. T., 119, 120, 121
Stecker, Robert, 244
Sterne, Laurence, 52, 104
Stradling, Robert, 229
Stravinsky, Igor, 202
Stringfellow, Frank, 44–45
structural irony: defined, 51, 53, 236; and dramatic/tragic irony, 52; in *Praise of Folly,* 76, 83; and Romantic irony, 52, 108; of Shostakovich's Fifth Symphony, 228; and Socratic irony, 52, 109; and verbal irony, 51, 83, 112–13
Suleiman, Susan, 37–38
surrealism, 177–82, 194–99; associated with irony, 177–78; and conceptuality, 194; contrasts in, 195–96; and dreams, 195; and the grotesque, 177; incongruities in, 194–96; ironic interpretations of, 180–82; Magritte, 178–81, 182, 194–99; representations of space in, 194–99
Swift, Jonathan, 17, 51, 56
symbol, 25, 206–7
synecdoche, 94
Szuman, Stefan, 214

Tan, Margaret Leng, 173–74
Taoism, and paradoxical language, 119
television, 148. *See also* film and filmic irony
Temple, Julian, 161
Tenth Symphony (Shostakovich), 238–39
Teresa of Avila, Saint, 119
Testimony: The Memoirs of Dmitri Shostakovich (Volkov, ed.), 225
theater. *See* drama and theater
Theophrastus, 86, 113, 122–23
Theorie der Ironie (Japp), 107
"Theory of Ironic Speech Acts, The" (Amante), 40
Theory of Parody, A: The Teachings of